New Context

Cornelsen

New Context

Im Auftrag des Verlags herausgegeben von	Prof. Hellmut Schwarz, Mannheim
Erarbeitet von	Barbara Derkow Disselbeck und Allen J. Woppert; Dr. Jens-Peter Green, Oldenburg; Angela Ringel-Eichinger, Bietigheim-Bissingen; Dr. Jana Schubert, Leipzig; Hellmut Schwarz, Mannheim; Sabine Tudan, Erfurt; Mervyn Whittaker, Bad Dürkheim
Verlagsredaktion	Michael R. Ferguson (Projektleitung), Dr. Marion Kiffe, Neil Porter (verantwortlich), Marc Proulx Dr. Ilka Soennecken, Dr. Bettina Schaschke (Assistenz)
Beratende Mitwirkung	Dr. Doris Breitenbach, Zittau; Dr. Helga Hämmerling, Jena; Sieglinde Spranger, Chemnitz *sowie* Kerstin Conrad, Meiningen; Martina Klötzer, Klipphausen; Dr. Gabriele Kugler-Euerle, Murrhardt; Petra Oehme, Jena; Rainer Schulz, Havelberg; Elke Wollenschläger, Benshausen
Umschlag	Knut Waisznor
Gestaltung und technische Umsetzung	Gisela Hoffmann
Text- und Bildquellen	s. Verzeichnis auf Seite 271
Weitere Bestandteile des Lehrwerks	Workbook: Bestellnummer 310477 Teacher's Manual: 310469 Listening Comprehension Doppel-CD: 310485 Video: 310493 bzw. DVD: 36014-8

Cornelsen online http://www.cornelsen.de

1. Auflage Druck 8 7 6 5 Jahr 07 06 05 04

Alle Drucke dieser Auflage sind inhaltlich unverändert
und können im Unterricht nebeneinander verwendet werden.

Druck: CS-Druck CornelsenStürtz, Berlin

ISBN 3-464-31045-0

Bestellnummer 310450

Gedruckt auf säurefreiem Papier,
umweltschonend hergestellt aus chlorfrei gebleichten Faserstoffen.

abbreviations

adj	adjective	i.e.	(Latin) id est = that is
abbr	abbreviation	infml	informal
AE	American English	l., ll.	line, lines
BE	British English	n	noun
cf.	confer, see	p., pp.	page, pages
derog	derogatory	sb.	somebody
ed., eds.	editor, editors	sl	slang
e.g.	(Latin) exempli gratia = for example	sth.	something
esp.	especially	pl	plural
etc.	(Latin) et cetera = and so on	usu.	usually
ff.	and the following lines/pages	v	verb
fml	formal	☆	American pronunciation follows

1 Finding Myself

A Land/scape Nadia Wheatley

Here is the longest text you will find in this English coursebook – an extract from a long Australian short story. The questions in the middle and at the end of the story will help you to enjoy and understand it better. Working with this text will also help you to assess your strengths and weaknesses in learning English.

Self-assessment. Before you start reading, fill in Section I ('Learning English so far') of the self-assessment questionnaire. (The self-assessment sheets can be found in the Workbook and the Teacher's Manual.)

➤ Skimming (p. 236)

Skim section i (pp. 8–10) of 'Land/scape' and speculate on what the story might be about. Then read sections i–iii in closer detail.

(i) Holding Pattern

'This is Captain Klein speaking. Unfortunately there is a bit of a queue here at Tullamarine today, so we are entering a holding pattern. Our estimated arrival time will now be 2.10 pm ...'

The rest of the passengers sighed, tapped their watches, ostentatiously took out again the company reports that they'd stowed in their briefcases. Ant grinned. A short reprieve.

Ant was dreading the thought of five days with his father: it would be the longest time they had spent together since Tony had gone. Ant had been in Year 5 then. He was in Year 10 now. Quite a different person, in many ways. It wasn't just a matter of pubic hair, deeper voice, pimples and the height problem (Ant was 199

The Greater Public Schools Regatta (left); students at one of Australia's elite schools (below).

centimetres, and rising), but internal changes, to the way the brain thought about things. At ten, Ant hadn't had opinions on matters like Land Rights, the Mabo decision, nuclear energy, woodchipping, American military involvement in the Gulf, school uniforms, the republic, compulsory enrolment in the cadets; now he did. And he knew that his father would have different opinions.

Tony was a barrister. A member of the Establishment. As witnessed by the school that he made Ant go to: one of the most famously conservative boys' private schools in the country. It produced footballers, cricketers, graziers, senior executives, lawyers, doctors, and politicians of the Liberal and National parties. It had produced Ant's father (Captain of the First XI; Dux of the School; Head Prefect; Barrister) and Ant's grandfather (Captain of the First XV; Sports Captain; Prefect; Judge). Ant had to sit beneath their names and achievements written in gold on the polished oak boards in the chapel every morning. Had to blush with shame every time the sports teachers said 'I would have expected better of *you*, Hindmarsh', whenever he bowled a mullygrubber, set up a try for the opposing team, served double faults into the net for an entire tennis match, or (on one spectacular occasion) managed to capsize the eight when they were only half a metre from the finishing line in the Greater Public Schools Regatta.

Why? Ant always wondered. Sure, in a general way he could see why they expected sporting ability from him: he should have had the genes for it. But – given that he didn't – why keep on expecting him to be able to do it? When every time he failed?

It was the same with the other teachers. Ant was bright enough to be in the A class, bright enough always to pass everything, even Maths and Chemistry. But he was always in the bottom half. Unlike Tony (his teacher told him), who had topped his year every year from Kindergarten to Leaving. 'I would have expected more of *you*, Hindmarsh,' his English/History/Maths/Chemistry/Physics and even Japanese teachers always said. It was the kind of school where staff stay on forever, so most of them could actually remember teaching Tony, and one old codger even claimed to have taught the judge. Ant wished he was stupid so he could get into the Special class: they did Art, Metalwork, Woodwork, Tech Drawing,

■ **1** holding pattern *circular path of an aircraft waiting for permission to land* **5** ostentatiously [- - '- - -] *very obviously* **7** reprieve [rɪ'priːv] (n) *delay before sth. bad happens* **18** the Establishment *the people in society who have influence and usu. are against change* **21** grazier ['greɪziə] *sheep farmer* **22** First XI *top school cricket team* **23** Dux *Schulsprecher* **24** First XV *top school rugby team* **27** Hindmarsh ['haɪndmaːʃ] **27** mullygrubber *bad throw in cricket* **28** try (n) *(in rugby) act of scoring points by touching the ground with the ball behind your opponents' goal line* **29** eight (n) *rowing boat for eight people* **42-43** old codger (sl) *stupid old man*

■ **52** Koorie *Aboriginal*
67 bight [baɪt] *long curve in a coast*

Carving and Casting, Photography, Screen Printing and Excursions. Even more to the point, Ant wished he could go to the Creative Arts High School two suburbs down the train line from where he lived. But Mum said not to waste his breath even asking Tony about it. The school Ant went to was a family tradition, from which Tony wouldn't budge, Mum said.

'We have now been given the clearance from the air traffic controller ...'

Ant sighed, stowed away his sketch book and pencils in his shoulder bag, which was bright yellow with the Koorie flag on it and the words 'Land is Life'.

He tapped at his watch. It was 2.14. Oh well. Look on the bright side. Most of Day 1 was nearly over. Then there'd just be Day 2, Day 3, Day 4 and on Day 5 he'd be travelling back home again. After that there'd still be nine days of holidays left for him to do what he liked doing: pottering around by himself at home, drawing, painting, developing photos, mucking about with the graphics program on his Macintosh, or simply lying on his bed for hours to recoup the energy that his growing body seemed to drain from him. Ant hated the sort of holiday in which you had to rush about and *do* things all the time.

There was a nasty jolt as the wheels touched the ground, then a sort of shudder seemed to run through the body of the plane, and now they were taxiing towards the terminal and Ant's father.

(ii) In the Wilds

It was half past five when they arrived at Cape Otway. The map showed this as just about the southernmost bit of the mainland, the beginning of the Great Australian Bight. To the south, there was nothing between here and Antarctica, Tony reckoned.

Despite himself, Ant grinned. When he was a little kid they used to have a map of the world on the back of the toilet door, and whenever his father took him in

Cape Otway.

there, Ant would get him to point out the big white land at the bottom, with its magic first three letters that Ant himself could read. He and Tony used to pretend that Antarctica belonged to Ant, and even that one day they would go there. Ant glanced at his father now, to see if he remembered, but Tony was just saying how, this far south in mid winter, it would be dark in half an hour. 'So we'd better get a move on with this tent,' he added in the kind of voice that adults use to make an order sound polite.

Sometimes Ant's mind would seem to click out of his body for a moment, and he would see himself and the scene he was in as if it were a picture that he was photographing. That happened now: into his mind came an image of two extremely tall thin people, trying to put up a tent in sandy scrubby country as a high wind kept pulling at the canvas and ballooning it out of their control.

Then Tony yelled something and Ant was back in the real picture.

Not that Ant could see all that much of the real picture, because now drizzle was drizzling down inside his specs, so he wasn't being very helpful as Tony kept yelling stuff like *'Hang on to that guy rope!'* and *'Just pull on the fly!'*

The fly?

As far as Ant knew, flies were either insects or things in trousers. He stood there gawping.

'Don't stand there gawping!' his father said.

It wasn't Ant's fault he'd never been camping before. His father should have taken him when he was a little kid. But Tony was always so busy working that Ant couldn't remember a holiday of any variety that he'd ever been on with his father; nor for that matter could he remember his father going off camping with a bunch of mates, as some men did.

So why this?

Ant had a terrible feeling that Tony wanted this to be one of those Father-and-Son trips that happen in American books and television shows: where out in the wilds amongst the grizzly bears and snowcapped mountains, Dad and Junior subsist on root beer and wienies while they discuss the Facts of Life, the Meaning of Life, or whatever. How else could you explain why his father was taking him camping for five days in the middle of winter in a place that was just about at the South Pole?

At last the tent was up, the gas lamp was burning. Tony had even managed to get a fire going (he'd been a Queen's Scout when he was Ant's age, he informed his son) and was grilling sausages.

Ant was standing uselessly in the rain, with the water running down the inside of his specs.

'Why don't you get the sleeping bags out of the car? Make up the beds?'

So Ant got the bags, crawled into the tent with them and spread them in two parallel lines, trying to leave as much room as possible between them. The thought of sleeping so close to his father was somehow embarrassing.

He needn't have worried. As Ant backed out of the tent and stood up, he tripped over the guy rope and onto the upright aluminium pole at the opening of the tent, which snapped as he went down with it and then pierced upwards, slashing a great hole through the fly sheet. Meanwhile, as Ant lay there swatched in canvas, the drizzle abruptly changed to a downpour so fierce that it was as if not buckets

78 click out of your body *(here) leave your body and watch it from the outside* **89** gawp [gɔːp] *stare in a stupid way* **100** wienie (sl) *sausage* **100** Facts of Life *information about the body and sex*

■ **121** snap *say sth. angrily* **123-124** 20/20 vision *perfect eyesight*

but bathtubs of water were being dumped from the sky. And by the time Tony had pulled Ant and the tent pole and the drenched bags out of the wreckage, the fire had gone out and the half-raw, half-charred sausages were cold and wet.

'How on earth did you manage that?' Tony snapped.

Ant said nothing. How could he explain disability to a man who had been a Queen's Scout, Head Prefect, Captain of Cricket and (obviously) possessor of 20/20 vision? How could he say that he simply was not able to see with the rain coming down inside his specs?

Ant, however, was able to see his father making an effort to control himself, not to lose his temper completely. In a strained voice, Tony added, 'Oh well, nothing for it but to pack up and head back to Apollo Bay and look for a motel, I guess. I just hope we can find a vacancy in one that's not too expensive.'

Again Ant said nothing. His father seemed to interpret this as some sort of challenge to his last statement. 'I'm not *made* of money, you know,' Tony said tersely.

Aren't you? Ant wondered as he stashed the two sodden sleeping bags in the boot of the car. Aren't you? Tony would have to be earning a packet. Ant and his mother were certainly well provided for – Mum didn't work, she did uni courses; and the fees must be astronomical at Ant's horrible school.

Tony sighed, and took the wet sleeping bags out again. Ant had just put them on top of his father's bag of dry clothes.

(iii) His Father's Footsteps

Day 2 at least had good weather. A still, bright winter's day. The ocean as they headed west along the coast road was a blue that Ant tried to find from the little palette of colour words that he held in the thesaurus of his brain.

Ultramarine, cobalt, Prussian, indigo, lapis lazuli, sapphire, turquoise, peacock ...

If he were painting it he would mix a big blob of Prussian blue with a fraction of lemon yellow and a slightly bigger dab of cobalt, then blend in white for tone and lightness. Making the colours was one of Ant's favourite bits of painting, more important to him sometimes than the images he got down. He hadn't brought his paints on the holiday – it was too messy to travel around with oil drying on canvas boards – but he did have his sketch pad and a bundle of 8B pencils in his Land Rights bag. Would he dare get them out? Wouldn't Tony think it – sissy somehow, or stupid, or just a sheer waste of time? Tony would no doubt prefer bush-walking, hiking, rock climbing, clambering up mountains, or plunging down caves into the bowels of the earth.

Ant was aware that the car had turned off the bitumen onto a sandy track leading through coastal scrub towards the sea. 'Thought we'd have a bit of a hike. Stretch our legs,' Tony said, right on cue.

Ant left his sketch pad down the bottom of his bag but did wear his camera around his neck as they set off along the bank of the wide river outlet that took them to a deserted stretch of beach between two rocky promontories.

He glanced at his father: cameras were respectable, weren't they? Not wimpy or anything? After all, he was a tourist ...

His father nodded towards the camera, as if trying to take an interest. 'What sort is it?'

Here we go, Ant thought. Difference-of-opinion time. 'A Zenit,' he said defiantly. 'It's a Soviet brand.' Expecting his father to splutter in outrage at his possession of a Communist camera.

But Tony just said, 'They make great lenses, the Eastern Europeans,' and strode on along the hard strip of beach at the surf's edge. Ant floundered through the soft sand a few metres to his father's left. He was damned if he'd move across and walk in his father's footsteps.

Reaching the further promontory Tony stopped, and Ant took a couple of photos. They were too low down however for the view he wanted, looking back over the dunes to include the river estuary. Tony saw his problem, produced the solution. 'If you were to climb that hill ...'

So they clambered up the dunes, and up the nearest hill, but now the sun was in the wrong position, Tony noticed. He thrust on ahead to the next hill, so Ant could get his shot.

Pushing his way through the maze of scrub behind Tony, Ant again found himself hampered by his spectacles, for the ricochet of the branches swinging back behind his father kept nearly knocking them from Ant's face.

At last they reached the second hill and Tony pointed out a place where Ant could tuck himself into the slope to avoid the sun getting into the lens. Ant took

■ **151** sissy *not manly, effeminate* **155** bitumen ['bɪtʃəmen ☆ bəˈtuːmen] *black substance used for covering roads* **163** wimpy *feeble, weak, childish* **172** be damned if ... *not be willing to (do sth.)*

the lens cap off, checked the light, focused, clicked, but got no joy from taking the photograph that his father had set up. It wasn't his picture any more.

'Ready to go back to the car now?' Tony inquired politely before spurting ahead again. This time, to avoid the backlash of branches, Ant stayed some distance behind.

And predictably was soon lost.

This scrub was really horrible: sappy green coastal bushes just a little higher than Ant's head, so he couldn't see his way through the maze.

But think now.

Stay calm.

The ocean had to be on that side – didn't it?

And the river had to be over there – hadn't it?

And the car must be . . .

It took an hour of burrowing headlong through tunnels of scrub, following pathways that petered out in gullies, fiddling back and forth, even gazing helplessly up to try to get his bearings from the noonday sun. (If he were a Queen's Scout, he'd have a compass.)

At last out he popped into a clearing that contained the red car and his father.

Tony was peeling a mandarin. He just nodded, tossed another one to Ant.

Ant peeled it. He hated mandarins. Didn't his father remember anything? He'd always hated mandarins, ever since he was a baby. Mum knew that, and never bought them.

1 Can you think of a word other than 'landscape' that has the syllable 'scape' in it? Discuss in class why the author used the punctuation she did in her title.

2 Describe the relationship between Ant and his father. What information are we given that would explain the relationship?

3 What hints are there to show how the relationship might develop in the course of the story? Find as many as you can and speculate as to how the story might continue.

➤ Glossary: Imagery (p. 268)

4 The headings in the story all have a literal and a figurative meaning. The first, 'Holding Pattern', is, literally, when a plane has to wait in the air for permission to land. But the author also uses 'holding pattern' figuratively to describe Ant's nervousness as he has to wait even longer for the moment when he sees his father again. Explain the literal and figurative meanings of the second and third headings in the story.

Self-assessment. Fill in Section II ('Working with the First Part of "Land/scape" ') of the self-assessment questionnaire.

CD

Now listen to a recording of sections ix–xi, which your teacher will play to you. (Sections iv–viii have been left out.) It is a few days later and Ant and his father have decided to go on a tour to a cave.

5 Describe the feelings that the cave inspires in Ant.

6 What does Ant see and feel when the lights go out?

7 Explain what problem Tony has in the cave.

8 a Recount the event that Ant remembers once he is outside the cave.

b Speculate on why he remembers it now.

9 Analyse how the incident in the cave alters the relationship between Ant and Tony.

Self-assessment. Fill in Section III ('Working with the Second Part of "Land/scape" ') of the self-assessment questionnaire.

Now read the end of the story. (Sections xii–xiii have been left out.)

(xiv) The Fine Art of Conversation

Later that night, lying in darkness in their room, Ant listened to the tempest. The roof had come off the fish cannery at Port MacDonnell, the publican had told them, and the harbour was closed at Portland. Some of the old-timers reckoned they couldn't remember a storm quite this bad.

From the other bed, Tony asked tentatively, 'You okay there? Not scared or anything?'

'No,' Ant said. The pub was an old stone building, huddled down into the earth. It felt safe.

But now that Tony had started talking, Ant wanted to keep going, wanted to say something – but how? Even in the dark, it wasn't easy.

Just start ...

'Um,' Ant said.

After a while came the reply: 'Um what?'

'Um, can I ask you something?'

'Go on.'

Losing courage: 'It doesn't matter.'

'Yes it does.'

'No it doesn't.'

Losing patience: 'Come on, Antony. Out with it.'

'Well. Um. You know how you're really broke?'

'No,' said Ant's father. 'I am not really broke. I am just not really rich.'

'Yeah, well, I was thinking ...'

Silence.

'Thinking what?'

All in a rush: 'Thinking about how, if I changed over to the Creative Arts High School, then you wouldn't have to pay my school fees?'

'I am happy to pay the fees for your school.'

'Yeah but ...'

'I went there, and I am happy for you to go there.'

So that was that. Mum had said not to waste his breath.

Then out it spluttered.

'Yeah but I'm not happy to go there. How do you think I feel, going somewhere you went? Hearing about you from the teachers, every day of my life? Looking at your name, on the board in the chapel? Having the same name, and being told all the time that I don't live up to it? How do you think I feel?'

'It was the same for me, remember?' Tony's voice murmured. 'I followed Grandpa there.'

'Yeah, but you were good at the same things as him. I'm different.'

Silence for a moment.

'I just don't fit in there. And anyway, I hate it.'

'Is it that bad?'

'Worse. And I want to go to the Creative Arts School, and learn something useful.'

After a while: 'It was your Grandfather that put your name down for the school. Day you were born. I guess I just went along with it.' Silence again. 'I'd have to talk to your mother about it.'

'Thanks, Dad.' It was the first time he'd called his father that for a long time.

Outside, the wind suddenly dropped, as if the storm had blown itself out like a candle.

(xv) Day Five

Pancake time again.

Ant was studying the map. Working out a route that would take them back to Melbourne a different way from how they'd come. His flight went at 4.00 pm. Eight hours from now. Mum would pick him up from Mascot; he'd be home in time for tea. Then he'd have nine days to potter about before school started.

'I guess we could head inland to Winnap,' he read off the map. 'Then up a bit to Casterton. Join the highway and come down through Hamilton, back to Geelong, and up to Melbourne. Or after Hamilton we could just head east towards Ballarat, then come down to Melbourne.'

Tony squeezed lemon over his pancake, sprinkled sugar. 'Which way would you like to go?'

Broken Hill: one of Australia's leading artists' colonies.

Ant's eyes scanned the map, flicking over exotic place names, blue threads of rivers, green patches of national park, an ochre colour towards the centre ...

'The way I'd like to go,' he joked, 'is straight up north, to the Little Desert National Park, then on from Dimboola, through Hopetoun – there's another national park there – to Ouyen, or however you pronounce it. Up through the Huttah-Kulkyne National Park to Mildura, then all the way up the Silver City Highway to Broken Hill.' Ant laughed, scoffed down his orange juice.

'Okay,' Tony said. 'Better ring your mother and tell her not to meet you.'

'What?' Ant's eyes were on his father. He had to be teasing.

'Why not?' Tony asked. 'You've got another week of holidays, I haven't got any work till August. We can go up to Broken Hill, poke around a bit, and then I can drive you back to Sydney. Check out this school you're so keen on, have a word with Mum about it ...'

'Broken Hill! Do you really mean it?' Ant had read about it in an art magazine: lots of painters lived there. Just from photographs Ant knew why: it was the colours of the landscape. Then he thought of something: 'What about, um, money? Won't a trip like that cost a lot?'

His father smiled. 'We'll cash in your ticket – that should cover the petrol. And anyway, there should be a disposal store in one of the bigger towns, where we could buy another tent pole and fly sheet. I don't know about you, but I feel like going camping.'

'Great,' Ant agreed, and meant it.

(xvi) Recording the Journey

Heading inland, the road began to open out before the windscreen. Even the sky was getting bigger.

Ant propped his sketch pad against the flap of the glovebox, got out a pencil, began a rapid record of the journey.

Glancing over as the folds of the landscape began to flow across the page, Tony asked, 'How on earth do you do that?'

'It's easy,' Ant told him. 'You just put down what you want to remember.'

(From: 'Land/scape', *The Night Tolkien Died*, Random House Australia, Sydney, 1994)

Useful words and phrases

Through the description of Tony's face when ..., the reader is being told indirectly that ...
As we can see when Ant ..., he is a ... boy.
The description of ... suggests that ...
The increasingly stormy weather reflects/ develops parallel to ...
Ant's passion for colours/ ..., as shown in lines ..., is in direct contrast to / a sign that ...

10 Say to what extent the story's ending matched your expectations (cf. p. 14, **3**).

11 Why does Tony think being at his old school is the same for Ant as it was for him? Why does Ant think it is different?

12 **a** Early in the story Ant feels unable to take out his sketch book (p. 12, ll. 147–154). Why can he take it out at the end?
b Describe the change in the relationship between Ant and his father, giving examples from the text. How do they feel towards each other now?

13 Is 'Land/scape' a coming-of-age story? Explain your answer.

➤ Glossary: Coming-of-age Story (p. 255)

14 Ant wants to go to the Creative Arts High School. Analyse the role Ant's passion for creative art plays in the story.

15 What role does the changing weather (wind, light, temperature, etc.) play in the story?

16 **Creative writing.** Write a short account of a family trip – real or fictional. Give it a title and at least two sub-headings. Try to find headings with both a literal and a figurative meaning.

B **Young, Talented and Rebellious** Anne-Marie Sapsted

➤ Glossary: Feature Story (p. 263)

Now read this feature story from a newspaper.

Alexandria had always excelled in dance, music and art and shone academically, too. Her parents sent her to a top private school, but when it came to university applications, Alexandria refused to take her school's advice. To her parents' consternation she stuck to her childhood dream of becoming an actress.

Her father was furious. How could a bright, intelligent girl not grasp the wonderful opportunities before her? He himself had left school at 15 and although he had become a successful and wealthy businessman, had always regretted his lack of a university degree.

Reluctantly, he agreed that she could study drama, but at university rather than drama school, so that she could at least get a decent degree. But her A-level results were not as good as expected, except in drama where she got an A grade, despite little help from her school. It was not considered a serious subject. She refused to take up any of the university places offered and after a year of casual jobs is now – with her parents' blessing – auditioning for drama school. [...]

Professor Joan Freeman, a developmental psychologist at Middlesex University, has been studying gifted children for almost 30 years and has just published the third in a series of books on the subject. She has followed 210 such children, many of whom turned their backs on education in their teens.

'It's basically rebellion,' she says, 'often against high-pressure parents. It's cutting the parental apron strings in a way that is most extreme. Some who go along with what everybody wants them to do, end up later on uncomfortable and unhappy with a feeling that their youth has gone and wishing they had rebelled. That's more poignant.' [...]

'I knew one boy who was truly gifted at everything, especially music and science,' she says. 'He was pushed towards sciences and studied medicine, but gave it up to become a music agent. He wanted to be a professional musician, but felt he had left it too late.'

John Coleman, who is the director of the Trust for the Study of Adolescence, believes that this form of rebellion is part of the adolescent identity development process. 'It's a healthy process, but some children feel they have to do something completely different to define themselves as being different from their parents,' he says. 'Very bright children often can't cope with being constantly tested. At the

■ **1** shine – shone – shone *do very well* **14** audition for sth. *give performances, etc. in order to get into sth.* **20** cut the parental apron strings *break free from your parents*

more extreme end, it can lead to serious depression and mental health problems. There is enormous stress on young people, and almost too much choice. The opportunities are so great now for them to travel and see and do amazing things. For some, it's a fear of choice.'

Professor Freeman feels that many parents have to learn to let go. Parents, she says, want their children to take advantage of the opportunities they never had. But some try to live their lives through their children. She feels that gifted children, particularly, need professional counselling and support.

'Parents should talk to their children and find out what they want to do. There should be a lot of interaction with schools and parents so these children do not feel too pressured. Bright children are often gifted in a number of areas and there are specialist tests that can give an indication of what would suit them best. But life experiences are never wasted and many of the ones who do rebel will go back to education.'

(From: 'Young, Gifted but Rebellious', *The Sunday Telegraph*, 16 February, 2002)

Work with a partner on tasks **1–6**. Answer **1–4** alternately and discuss tasks **5** and **6** together. When it is your turn to speak, try and speak as fluently as possible. When you are listening to your partner, make a note of any mistakes he or she might have made and tell him or her about them afterwards.

1 Should Alexandria have taken her parents' advice or not? Explain.

2 What reasons does Freeman give for gifted teenagers turning their backs on education? How does Coleman see the same problem?

3 What is Freeman's advice to parents? Do you agree with it? Explain your answer.

4 What does Alexandria's story have in common with Ant's?

5 Which text do you feel gives the greater insight into how parents think? Explain your answers, giving examples from the texts. How does the text form (short story or feature story) affect your answer?

➤ Glossary: Short Story (p. 255), Feature Story (p. 263)

6 Discuss the idea that 'life experiences are never wasted' (l. 52)

7 **Creative writing.** Write a short article for your school magazine on a youth-related topic. The following phrases from the feature article might help to inspire you: 'high-pressure parents', 'cut the parental apron strings', 'too much choice'.

Self-assessment. Fill in Section IV ('Working with the Final Part of "Land/scape" and with "Young, Talented and Rebellions"') of the self-assessment questionnaire.

Self-assessment. Now that you have finished this chapter and evaluated your work on it, you should be able to assess your strengths and weaknesses in learning English. To do this, fill in Sections V, VI and VII of your self-assessment questionnaire. Use your findings to develop a plan of action for improving your English over the next two years by referring back to it at the end of each of the next three half-years.

Mother abandons baby

Single parent families on the increase

More fathers take paternity leave

Unmarried couples can adopt

DESIGNER BABY BORN TO CHILDLESS COUPLE

Pop star marries childhood sweetheart

➤ Mind Mapping (p. 222)

1 a When you think about the word 'family', what words and phrases come to mind? Make a list or mind map.
b Compare your choices with those of a partner. Keep adding to your list or mind map as you work through this chapter.

➤ Working with Pictures (p. 223)

2 a Now look at the painting by Norman Rockwell on p. 21. What image of 'the family' does Rockwell convey? What elements give the painting its atmosphere?
b Choose one of the people in the picture and write down their thoughts about the event and about at least two of the other people round the table.

➤ The Stages of Writing (p. 244)

➤ Glossary: Text Forms (pp. 262–264)

3 **Creative writing.** Look at the headlines above. Choose one of them and collect useful vocabulary dealing with the issue it refers to. Then write an article in one of these forms:
a) a news story, b) an interview,
c) a feature article for a teen magazine,
d) a letter to the editor of a newspaper.
If you choose c) or d), remember to give your own viewpoint.

4 a Choose either Rockwell's painting or one of the headlines above and write down how it relates to your view of the family – as it is today or as it might be in the future.

Useful words and phrases

My grandmother/... lives with us; I like having three generations together.
I think one-parent families/... are fine/sad/stronger/ ...
I think it's right/wrong that scientists/parents ...
The family of the future might ...

b Find someone in your class who has made the same choice as you. Compare your views. Report back to the class on what you agree or disagree on.

'Freedom from Want' by Norman Rockwell (1943).

1 The Trouble with Mother

With a partner, read and work on this article from a magazine for teenagers. Each of you reads different parts of the article; then you exchange information to find out what the text as a whole is about.

Partner A

1 a Partner B: Go to p. 25.
Partner A: You have the beginning of the text. Read it, then do **b** and **c** below.

I suppose my family's always been pretty strict. When we were younger, my sister and I were never allowed out as late as everyone else. Mum's always had firm rules about where we're going, who we're seeing, stuff like that and it was OK until a couple of months ago, but now things are unbearable.

The problem is, I don't seem to have any privacy in my life at all and the only time I do get any peace is at school. I suppose what my older sister Suzanne went through is mainly to blame but I don't think I should be the one getting all the hassle!

Suzanne moved out a few months ago, against my parents' wishes, to live with her boyfriend. Of course Mum went mad when Suzanne announced it, but since she's 21 and old enough to make her own decisions there wasn't very much they could do about it and that just made everything worse. It wasn't as if she was particularly wild or anything – she's only ever had two proper boyfriends and the second one is the one she's with now! Mum and Dad reckoned they should get married but Suzanne was dead against rushing things – they just couldn't agree with her views and the atmosphere in the house was terrible. It was like creeping around waiting for an explosion and things got pretty tense.

Anyway, after weeks of arguments and rows, Suzanne finally decided that she'd had enough and moved out. Mum hasn't spoken to her since and although she phones my dad sometimes, that's really all the contact there is.

I really miss Suzanne but I can't help feeling a little jealous that she's completely out of it while I'm still stuck at home living with the aftermath. Since Suzanne left, my mum demands to know *everything* I do – it's almost as if she's lost trust in me completely. It's not as if I'm the rebellious sort either – in the past I've been happy enough to explain where I'm going, when I'll get back, who with and stuff like that. I know Mum worries and I didn't really mind until the disco incident.

Last week, I'd arranged to go to a local disco with a crowd of mates for a girls' night out. I'd told Mum where it was, who I was going with and reassured her that I'd booked a taxi to bring us home at 11.30 p.m. so there'd be no late-night journeys or lifts from strange guys! That was all OK anyway, so we had a great night, spoke to a few guys and eyed up the talent.

(From: 'She Opened My Mail', *Jackie*, 15 June, 1991)

4 unbearable [ʌn'beərəbl] *so terrible that you cannot stand it*
7 hassle (n; infml) *trouble*
14 dead (adv; BE infml) *very (much), completely*
14 rush sth. *make sth. happen quickly*
17 row [raʊ] (BE infml) *(usu. loud) argument*
21 aftermath *situation that exists after sth. unpleasant has happened*
27 reassure sb. [ˌriːə'ʃʊə] *tell sb. sth. in such a way as to make them feel better*
30 eye up the talent (sl) *(here) look at boys*

b Tell your partner the main ideas of your text. You should be able to do so in no more than six sentences, one for each paragraph. Here is an example:
'The narrator says that her mother has always been … . She says she has no … .'
Answer any questions your partner may have.

c Now listen to your partner's summary of the next part of the text. Ask questions if there is anything you do not understand.

2 **Creative writing.** Write an ending to the story in two or three paragraphs. Try to make your conclusion sound as much like the original as possible.
Compare your text with the copy your teacher will give you.

➤ The Stages of Writing (p. 244)

Useful words and phrases

The expressions in this box will help you when doing the tasks below, and they will be useful when talking about other texts.

a fictional/non-fictional story
use colloquial/informal expressions/ English
authentic (use of) language
the way sb. talks in an informal setting / a formal situation
refer to sb./sth.
help the reader to identify with the narrator
create empathy with sb.
be more/less appropriate for/to sth.
a first-person account
be told in the first person
write in the first/third person

⚠ **Trouble spot**
identify with sb. = *sich mit jdm identifizieren.;*
identify oneself with sb. = *(eine Gruppe, Partei usw.) unterstützen*

3 The magazine presents the article as a true story, i.e. as non-fiction. What makes it feel real? Consider:
- the way the story is told (the 'form');
- the content.

4 **a** Collect at least five sentences with informal language from the text. Examples might be:
- use of short forms, e.g. 'My family's always been ...' (l. 1);
- use of informal words, e.g. 'pretty' (l. 1), 'stuff like that' (l. 3).

b Try to rewrite your examples using more formal English. In what situations would your more formal versions be appropriate?

➤ Glossary: Register (p. 265)

5 **Role play.** Work in groups of three to act out a scene in which a teenager and his or her mother or father are appearing on a chat show to talk about their problems with one another. Before you start, discuss the people (parent, child, chat show host) and prepare role cards for each. The role cards should include:
- the person's name;
- the characteristics you agree on for that person;
- why the person behaves the way he or she does;
- what the problem is and a possible solution;
- words and phrases which that person might want to use.

⚠ **Trouble spot**
discuss sb./sth.
Not: ~~discuss about sb./sth~~

Suggestions for words and phrases can be found on the following page.

Useful phrases

act crazy
be afraid of losing sb.
be reasonable/unreasonable
check up on sb.
discuss sth. sensibly
force sb. to do sth.
give sb. sth. to worry about
have something/nothing to worry about
put yourself in sb. else's position
rebel against sb./sth.
try and see things from sb. else's point of view
try to find / come to a compromise
approve/disapprove of sth.
be more understanding
behave disgracefully/maturely
defend sb.'s actions
drive sb. crazy
drive sb. out of the house
get in with the wrong crowd
invade sb.'s privacy
put sb.'s mind at ease
solve your/sb.'s problems
work out a solution to your/sb.'s problems

⚠ **Trouble spot**
sensible ≠ *sensibel*
sensible = reasonable
sensitive = understanding, caring

CD

6 Not all mother–daughter relationships are like the one in 'The Trouble with Mother'. Listen to 'Sex Columnist', a conversation from a phone-in segment on an American radio station.

a As you listen for the first time, collect as much information as you can about Kaley (her age, where she is from, where she attends school, what she does there, etc.). Compare notes with your classmates afterwards.

b Listen again, then answer the following questions:
- How did Kaley get the job as sex columnist?
- How comfortable is Kaley's mother with her daughter's job? Has their relationship changed at all because of Kaley's column? Explain.

c What is the 'walk of shame'?

7 How would you describe a good relationship between a mother and daughter or father and son?

'So I blame you for everything – whose fault is that?'

1 The Trouble with Mother

Partner B

You have the second part of the text. Read your part, then do **b** and **c** below.

As it happened the disco finished early, so we all went over to a nearby chip shop to get something to eat. I was waiting outside with a few mates, looking out for the taxi when my mum's car pulled up and she started shouting at me in front of everyone. She called me a liar and a sneak – for some reason she'd got this idea into her head that I wasn't going to the disco at all and it was just an excuse to meet a boy! So she accused me of never setting foot in the disco – by this time there wasn't much point in arguing back, I knew that by now, so I just sat silently as she dragged me off home leaving my mates wondering what on earth was going on.

That hasn't been the only embarrassing occasion either – I've caught my mum accidentally-on-purpose bumping into me while I'm shopping with my mates and waiting outside school to pick me up straight afterwards. For anybody else it might mean a concerned mum, but to me it seemed as if she was constantly watching my every move. I suppose I got a bit paranoid about it, but she started double-checking everything I told her and, embarrassingly, has taken to ringing my mates' house when I say I'm going there for the evening.

I'm quizzed endlessly about anyone I bring home and I only have to *mention* a boy's name in the house to start the third degree! It's got to the stage where I just avoid my mates coming back as much as I can because I'm totally embarrassed by the way she carries on. Even when I do, she always 'pops in' to check everything's OK. I really wouldn't be surprised if she stood listening at the door half the time to hear what we were talking about.

All this has been bad enough but I think the worst thing Mum did was opening my mail. After my sister moved out she wrote me a couple of letters inviting me to visit and telling me how she was getting on. I never saw them until days afterwards when Dad found them in Mum's handbag and he passed them on, causing yet another row. Suzanne's *my* sister and I don't know what gave my mum the idea she has the right to stop us keeping in touch. This wasn't the only time either – she opened all my birthday cards too, despite me asking her not to after the first time. I've asked my penpal to re-address her letters to my mate's house because Mum doesn't seem to understand that I need some privacy in my life, even if it's only writing to a friend in confidence.

I get so envious when my friends talk about how well they get on with their own mums – I wish my family could be like that too instead of these constant questions and accusations. It's not as if I've ever been a very secretive sort of person anyway but that's changing – things either take too long to explain to Mum properly or she'd take them the wrong way, so I say as little as possible.

(From: 'She Opened My Mail', *Jackie*, 15 June, 1991)

■ **4** liar ['laɪə] *person who lies* **4** sneak (n; infml) *(here) person who does things secretly* **10** accidentally-on-purpose *done on purpose but made to look as if done by accident* **10** bump into sb. *meet sb. by accident* **14** take to sth. *start to do sth.* **17** the third degree (infml) *verschärftes Verhör* **18** come back *come home with sb.* **26** row [raʊ] (BE infml) *(usu. loud) argument*

b Listen to your partner's explanation of the opening paragraphs. Ask questions about anything you do not understand.

c Now tell your partner the main ideas of your text. You should be able to do so in no more than five sentences, one for each paragraph. Here is an example:
'After the disco had finished, the narrator … . There have also been cases when … .'

Now return to task **2** on p. 23 for further work on the text.

2 This Be the Verse Philip Larkin

They fuck you up, your mum and dad
They may not mean to, but they do.
They fill you with the faults they had
And add some extra just for you.

But they were fucked up in their turn
By fools in old-style hats and coats,
Who half the time were soppy-stern
And half at one another's throats.

Man hands on misery to man.
It deepens like a coastal shelf.
Get out as early as you can,
And don't have any kids yourself.

(From: *High Windows*, 1974)

[1] fuck sb. up (vulg sl) *cause sb. emotional or mental problems* [7] soppy-stern *sentimental and strict at the same time* [8] at sb.'s throat *aggressive towards sb.* [10] coastal shelf *(in Erdkunde) Festlandsockel*

1 State in one sentence the advice the speaker in the poem gives and his reasons for giving it.

2 Do you agree with the speaker's views on parents in the first stanza? Explain your answer.

3 a What are the rhyme scheme and the metre of 'This Be the Verse'? Do either contribute to the mood of the poem and if so, how?

b What effect does Larkin's use of language that is considered taboo have?

4 a Read the poem again and look at the photos. Discuss how the photos relate to the poem.

b **Creative writing.** Either write one more stanza which is critical of parents for the poem, or write another short poem in which you present parents in a more positive light.

➤ Reading Poetry (p. 241), Glossary: Rhyme (p. 256), Metre (p. 257)
➤ Glossary: Register (p. 265)

3 Households and Families: 1990 and 2000

Below you can see three different ways of presenting information. They are taken from a report by the US Census Bureau.

The number of households grew by over 13 million since 1990

Overall, the number of households in the United States increased 15 percent, from 91.9 million in 1990 to 105.5 million in 2000. Family households increased 11 percent, from 64.5 million in 1990 to 71.8 million in 2000, while non-family households increased faster, 23 percent, from 27.4 million in 1990 to 33.7 million in 2000.

[...] The vast majority of family households in 2000 – households containing at least one person related to the householder by birth, marriage, or adoption – were married-couple households (54.5 million). Family households maintained by women with no husband present numbered 12.9 million, almost three times the number maintained by men with no wife present (4.4 million). Among nonfamily households, one-person households predominated (27.2 million) and were more than four times as common as non-family households with two or more people (6.5 million).

Despite increases in both the number of households and of people in the United States since 1990, both the average household size and the average family size decreased over the decade – from 2.63 to 2.59, and from 3.16 to 3.14, respectively[1]. These declines continue the downward trends in these indicators since the end of the Baby Boom in the 1960s.

The number of households within each category type increased in the last 10 years, including married-couple households, from 50.7 million in 1990 to 54.5 million in 2000. Despite this increase, Figure 1 shows that in 2000, 52 percent of all households were married-couple households, down from 55 percent in 1990. For each of the other types of households, both the numbers and the percentage share increased slightly from 1990 to 2000.

[1] Family members include only people related to the family householder by birth, marriage, or adoption.

■ household *family or group of people living together in a house or flat* **7** vast majority *überwiegende Mehrzahl* **12** predominate [- '- - -] *be larger in number (than sth. else)* **18** respectively *in the same order as the things mentioned beforehand* **19** Baby Boom *(in the USA) period between 1946 and 1964 when there was an increase in children being born* **24-25** percentage share *Prozentanteil*

Figure 1
Households by type: 1990 and 2000 (in percent)

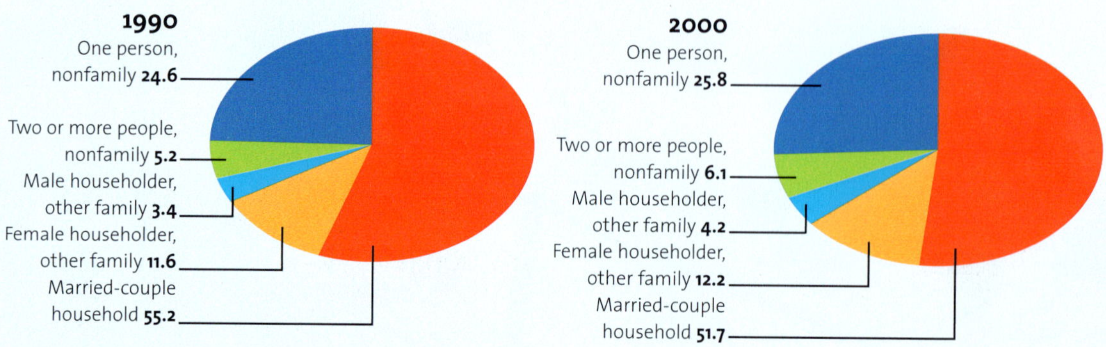

Table 1

Households and families for the United States: 1990 and 2000

All households		Percent of households in 2000 which were:										Average number of people in 2000	
		Family households						Nonfamily households					
		Married-couple households		Female family households		Male family households							
April 1, 1990	April 1, 2000	Total	With children under 18 yrs	Total	With children under 18 yrs	Total	With children under 18 yrs	One person	Two or more people	Unmarried partner households	Multigenerational households	Per household	Per family
91,947,410	**105,480,101**	**51.7**	**23.5**	**12.2**	**7.2**	**4.2**	**2.1**	**25.8**	**6.1**	**5.2**	**3.7**	**2.59**	**3.14**

(From: The website of the *US Census Bureau*, November 2001)

➤ Working with Numbers (p. 226)

1 What one fact from the text, pie charts or table did you find most interesting or surprising? Try to think of reasons that may explain that particular fact, then tell the class your ideas.

2 Compare the different methods of presenting information. Which is or are used to:
- present exact numbers or percentages?
- present facts for a quick comparison?
- explain and interpret facts?

Which method is most limited in what it can present?

3 **a** Collect expressions from the text for talking and writing about statistical changes over time, e.g. 'the number of ... increased ... percent', etc.

b Now collect expressions from the text for making comparisons between numbers, e.g. 'almost three times the number', etc.

c Write two to three paragraphs about one or both pie charts in Figure 1. Use as many of the expressions you have collected as possible.

4 Divide the class into groups of four. Half the groups will argue that the traditional family is a thing of the past, while the others will argue that the traditional family is alive and well. Prepare arguments based on a combination of personal observation, logic and statistics to support the view that your group has been assigned. (It does not matter whether you agree with this view personally.) Present your arguments to the class in not more than two to three minutes – the box below will help you to talk about any statistics you may want to use. The class then votes to decide which group has argued its case most convincingly.

Useful words and phrases

The facts clearly show that ...
As you can see from the statistics, ...
That's why I believe that ...
The numbers suggest that ...
It's plain to see ...
Going by the numbers, it seems fair to say that ...
The facts definitely support me when I say that ...
While it's true that ..., it is still ...
I think you will agree that ...
In conclusion, I would like to say that ...

CONTEXT BOX

Changing Families

The word 'family' can mean different things to different people and indeed many different forms of family are accepted in our world today. In the West, until recently, the norm has been the nuclear family – mother, father and children (natural or adopted). But this almost counts as old-fashioned these days. Many children grow up in one-parent families, either because their parents' marriage has broken up and their parents have separated or divorced or because their mother (or father) decided to stay single in the first place.

Even within the nuclear family there have been many changes in the last fifty years. Traditionally the father was the breadwinner who supported the family financially, and the mother was the homemaker who looked after the family from day to day. Now in many families both mother and father work, bringing in a double income, and in some, where the mother is the better or only breadwinner, it is the father who takes on the main burden of childcare.

While in our culture the family unit is usually small, in many other cultures it is much larger. The extended family can include grandparents, aunts and uncles all living together under one roof or close by. Often this is an economic necessity, but for many such families it is at least as much a matter of respect, kindness, mutual responsibility and ... preference.

And how will people bring up their children in the future? What will family values look like in the future? A gay couple in Britain have successfully adopted the twin daughters they had conceived with a surrogate mother, test-tube babies are now quite common, and the cloning of human beings may already be reality.

Nuclear family.

Extended family.

Gay parents.

1 **a** Check that you understand the meaning of all the highlighted words and phrases. Then list them under one of the headings *traditional families* or *new kinds of families*. Many may fit into both lists. Explain why.

b Pick four of the highlighted words and with the help of a dictionary write down as many different forms of the words as you can, e.g. *adopt, adopted, adoption, adoptive*.

c Choose five of your new words or phrases and use each one in a sentence, e.g.
Growing up in a nuclear family is nice, but I think a child can be just as happy living in a one-parent family.

d Find other useful words and phrases in the text which you can add to your word list dealing with the family (cf. p. 20, **1**).

4 Family Life

A Giving Thanks Laurie Halse Anderson

What festivals do you celebrate with your family? What preparations does each of you make for these festivals? If the choice were yours, would you celebrate differently? Now read the following excerpt from a novel in which an American family prepares to celebrate Thanksgiving together.

The Pilgrims gave thanks at Thanksgiving because the Native Americans saved their sorry butts from starving. I give thanks at Thanksgiving because my mother finally goes to work and my father orders pizza.

My normally harried, rushed mother always turns into a strung-out retail junkie just before Turkey Day. It's because of Black Friday, the day after Thanksgiving, the start of the Christmas shopping season. If she doesn't sell a billion shirts and twelve million belts on Black Friday, the world will end. She lives on cigarettes and black coffee, swearing like a rap star and calculating spreadsheets in her head. The goals she sets for her store are totally unrealistic and she knows it. She can't help herself. It's like watching someone caught in an electric fence, twitching and squirming and very stuck. Every year, just when she's stressed to the snapping point, she cooks Thanksgiving dinner. We beg her not to. We plead with her, send anonymous notes. She doesn't listen.

I go to bed the night before Thanksgiving at 10 p.m. She's pounding on her laptop at the dining-room table. When I come downstairs Thanksgiving morning, she's still there. I don't think she slept.

She looks up at me in my robe and bunny slippers. 'Oh, damn,' she says. 'The turkey.'

■ **2** save their sorry butts (infml) *ihre armselige Haut retten (butt = Hintern)* **4** harried *gehetzt* **4** strung-out (infml) *very nervous* **4-5** retail junkie *person who spends all their time in shops* **8** calculate spreadsheets *die Buchhaltung machen* **9** set goals *aim for sth.* **11** stuck *unable to move* **12** snapping point *breaking point* **17** robe (AE) *long loose piece of clothing which is worn over your nightclothes*

■ 22 hack at sth. *cut sth. up in a rough manner* 22 guts *Innereien* 23 body parts *(hier) Innereien* 27 Kodak logic *reference to an advert for Kodak in which 'those special family moments' are shown* 28 commercial *advertisement* 32 #1 (AE) *number 1* 34 scabby *schorfig* 36 hang up *put the phone down* 41 confectioner's sugar *Puderzucker* 41-42 bum around (sl) *hang around* 43 motion (v) *signal* 44 cord *Schnur* 45 stake *Brandpfahl* 45 drumstick *lower part of the turkey's leg* 45-46 poke out *herausragen* 47 thaw *no longer be frozen* 50 rip-roarer (infml) *very loud argument* 52 wade through sth. *struggle through sth.* 57 oven mitt (AE) *type of glove used to hold hot pots with* 60 chopping block *Hackklotz* 60 hatchet *small axe* 70 stuffing *Füllung* 75 wince *zusammenzucken* 78 fake (adj) *acted, not real* 79 screw up (infml) *do sth. very badly* 81 burp *rülpsen*

I peel potatoes while she gives the frozen turkey a hot bath. The windows fog up, separating us from the outside. I want to suggest that we have something else for dinner, spaghetti maybe, or sandwiches, but I know she wouldn't take it the right way. She hacks at the guts of the turkey with an ice pick to get out the bag of body parts. I'm impressed. Last year she cooked the bird with the bag inside.

Cooking Thanksgiving dinner means something to her. It's like a holy obligation, part of what makes her a wife and mother. My family doesn't talk much and we have nothing in common, but if my mother cooks a proper Thanksgiving dinner, it says we'll be a family for one more year. Kodak logic. Only in film commercials does stuff like that work.

I finish the potatoes. She sends me to the TV to watch the parades. Dad stumbles downstairs. 'How is she?' he asks before he goes in the kitchen. 'It's Thanksgiving,' I say. Dad puts on his coat. 'Doughnuts?' he asks. I nod.

The phone rings. Mom answers. It's the store. Emergency #1. I go into the kitchen for a soda. She pours me orange juice, which I can't drink because it burns my scabby lips. The turkey floats in the sink, a ten-pound turkey iceberg. A turkeyberg. I feel very much like the *Titanic*.

Mom hangs up and chases me with instructions to take a shower and clean my room. I soak in the bathtub. I fill my lungs with air and float on top of the water, then blow out all my breath and sink to the bottom. I put my head underwater to listen to my heart beat. The phone rings again. Emergency #2.

By the time I'm dressed, the parades are over and Dad is watching football. Confectioner's sugar dusts the stubble on his face. I don't like it when he bums around the house on holidays. I like my Dad clean-shaven and wearing a suit. He motions for me to get out of the way so he can see the screen.

Mom is on the phone. Emergency #3. The long curly cord snakes around and around her thin body, like a rope tying her to the stake. Two drumstick tips poke out of an enormous pot of boiling water. She is boiling the frozen turkey. 'It's too big for the microwave,' she explains. 'It will be thawed soon.' She puts a finger in her free ear to concentrate on what the phone is telling her. I take a plain doughnut from the bag and go back to my room.

Three magazines later, my parents are arguing. Not a rip-roarer. A simmering argument, a few bubbles splashing on the stove. I want another doughnut, but don't feel like wading through the fight to get it. They retreat to their corners when the phone rings again. Here's my chance.

Mom has the phone to her ear when I walk in the kitchen, but she isn't listening to it. She rubs the steam from the window and stares into the back yard. I join her at the sink.

Dad strides across the back yard, wearing an oven mitt and carrying the steaming turkey by one leg. 'He said it would take hours to thaw,' mutters Mom. A tiny voice squeaks from the receiver. 'No, not you, Ted,' she tells the phone. Dad lays the turkey on the chopping block and picks up his hatchet. Whack. The hatchet sticks in the frozen turkey flesh. He saws back and forth. Whack. A slice of frozen turkey slides to the ground. He picks it up and waves it at the window. Mom turns her back to him and tells Ted she's on her way.

After Mom leaves for the store, Dad takes over the dinner. It's the principle of the thing. If he gripes about the way she handled Thanksgiving, then he has to prove he can do a better job. He brings in the butchered dirty meat and washes it in the sink with detergent and hot water. He rinses off his hatchet.

Dad: 'Just like the old days, right, Mellie? Fellow goes out into the woods and brings home dinner. This isn't so difficult. Cooking just requires some organization and the ability to read. Now get me the bread. I'm going to make real stuffing, the way my mother used to. You don't need to help. Why don't you do some homework, maybe some extra-credit work to pull those grades up. I'll call you when dinner is ready.'

I think about studying, but it's a holiday, so I park myself on the living-room couch and watch an old movie instead. I smell smoke twice, wince when glass shatters on the floor, and listen in on the other phone to his conversation with the turkey hot-line lady. She says turkey soup is the best part of Thanksgiving anyway. He calls me into the kitchen an hour later, with the fake enthusiasm of a father who has screwed up big-time.

Bones are heaped on the cutting board. A pot of glue boils on the stove. Bits of gray, green, and yellow roll in the burping white paste.

Dad: 'It's supposed to be soup.'

Me:

Dad: 'It tasted a bit watery, so I kept adding thickener. I put in some corn and peas.'

Me:

Dad: [pulling wallet from his back pocket] 'Call for pizza. I'll get rid of this.'

I order double cheese, double mushroom. Dad buries the soup in the back yard next to our dead beagle, Ariel.

(From: *Speak*, Farrar Straus Giroux, New York, 1999)

1 How does the way the mother sees her role – at home and at work – affect the story?

2 Look at ll. 83 and 86. What is the writer trying to show?

3 Look again at p. 21 and compare the scene in Rockwell's painting with the scene described at the end of the story.

4 What devices does the writer use to introduce humour into the story?

➤ Glossary: Humour (p. 265)

5 **Creative writing.** Choose one section of at least ten lines and rewrite it in the third person. Read your section to a partner and listen to your partner's section. Discuss the effects of the changes each of you has made.

6 **Creative writing.** Read ll. 40–63 again. Now rewrite this section from the father's point of view.

➤ Glossary: Narrator and Point of View (p. 258)

B Taking Responsibility

VIDEO

In all families there are typical behaviour patterns. Watch the two short extracts from the BBC sitcom *My Family*.

1 **a** List all the situations you consider to be typical of family life. Compare your list with that of a partner.

b Now add any other typical situations you can think of.

➤ Viewing Skills (p. 227), Glossary: Sitcom (p. 257)

2 Watch the extracts again and write down all the features that are typical of a sitcom.

GETTING ALONG IN ENGLISH

An Invitation to Dinner

Imagine you are in a school or on work placement in an English-speaking country. Someone from the school or work place invites you home to dinner with their family. What do you know about:

- how to accept an invitation?
- whether to take anything with you?
- what time you should arrive?
- what to talk about before the meal?
- during the meal how to get the potatoes from the other end of the table?
- how to ask where the toilet is?
- when to leave and what to say when you do?
- what to do the following day?

Working through this page will give you confidence to deal with all these situations.

CD

1 List words and phrases you already know to deal with some of the above. Then listen to the first set of dialogues. Collect useful phrases and make notes on different customs.

2 Before you go to visit your friend's family think about what you can say while you are there.

a With a partner, try to anticipate questions your hosts may ask you and think how you would answer them. Here are some examples:

Host: How do you like it here?
You: Very much, thank you. Life here is so relaxed/ ....
I like it a lot – everyone is so kind, but I miss ....
I love ..., but I have a bit of a problem with ....
...
Host: Are the schools/offices/factories/... where you come from very different to ours?
You: Well, yes. In my country the schoolday usually ends at lunch time. / ...

b With your partner, list phrases you might use for talking about these and other topics. Here are some examples:

The weather: It's been so hot/rainy/... these last few days; is it always like this at this time of year?
Sport: Did you see the game last night? It was very exciting/..., wasn't it?
Films: Have you seen ... yet? What did you think of it?

CD

3 Listen to the second set of dialogues – they deal with some practical aspects of being invited into someone's home. Collect useful phrases and make notes on different customs.

4 In groups of four prepare new two-to-three-minute dialogues for the dinner table at a friend's house. Act them out for the class.
Evaluate the different dialogues in a classroom discussion.

5 Prepare a short thank-you phone call dialogue with a partner or write a thank-you note.

WATCH YOUR LANGUAGE

Looking carefully at your teacher's corrections on your homework or a test will help you to avoid making the same mistakes in the future.
Look at these paragraphs from a paper about family problems. The teacher has underlined the mistakes.

The problem is typical for parents and children. The mother just don't trust her daughter. They have to sit and discuss about their problems. Maybe the girl will find out that she is just being too sensible, and the mother will understand that she hasn't to be so strong with her.

They should speak a counsellor – he could help them and explain them what their problems really are. And maybe they will even learn that they agree on each other more than they thought.

1 a Correct as many of the mistakes in the paragraphs above as you can without consulting a dictionary or grammar book.

b With a partner, look at the mistakes you were not able to correct and decide where to look up the correct forms. Then make the necessary corrections.

➤ Using a Monolingual Dictionary (p. 234), Using a Grammar Book (p. 235)

2 Look again at the mistakes in the paragraph above. What areas does the student need to study more closely? What might he or she do to improve his or her English?

3 Prepositions

a *How do you say ...?* – Translate the phrases below, then use them in one or two sentences.

1 'typisch für'
2 'ein Symbol für'
3 'ein Gedicht von Larkin'
4 'im Fernsehen'
5 'im Radio'
6 'im Kino'

b *What's the difference?* – Find out the differences in meaning and usage, then make sentences for each pair of words to show that you have understood the expressions.

1 agree on / agree with
2 think of / think about
3 look at / look for
4 ask about / ask for

c *With or without?* – Translate the following sentences into English. Sometimes you need a preposition, sometimes using a preposition is wrong.

1 'Morgen wollen wir über die Adoption von Kindern durch Schwule diskutieren.'
2 'Wenn ich meinen Bruder darum bitte, tut er alles für mich.'
3 'Hast du eigentlich eine gute Beziehung zu deinen Eltern?'
4 'Die Freunde meines Vaters verlassen sich ziemlich auf ihn.'
5 'Wir stimmen in einem überein: die Familie ist wichtig.'

Has this page pointed out any areas of difficulty for you that you had not yet noticed? If so, they should be added to your self-assessment 'plan of action' (cf. Workbook).

YOUTH Culture

1 Brainstorm the idea of 'youth culture'. Collect words and phrases to describe activities, venues, musical tastes, feelings, etc. that belong to today's youth culture as you see it. Classify your words and phrases according to positive or negative aspects of youth culture. As you go through the chapter, add to your list or mind map.

2 **a** Speculate on what aspects of youth culture the photos on these two pages show. Give each photo a title. Then comment on the one you find most interesting.

b Describe what is happening in each photo. What do you know or what can you find out about them? Can you assign each to a country? What chronological order would you put them in? Explain. (If you have difficulty, try asking your parents or grandparents.)

c What aspects of youth culture seem to you to be the same in each of the pictures? What aspects seem to be different?

Useful words and phrases

The photo above / bottom left / top right / ... shows the trend towards ...
Youth fads like ... often shock/amuse/... adults
Consumerism/hysteria/permissiveness/... was a feature of the nineties/...
The craze for ... was typical of the fifties/...
Dressing/behaving/... outrageously/... to grab attention is ...

⚠ **Trouble spot**
typical of
Not: ~~typical for~~

Youth Culture

YOUTH CULTURE

CULTURE

3 Bring a picture to class that you feel represents youth culture today. Describe the picture and explain why you find it representative. Do you see in it any similarities to youth culture as portrayed in the photos on these pages? Explain.

➤ Working with Pictures (p. 223)

4 Here is a piece of advice for modern youth from the popular 1997 song 'Everybody's Free (to Wear Sunscreen)':

⚠ Trouble spot
a piece of advice = *ein Ratschlag*
Not: ~~an advice~~

> Enjoy the power and beauty of your youth.
> Never mind, you will not understand the power and beauty of your youth until they've faded.
> But trust me, in twenty years, you will look back at photos of yourself and recall in a way you can't grasp now, how much possibility lay before you and how fabulous you really looked.

a Listen to the song once. Then listen again and, using the worksheet your teacher will give you, spot and tick off as many of the speaker's recommendations as you can.

CD

b Describe the tone of the speaker. Give examples to illustrate your answer.

➤ Glossary: Tone (p. 265)

c How do you feel when older people try and give you advice? Why?

d Choose three recommendations from the song and decide whether you agree or disagree with the advice. Give reasons.

1 This Thing Called 'Youth Culture' Katie Milestone

1 emergence [ɪ'mɜːdʒəns] *appearance* **5** rite of passage *ceremony or event that marks an important stage in sb.'s life* **7** Brylcreem *brand of men's hair cream which was popular in the 1950s* **7** crepe sole [kreɪp] *type of strong rubber shoe sole* **9** package sth. as sth. else *etwas als etwas anderes vermarkten* **15** defining moment *key event*

20 ted (abbr) = Teddy boy *(in the UK) member of a group of rock 'n roll fans in the 1950s who had their own style of dressing* **20** mod *(in the UK) member of a group of youths in the 1960s who wore neat, fashionable clothes and rode motor scooters* **27** revival [rɪ'vaɪvl] *process in which sth. becomes popular or fashionable again*

The emergence of this thing called 'Youth Culture' is a distinctly 20th-century phenomenon; the collision of increased standards of living, more leisure time, the explosion of post-war consumer culture and wider psychological research into adolescents all contributed to the formation of this new social category defined by age. Previously, the rite of passage between childhood and adult life had not been so clearly demarcated – this is not to say that young adults didn't have their own activities before the invention of Brylcreem and crepe soles (youth gangs were common in Victorian Britain, for example) – but it hadn't before been defined or packaged as a culture.

Once 'invented', the 'youth culture' provoked a variety of often contradictory responses: youth was dangerous, misunderstood, the future, a new consumer group. British post-war youth culture emerged primarily in response to the American popular culture centred on rock 'n' roll. The 1955 film *Blackboard Jungle*, with its soundtrack featuring Bill Haley and the Comets' 'Rock Around the Clock', was a defining moment, inspiring people to dance in the aisles (and some to slash seats). The fear was not only of hoodlums but also of the creeping Americanisation of British culture. But the impact of imported US films and music did not lead to a homogenisation; instead it inspired a series of spectacular – and distinctly British – youth subcultures from the mid-50s to the late 70s: teds, mods, skinheads, punks. [...]

Britain also led the way in the study of youth, and its celebration of creativity and resistance, though these studies, naturally, have their favourite subcultures, often overlooking others. (Still, the kiss of death for any subculture is to be 'understood' by a sociologist.) By the late 70s and early 80s, youth subculture began to change, and became less gang oriented. The regular emergence of new subcultures slowed down, and the first major period of revivals began. It became difficult to identify distinct subcultures, rather than just musical styles. In fact, something weird happened: everyone started behaving like a teenager. By the 90s 'proper' grown-ups had started to complain that contemporary youth were dull and conformist.

(From: *The Guardian*, 18 December, 1999)

1 a Look at each paragraph and find one or two key sentences which contain the most important points the writer wishes to make. Find a heading for each paragraph.

➤ Summary Writing (p. 248)

b Using your headings and key sentences, write a summary of the text.

2 Read the article again. Find words or phrases that relate to your life as a teenager. Add them to your collection (cf. p. 36, **1**). The words and phrases you have so far may help you with tasks **3a** and **b**.

3 a Explain what the writer means by 'The kiss of death ... a sociologist' (ll. 24–25) and 'By the 90s ... conformist' (ll. 29–31).

➤ Writing Letters (p. 250), Glossary: Letter to the Editor (p. 264)

b Do you agree with these views or not? Write a letter to the editor of the *Guardian*. Refer to this article and state your opinion.

CONTEXT BOX

A New Consumer Group

With the baby boom that followed the Second World War, the 1950s and early 1960s saw a huge increase in the teenage population of Great Britain and the USA. These young people were freer to enjoy themselves than their parents had been in the difficult post-war period. What's more, they had more money – or, as the economists (and manufacturers) saw it: 'spending power'. They had, in fact, become a major force in the market. The producers of records, magazines, clothes, make-up, etc. recognized this. And so did the advertisers. Suddenly teenagers found themselves the target of marketing campaigns for everything from socks to hair cream. And what the advertisers could not achieve, peer pressure did: it was your own friends who would laugh at you if you were not wearing the right clothes or listening to the right music.

But throughout the fifties and into the sixties teenagers became increasingly aware of the power they wielded – through numbers, if nothing else. Their taste in music dominated the market, films were made for them, magazines were invented for them and, for the first time, fashion designers, such as Mary Quant, turned the spotlight on them. Bright, attention-grabbing clothes came on the market, expressing the new self-confidence of the youth culture of the time.

Gradually, however, the manufacturers, instead of satisfying new needs amongst the young people of the day, began to create needs the teenagers never knew they had. It became important not just to wear jeans, for example, but to wear jeans with a particular designer label. And now the advertisers began to create a whole world of beautiful, slender, blemish-free youngsters who seemed to cry out from TV screens, hoardings and the glossy pages of magazines: 'Buy my product and you buy into my beauty and my lifestyle. You, too, can be one of the in-crowd!'

1 **a** Check that you understand all the highlighted words and phrases and add those that are appropriate to your list or mind map (cf. p. 36, **1**).

b Using words and phrases you have collected, write an essay of about 400 words on 'Youth Culture: breaking free or giving in to peer pressure?'

2 The film *Spiderman* broke all Hollywood records by earning $40 million on its first day in May 2002. 'The film's central character is a teenager – that's in the peer group of the most frequent moviegoer', said a spokesperson.
How does this statement fit the information above?

2 My Music

A

I'm Britain's top teen DJ!

16-year-old Joe is officially Britain's top teen mixmaster! Here's his spin-tastic story…

Joe knows how to drive a crowd wild!

When I was 15, I bought my first decks with some money I'd been given for Christmas. I probably spent about £250 initially on records, a mixer, amp, speakers and headphones. To be honest, mixing came quite naturally to me, as I found it pretty easy to pick up the beat.

Mum was all for it, but Dad wasn't so keen! I don't think that most older people get the whole dance music thing – it's just repetitive noise to them. Plus, Dad was never over the moon when he came in from work to hear me practising, but I guess he got used to it! After a year or so, I started doing mobile discos with a friend. We just took our decks along to friends' birthday parties and had a laugh, so it was hardly professional!

DJ Funk

Then, about six months ago, I saw a flyer for the Young UK DJ Of The Year competition at a *ukclubculture* gig in Romford, Essex. It sounded like a good opportunity, so I sent in a tape of my mixing skills. I needed a DJ name, so I chose DJ Funk as that's the kind of music I play – fresh, funky house!

> "I found it pretty easy to pick up the beat"

A week later, a letter arrived telling me I was through to the heats! I was over the moon, but I knew I'd have to stay calm as it was only the first step of a really long process. I just kept on practising inbetween getting through each stage. I usually practise for two or three hours a day anyway!

My regional heat was the first time I'd played in a real club. I played a set at Zeus in Chelmsford and I loved it! When I got through to the final, I thought I had a chance of doing well 'cause I'm so dedicated. But, when one of the other finalists told me he'd improved loads since the last heat, I got quite nervous.

Go bananas

The judges at the final included top DJs, Carl Cox and Boy George. Carl's always been my inspiration – he's just amazing and it was great to get to meet him. I had a quick chat and he said how impressed he was with me. He was really down to earth and wished me luck for the future, which meant a lot coming from him. When I found out I'd won, I wasn't *too* shocked as I think I'm good at what I do – I love it and it shows! I gave the crowd what they wanted and everyone went bananas – it was fantastic!

Joe with his award – and his DJ heroes.

The prize was £200 worth of the latest eJay music software titles, two Vestax turntables, a PMC Mixer and PlayStation 2, plus an exclusive contract with Big Bang Management.

They've already booked me to do a couple of gigs next month, at Time And Envy in Romford, and the Liquid Rooms in Luton.

If I could DJ anywhere at all, my dream gig would be at Space in Ibiza, alongside the real DJ-ing masters like Carl Cox, Sacha and Pete Tong. In the meantime, I'm happy just working towards my ambition of DJ-ing full time.

Rock DJ!

Joe's top tips for DJing success…

★ Believe in yourself.
★ Practise your technical skills like mad!
★ Work on your own individual style – don't try to copy someone else.
★ Do it because you love the music, not the recognition.
★ Be flexible and read the crowd – if they want harder music you've got to keep up!

If you've got an experience you'd like to share, send a brief outline with your phone number to *Your stories* at the usual **Sugar** address, or email it to us at **sugarreaders@sugarmagazine.co.uk** If it's published, you could receive payment.

■ amp (infml) = amplifier *Verstärker* • pick up the beat *find your way into the rhythm of a piece of music* • get sb./sth. (infml) *understand sb./sth.* • heat *round in a competition* • loads (infml) *a lot* • eJay *brand of software for making or mixing music* • read the crowd *work out what the crowd wants*

(From: *Sugar*, March 2002)

1 How did Joe become 'officially Britain's top teen mixmaster'?
2 Is Joe modest about his skills or not so modest? Find quotations to support your view.
3 List all the words and phrases in the article which are informal (infml) or slang (sl). Then look again at the article. How much of it is written in informal language or slang? What effect does the writer achieve by using this kind of language?

➤ Glossary: Register (p. 265)

4 Joe says in the article: 'I don't think that most older people get the whole dance music thing – it's just repetitive noise to them' (cf. 2nd paragraph).
In a *Newsweek* report on young people a journalist wrote that 'adolescents of every era have carved out their own secret worlds, inventing private codes of style and behavior designed to communicate only within the in-group and to exclude or offend adults.'
Do you agree with either or both opinions? Explain.

⚠ **Trouble spot**
all – every – each
Do you know the difference? All three are used on this page.

5 **Creative writing.** Write a one-page article for a teen magazine like *Sugar* about a real or imagined success in your favourite activity. Add a 'Top Tips' box to encourage your readers to take up your activity. Think about the style and vocabulary that would be appropriate. Finally, lay out your article on a page and add illustrations.
When your page is finished, swap with another student and read what he or she has written. Give constructive criticism on how to improve the piece. Then rewrite your own piece in the light of your partner's corrections and comments.

➤ The Stages of Writing (p. 244)

B Two Generations of Pop

CD

Listen to the two song extracts. 'Whiter Shade of Pale' was a hit in the 1960s, and the rap song 'Because I Got High' dates from 2001.

1 What strikes you as similar or different about the two songs? Listen again and give examples.
2 List the main characteristics of the musical style of each song. What else about the songs links or separates the teenagers of the 1960s and those of the first decade of the 21st century?
3 **a** What music do you like to listen to? Why do you like it?
b Choose your favourite track of the moment and write a review of it.

➤ Writing Reports and Reviews (p. 251)

4 **Project work.** Form small groups. Each group is to prepare a five-minute segment of a music radio station's programme for teens. The segment should include two minutes of chat about music (a recommendation, gossip about the stars, news of a new craze, etc.) and three minutes of music. If you are a DJ, musician or singer-songwriter you may choose to record the segment at home with your group.
At the end of the lesson vote on the kind of music that is most popular in your class right now and on the best radio segment.

3 How I See Me, How I See You

A Diet-crazy Girls ... and Boys Cahal Milmo

British teenagers of both sexes are increasingly fixated with their weight as a combination of low self-esteem and concern about image drives them into unnecessary dieting, a study said yesterday.

The survey, which sought the opinions of nearly 37,000 British school children aged from 10 to 15 on health matters, found that 60 per cent of girls aged between 14 and 15 believe they are fat and need to lose weight.

Researchers at the Schools Health Education Unit in Exeter found that a youth culture increasingly focused on appearance is driving some female pupils to go without food for the entire school day.

The report found that 18 per cent of 14- to 15-year-old girls skip breakfast and 15 per cent miss lunch, while 4.5 per cent miss both meals, despite the fact that fewer than one in eight females of that age are clinically overweight.

Dr David Regis, research manager for the project, said: 'We can relate this desire to low self-esteem and general anxiety about appearance. It's certain that most of these young women do not need to lose weight.'

A rising proportion of boys were also found to be worried about their weight, with 28 per cent saying they would like to lose a few pounds to conform with their 'ideal' shape.

Dr Regis said teenagers were more aware of how to eat healthily by choosing fresh fruit and vegetables, but he called for greater efforts in the media to make youngsters comfortable with their bodies.

Health campaigners, who called the findings 'disappointing', said schools needed to do more to encourage youngsters to be sceptical about the images presented to them by the outside world. Steve Bloomfield, spokesman for the Eating Disorders Association, said: 'It is disappointing that the figures for teenagers who consider themselves overweight should be so high.'

'Dieting is no solution – it is much better to eat healthily and exercise. Children should be educated to make them question what they are presented with by the media rather than striving to conform.'

(From: 'Fixation with Image Drives Teenage Girls and Boys into Needless Dieting', *The Independent*, 16 October, 2000)

⚠ **Trouble spot**
... aged from 10 to 15 ...
Note the position of the participle clause. What does it refer to? How else could it be expressed? There are two more examples of this construction in the article.

2 low self-esteem *not being happy with who you are* **8** appearance *way that sb./sth. looks* **8-9** go without sth. *auf etwas verzichten* **12** clinically *from a medical point of view* **12** overweight *(of a person) too heavy and fat* **25** eating disorder *Ess-störung*

➤ Summary Writing (p. 248)

➤ Mind Mapping (p. 222)

1. Summarize the findings of the study which the article discusses. Do you think a similar survey in Germany would have had the same results? Explain.
2. Start a new word list or branch of your mind map on 'the problems of youth culture'. Collect words and phrases from the article; you might include the word fields 'health', 'self-image' and 'eating disorders', among others. Add words or phrases you already know.
3. According to health campaigners, youngsters should be 'sceptical about the images presented to them by the outside world' (ll. 23–24). Find one picture, article or advert that tries to present an image to young people of how they should be. Analyse its aim, method and effect.

4 Look at the expression 'go without food' (ll. 8–9). How many expressions do you know that use the verb 'go'? Make a list of ten. (Check or find expressions in your monolingual dictionary.) Then swap lists with a partner and use each phrase from your new list in a sentence.

➤ Using a Monolingual Dictionary (p. 234)

5 What reasons can you think of for low self-esteem amongst young people today? What are the effects you have observed?

B **Sonnet 130** William Shakespeare

CD

My Mistress' eyes are nothing like the sun;
Coral is far more red than her lips' red;
If snow be white, why then her breasts are dun;
If hairs be wires, black wires grow on her head.
I have seen roses damask'd, red and white,
But no such roses see I in her cheeks;
And in some perfumes is there more delight
Than in the breath that from my mistress reeks;
I love to hear her speak, yet well I know
That music hath a far more pleasing sound;
I grant I never saw a goddess go, –
My mistress when she walks treads on the ground.
And yet by heaven I think my love as rare
As any she belied with false compare.

(Source: *Complete Sonnets*, Dover, New York, 1991)

1 In this sonnet, Shakespeare compares his 'Mistress' (his love) to the ideal of beauty in his time.
   a List the characteristic features of this ideal of beauty.
   b What points is Shakespeare trying to make about this ideal and his love in particular?
2 List the stylistic devices Shakespeare uses and comment on their effectiveness.
3 Identify the rhyme scheme and metre of the sonnet. Explain the effect of the change in the rhyme scheme in the final couplet.
4 'Beauty is in the eye of the beholder.' How does this saying apply to
   a the sonnet?
   b the pictures?
   c the text 'Diet-crazy Girls ... and Boys' (p. 42)?
5 **Project work.** Bring pictures to class which illustrate ideas of beauty from different periods in time. Collect all the class's pictures and put them onto a time line. How have ideals changed?

➤ Glossary: Stylistic Devices (pp. 267ff.)
➤ Reading Poetry (p. 241)
➤ Glossary: Sonnet, Rhyme, Metre (pp. 256–257)

■ **3** dun *greyish-brown* **4** wire *(here) gold thread* **5** damask'd ['- -] (old-fashioned) *of damask (the greyish-pink colour of the damask rose)* **8** reek *ausströmen* **12** tread [tred] *step firmly* **14** as any ... compare *wie jede andere Sie, die man mit falschen Vergleichen belog*

4 The Morning After

➤ Glossary: Advertisement (p. 264)

Look at the advert below, which the UK government placed in different teen magazines.

A Sex After Drinking

(From: *J-17*, December 2001)

■ hangover [ˈ- - -] *headache and sick feeling the day after drinking too much alcohol* • likely (adj) *expected, probable* • contraception [ˌ- - ˈ- -] *Empfängnisverhütung*

1 When you looked at the advert, what attracted your attention first? Why? Do you think the ad was meant to speak only to girls, or to boys, too? Discuss.

2 How does the ad try to get its message across? Pick out as many points as you can.

➤ Working with a Monolingual Dictionary (p. 234)

3 **a** Look up the different meanings of the word 'nurse' in your dictionary and say which are implied in the ad. Then explain how the slogan is linked to the picture.

b Now do the same with 'sober'. Find any other double meanings in the ad.

B

Doctor Sarah Brewer says...

Excess alcohol intake can lead to raised blood pressure, death from abnormal heart rhythms, alcoholic hepatitis, liver fibrosis, liver cirrhosis, addiction and reduced fertility. If you get pregnant after drinking excess amounts of alcohol, there is also a danger that your baby could be born with physical or mental abnormalities.

Binge drinking increases the risk of sudden death from abnormal heart rhythms and puts strain on the liver. If you are drunk, you may be taken advantage of sexually, there is more risk of serious accidents and accidental death.

If a friend gets very drunk, the first thing you should do is try and persuade them not to drink any more! Get them to drink water, have something to eat if they can and make sure they're not left alone as there is a danger of their blood glucose level failing very low (occasionally enough to kill) or of them vomiting and inhaling vomit (this can also be fatal).

If you are in any doubt, then seek medical advice about how to treat your friend as they may need treatment, or even admission to hospital.

If you *are* going to drink always drink in moderation. Drink on a full stomach (i.e. after a meal); try and alternate alcoholic with non-alcoholic drinks and ***never*** drink alcohol if you are driving.

Remember, it is illegal to buy alcohol if you are under 18. It is also illegal for under 18s to drink alcohol in a public place.

(From: *Sugar*, May 2001)

1 **a** Skim text **B**, an advice column from a teen magazine. What are your impressions of the language and presentation as compared to that of the ad?

b Now read the column. What is its main message?

c Make a keyword outline. Compare the length of your outline with that of the column. What does this tell you about the column?

2 Compare the effectiveness of an advert (**A**) and a column (**B**) for use in a campaign to stop young people from drinking. Which text type has more short-term impact, which more long-term impact?

3 **Project work.** Imagine the following situation: A girl from a sixth-form college in the UK has died at a disco after taking Ecstasy. The college asks interested students to start a leafleting campaign to discourage teenagers from taking drugs or drinking alcohol in excess.

a Form groups of four or five to work on the campaign. Begin by deciding where and how you are going to distribute your leaflet.

b Now decide on the content: Will your leaflet try to scare/shock/inform/help those already in difficulties/... ? If necessary, assign research tasks to members of your group (e.g. Are there self-help groups in your neighbourhood? Is there helpful medical information you could offer?).

c Once you know what sort of leaflet you want and what information you think is important to provide, think about how best to achieve the desired effect. Is there a place for colour/humour/photos/... in your approach?

d Make your leaflet.

e Finally, present your group's leaflet to the class. Vote on the best or most effective leaflet in your class. Discuss what makes it the best.

➤ Skimming (p. 236)
➤ Glossary: Column (p. 263)
➤ Writing Outlines (p. 244)

4-5 liver fibrosis [faɪ-] *disease of the liver, usu. caused by unhealthy eating and drinking* **5** liver cirrhosis [sə'rəʊsɪs ☆ -'roʊ-] *Leberzirrhose* **6** fertility *state of being able to produce babies* **12** binge drinking [bɪndʒ] *drinking large quantities of alcohol in a short time*

➤ Giving a Talk or Presentation (p. 254)

GETTING ALONG IN ENGLISH

Communicating by Chat and E-mail

Imagine you are planning to attend a language school in Malta to improve your English. The language school's website gives you the chance to chat with someone from the school during certain hours or to send them an e-mail.

➤ Writing Letters (p. 250)

1 During the six weeks you plan to be in Malta, you would like to spend the first three weeks at the school, go sailing for a week, then do another two weeks of classes. The school only offers two, four and six-week courses. You would like to know whether it is possible to do what you want to do and what the price would be.
Draft an e-mail to the school to find out. You should:
- use a meaningful subject line ('Information' is not very helpful);
- start and finish your e-mail as in a business letter;
- be as brief and precise as possible about what you want;
- 'sign' with your name and e-mail address.

2 You still have some questions and decide to chat with a school employee online. First look at the following chat transcript between a student and the school and answer the questions below. Then write your chat dialogue with a school employee.

LinguaFranca:	Welcome to LinguaFranca, my name is Mark. How can I help you?
Guest:	Hi, I'm Monika Bretow. I have some questions.
LinguaFranca:	ok, hope I can help
Guest:	First, I've lost the e-mail address of my host family. Can you give it to me?
LinguaFranca:	have to get your file. brb
Guest:	OK.
LinguaFranca:	got it. RDavies@mail.mt
Guest:	Thx. Also, is it ok if I arrive a day later?
LinguaFranca:	no prob. it's €5 more for transfer tho. Anything else?
Guest:	No, that's it. Thx again.
LinguaFranca:	ur welcome. cu in aug
Guest:	Yes, cu. :-)

a Find the abbreviations, short forms and the smiley in the transcript. If you do not know what they mean, try and guess what they could stand for.
Do you know any other such conventions?

b How do you say the e-mail address in English?

c Look again at Mark's words. What other conventions do you notice regarding:
- spelling?
- punctuation?
- grammar?

3 The language school has asked you to e-mail your host family to introduce yourself and to tell them of any special needs you may have (e.g. special diet, allergies). You also want to tell them when they can expect you and what you want to get out of your home-stay. Write the e-mail, using what you have learned above. Consider, too, what register to use (e.g. should you use abbreviations and smileys in this context?).

5 Y2K.CHATRM43 Alden R. Carter

Do you think it is important to inform yourself about world affairs? Why or why not? Read this story about some young people who do just that.

At the end of this story I'm supposed to turn off my computer and go outside to enjoy a beautiful autumn evening: the real world as opposed to cyberspace, reality as opposed to the electronic void, blah blah ... Well, I guess we'll have to see what happens. But beginnings first.

The bus let us off at the corner of Marathon and Peach in the late October dusk. As usual, I walked the last couple of blocks to my street with Adrien Koudalakian, who's Lebanese-Armenian and looks it. We've never been boyfriend and girlfriend, just friends and neighbors for just about forever. I guess it's a condition that Adrien feels gives her the right to rip on me every so often – actually, pretty often. Tonight was one of those nights.

'You ought to get involved in some stuff, Joel,' she snapped. 'It'd give you a better attitude. Today in Mod Prob you were so depressing, I felt like hitting you with a textbook. A big, heavy one.'

'Well, school violence is another modern problem we ought to discuss. Bring it up tomorrow.'

She glared at me. 'In your case a whack alongside the head would be therapy. How come you see the dark side of everything? This is going wrong, that's falling apart, disaster is right around the corner. You're a gloomy Gus.'

'That's an old one,' I said.

'I know. That's what my grandma calls my grandpa when he starts in on how the world's going to hell.'

'He's probably got a point.'

■ **9** rip on sb. (AE sl) *criticize sb. strongly*
12 Mod Prob *class in Modern Problems*
18 a gloomy Gus *a negative or depressed person*

'Oh, pooh. There are lots of reasons to be optimistic about the future.'

'Name a dozen and I'll name two dozen why you're wrong.'

She turned on me, stamping a foot she was so mad. 'Just take a break, will you? Get away from your computer. Get out of your dumb chat room and spend some time around real people. I remember when you used to be in band and lots of things. Now you're gone in hyperspace every spare minute you've got.'

'Cyberspace, not hyperspace.'

'Whatever. The point is, all you do anymore is play with your computer.'

She'd finally hit a nerve. 'I don't *play* with my computer! I use it. And, by the way, how's that new Power Mac I helped you set up last summer?'

'It's fine! And I get your point. But there's a difference: I use my computer to get my homework done so I can get on to other things. You? You almost live on the Web.'

'So? It happens to be what I like to do. And don't tell me my chat room is dumb. We're doing important stuff there. We're trying to solve some problems.'

'Yeah, yeah. You told me all about your chat room. Trying to solve the problems of the twenty-first century while there's still time. But three hours every night, Joel? Don't you get depressed worrying about the world's problems every night?'

I glared at her. 'Yeah, I get depressed about the world's problems, Adrien. But at least I'm doing something about them. Or trying to.'

She returned the glare and then huffed off. I went in to help with supper. [...]

I guess this brings me to the point where I have to explain how I became a Webdict. (Web plus addict. Clever, huh?) It's not much of a story. I just dig the Web and have since the first time I got on a computer powerful enough to really cruise. For a long time I was happy jumping from one chat room or newsgroup to the next. (I guess Adrien could call me a hyper cybersurfer if she ever got her terms straight.) But after a few months the stupid talk in the chat rooms really started to irritate me. I mean, I could go all over the Web, learning stuff that was happening all over the world. But when I went to a chat room to talk about it, here were these people flaming each other just for the heck of it: 'suck my toe jam'; 'eat my shorts'; 'hey the snot you just sneezed was really your brains man.'

Just junk like that. And stupid me, I decided to try to do something different: I opened Y2K.CHATRM43.

Y2K.CHATRM43 is supposed to discuss the problems of the new millennium. Rules: teenagers only; keep to the nightly topic; serious comments only; don't monopolize; keep your mind open; no flaming.

Amazingly, the chat room caught on. Not that it was any big fad or anything, but a lot of people stopped by. Most only hung around a few minutes, dropped a comment or two, and then cruised off into cyberspace. But a few stayed and kept coming back night after night. Most of the regulars were from around the U.S., but we had quite a few international log-ins despite the problems of language and time zones. In all, I counted some thirty countries over the course of six months. A few of the log-ins might have been fakes. (One kid from North Carolina claimed to be from Tahiti until we caught him in a lie.) Still, I was pretty sure that most of them were for real.

For quite a while the rules actually worked. Cyberpunks would check through, decide we were boring, drop an obscene comment or two, and then boost off for

the next chat room. We'd go back to business. Our discussions didn't find magic solutions to anything big. We didn't find any way to defuse the population bomb, close the hole in the ozone layer, end terrorism, or cure AIDS. Still, we talked through a lot of things.

But after a few months all the talk about big, big problems without any solutions started getting big-time depressing. I don't know what I expected. Were we going to wow the United Nations with some radical and painless solution to a problem? Were we going to find a magic bullet to shoot one of the world's really nasty werewolves? No, I don't think any of us were that naive. But when nothing new happened, people started losing interest. A lot of the regulars just dropped out. Those who remained started wanting to talk more and more about smaller and smaller issues: tattooing, dating, clothes, school rules, getting along with parents.

Hard as I tried as the chatmaster, I couldn't keep them on the nightly subjects for very long. I wasn't about to admit it to Adrien, but she was right: The chat room was taking far too much of my time and leaving me depressed just about every minute of the day. I had to break free, but it was tough. I'd had a lot of hopes and it was hard to let them go.

Logging on to my server, I told myself that maybe tonight would be better, that maybe tonight I'd find enough reason to go on believing. But I wasn't really hopeful. No, this was it. Time to shut down Y2K.CHATRM43 while I still had something like a life.

I'd set up the evening's question the night before: *What do you see as the future of international peacekeeping? When should NATO, the UN, or other international organizations deploy armed forces?*

The subject was a downer. Fred (Texas) and I kicked it back and forth for a while. Fred's a conservative let-them-solve-their-own-problems-even-if-they-blow-themselves-to-hell sort of guy. But I like him. He's tough but he listens.

I hoped Vlad (Bosnia) would log in, since he'd had some real experience with international peacekeepers. But he didn't and that made me uneasy. Vlad had been telling us for months about the problems in his country: the threat of renewed civil war; the poverty; the poor sanitation; the closed hospitals; the unexploded artillery shells lying around. Altogether, some pretty nasty stuff. But he hadn't been around in a few days, and I was beginning to have some doubts. Maybe he was just another American kid masquerading as something he wasn't, an American kid who'd had his fun and wandered off to make trouble somewhere else. Still, I wanted to believe in Vlad. And if he was real, I just hoped he was okay.

Suddenly, Sonja (Norway) popped into the middle of an exchange between Fred (Texas) and me.

Sonja (Norway): hey kids. i'm here. want hear news?

I sighed and dropped my fingers to the keyboard, figuring I'd better get her under control right from the start. But Fred, who has a lot more patience with distractions than I have, had already begun to type.

Fred (Texas): new pair of skis sonja?

Sonja (Norway): no that is last week news.

Fred (Texas): new boyfriend?

Sonja (Norway): oh they come and go. i don't worry.

Fred (Texas): sven's history, huh?

23 pooh (infml) *nonsense* **25** turn on sb. *attack sb. suddenly* **43** huff off (infml) *leave in a way that shows you are offended or annoyed* **45** dig sb./sth. (sl) *like sb./sth. very much* **52** flame sb. (infml) *send sb. angry and insulting messages on the Internet* **52** toe jam (sl) *smelly substance which collects between the toes* **53** snot (infml) *Rotz* **69** boost off (infml) *leave, log out* **75** big-time (infml) *extremely* **94** downer (infml) *sad or depressing topic, event or experience*

Sonja (Norway): no he still here. and erik and jon.
Jill (Oregon): how many do you keep at once?
Sonja (Norway): i do no count.
[...]

I dropped my hands to the keyboard, fingers ready to fly, and stopped. Vlad (Bosnia) had logged into the chat room.

Vlad (Bosnia): hi everyone. sorry i gone three days. little brother hurt by land mine expluding. right no foot no leg. other better. he in hospital. sorry...things not so good hear.

There was a long pause. Finally I typed:

Joel (Wisconsin): hey sorry vlad. hope he comes thru ok.

The others came in, one by one:

Fred (Texas): ya sorry vlad. thats tough.
Jill (Oregon): say we're thinking of him huh?
Art (Kansas): sorry vlad. lousy land mines. we ought to talk about them some night joel.

A few more said sorry and then Sonja took her turn.

Sonja (Norway): sorry vlady. really really sorry. give him our love. and joel i'm sorry i got everyone talking about navels and stuff. tell us the big question again.

I've got all sorts of questions for you, I thought. I typed:

Joel (Wisconsin): international peacekeeping. when is it justified? who should do it? how much force is ok? you first sonja.

I could almost feel Sonja hesitate. This is it, I thought. Are we going to stay open or not? Make or break is in your hands. She started in:

Sonja (Norway): i think when many innocent people are dying then the world has to do something. if it takes peacekeepers with guns then maybe thats how it has to be.
Fred (Texas): problem is it always seems like the u.s. sends the troops and foots the bill.
Pero (Rome): italians help sometimes. in africa we do much with no help.
Cal (London): and brits too. with iraq lots of countries helped.
Fred (Texas): ya, but that wasn't really peacekeeping. that was kicking saddam's butt so everybody could have oil.
Art (Kansas): lets stick to the question. does peacekeeping work well enough for the cost. and i mean the cost in lives.
Don (Illinois): i say yes. most of the time anyway. i give a rap about those kids caught up in all that crap in yugoslavia and bosnia and those places.
Jill (Oregon): i'm with sonja and don. sometimes we need to do something.

The discussion went on that way until the end, everybody keeping cool and thinking hard. Jill and Art (who I figure are going to look each other up someday and get married) went round and round about the United Nations but didn't lose their tempers. Vlad (Bosnia) typed a long, careful comment on Bosnia and NATO. He apologized about five times for his grammar, but the grammar didn't make any difference. The guy was for real – had been there and was there, God help him.

It was closing time. I leaned forward and typed:

Joel (Wisconsin): thanks everybody. have courage. remember, no fear. sonja meet you out front in five minutes.

I leaned back and smiled when I got the response.

Sonja (Norway): ???!!!

So I guess the story ends pretty much like it was supposed to. I put my computer to sleep and went out to enjoy the autumn evening. My parents were still arguing in the kitchen, so I left by the front door. Three houses away, Adrien came down from her porch, pulling on a light jacket. She didn't look hugely happy with me.

'Okay, how'd you know?' she snapped.

'Oh, it's a small world.' I started walking toward the park, and she followed.

'Come on, Joel. How'd you know?'

'You let on things. A couple of weeks ago you didn't know that the Norwegian hockey team had won an exhibition against the Russians. Real big stuff in Norway. Tonight ... well, come on. Belly button? What Norwegian kid is going to call it that? Then every time you got serious, you'd forget to leave out words and to mess up your tenses. You sounded just like you.'

She looked at me. 'How mad are you?'

'Not very. You didn't hurt anything and whenever you got serious you had good stuff to say.'

'Well, thanks. I guess ... It was hard not to be serious after Vlad logged on. I just can't get it out of my head about his little brother getting his leg blown off. I just hate to think there's nothing we can do but talk about land mines some night. There ought to be more.'

'I think there are some organizations that work on the issue. We could look into it. They're bound to have Web pages.'

'Yeah, but guys like Fred and Art aren't going to go along with raising money for any Princess Diana Fund.'

'Hard to say. We'll have to talk about it.'

'I guess that's the place to start,' she said.

We walked on for a few minutes without saying anything. Gosh, it was an incredible evening, what with the stars out, a moon rising, and all the smells of leaves and autumn and frost in the air. 'I've got one question,' I said. 'Why'd you do it? I thought you hated the chat room.'

She shrugged. 'Oh, I figured somebody should keep an eye on you.'

I laughed. 'Why? Did you think I'd get seduced by some babe from the chat room? That I'd run away to meet her in Las Vegas or some place?'

She shrugged again. 'Something like that ... So you guessed all along that I was Sonja Norway, huh?'

'Oh, not all along, but I was pretty sure you were an American after a couple of weeks. The last couple of days I kind of wondered if it was you. Tonight cinched it.'

She sighed. 'Darn. I really wanted to be Sonja Norway. Tall, blond, athletic. Some Nordic goddess on skis.'

'I'll call you Sonja if you like.'

'Na, that's okay. I don't really fit the name.'

'I like Adrien better, anyway. And I've always liked small and sultry better than tall and blond.'

She gave me a skeptical look. 'Is that supposed to mean something?'

'Maybe.'

■ **144-145** foot the bill (infml) *carry the cost* **147** iraq *reference to the 1991 Gulf War* **148** saddam = Saddam Hussein *President of Iraq (1979–2003)* **148-149** kick sb.'s butt (AE sl) *punish or defeat sb.* **152** give a rap (about sth.) (sl) *care (about sth.)* **188** Princess Diana Fund *organization whose work includes campaigning against landmines* **192** what with sth. *(etwa) mit ...* **195** shrug *(mit den Achseln) zucken* **201** cinch sth. [sɪntʃ] (AE infml) *finalize sth., make sth. certain*

'Something about you and me?'

'We could give it a try.'

She considered. 'I'm not going to compete with your computer. At least not all the time.'

'Not a problem. I'm thinking of cutting back the chat room to an hour and a half every other night and letting Fred or Vlad or somebody else do the hosting half the time.'

'Why not just end it? Try something new for a change?'

'Do you think we should?'

'Oh, it's we now, huh?'

'Well, I'd like to hear your opinion.'

She thought for a long minute. 'No, I guess we should keep talking.'

'That's what I figure,' I said, and took a breath because I wasn't sure how this next part was going to sound. 'The way I see it, everybody's got to remember that we're all connected. That we're all caught in the same web together.'

'Not caught. Part of the same web.'

'Yeah, you're right. Part of the same web. And if we remember that and keep talking, then maybe we'll all come through all right. Maybe we'll be able to handle what's coming.'

She slipped her arm through mine. 'All of us coming through all right,' she said. 'Yeah, I think we've got to believe that.'

And after the chill of cyberspace, her hand was warm, firm reality in mine.

(From: Donald R. Gallo, ed., *Time Capsule – Short Stories about Teenagers Throughout the Twentieth Century*, Delacorte Press, New York, 1999)

1 Contrast the beginning and ending of the story. What has changed?

2 What are Adrien's arguments against Joel's chat room, and why does she choose to go into the chat room anyway?

3 Look at 'Sonja's' chat again (cf. ll. 108–165). When does her English suddenly become better? What reasons can you find for this change?

➤ Glossary: Coming-of-age Story (p. 255)

4 Do you think 'Y2K.CHATRM43' is more a love story or a coming-of-age story? Explain, using examples from the story.

Useful words and phrases

On the whole, ...
The overall impression you get is that ...
I would argue that ...
I don't really think you can call it a ... because ...

To be a ..., it would have to ... . But ...
Although the story does have elements of ...
On the one hand, you could say ... . On the other hand, ...

⚠ **Trouble spot**
overall ≠ *überall*

5 Explain why you liked or did not like the story. Consider the language, the plausibility of the characters, the originality or predictability of the plot, etc.

6 **Creative writing.** Imagine Adrien and Joel go to universities in different places, but they still keep in touch. Outline how their relationship might develop, and write the first two or three e-mails they exchange.

7 What do you consider the most urgent 'problems of the twenty-first century' (ll. 38–39)? Do you believe young people can make a difference to them? If not, why not? If so, how?

WATCH YOUR LANGUAGE

Look at these sentences from student essays on the chapter 'Youth Culture'.
The teacher has copied them onto a handout and marked the mistakes.

1 Too much old people think our music is not as good their music was.
2 It's worser to diet all the time as to live with a few extra pounds.
3 The worse thing about the advertising is that it always tell us what to wear.
4 After the study, spending too much time on the Internet is not so bad how people think.
5 I mean it's little important what people think than how you feel about yourself.

1 a Correct as many of the mistakes in the sentences above as you can without consulting a dictionary or grammar book.

b With a partner, look at the mistakes you were not able to correct and decide where to look up the correct forms. Then make the necessary corrections.

➤ Using a Monolingual Dictionary (p. 234), Using a Grammar Book (p. 235)

2 Look again at the mistakes in the sentences above. What areas does the class need to revise?

3 Making comparisons

a Make as many sensible comparisons as you can. Use adjectives from the box (or adverbs made from them) or others that you can think of. (Hint: Think opposites!)

1 Jewel – Madonna
2 Palace of Westminster – United States Capitol – Reichstag
3 MTV – VIVA – CNN
4 football – rugby
5 Günther Jauch – Thomas Gottschalk
6 Paris – London – Rome – Berlin
7 Maths – Physics

Vocabulary box
awe-inspring • confusing • dangerous • exciting • far • funny • good-looking • impressive • informative • international • silly • sophisticated • talented • violent

b For each question below, think of three people, animals or things and compare them:

1 How beautifully can they paint?
2 How well are they made?
3 How intensively do they train?
4 How attractively do they dress?
5 How skilfully were they constructed?
6 How practically were they designed?
7 How well are they trained?
8 How ...?

Example: *Of all the painters I know, Chagall paints the most beautifully. Turner paints beautifully too, but I'd say Van Gogh paints even more beautifully than him.*

Has this page pointed out any areas of difficulty for you that you had not yet noticed? If so, they should be added to your self-assessment 'plan of action' (cf. Workbook).

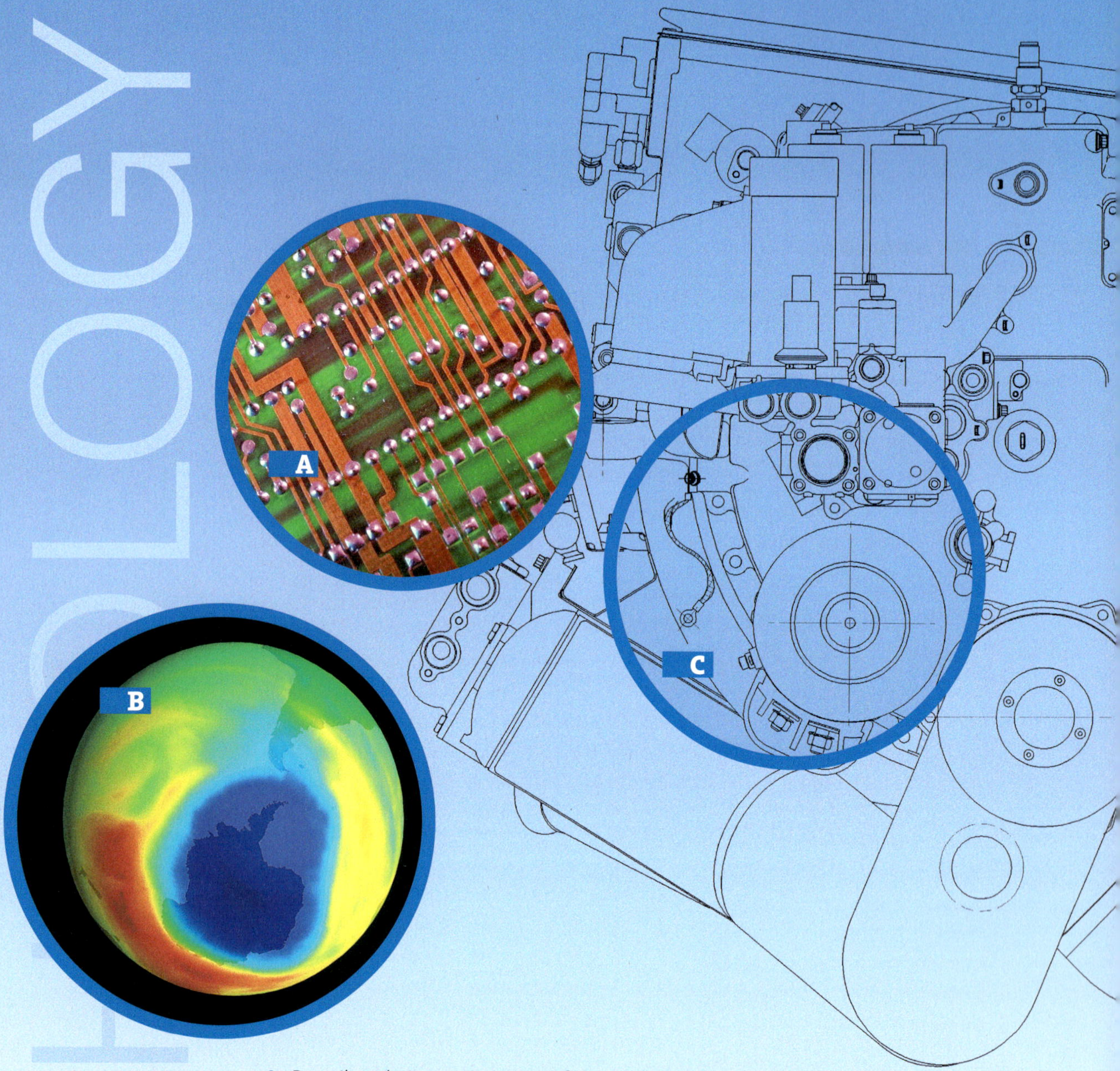

➤ Working with Pictures (p. 223)
➤ Using a Monolingual Dictionary (p. 234)

1 Describe what you see in two of the pictures above (A–D). Be as precise as possible. The words in the box below will help you. (Use a dictionary to check meanings and pronunciations.)

Useful words and phrases

Shapes	Textures	Colours, shades, etc.
round, oval, spherical	smooth, rough, bumpy	a deep/dark/light shade of red/...
rectangular, square	coarse, fine	a sort of brownish-orange/...
triangular	jagged/soft/hard edges	a stark contrast
curved, straight	form a sharp edge	a soft transition from ... to ...
shaped like a ..., ...-shaped	a(n) regular/irregular pattern	different shades of the same colour
be at a 45° angle (to sth.)	has a surface like a ...	clear, blurry
run parallel to sth.		

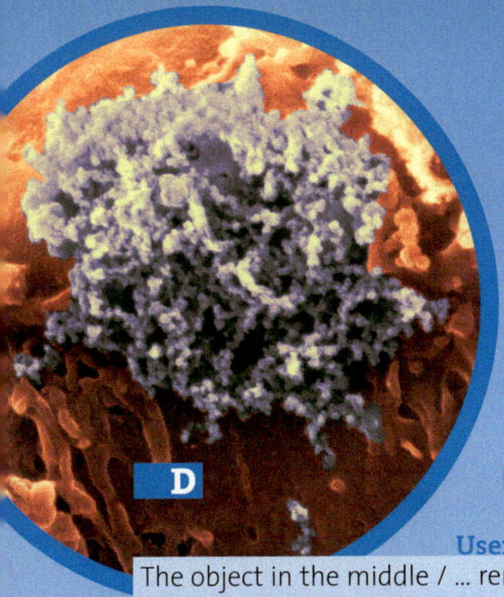
D

SCIENCE

2 a Try to guess what each of the pictures shows. Feel free to speculate, but say why you think each photo might be what you think it is.

Useful words and phrases

The object in the middle / ... reminds me of ... / looks like it might be a ...
I've seen similar images in the past, and they ...
If you look closely, you can see ..., so my guess would be that it's ...
This appears to be a close-up / highly enlarged / satellite / an enhanced photo of ...
The date/... makes me think it might be / come from ...

b What branches of science or technology do you think the photos represent? The words below will help you.

aeronautics [ˌeərəˈnɔːtɪks] • astronomy [- ˈ- - -] • biology [- ˈ- - -] • botany • chemistry • climatology [ˌklaɪməˈtɒlədʒi ☆ -tɑː-] • drafting • electronics • engineering • geography • geology • mathematics • mechanics [- ˈ- -] • medicine • meteorology [ˌmiːtiəˈrɒlədʒi ☆ -ˈrɑː-] • oceanography [ˌ- - ˈ- - -] • physics • zoology [zəʊˈɒlədʒi ☆ zoʊˈɑːl-]

⚠ **Trouble spot**
technology ≠ technique
Check your dictionary to find out the difference.

c What is the difference between 'science' and 'technology'?

3 a With a partner, do some research on a famous person in science or technology, living or dead. Include information on their background, education and motivation.

b Present your findings to the class, including a one-page handout.

➤ Doing Research (p. 230)

➤ Giving a Talk or Presentation (p. 254)

Leonardo da Vinci: scientist, engineer, universal genius

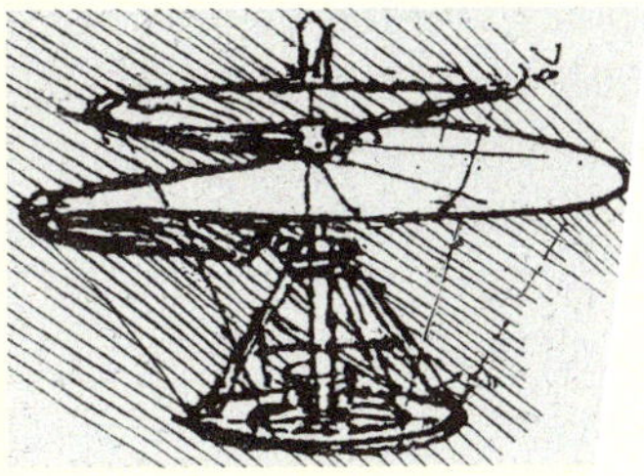

Leonardo (self-portrait), 1452–1519
Da Vinci's drawing of an 'aerial screw' (ca. 1485), thought by many to be the ancestor of the modern helicopter

James Watson, Francis Crick and the discovery of DNA

Nobel Prize-winners Watson and Crick ...

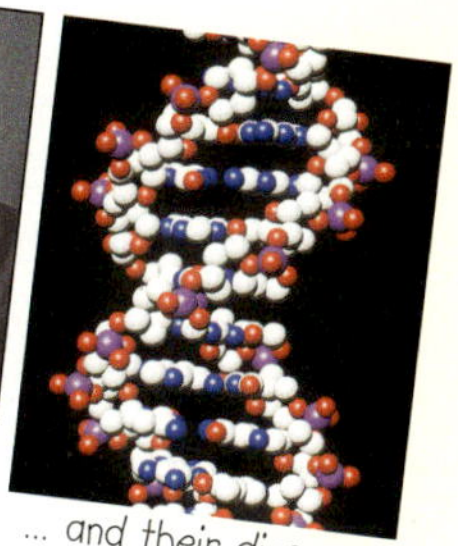
... and their discovery

4 a Choose a particular branch of science or technology and collect useful words and collocations having to do with it. Add more terms having to do with science and technology as you work through the chapter.

b Now try to imagine life without the discoveries and advances of the branch of science or technology that you have chosen. What would be different? Write a short text, either in essay form or as fiction.

➤ The Stages of Writing (p. 244)

1 Who's Boss?

A From Calculator to Typewriter Douglas Adams

Look at the title of this text and the illustrations and speculate on what the text might be about. What key words might you want to look for as you read it?

I remember the first time I ever saw a personal computer. It was at Laskys, as was, on the Tottenham Court Road, and it was called a Commodore PET. It was quite a large, pyramid shape, with a screen at the top about the size of a chocolate bar. I prowled around it for a while, fascinated. But it was no good. I couldn't for the life of me see any way in which a computer could be of any use to a writer. However, I did feel the first tiniest inklings of a feeling that would go on to give a whole new meaning to the words 'disposable income'.

The reason I couldn't imagine what use it would be to me was that I had a very limited idea of what a computer actually was – as did we all. I thought it was a kind of elaborate adding up machine. And that is exactly how 'personal' computers (a misleading term as applied to almost any machine we've seen so far) were for a while developed – as super adding machines with a long feature list.

Then, as our ability to manipulate numbers with these machines became more sophisticated, we wondered what might happen if we made the numbers stand for something else, like for instance the letters of the alphabet.

Bingo! An extraordinary, world changing breakthrough! We realised we had been myopically short-sighted to think this thing was just an adding machine. It was something far more exciting. It was a typewriter! So we began to develop it as a super typewriter. With a long and increasingly incomprehensible feature list.

■ calculator *machine for dealing with numbers* • typewriter *Schreibmaschine* **2** Laskys *first cheap computer shop in London* **2** as was *which no longer exists* **6** prowl *move quietly and carefully around sth., esp. when hunting* **9** inkling (n) *idea of sth. that is going to happen* **10-11** disposable income *money left to be spent after essentials have been paid for* **21** myopically short-sighted *sehr kurzsichtig*

Users of Microsoft Word will know what I'm talking about.

The next breakthrough came when we started to make these numbers, which were now flying round inside these machines at insane speeds, stand for the picture elements of a graphical display. Pixels.

Aha! we thought. This machine turns out to be much more exciting even than a typewriter. It's a television! With a typewriter stuck in front of it!

And now we have the world wide web (the only thing I know of whose shortened form – 'www' – takes three times longer to say than what it's short for) and we have yet another exciting new model. It's a brochure. A huge, all-singing, all-dancing, hopping, beeping Flash-ridden brochure.

Of course, the computer isn't any of these things. These are all things we were previously familiar with from the real world which we have modelled in the computer, so that we can use the damn thing.

Which should tell us something interesting.

The computer is actually a modelling device.

Once we see that, we ought to realise that we can model anything in it. Not just things we are used to doing in the real world, but the things the real world actually prevents us from doing.

(From: 'From Calculator to Typewriter to TV to Whatever You Want', *The Independent on Sunday*, 19 March, 2000)

■ **33** Flash-ridden *full of quick, bright animations which are made with the computer program Flash*
41 prevent sb./sth. from doing sth. *stop sb./sth. from doing sth.*

1 Summarize the article and comment on Adams's conclusion.
2 Identify the tone of the article (serious, scientific, humorous, tongue-in-cheek, etc.), using quotations from the article to support your view.
3 Which branch(es) of science or technology does the computer belong to (cf. p. 55, **2b**)? Add any words from this article that are not already on your list (cf. p. 55, **4a**).
4 Trace the development of another machine that is now a part of our everyday lives. Write up your findings either as a report or as a feature article.

➤ Summary Writing (p. 248)
➤ Glossary: Tone (p. 265)

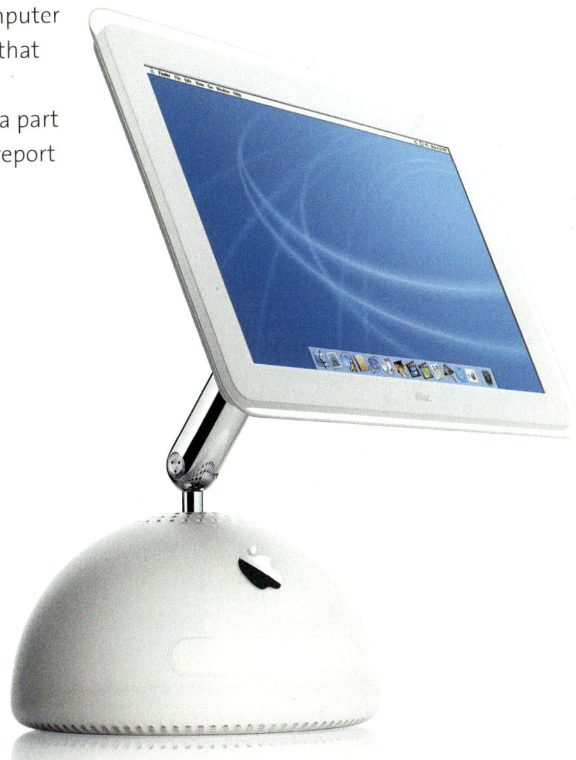

■ **1** appliance *household machine* **2** drive sb. insane *make sb. more and more annoyed or angry, usu. over a long period of time* **7** be out of sth. *not have sth. any more* **8** gym [dʒɪm] *Fitnesscenter* **9** with all due respect *bei allem Respekt* **10** crack *type of illegal drug* **22** foolproof *idiotensicher* **24** Jell-O (AE) *Götterspeise* **26** nuts (infml) *crazy*

B **Remote Control** Dave Barry

Recently the *Washington Post* printed an article explaining how the appliance manufacturers plan to drive consumers insane. Of course they don't say they want to drive us insane. What they say they want to do is have us live in homes where 'all appliances are on the Internet, sharing information' and appliances will be 'smarter than most of their owners.' For example, the article states, you could have a home where the dishwasher 'can be turned on from the office' and the refrigerator 'knows when it's out of milk' and the bathroom scale 'transmits your weight to the gym.'

I frankly wonder whether the appliance manufacturers, with all due respect, have been smoking crack. I mean, did they ever stop to ask themselves why a consumer, after loading a dishwasher, would go to the office to start it? Would there be some kind of career benefit?

Your Boss: What are you doing?
You: (tapping computer keyboard) I'm starting my dishwasher!
Your Boss: That's the kind of productivity we need around here!
You: Now I'm flushing the upstairs toilet!

Listen, appliance manufacturers: We don't need a dishwasher that we can communicate with from afar. If you want to improve our dishwashers, give us one that senses when people leave dirty dishes on the kitchen counter, and shouts at them: 'Put those dishes in the dishwasher right now or I'll leak all over your shoes!'

Likewise, we don't need a refrigerator that knows when it's out of milk. We already have a foolproof system for determining if we're out of milk: We ask our wife. What we could use is a refrigerator that refuses to let us open its door when it senses that we are about to consume our fourth Jell-O Pudding Snack in two hours.

As for a scale that transmits our weight to the gym: Are they nuts? We don't want our weight transmitted to our own eyeballs! What if the gym decided to transmit our weight to all these other appliances on the Internet? What if, God forbid, our refrigerator found out what our weight was? We'd never get the door open again!

But here is what really concerns me about these new 'smart' appliances: Even if we like the features, we won't be able to use them. We can't use the appliance features we have now. I have a feature-packed telephone with 43 buttons, at least 20 of which I am afraid to touch. This phone probably can communicate with the dead, but I don't know how to

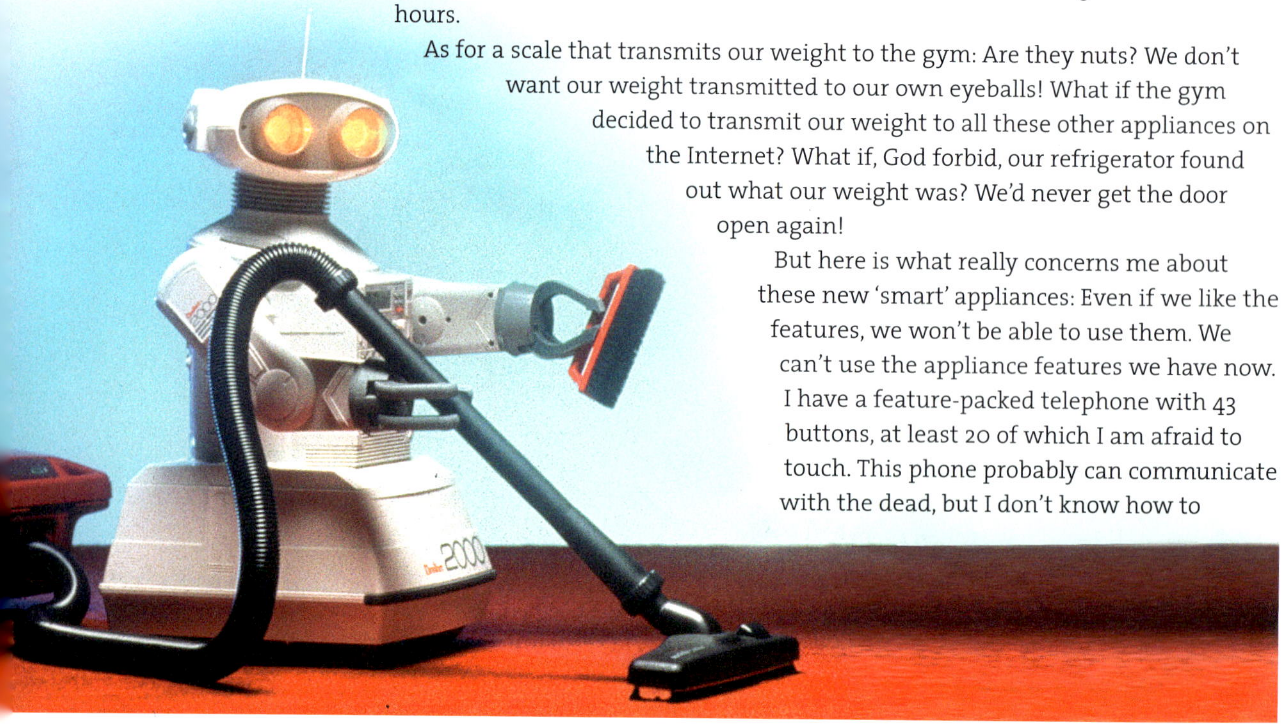

operate it, just as I don't know how to operate my TV, which has features out the wazooty and requires three remote controls. One control (44 buttons) came with the TV; a second (39 buttons) came with the VCR; the third (37 buttons) was brought here by the cable man, who apparently felt that I did not have enough buttons.

So when I want to watch TV, I'm confronted with a total of 120 buttons, identified by such helpful labels as PIP, MTS, DBS, F2, JUMP and BLANK. There are three buttons labeled POWER, but there are times – especially if my son and his friends, who are not afraid of features, have changed the settings – when I honestly cannot figure out how to turn the TV on. I stand there, holding three remote controls, pressing buttons at random, until eventually I give up and go turn on the dishwasher. It has been, literally, years since I have successfully recorded a TV show. That is how 'smart' my appliances have become.

And now the appliance manufacturers want to give us even more features. Do you know what this means? It means that some night you'll open the door of your 'smart' refrigerator, looking for a beer, and you'll hear a pleasant, cheerful voice – recorded by the same woman who informs you that Your Call Is Important when you call a business that does not wish to speak with you personally – telling you: 'Your celery is limp.' You will not know how your refrigerator knows this, and, what is worse, you will not know who else your refrigerator is telling about it ('Hey, Bob! I hear your celery is limp!'). And if you want to try to make the refrigerator stop, you'll have to decipher Owner's Manual instructions written by and for nuclear physicists ('To disable the Produce Crispness Monitoring feature, enter the Command Mode, then select the Edit function, then select Change Vegetable Defaults, then assume that Train A leaves Chicago traveling westbound at 47 mph, while Train B ...').

Is this the kind of future you want, consumers? Do you want appliances that are smarter than you? Of course not. Your appliances should be dumber than you, just like your furniture, your pets and your representatives in Congress. So I am urging you to let the appliance industry know, by phone, letter, fax and e-mail, that when it comes to 'smart' appliances, you vote NO. You need to act quickly. Because while you're reading this, your microwave oven is voting YES.

(From: *The Washington Post*, 5 March, 2000)

■ **40-41** out the wazooty (AE sl) *in larger numbers than you can imagine* **42** VCR (abbr) = video cassette recorder **50** at random *not according to a plan* **58** limp *welk* **61** decipher sth. [-'saɪ-] *etwas dechiffrieren; etwas entziffern* **62** disable sth. *(here) turn sth. off* **62** produce ['prɒdjuːs ☆ 'proʊduːs] (n) *fruit and vegetables* **62** crispness *freshness* **65** mph (abbr) = miles per hour **67** dumber (infml) *more stupid*

1 Describe Barry's attitude to appliance manufacturers. Use quotations from the article to illustrate your answer.

➤ Quoting (p. 232)

2 What criticisms does Barry make, directly or indirectly, of owner's manuals?

3 Using quotes from the text, show what stylistic features make it a humorous text.

➤ Glossary: Humour (p. 265)

4 Discuss which of the two writers, Adams (cf. p. 56) or Barry,
a) writes the funnier prose, b) argues his case better, and c) is more enjoyable to read?
When arguing your case, use examples or quotations from both texts.

5 Who is the boss: man or machine? What do Adams and Barry think? What do you think?

6 **a** Devise one 'smart' appliance and describe its functions and speech features.
b Write a dialogue between you and your boss (cf. ll. 13–16) arising out of one of the functions of your appliance.

2 Genie in the Bottle

A The Flying Machine Ray Bradbury

Read the title and first sentence of this short story and speculate on what it might be about. Then read the whole story.

■ genie in the bottle *Flaschengeist* **5** fan sb. *jdm. zufächeln* **6** tile *Fliese* **9** bow [baʊ] *move the top half of your body forwards and downwards as a sign of respect*

In the year A.D. 400, the Emperor Yuan held his throne by the Great Wall of China, and the land was green with rain, readying itself toward the harvest, at peace, the people in his dominion neither too happy nor too sad.

Early on the morning of the first day of the first week of the second month of the new year, the Emperor Yuan was sipping tea and fanning himself against a warm breeze, when a servant ran across the scarlet and blue garden tiles, calling, 'Oh, Emperor, Emperor, a miracle!'

'Yes,' said the Emperor, 'the air is sweet this morning.'

'No, no, a miracle!' said the servant, bowing quickly.

'And this tea is good in my mouth, surely that is a miracle.'

'No, no, Your Excellency.'

'Let me guess then – the sun has risen and a new day is upon us. Or the sea is blue. That now is the finest of all miracles.'

'Excellency, a man is flying!'

'What?' The Emperor stopped his fan.

'I saw him in the air, a man flying with wings. I heard a voice call out of the sky, and when I looked up, there he was, a dragon in the heavens with a man in its mouth, a dragon of paper and bamboo, colored like the sun and the grass.'

'It is early,' said the Emperor, 'and you have just wakened from a dream.'

'It is early, but I have seen what I have seen! Come, and you will see it too.'

'Sit down with me here,' said the Emperor. 'Drink some tea. It must be a strange thing, if it is true, to see a man fly. You must have time to think of it, even as I must have time to prepare myself for the sight.'

They drank tea.

'Please,' said the servant at last, 'or he will be gone.'

The Emperor rose thoughtfully.

'Now you may show me what you have seen.'

They walked into the garden, across a meadow of grass, over a small bridge, through a grove of trees, and up a tiny hill.

'There!' said the servant.

The Emperor looked into the sky.

And in the sky, laughing so high that you could hardly hear him laugh, was a man; and the man was clothed in bright papers and reeds to make wings and a beautiful yellow tail, and he was soaring all about like the largest bird in a universe of birds, like a new dragon in a land of ancient dragons.

The man called down to them from high in the cool winds of morning. 'I fly! I fly!'

The servant waved to him 'Yes, yes!'

The Emperor Yuan did not move. Instead, he looked at the Great Wall of China now taking shape out of the farthest mist in the green hills, that splendid snake of stones which writhed with majesty across the entire land. That wonderful wall which had protected them for a timeless time from enemy hordes and preserved peace for years without number. He saw the town, nestled to itself by a river and a road and a hill, beginning to waken.

'Tell me,' he said to his servant, 'has anyone else seen this flying man?'

'I am the only one, Excellency,' said the servant, smiling at the sky, waving. The Emperor watched the heavens another minute and then said, 'Call him down to me.'

'Ho, come down, come down! The Emperor wishes to see you!' called the servant, hands cupped to his shouting mouth.

The Emperor glanced in all directions while the flying man soared down the morning wind. He saw a farmer, early in his fields, watching the sky, and he noted where the farmer stood.

The flying man alit with a rustle of paper and a creak of bamboo reeds. He came proudly to the Emperor, clumsy in his rig, at last bowing before the old man.

'What have you done?' demanded the Emperor.

'I have flown in the sky, Your Excellency,' replied the man.

'What have you done?' said the Emperor again.

'I have just told you!' cried the flier.

'You have told me nothing at all.'

The Emperor reached out a thin hand to touch the pretty paper and the birdlike keel of the apparatus. It smelled cool, of the wind.

'Is it not beautiful, Excellency?'

'Yes, too beautiful.'

'It is the only one in the world!' smiled the man. 'And I am the inventor.'

'The only one in the world?'

'I swear it!'

'Who else knows of this?'

■ **33** reed *Schilf* **40** mist *thin fog* **41** writhe [raɪð] *sich winden* **43** nestle [nesl] *be situated in a position that is protected* **50** cup your hands to your mouth *shape your hands like a cup around your mouth* **54** alight – alit – alit (fml) *(of a bird or insect) land* **54** rustle ['rʌsl] *knistern* **55** rig *equipment*

■ **69** (be) mad with the sun *(hier) einen Sonnenstich haben* **87** serene [sə'ri:n] *calm* **90** wind – wound – wound sth. up [waɪnd] *make sth. work by turning a key* **91** set sth. going *start sth.*

'No one. Not even my wife, who would think me mad with the sun. She thought I was making a kite. I rose in the night and walked to the cliffs far away. And when the morning breezes blew and the sun rose, I gathered my courage, Excellency, and leaped from the cliff. I flew! But my wife does not know of it.'

'Well for her, then,' said the Emperor. The sun was full in the sky now, and the smell of the grass was refreshing. The Emperor, the servant, and the flier paused within the huge garden.

The Emperor clapped his hands. 'Ho, guards!'

The guards came running.

'Hold this man.'

The guards seized the flier.

'Call the executioner,' said the Emperor.

'What's this!' cried the flier, bewildered. 'What have I done?' He began to weep, so that the beautiful paper apparatus rustled.

'Here is the man who has made a certain machine,' said the Emperor, 'and yet asks us what he has created. He does not know himself. It is only necessary that he create, without knowing why he has done so, or what this thing will do.'

The executioner came running with a sharp silver ax. He stood with his naked, large-muscled arms ready, his face covered with a serene white mask.

'One moment,' said the Emperor. He turned to a nearby table upon which sat a machine that he himself had created. The Emperor took a tiny golden key from his own neck. He fitted this key to the tiny, delicate machine and wound it up. Then he set the machine going.

The machine was a garden of metal and jewels. Set in motion, birds sang in tiny metal trees, wolves walked through miniature forests, and tiny people ran in and out of sun and shadow, fanning themselves with miniature fans, listening to the tiny emerald birds, and standing by impossibly small but tinkling fountains.

'Is it not beautiful?' said the Emperor. 'If you asked me what I have done here, I could answer you well. I have made birds sing. I have made forests murmur, I have set two people to walking in this woodland, enjoying the leaves and shadows and songs. That is what I have done.'

'But, oh, Emperor!' pleaded the flier, on his knees, the tears pouring down his face. 'I have done a similar thing! I have found beauty. I have flown on the morning wind. I have looked down on all the sleeping houses and gardens. I have smelled the sea and even seen it, beyond the hills, from my high place. And I have soared like a bird; oh, I cannot say how beautiful it is up there, in the sky, with the wind about me, the wind blowing me here like a feather, there like a fan, the way the sky smells in the morning! And how free one feels! That is beautiful, Emperor, that is beautiful too!'

'Yes,' said the Emperor sadly, 'I know it must be true. For I felt my heart move with you in the air, and I wondered: What is it like? How does it feel? How do the distant pools look from so high? And how my house and servants? Like ants? And how the distant towns not yet awake?'

'Then spare me!'

'But there are times,' said the Emperor, more sadly still, 'when one must lose a little beauty if one is to keep what little beauty one already has. I do not fear you, yourself, but I fear another man.'

'What man?'

'Some other man who, seeing you, will build a thing of bright papers and bamboo like this. But the other man will have an evil face and an evil heart, and the beauty will be gone. It is this man I fear.'

'Why? Why?'

'Who is to say that someday just such a man, in just such an apparatus of paper and reed, might not fly in the sky and drop huge stones upon the Great Wall of China?' said the Emperor.

No one moved or said a word.

'Off with his head,' said the Emperor.

The executioner whirled his silver ax.

'Burn the kite and the inventor's body, and bury their ashes together,' said the Emperor.

The servant retreated to obey.

The Emperor turned to his hand servant, who had seen the man flying.

'Hold your tongue. It was all a dream, a most sorrowful and beautiful dream. And that farmer in the distant field who also saw, tell him it would pay him to consider it only a vision. If ever the word passes around, you and the farmer die within the hour.'

'You are merciful, Emperor.'

'No, not merciful,' said the old man. Beyond the garden wall he saw the guards burning the beautiful machine of paper and reeds that smelled of the morning wind. He saw the dark smoke climb into the sky. 'No, only very much bewildered and afraid.' He saw the guards digging a tiny pit wherein to bury the ashes. 'What is the life of one man against those of a million others? I must take solace from that thought.'

He took the key from its chain about his neck and once more wound up the beautiful miniature garden. He stood looking out across the land at the Great Wall, the peaceful town, the green fields, the rivers and streams. He sighed. The tiny garden whirred its hidden and delicate machinery and set itself in motion; tiny people walked in forests, tiny foxes loped through sunspeckled glades in beautiful shining pelts, and among the tiny trees flew little bits of high song and bright blue and yellow color, flying, flying, flying in that small sky.

'Oh,' said the Emperor, closing his eyes, 'look at the birds, look at the birds!'

(From: *The Golden Apples of the Sun and Other Stories*, Doubleday, 1957)

■ **126** whirl sth. *etwas herumwirbeln* **138** bewildered [bɪ'wɪldəd] (adj) *verwirrt* **140** take solace from sth. ['sɒləs ☆ 'sɑːləs] (fml) *be happier because of sth.* **146** lope *run with long, relaxed steps* **146** sunspeckled (adj) *mit sonnigen Flecken*

1 State in no more than five sentences what happens in the story.

2 Explain why the story was or was not what you expected.

3 Compare the Emperor's views on his mechanical garden (cf. ll. 96–99) and the flier's on his machine. Explain how the Emperor's views lead him to remain firm in his decision to execute the flier.

4 a Consider whether the story is only about the events that happen in it. Quote from the text to support your conclusions.

b Analyse two or three of the images (e.g. similes) which Bradbury uses. Explain how they work and what effect they have.

➤ Glossary: Imagery (p. 268)

5 Comment on why you think the Emperor was right or wrong to execute the flier.

VIDEO

B Oppenheimer

J. Robert Oppenheimer (1904–1967).

The US nuclear scientist J. Robert Oppenheimer was put in charge of Los Alamos Laboratory in 1943. The scientists and engineers he gathered there had one task: to invent a nuclear bomb. Watch the two extracts from the documentary *The Day after Trinity* (1981) and the drama serial *Oppenheimer* (1981).

1 Compare and contrast the information available through each extract and the emotional effect of each. Which type of programme does what best?
2 Compare Oppenheimer with the flier in Bradbury's story.

Right: Wernher von Braun (1912–1977), a scientist with a Nazi past.

CD

C Wernher von Braun Tom Lehrer

Wernher von Braun was a German rocket scientist. During the Second World War he worked for the Nazis. He is mainly remembered for inventing the V2 rocket, which was used in the bombing of London. After the war he joined the US space programme. Listen to the song by US satirist Tom Lehrer.

1 What does Lehrer think of von Braun?
2 Lehrer sings: *Don't say that he's hypocritical.*
Say rather that he's apolitical.
Check the underlined words in a dictionary if you are not sure of their meanings. Then explain in your own words what they mean. Could either word apply to (a) the Emperor (b) the flier in Bradbury's story? Explain.
3 *'You can't "uninvent" something once it's been invented.'*
'It's the scientists' job to push the frontiers of knowledge as far as they can; it's the politicians' job to decide what to use and what not to use.'
Choose one of these statements and write a short essay on the topic. Use the short story, the documentary and the song – as well as any other information you have – to back up your views.

➤ The Stages of Writing (p. 244)

GETTING ALONG IN ENGLISH

Going to the Doctor

If you are abroad and you become ill or are injured, you will need to see a doctor. Could you cope if the doctor asked you the following questions?

- What can I do for you?
- Where does it hurt?
- What symptoms do you have?
- Do you have any allergies?

And what about the doctor's diagnosis, prognosis and suggested cure? Collect any words or phrases you already know in a mind map or list. Then work through this page and learn more useful vocabulary so that you can feel more confident about going to a doctor who you have to speak English with.

➤ Mind Mapping (p. 222)

1 Add to your mind map or list more words and phrases from the box below. Look up the words you do not know in a dictionary.

I feel sick/dizzy/... • I have a stomach ache / ... • It stings/throbs/burns/... Can you prescribe something to stop the pain/nausea/...? • I would prefer homeopathic/herbal medication • My temperature / the fever is going up/down Before I agree to surgery I'd like a second opinion

⚠ **Trouble spot**
In British English when you 'feel sick' it means you want to vomit (= *sich erbrechen*). In American English it means you do not feel well.

2 Listen to the first set of dialogues and collect any new words and phrases that cover common complaints for which you might need to consult a doctor. CD

3 Form groups. Write down five different complaints or injuries on separate pieces of paper, mix them up and draw one each. In turn explain to the group what your symptoms are and discuss diagnoses and cures.

4 When a doctor tells you his or her diagnosis and treatment, you need to be able to: CD
- understand him or her and
- ask questions to help you understand what you need to do.

a Listen to the second set of dialogues and then answer these questions:
1 What sort of illness is hay fever?
2 Who is going to strap up Mr Martin's ankle?
3 What is the informal word for an injection?
4 What will the doctor do if Michael's symptoms do not go away?

b Write down questions you might ask the doctor if you were the patient in each case. Then listen to the third set of dialogues.

c Now write a short dialogue between a doctor and a patient from the moment the patient enters the room to the moment he or she leaves. (Use situations other than those you have just heard.) Act it out with a partner. Then act out your partner's dialogue. Add any new words or phrases to your mind map or list.

'This is gonna hurt like hell.'

Coming Soon: The Hydrogen Car

The futurologists at Ford, GM and DaimlerChrysler all agree that when oil runs out, hydrogen is likely to be the fuel of choice. The stinky internal combustion engine will give way to clean electric motors run on hydrogen-fuel cells. The only question is when.

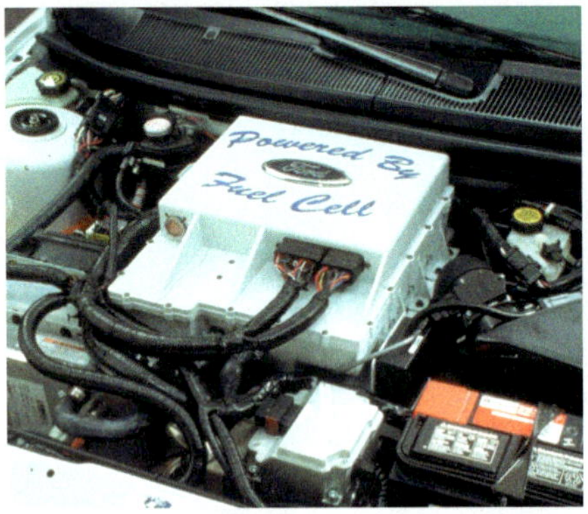

This fuel cell powers a prototype Ford of the near future.

Inside a Fuel Cell: Electricity From Hydrogen With No Waste

Like a battery, a fuel cell passes electrical energy between positive and negative poles. Unlike a battery, a fuel cell generates current rather than simply storing it.

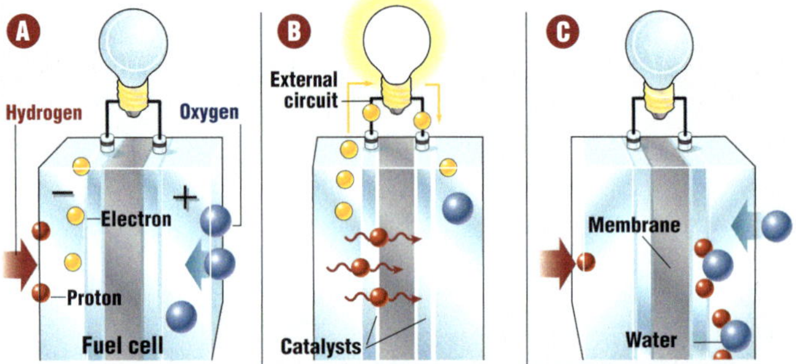

A **Hydrogen,** pumped to the cell's negatively charged side (–), divides into protons and electrons. Then oxygen is pumped into the positively charged side (+), which attracts electrons.

B A platinum membrane blocks electrons from moving directly to the the positive side, forcing them through an **external circuit** as usable current.

C **Protons,** which can pass through the membrane, join with oxygen to form water. When the water is expelled, oxygen refills the cell and the process begins again.

Getting the Hydrogen Out

Unlike ready-made fuels like oil and gas, hydrogen must be extracted from other substances.

From Water
Zapping H_2O with high-voltage electricity to break off the H is not cheap. Current cost for a kilo of hydrogen: about $2.40.

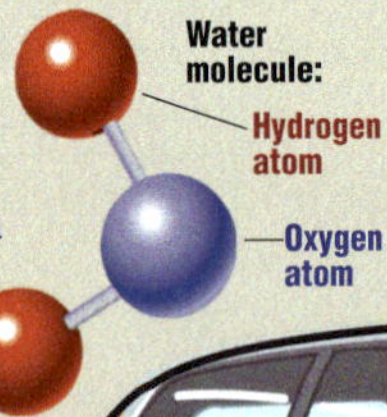

From Hydrocarbons
Combining hydrocarbons like methane with pressurized steam to break off hydrogen is less expensive. Current cost per kilo: 65¢.

Methane molecule

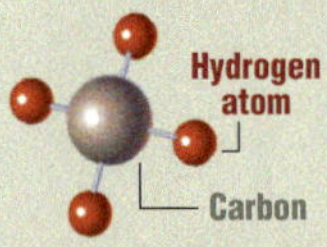

"H" Inside

On the outside, hydrogen-fueled cars look just like their gasoline-powered kin. Under the skin, though, unique parts abound.

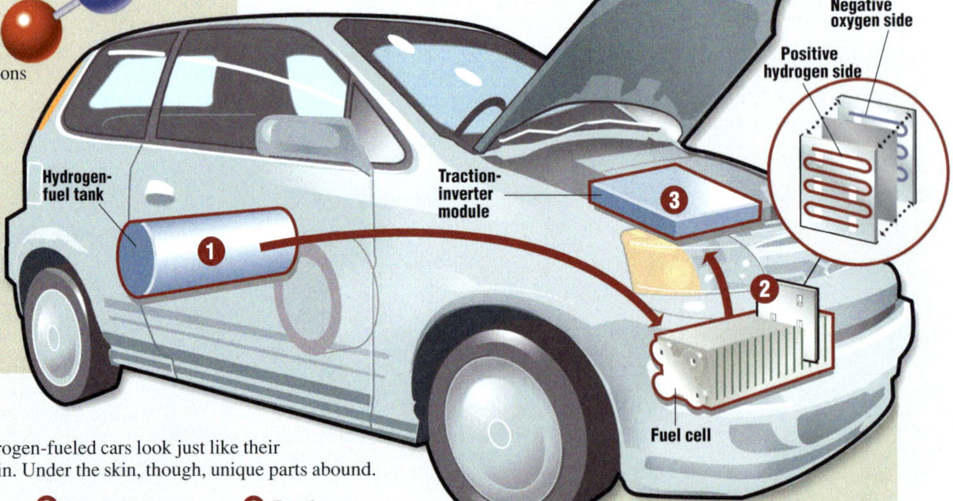

1 High-Pressure Fuel Tank stores hydrogen as a liquid or as a gas. Fill 'er up at the pump, just like a gas tank.

2 Fuel Cell generates electric current by combining hydrogen and oxygen, emitting only water from the tailpipe.

3 Traction-Inverter Module converts electrical energy from the fuel cell into mechanical energy to turn the wheels.

SOURCE: HOW STUFF WORKS.COM.
TEXT BY JOHN D. SPARKS, GRAPHIC BY TONIA COWAN—NEWSWEEK

OTHER USES: Besides powering cars and buses, fuel cells are used to provide power for orbiting spacecraft. Giant fuel cells get larger all the time and may one day power entire cities.

(From: *Newsweek*, 8-15 April, 2002)

3 How Things Work

Skim the material on the left to find out what it is about and what you might expect to learn from it. Now read one section at a time and make sure you understand the processes described before you continue reading.

➤ Skimming (p. 236)

Partner A

1 a For this task, find a partner. Partner B does task 1 on p. 68.
Partner A: Read the statements below. Check them against the text if necessary and decide which are true. Correct the ones that are false.
1 Energy is stored in a fuel cell, much in the same way as in a battery.
2 The platinum membrane in the fuel cell forces electrons to go through an external circuit.
3 You can tell a hydrogen car just by looking at it.
4 The high-pressure fuel tanks of hydrogen cars cannot be filled in the normal way.
5 The only emission from a hydrogen-powered car is in the form of water.
6 The electricity produced by the fuel cell is sent directly to the wheels of the car.
b Now read the statements above to your partner, who must try to identify and correct the mistakes. Try to help him or her without giving away the answers.
c Listen carefully to the statements which your partner reads out to you. Say whether they are correct; if not, try to correct the mistakes. Your partner will help you if necessary.

2 List the possible benefits of a hydrogen-powered car and state who might stand to lose because of such an innovation.

3 a Identify the grammatical form in the highlighted clauses in the following sentences from the text:
'Hydrogen, pumped to the cell's negatively charged side, divides into protons and electrons.'
'A platinum membrane blocks electrons from moving directly to the positive side, forcing them through an electric circuit.'
b Find at least one other way to express each of the sentences in English. Speculate on reasons why this construction is commonly used when describing technical processes.

4 a The following is the beginning of an article about 'remote-controlled rats'. Read it, then try to imagine how rats might be controlled from afar.
'By implanting electrodes in rats' brains, scientists have created remote-controlled rodents they can command to turn left or right, climb trees and navigate piles of rubble. Someday, scientists said, rats carrying tiny video cameras might search for disaster survivors.'
b Match the clauses on the left and right to complete the labels for the drawing.

1 A backpack receives signals, ...	a telling it it is going the way its controllers want it to
2 A small stimulus, ..., causes the rat to go right or left.	b passing them on to the appropriate areas of the brain
3 A stimulus to this part of the brain causes the rat to feel pleasure, ...	c sent to the part of the brain that controls the whiskers
4 The rat's whiskers, ..., help it to navigate in utter darkness.	d touched by objects as the rat walks

■ hydrogen (H) ['haɪdrədʒən] *Wasserstoff* • charge sth. pass electricity through sth. so that it is stored there • proton ['- -] *positively charged part of an atom* • electron [- '- -] *negatively charged part of an atom* • circuit ['sɜːkɪt] *configuration of wires through which electricity flows* • oxygen (O_2) ['ɒksɪdʒən ☆ 'ɑːk-] *Sauerstoff* • hydrocarbon *Kohlenwasserstoff* • 'er = her (infml) *the car*

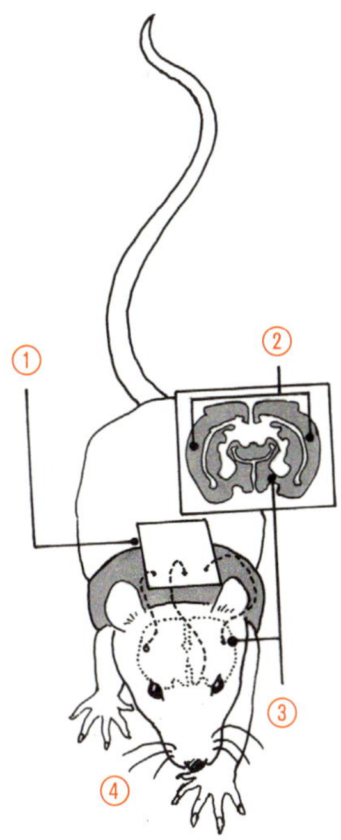

➤ Giving a Talk or Presentation (p. 254)

5 Choose a device (e.g. a coffee-maker) or a process (e.g. photosynthesis) and explain in one page how it works, using diagrams and text as on p. 66. Present your page to the class.

'I think I see a problem with your electric-car invention, Fred.'

Partner B

1 a Read the statements below. Check them against the text if necessary and decide which are true. Correct the ones that are false.

1 The fuel cell uses water to produce hydrogen and energy.
2 Once in the fuel cell, hydrogen separates into protons and electrons.
3 The electrons pass through the platinum membrane, which produces the electric current for the car.
4 Extracting hydrogen from water is cheaper than getting it from methane.
5 The traction-inverter module uses electricity to power the car's wheels.
6 It is unlikely that fuel cells could power anything larger than a bus or truck.

b Listen carefully to the statements your partner reads to you. Say whether they are correct; if not, try to correct the mistakes. Your partner will help you if necessary.

c Now read the statements in **a** to your partner, who must try to identify and correct the mistakes. Try to help him or her without giving away the answers.

Now go back to task **2** on p. 67.

CONTEXT BOX

Science, Technology and Controversy

If science is the attempt to understand the world around us, technology is the application of the knowledge gained through science. We humans are naturally curious, so we have tried to comprehend the natural phenomena that affect us. And because people have believed from early on that the stars influence the course of events on earth, astronomy was the first science to emerge.

Unfortunately for scientists, the knowledge gained from observation and experiment has not always fitted into the pre-conceived notions of the ruling classes. For example, in the 17th century the Catholic Church forced the astronomer Galileo to reject the view that the earth revolves around the sun.

In some societies today it is still not possible for researchers to publish the knowledge they have gained through their studies; even in 'open', Western societies, scientists sometimes find themselves at the centre of controversy because of their discoveries.

Today the field of study that is spawning the greatest controversy is the science of genetics and the technology that goes with it. This area deals with issues that touch the moral and religious foundations of our society in a way no other field does because it has to do with the nature of life itself.

Many scientists claim they are doing 'pure science', that their work furthers the cause of knowledge without them being responsible for what others do with that knowledge. A geologist, for example, might say that he or she cannot be held responsible for the destruction of an entire landscape through strip-mining simply because he or she discovered the relationship between certain geological features and the occurrence of a valuable mineral.

This scientific formula led ultimately to the creation of the atomic bomb and thus to the deaths of tens of thousands of people.

But what of those researchers who work under oppressive regimes, knowing that their discoveries might be used for further oppression by the regime? Or those whose findings are used to develop, say, weapons of mass destruction? To what extent can a scientist always foresee the consequences of his or her research?

Albert Einstein said: 'Concern for man himself and his fate must always form the chief interest of all technical endeavours [...] in order that the creations of our mind shall be a blessing and not a curse to mankind.' Today the ethics of science is a matter of public discussion. We can expect this debate to accompany us for a long time.

1 List reasons why a scientific discovery might prove controversial and provide examples to explain the problem.

2 **a** Choose five of the highlighted nouns and find the corresponding verb forms. Then choose five verbs and find the corresponding nouns.

b Read the text again to find out how the following things are expressed:
sich auf jdn. auswirken – der Lauf der Dinge – zum Leidwesen der Wissenschaftler – Kontroverse erzeugen – jdn. zur Verantwortung ziehen – inwiefern

c Write sentences using three of the words from **a** and three expressions from **b**, but leaving blanks for the words or expressions. Exchange papers with a partner and try to complete your partner's sentences.

3 Research a controversial scientific discovery or theory – past or present. Present your findings to the class, using as many of the highlighted words as possible.

➤ Doing Research (p. 230)

4 Can Science Save Us from Ourselves? Natasha Walter

➤ Reading Non-fiction (p. 237)

In what areas do we look to science to save us? Make a list. Now see whether Walter names any you did not think of.

A decision taken yesterday in the venerable atmosphere of the House of Lords would once have sounded as if it had been plucked straight from an Aldous Huxley novel or a Stanley Kubrick film. The Lords in their wisdom decided that scientists should be able to dabble in cells taken from cloned human embryos. But given the current rash of tales about 'designer' babies and genetic manipulation, such a decision has almost lost its potential to surprise us. Over the past few days we've been treated to the story that one baby will be selected so that its genetic material can save its brother and to the tale that another baby has been born after being selected to be free of the gene that predisposed her mother to Alzheimer's disease.

So much has been talked about designer babies that the public's perception of what is now possible in genetic science has already way outrun reality. Many people probably believe that if they were given their way, scientists could already clone dozens of dinky copies of themselves, grow embryos to term in plastic wombs outside women's bodies, manipulate the eye-colour or piano-playing ability of foetuses and, altogether, provide the perfect à la carte baby service.

Couples who can't conceive naturally are often shocked to realise that doctors cannot just wave a wand and create a baby for them and that fertility treatments still have high failure rates. When you look at the reality of the designer baby stories, what is in fact going on is a lot cruder than the science-fiction dreams. But all the talk about designer babies means that the decision taken by the House of Lords select committee to allow limited research using cloned human embryos hardly feels revolutionary.

This move promises to put Britain in the forefront of stem-cell research, and most people in this country are likely to welcome it. After all, manipulating the very structure of life is exactly what we have come to expect from scientists. People in the Western world are beginning to believe that life should be completely controllable. They are beginning to believe that all babies should be perfect: that nobody should suffer from diseases caused by genetic dysfunction; that research using the cells of embryos will be used to combat disabilities and intractable diseases such as Parkinson's and Alzheimer's; that old age itself should one day pretty soon – and hopefully in time for our retirement – be curable.

And why not? If our culture didn't have this impatient attitude to nature, this arrogant belief that physical and even mental illnesses can always be conquered, where would we be? Still thinking that 40 was a ripe old age and still having a dozen children in the hope that one would survive until adulthood, no doubt. [...]

Certainly we in the West can dream of perfect control over our health – we can listen to the tales of dazzling experiments resulting in cloned animals and the possibility of break-throughs that might, one day, make paraplegics walk again and give brain connections back to Ronald Reagan. We can fantasise that we might become a perfect race, each of us taken through a life of absolutely predictable health from a managed birth to a far-off, pain-free trip to the grave.

■ **1** venerable *wise and deserving respect* **2-3** Aldous Huxley (1894–1963) *English writer, famous for his novel* Brave New World *(1932), which depicts a scientifically controlled civilization* **3** Stanley Kubrick (1928–1999) *US film director who made such films as the futuristic* 2001: A Space Odyssey *(1968)* **4** dabble in sth. *work with sth., but not really seriously* **5** rash of sth. *series of (usu. unpleasant) things which happen over a short period of time* **7** be treated to sth. *be offered sth.* **9-10** predispose sb. to sth. *jdn. für etwas anfällig machen* **14** dinky (infml) *neat, attractive* **14** to term *for the full nine months* **17** conceive [kən'si:v] *become pregnant* **18** wave a wand *zaubern* **22** select committee *parlamentarischer Ausschuss* **32** curable ['kjʊərəbl] *heilbar* **39** paraplegic [ˌpærə'pli:dʒɪk] *Querschnittsgelähmte(r)* **40** Ronald Reagan (born 1911) *former US president who suffers from Alzheimer's*

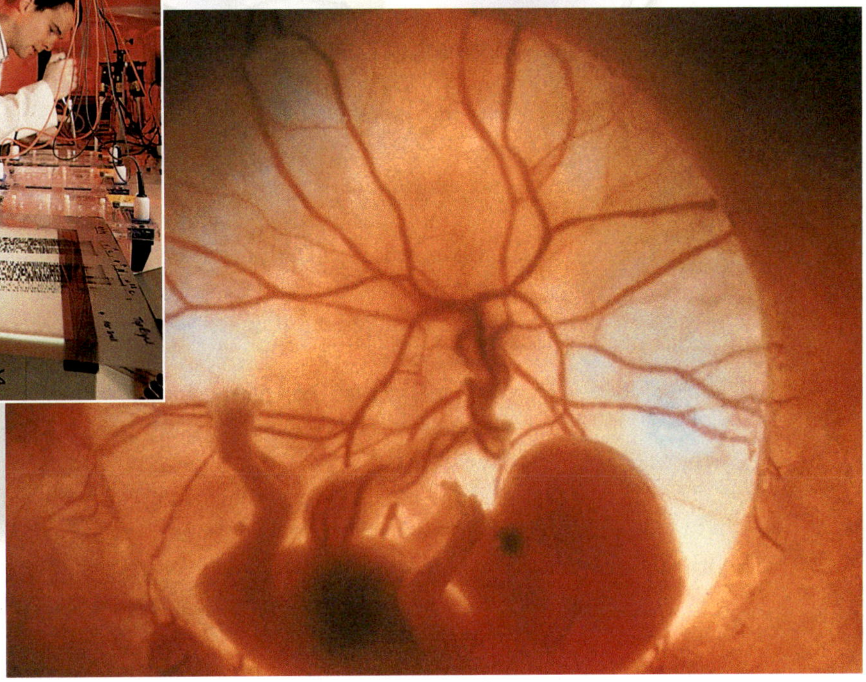

Stem-cell researchers at work (above).
A human embryo in its twelfth week (right).

If you buy into that dream, the Lords' decision yesterday to allow research using cells from cloned embryos is just part and parcel of a great story of progress. [...] As Robert Lanza, the vice-president of medical and scientific development at ACT, said after his company cloned the first human embryo in the US last year. 'Our intention is not to create cloned human beings, but rather to make life-saving therapies for a wide range of human disease conditions, including diabetes, strokes, cancer, Aids.' How can one argue with that?

One can't. But look again at the diseases that he said that cloned-embryo cell research is now expected to deal with: diabetes, strokes, cancer, Aids. And then look at some of the other health stories to have hit the headlines.

The story that, for instance, one in four five-year-old girls is showing early signs of diabetes due to the increase in childhood obesity. Or that a form of diabetes, previously known to affect only overweight adults, is now being identified in children as young as 13 because of their poor diets and lack of exercise. Or that the incidence of sexually transmitted diseases, including HIV, is rising steeply because young people refuse to wear condoms. Or that deaths from alcohol-related car crashes rose sharply last year. Or that young girls and boys are becoming increasingly heavy drinkers. Or that smoking has increased among people aged from 16 to 19.

■ **43** buy into sth. *believe sth., esp. an idea that many other people believe*
45 ACT (abbr) = Advanced Cell Technology *US company that researches and develops the genetic manipulation of cells*
54 obesity [əʊ'bi:sɪti ☆ oʊ-] *fatness* **57** incidence ['ɪnsɪdəns] *the number of times sth. (usu. unpleasant) happens*

66 haze *Rausch* **66-67** strap yourself into sth. *sich in etwas festschnallen* **69** ride a wave of sth. *enjoy a feeling of sth.* **71** holistic health care *ganzheitliche Medizin* **78** beggar belief *be too shocking to believe* **79** heritage *(here) what you have inherited from your parents*

This is where the dream of total control falls down – not in the achievements of scientists, but in the messy reality of our lives. What do we really want? We may think we want perfect health, a life lived in absolute control. And when we make rational choices for ourselves or for others, of course that's what we choose. But then we pour another glass to take the evening into a lovely haze, we strap ourselves into steel cages and roar around the country at 90 miles an hour, or we ride a wave of urgent passion without even remembering that packet of condoms sitting in the bathroom cabinet. Of course we do!

For all the trendy talk of holistic health care, what most people in the West want is the opposite – they want to eat what they like and do what they like and still live as long as they want. That's why the reality of our lives so often falls so far short of the dreams of both science and science fiction. Neither takes account of the messy irrationality of human desires – desires that seem to get even more messy and irrational, as our theoretical ability to control our lives increases.

Nor, of course, does the dream of total control take any account of the unspeakable inequalities in the world. Because it beggars belief that, while we have worked out how to save a baby in America from her own genetic heritage, we still haven't worked out how to save babies in other countries from dying of drinking dirty water.

That's not to say that the scientists are on the wrong track. Surely they are just doing what scientists do – expanding our knowledge and spelling out the secrets of life, day by day.

But perhaps we should put their glittering achievements into perspective. Because, although scientists might one day be able to save us even from our genes, they still won't be able to save us from ourselves.

(From: Natasha Walter, 'Science Can't Save Us from Ourselves', *The Independent*, 28 February, 2002)

1 List the human weaknesses Walter mentions that hinder total scientific control of our lives. Add as many more to the list as you can.

2 Walter's comment does not try to be objective in the way of, for instance, a government report. Explain how she reveals her views on stem-cell research, finding at least three words or phrases that show what she thinks. It might help to consider the overall message of the article.

3 The writer says that people are generally 'impatient' (l. 33) and 'arrogant' (l. 34) in their attitude to nature and the treatment of illnesses. To what extent would you agree or disagree?

4 Work with a partner. One of you looks at ll. 1–49, the other at lines 50–87. Each has to find five words or phrases and paraphrase them. He or she then reads them out and the other partner has to find the original words or phrases.

5 **Project work.**

➤ Doing Research (p. 230), The Stages of Writing (p. 244)

a Form groups and choose one scientific or technological advance of the last 20 years (that has not been covered in this chapter). Gather material on your topic and write a leaflet describing its pros and cons.

b Give your leaflet to another group. In your group discuss the leaflet you have been given. If you disagree with any points in it, justify your views.

c Choose one person from your group to report on your views to the other group. Listen to what the other group's representative says about your leaflet and revise it if you agree with what they say.

WATCH YOUR LANGUAGE

Look at these paragraphs from a student's paper on a famous scientist. The teacher has marked the mistakes.

ALBERT EINSTEIN

Albert Einstein, knowing as one of the world's greatest scientists, was born in Ulm in 1879. The young Einstein did not do well in a disciplined environment, and he left the school with 15, without a diploma. He later returned to the school and went on to study physics and mathematics. In 1905 a paper he wrote on molecular dimensions appeared in 'Annalen der Physik', earned him a doctorate from the university in Zurich. Four more papers appeared in the 'Annalen' that year, established Einstein as one of the greatest minds in physics.

Einstein travelled and lectured throughout Europe. He always travelled third class, his beloved violin holding under his arm wherever

1 a Correct as many of the mistakes in the above paragraphs as you can without consulting a dictionary or grammar book.

b With a partner, look at the mistakes you were not able to correct and decide where to look up the correct forms. Then make the necessary corrections.

➤ Using a Monolingual Dictionary (p. 234), Using a Grammar Book (p. 235)

2 Look again at the mistakes in the paragraphs above. What areas does the student need to study more closely? What might he or she do to improve his or her English?

3 Participle constructions

a Explain the use of the present and past participles in the sentences below.

Einstein got off the train, holding his violin under his arm.

Einstein got off the train, his violin held under his arm.

b Use the present or past participles of the verbs in the box on the right to complete the sentences below.

1 ... his German citizenship after Hitler became chancellor, Einstein left Germany.

2 Upon ... that the Germans were developing an atom bomb, Einstein wrote to US President Roosevelt, ... 'watchfulness and, if necessary, quick action' on the part of the United States.

3 Einstein, a pacifist, published the general theory of relativity, ... the basis for the deadliest bombs ... to humanity, the atomic and hydrogen bombs.

4 ... that the atom bomb might be used again, Einstein issued a statement ... world government under a constitution ... by the USA, Britain and the Soviet Union.

5 Largely ... in later life, Einstein quietly continued his research until his death in the USA in 1955.

c Translate the sentences above in as many ways as you can think of.

Vocabulary box

advocate • draft • frighten • give up • ignore • know • learn • provide • urge

Has this page pointed out any areas of difficulty for you that you had not yet noticed? If so, they should be added to your self-assessment 'plan of action' (cf. Workbook).

ENV

1 a In class, do a brainstorming in which you collect at least ten types of outdoor leisure activities.
b Divide the class into groups. Half the groups look at the list of activities and try to identify ways in which each activity is good for the environment or people's relationship with nature; the other groups try to show how each activity is harmful.
c Compare the results of the groups in class and discuss.

➤ Mind Mapping (p. 222)

2 Make a list or mind map of words and phrases to do with 'Nature and the Environment'. Continue to add to your list or mind map as you work your way through this chapter.

Now read the poem 'If the Earth' below and then do the tasks on the right-hand page.

If the Earth

were only a few feet in diameter,
floating a few feet above a field somewhere,
people would come from everywhere to marvel
at it. People would walk around it, marvelling at its
big pools of water, its little pools and the water flowing
between. People would marvel at the bumps on it, and the
holes in it. They would marvel at the very thin layer of gas
surrounding it and the water suspended in the gas. The people
would marvel at all the creatures walking around the surface
of the ball and at the creatures in the water. The people would
declare it as sacred because it was the only one, and they would
protect it so that it would not be hurt. The ball would be the
greatest wonder known, and people would come to pray to
it, to be healed, to gain knowledge, to know beauty and to
wonder how it could be. People would love it, and defend
it with their lives because they would somehow
know that their lives could be nothing
without it. If the Earth were only a few
feet in diameter.

Joe Miller, 1975

NATURE

3 Why do you think Miller chose to present his poem as a 'shape poem'?

➤ Glossary: Shape Poem (p. 256)

4 **a** Identify the themes in the poem. Say which lines deal with each theme.

b Evaluate the main image of 'If the Earth' as a means of getting Miller's point across.

➤ Glossary: Imagery (p. 268)

5 Some might say that 'If the Earth' is not really a poem at all. Give your opinion, stating your reasons for your view.

➤ Reading Poetry (p. 241), Glossary: Poetry (p. 256)

6 **a** Now look at the picture (1962) by René Magritte below. Describe the picture in as much detail as you can.

➤ Working with Pictures (p. 223)

Useful words and phrases

tree stump • wood chips • root • axe • chop sth. down

b Give the picture a title. Exchange titles with a partner and explain why you chose your title. Then say whose title you think fits the picture better.

7 Compare 'If the Earth' and the picture by Magritte. Discuss what they have in common and in what ways they are different.

1 'Where the Cricket Sings'

'The Lake at Petworth' (1828).

A The Lake at Petworth J.M.W. Turner

➤ Working with Pictures (p. 223)

1 Describe the landscape painting above. What atmosphere does it convey? How does Turner use colour and light to achieve this?

2 Add as many words and phrases to do with 'landscape' as you can to your word list or mind map (cf p. 74, **2**). Remember, there are many types of landscape – natural, artificial, industrial, etc.

3 **Project work.** Form groups. Each person chooses an outdoor place near his or her home. Make notes on it and bring in any materials you might have – a picture, a bunch of flowers, etc. Then, with the help of your materials, describe the landscape in detail to your group, using at least five new words or phrases. Let the group really feel what the place is like – the look of it, its smells, sounds, etc.

Useful words and phrases

The view is wonderful/breathtaking/...
The surroundings are a bit grim/..., but this place is ...
Even though you can hear ..., it is very tranquil/... here.
The rough/smooth/cool/ ... feel of the ... is exciting/soothing/ ...
The smell of the ... takes me back to / reminds me of ...
This photo/leaf/... shows you / gives a sense of what ...

The group chooses its favourite place and together you visit it and prepare a presentation for the class by taking photos, making drawings and recordings, etc.

➤ Giving a Talk or Presentation (p. 254)

B The Lake Isle of Innisfree William Butler Yeats

CD

I will arise and go now, and go to Innisfree.
And a small cabin build there, of clay and wattles made:
Nine bean rows will I have there, a hive for the honey-bee,
And live alone in the bee-loud glade.

And I shall have some peace there, for peace comes dropping slow
Dropping from the veils of the morning to where the cricket sings:
There midnight's all a glimmer, and noon a purple glow,
And evening full of the linnet's wings.

I will arise and go now, for always night and day
I hear lake water lapping with low sounds by the shore:
Where I stand on the roadway, or on the pavements grey,
I hear it in the deep heart's core.

(From: *The Rose*, 1893)

■ **2** clay *Ton* **2** wattle *stick* **3** hive *structure bees live in* **4** glade *open area of grass in forest* **6** veil [veɪl] *Schleier* **6** cricket *Grille* **7** be all a glimmer *have a pale, unsteady light* **7** glow (n) *dull, steady light* **8** linnet *type of small bird (German: Bluthänfling)* **10** lap (v) *(of water) touch (sth.) gently and regularly* **12** core *Kern*

1 Describe the sort of life the speaker seems to want. Support your view with quotes from the poem.

➤ Quoting (p. 232)

2 Show how the rhythm of the poem reflects the content. It will help you if you read the poem aloud.

➤ Reading Poetry (p. 241), Glossary: Poetry (p. 256)

3 Turner's painting and Yeats's poem both feature lakes. Which one transports you to a lakeside more effectively? Explain your reaction.

C It Was a Lover and His Lass William Shakespeare

CD

Listen to the song from Shakespeare's play *As You Like it* (1600).

1 **a** Fill in the missing words on the worksheet your teacher gives you.
b In a few sentences say what the song is about.

2 Listen again and decide what the song has in common with either the painting 'The Lake at Petworth' or the poem 'The Lake Isle of Innisfree'.

■ 4 thingy (sl) *Dingsbums* 6 telly (sl) *TV* 9 bommy night (sl) *Bonfire night (which is celebrated on November 5th)*

D **Nice Places** Willy Russell

In this extract from a play, a group of English inner-city schoolchildren are on a day trip to the sea. In the coach, on the way there, one of the students talks to her teacher.

[Carol, who is sitting next to Mrs Kay, is staring out of the window.]

Carol: Isn't it horrible, eh, miss.

Mrs Kay: Mm?

Carol: Y' know ... all the thingy like. The dirt an' that. *[Pause]* I like them nice places.

Mrs Kay: Which places?

Carol: Y' know them places on the telly. Where they have gardens an' trees outside an' that.

Mrs Kay: You've got trees in Pilot Street, haven't you?

Carol: We did have till last bommy night – the kids chopped 'em all down an' burnt them all. *[Pause]* Miss, y' know when I grow up, miss. Y' know if I started to work hard now an' learned how to read, eh? Well, d' y' think I'd be able t' live in one of them nice places?

[Pause]

Mrs Kay: Well you could try, couldn't you, love. Eh?

Carol: Yeh.

(From: *Our Day Out*, 1976)

1 Describe Carol's feelings about the area she lives in, based on the information in the short extract.

2 **a** Examine the language Carol uses and compare it to the way Mrs Kay speaks.
b Explain what this tells you about their backgrounds.

➤ Writing Letters (p. 250)

3 **Creative writing.** It is twenty years later. Write a letter from Carol to Mrs Kay. Say what Carol does now, where she lives, and how she feels about living there.

CD

4 Listen to the extract from the radio programme 'Country of Our Time'.
a Compare the views Carol in 'Nice Places' and Gloria Williams in the programme have on their environment.
b List the advantages named in the programme of living in 'a pleasant landscape'.

GETTING ALONG IN ENGLISH

Going on a Tour

You and a friend have saved for a trip to Australia when you finish school. What you are most looking forward to is a trip into the rainforest. On your arrival in Brisbane you want to fix one up. Do you know how to:

- ask all the right questions before booking?
- break the ice with the other tour members?
- thank your tour guide in an appropriate way?

Working through this page will give you the confidence to deal with all these points.

1 You are about to visit 'Bruce's Tours' to book a 'Rainforest Tour'. Work with a partner (who is your travelling companion) and together make a list of important questions you will need to ask and the polite way of asking them. Here are a few ideas to start you off. Note that very direct questions, e.g. 'How much ...?', are generally considered impolite in English.

- Good morning/ ..., we'd like to enquire about your tours/prices/....
- Could you tell us what weather/... to expect?
- Do you have a list of things we need to bring?
- Thank you so much, we are really looking forward to the tour.

2 **a** Now listen to the CD and see if you can find answers to the questions you prepared. Were there questions in the dialogue that you would like to have asked? Could you follow all the answers? If not, what did you find difficult to understand? CD
b Did the people on the CD phrase their questions differently / more politely than your questions? Listen once more and see whether you can improve your questions in any way.

3 **a** Today's the day: you are about to meet the other people on the tour. Listen to the CD to see what Bruce does to help make the people feel more at ease with each other. CD
b Now ask your partner to tell you a short anecdote about something that happened to him or her when travelling. Try and give an appropriate response at the end of your partner's story. If you have been telling the story, remember that it is polite to ask your partner to tell one, too.

4 The tour has come to an end. Listen to the CD and collect appropriate phrases for thanking someone. Then make a second list with all the intensifiers you can remember: *really, very, ...* CD

5 In groups of five, prepare and act out a short dialogue between strangers doing a guided walk in your area. One of you should be the guide. Try to use words and phrases you have heard and collected in this section.

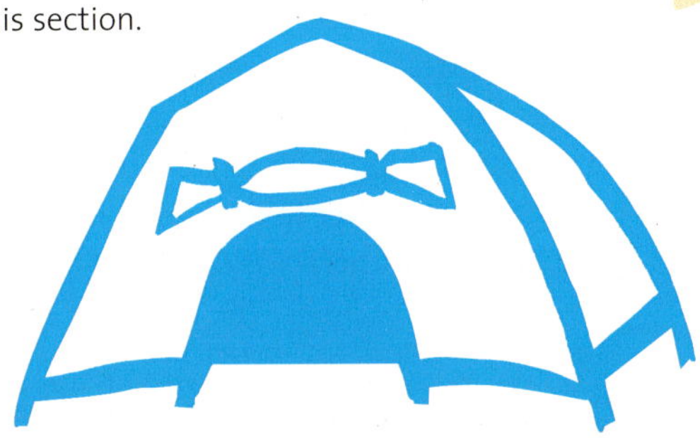

CD

2 What Happened during the Ice Storm
Jim Heynen

As you read the following short short story, stop after each paragraph, close your eyes and imagine the scene. Try to make use of all your senses.

One winter there was a freezing rain. How beautiful! people said when things outside started to shine with ice. But the freezing rain kept coming. Tree branches glistened like glass. Then broke like glass. Ice thickened on the windows until everything outside blurred. Farmers moved their livestock into the barns, and most animals were safe. But not the pheasants. Their eyes froze shut.

Some farmers went ice-skating down the gravel roads with clubs to harvest pheasants that sat helplessly in the roadside ditches. The boys went out into the freezing rain to find pheasants too. They saw dark spots along a fence. Pheasants, all right. Five or six of them. The boys slid their feet along slowly, trying not to break the ice that covered the snow. They slid up close to the pheasants. The pheasants pulled their heads down between their wings. They couldn't tell how easy it was to see them huddled there.

The boys stood still in the icy rain. Their breath came out in slow puffs of steam. The pheasants' breath came out in quick little white puffs. One lifted its head and turned it from side to side, but the pheasant was blindfolded with ice and didn't flush.

The boys had not brought clubs, or sacks, or anything but themselves. They stood over the pheasants, turning their own heads, looking at each other, each expecting the other to do something. To pounce on a pheasant, or to yell Bang! Things around them were shining and dripping with icy rain. The barbed-wire fence. The fence posts. The broken stems of grass. Even the grass seeds. The grass

■ 4 livestock *animals* 5 pheasant ['feznt] *Fasan* 6 club *heavy stick with one end thicker than the other* 12 huddle *stand or lie close together* 15 blindfold sb./sth. *cover the eyes of sb./sth. so that they cannot see* 16 flush *fly away quickly, e.g. due to fear* 19 pounce on sth. *jump on sth. in order to catch it* 20 barbed wire [ˌ- '-] *Stacheldraht* 22 seed *Samen(korn)* 22 yolk [jəʊk] *yellow part of an egg* seeds looked like little yolks inside gelatin whites. And the pheasants looked like unborn birds glazed in egg white. Ice was hardening on the boys' caps and coats. Soon they would be covered with ice too.

Then one of the boys said, Shh. He was taking off his coat, the thin layer of ice splintering in flakes as he pulled his arms from the sleeves. But the inside of the coat was dry and warm. He covered two of the crouching pheasants with his coat, rounding the back of it over them like a shell. The other boys did the same. They covered all the helpless pheasants. The small gray hens and the larger brown cocks. Now the boys felt the rain soaking through their shirts and freezing. They ran across the slippery fields, unsure of their footing, the ice clinging to their skin as they made their way toward the blurry lights of the house.

(From: *The One-Room Schoolhouse*, Vintage Books, New York, 1993)

1 In no more than three sentences, write down what the story is about.

2 **a** Describe to a partner what you saw, heard, felt – and maybe even smelled and tasted – as you read the story. Were your experiences similar to your partner's?

b Identify the passages which speak to each of the senses and examine the images. Do they cover all the things you saw, heard and felt, or did you experience other things? Why do you think that is?

➤ Reading Narrative Prose (p. 238)
➤ Glossary: Imagery (p. 268)

3 How much does the author reveal about the setting and the characters? Analyse the effect this has on the reader.

➤ Glossary: Setting (p. 262), Character and Characterization (p. 260)

4 **Hot seating activity.** The class is divided into two, with four students forming the 'boys' group and the rest the 'interviewers'.
The 'boys' collect ideas about how they felt and why they behaved as they did, while the 'interviewers' write down questions they would like to ask them, e.g. about their behaviour, what they were thinking, etc.
Then the 'boys' sit in front of the class, and the 'interviewers' ask them their questions.

CONTEXT BOX

Nature and the Environment

Although the concept of humanity living in harmony with nature is an old one, it has rarely been achieved except in smaller, 'primitive' societies. Larger, industrialized 'modern' societies have failed to develop a sustainable lifestyle which gives back to the land as much as it takes away from it.

Just how wise or unwise use of land can affect the earth can be seen in the Sahara Desert in northern Africa: a few thousand years ago much of this area was covered with forests until the needs of ship-building nations led to its deforestation.

The reduction of oxygen-giving forests, especially the tropical rainforests, is one component of the climate change that scientists have been observing over the past few decades. This global warming appears to be causing the polar ice caps to melt, which could flood many coastal regions.

At the same time as we rob the earth of its natural resources, we pollute the air and water with the waste products of those resources. Some of the emissions our technology produces are to blame for the greenhouse effect, which further contributes to the global warming phenomenon. Other emissions are responsible for the depletion of the protective ozone layer in the upper atmosphere. Without this protection, damaging radiation reaches the earth's surface unfiltered, causing increased rates of skin cancer.

'Where there's smoke, there's money.'

Environmental awareness has increased over the last few decades, and some small steps have been taken to help to save the planet: most people now separate their rubbish and most communities have recycling programmes; cars consume less fuel than they did before, and many poisonous emissions have been drastically reduced; environmental groups are taken seriously – even individual 'eco-warriors' have been able to sway public opinion.

But much remains to be done: business concerns are reluctant to conserve resources or reduce pollution as such steps are seen as bad for profits. Governments are afraid to pass strict environmental protection laws in case they drive away businesses to other countries where the laws are less restrictive. For that reason, and because pollution knows no borders, international cooperation is essential for making significant improvements to the environment. But efforts to deal with the problems of pollution and the use of resources on an international level have been hampered by the failure of some countries – most notably the United States of America – to cooperate.

1 With a partner, check whether you understand the words which have been highlighted in the text: ask each other to paraphrase the terms, giving examples of how they are used where possible. Then add any appropriate words to your list or mind map of words and phrases dealing with 'Nature and the Environment' (cf. p. 74, **2**).
2 Give examples of what is meant by 'living in harmony with nature'.
3 Put together a one-page fact sheet about global warming using vocabulary from the Context Box.

3 Earth Awareness

A Too Much Trouble? Erin Jackson

The following text was written for a web magazine by a 20-year-old Canadian student.

One hundred children are singing on a stage. They're wearing bright, multi-coloured T shirts and waving orange and blue streamers. Their eyes sparkle with enthusiasm. 'We are able. We are able. We can't wait. It's far too late. Won't you join us now?' they chant.

Almost ten years have passed since I stood on stage singing in our school's earth-themed production and I still remember most of the words. Unfortunately, things seem to have changed and these days I often wonder why so many of the classmates who sang along with me have become apathetic.

The musical we performed dealt with issues such as the ozone depletion, energy conservation, car-pooling and recycling. We were passionate about these things and the songs sprang from our collective conscience. We were ecological warriors who wanted to change the world, young dynamos determined to spread a message of environmental awareness.

And we didn't just sing about the environment – we got active. We recycled whenever possible – dutifully compacting cans and flattening tetra boxes – and held 'garbage-less' lunch days. We were convinced that by taking small steps like these the world would be a greener place.

On Earth Day, we made posters and cleaned up the schoolyard. It was a big deal. 'I remember my mom made a cake and we sang songs in the gym about the environment,' recalls Jennie Mester, 20.

That was then, but this is now: the assault on the ozone layer continues; air pollution is pandemic; landfills overflow with garbage. And all our enthusiasm seems buried in the debris.

Despite the deplorable state of the earth, our once keen efforts have become sporadic. The blue box still gets put out on collection day, but our childhood passions are all but gone.

I can't say for certain what happened to our environmental consciousness, but I can hazard a guess. At least in part, it's because convenience became the new mantra.

If an eco-friendly practice is not too much trouble, we still do it. For example, separating bottles and cans for recycling is a habit most of us have kept. But if an activity is inconvenient, it's likely abandoned.

'I find it harder to do garbage-less lunches now,' says Mester. 'I don't think it's realistic to lug the whole Tupperware set downtown and back every day. Convenience takes precedence over what's environmentally friendly. It's unfortunate.'

Nowhere is this craving for convenience more evident than in our dependence on cars. At 16, most teenagers develop an unbreakable bond with the automobile and driving replaces walking as our main form of transportation. [...]

Coupled with this penchant for doing things the easy way is the creeping effect of consumerism. From a very early age, we are bombarded with advertisements.

■ [2] streamer *long, narrow strip of coloured paper* [9] depletion [dɪ'pliːʃn] *Verringerung* [10] car-pooling *Fahrgemeinschaft* [12] dynamo *person with a lot of energy* [15] compact sth. [-'-] (v) *make sth. flat* [16] garbage-less (AE) *without creating rubbish* [21] assault [ə'sɔːlt ☆ -'sɑːlt] (n) *attack* [22] pandemic [pæn'demɪk] *(usu. of a disease) widespread* [22] landfill *site where rubbish is buried* [23] debris ['debriː ☆ də'briː] *Schutt, Trümmer, Abfall* [24] deplorable *terrible* [25] blue box *(in Canada) open, blue plastic box in which recyclable rubbish is placed and then collected* [28] hazard a guess *make a guess* [29] mantra *word or phrase that is repeated again and again* [34] lug sth. (infml) *carry sth.* [35] take precedence over sth. ['presɪdəns] *come before sth.*

■ **42** jingle *short, catchy song used in an advertisement* **44** degradation [ˌdegrəˈdeɪʃn] *process of damaging sth.* **48** sorry (adj) *sad* **50** belt sth. out *sing sth. loudly*

Commercial jingles replace nursery rhymes and ring in our heads. Over the years the message gets through: you are what you consume. [...]

Consumerism is a major factor in the degradation of the earth. Huge amounts of the earth's resources are being used up to produce the stuff we buy, much of which gets thrown away when something 'new' comes along.

It's no wonder that we hear stories of overflowing landfills and that the planet sometimes seems beyond repair. If my generation ever hopes to reverse this sorry state of affairs we'd better rediscover the environmental awareness that we once had – back when we belted out tunes in the school auditorium and took our activism seriously.

(From: 'Earth Awareness: Where Did It Go?', the website of *Envirozine*)

1 **a** List the measures which Erin and her schoolfriends used to take to protect the environment.
b Write two or three sentences to explain what each measure consists of and how it might help.

2 **a** What reasons does Erin find for the loss of enthusiasm she and her friends have experienced?
b Find other reasons why people become less enthusiastic about environmental awareness as they grow up.
c List at least three ideas for action that might encourage people to renew or take up an interest in the environment.

3 **Project work.** Not all young people settle for convenience. Julia 'Butterfly' Hill spent 738 days and nights on a platform 55 metres above the ground at the top of a Californian redwood tree which was scheduled to be cut down. She saved the tree and later wrote a book called *One Makes the Difference*. Here is a brief extract:
'THE "FIVE R" MANTRA
One of the easiest ways to get started making the difference in our environment is to embrace the "Five R" mantra: Respect, Rethink, Reduce, Reuse, Recycle. It may seem simplistic, but its applications are bountiful.'
Divide the class into five groups. Each group takes one of the 'Five R's' and discusses it, does some research on it where necessary and then prepares a detailed presentation for the class of how it can be put into action.

➤ Doing Research (p. 230)
➤ Giving a Talk or Presentation (p. 254)

B What Is 'Eden' about? Tony Kendle

The original Garden of Eden is a symbol of paradise, but also of mankind's rejection from it. Historically conservation policies have also assumed that the best quality environments are untouched by people and that environmental care meant keeping people out of them. The real situation is more complex than that.

Humans have caused lots of problems in the world, but there are also places where we have lived in harmony with nature without complete destruction, and sometimes with a beneficial effect. Many of the challenges that lie ahead can only be met by people being here, not by their walking away. Communities have already begun to make steps to be effective stewards of the world. The Eden project is here to showcase those steps.

(From: *Eden, the Guide*, 2001)

■ **7** beneficial [ˌbenɪˈfɪʃl] *positive* **8** meet sth. *successfully carry sth. (e.g. a challenge) out* **9** steward *sb. who looks after sth.* **10** showcase sth. *display sth.*

The Eden Project, which opened in Cornwall in 2001, had 1.5 million visitors in its first year.

1 What is Eden about?

a Make a list of questions you would ask Dr Kendle if you could interview him.

b Do some research about the Eden Project, and see how many of your questions you can answer for yourself.

➤ Doing Research (p. 230)

C Economists Are Also Environmentalists Paul Krugman

Skim this text by a leading US economist. What do you think it might be about? Then scan it for references to: lifestyle, taxation, payoff. Define these terms in your own words (check in a dictionary if necessary). Now read the text.

➤ Skimming (p. 236)
➤ Scanning (p. 236)
➤ Reading Non-fiction (p. 237)

Many economists are also enthusiastic environmentalists.

Partly this is just because of who economists are: Being by definition well-educated and, for the most part, pretty well-off, they have the usual prejudices of their class – and most upper-middle class Americans are sentimental about the environment, as long as protecting it does not impinge on their lifestyle. (I bring bags and bottles to the recycling center in my gas-guzzling sports utility vehicle.) But my unscientific impression is that economists are on average more pro-environment than other people of similar incomes and backgrounds. Why? Because standard economic theory automatically predisposes those who believe in it to favor strong environmental protection.

This is not, of course, the popular image. Everyone knows that economists are people who know the price of everything and the value of nothing, who think that anything that increases gross domestic product is good and anything else is worthless, and who believe that whatever free markets do must be right. [...]

But won't protecting the environment reduce the gross domestic product? Not necessarily – and anyway, so what?

At first sight, it might seem obvious that pollution taxes will reduce GDP. After all, any tax reduces the incentives to work, save and invest. Thus a tax on exhaust emissions from cars will induce people to drive cleaner cars or to avoid driving altogether. But since it will also in effect lower the payoff to earning extra money (since you wouldn't end up driving the second car you could buy with that money anyway), people will not work as hard as they would have without the tax. The result is that taxes on pollution (or anything else) will, other things being equal, tend to reduce overall monetary output in the economy – which is to say, GDP.

5 impinge on sth. [ɪm'pɪndʒ] (fml) *have a negative effect on sth.* **6** gas-guzzling (AE infml) *using lots of gas (BE: petrol)* **6** sports utility vehicle *Sportgeländewagen* **9** predispose sb. to do sth. *make it likely that sb. will do sth.* **13** gross domestic product (GDP) *Bruttoinlandsprodukt* **24** monetary output *Ausgaben*

But things need not be equal, because there is already a whole lot of taxing and spending going on. Even in the United States, where the government is smaller than in any other advanced country, about a third of GDP passes through its hands. So existing taxes already discourage people from engaging in taxable activities like working or investing. What this means is that the revenue from any new taxes on pollution could be used to reduce other taxes, such as Social Security contributions or the income tax (but not, of course, the capital-gains tax). While the pollution taxes would discourage some activities that are counted in the GDP, the reduction in other taxes would encourage other such activities. So measured GDP might well fall very little, or even rise.

Does this constitute an independent argument for taxing pollution, quite aside from its environmental payoff? Would we want to have, say, a carbon tax even if we weren't worried about global warming? Well, there has been an excruciatingly technical argument about this, mysteriously known as the 'double dividend' debate; the general consensus seems to be no, and that on balance pollution taxes would be more likely to reduce GDP slightly than to increase it.

But so what? 'Gross domestic product is not a measure of the nation's economic well-being' – so declares the textbook as soon as it introduces the concept. If getting the price of the environment right means a rise in consumption of nonmarket goods like clean air and leisure time at the expense of marketed consumption, so be it.

Isn't this amazing? Not only do thousands of economists agree on something, but what they agree on is the warm and cuddly idea that we should do more to protect the environment. Can 2,500 economists be wrong?

(From: *The Accidental Theorist and Other Dispatches from the Dismal Science*, Norton, New York, 1998)

1 What reasons does Krugman give for economists to be enthusiastic environmentalists?

2 **a** Explain in your own words how taxes affect the economy.
b How does Krugman nonetheless justify a pollution tax?

➤ Summary Writing (p. 248)

3 Pick one or two key sentences for each paragraph. Now write a summary of the text.

4 Examine how the writer tries to convince his readers of his arguments. Evaluate how effective his methods are.

5 **Role play.** In groups of six prepare role cards for and act out the following role play: The local council wants to chop down a beautiful wood near your town or village in order to build cheap housing for poorer people in a nearby city. There are protests from local nature-lovers, parents and environmentalists. A public meeting is to be held at which the following people will speak: a town councillor, a local shopkeeper, a homeless person from the city, a teenage environmentalist, the mother of a small child and a bird-watcher.

■ **28** discourage sb. from (doing) sth. *make sb. not want to do sth.* **29** revenue ['revənju: ☆ -nu:] *Steueraufkommen* **31** capital-gains tax *Kapitalertragssteuer* **37** excruciating [ɪk'skru:ʃieɪtɪŋ] *very painful* **44** nonmarket goods *things that are not, or cannot be, bought and sold* **45** so be it *(hier) sei's drum*

D Cartoons Dealing with the Environment

With a partner, do the following information gap exercise. Partner A remains on this page, while Partner B goes to p. 88.

➤ Working with Cartoons (p. 225)

Partner A

Look at the cartoon at the bottom of this page.

1 **a** Describe the picture to your partner.
b He or she then reads out four captions. Discuss and decide together which caption is the correct one.

2 Now listen to your partner's description of his or her cartoon. Then read out your four captions:
1 'I hate long car journeys, everything looks the same.'
2 'Funny how nothing changes when you cross the border into Canada.'
3 'They have very strict anti-pollution laws in this state.'
4 'I liked the last environment better.'
Discuss and decide together which is the right caption.

Useful words and phrases
As there's a lot of / are no ... in the picture, the caption about ... can't/must be right.
If the flag/... is American/..., then ...
The first/... caption isn't relevant/funny/... so I don't think it's the right one

Partner B

1 Listen to your partner's description of his or her cartoon. Then read out your four captions:

1 'If the water shortage continues our farmers will be in serious trouble.'

2 'And the next person to mention the weather is fired!'

3 'Gentlemen, it's time we gave some serious thought to the effects of global warming.'

4 'The Queen is very worried about the situation.'

Discuss and decide together which is the right caption.

2 a Describe the cartoon below to your partner.

b He or she then reads out four captions. Discuss and decide together which caption is the correct one.

Useful words and phrases

As there's a lot of / are no ... in the picture, the caption about ... can't/must be right.
If the flag/... is American/..., then ...
The first/... caption isn't relevant/funny/... so I don't think it's the right one

VIDEO

E The Destruction of Habitats

In this section you have given some thought to the relationship between humans and nature. Would you say that humanity is basically destructive? Write down your opinion in a few sentences giving examples.
Now watch the extract from the documentary film *State of the Planet* (2000).

1 Does the information in the documentary change your opinion at all? Explain your answer.

2 a Why, according to the scientist Edward Wilson, have humans always destroyed the environment?

b Was this necessarily a bad thing?

c What has changed that makes humans in the present age more dangerous to the environment?

➤ Viewing Skills (p. 227)

3 List some of the film techniques that are used in this extract, and explain their use.

WATCH YOUR LANGUAGE

Look at these paragraphs from a student essay on the environment. The teacher has marked the mistakes.

There was a study about recycling and peoples' attitudes towards it. The researchers found, that most people don't mind to separate their rubbish if it is easy. When it is complicated, they stop to do it.
I think the same is true of save petrol and other ressources. When it is easy, people will do it; when it is not, they won't. For example, to turn off the engine when you have to stop the car for a time is something a lot of people don't do, but it's easy to remember. Start slowly from a traffic light is more difficult to remember, especially when you're in a hurry. Even if people remember doing that for a time, they usually forget doing it later.
So, as with most things, educate people about conserve energy is what's most important.

1 **a** Correct as many of the mistakes in the paragraphs above as you can without consulting a dictionary or grammar book.
b With a partner, look at the mistakes you were not able to correct and decide where to look up the correct forms. Then make the necessary corrections.

➤ Using a Monolingual Dictionary (p. 234), Using a Grammar Book (p. 235)

2 Look again at the mistakes in the paragraph above. What areas does the student need to study more closely? What might he or she do to improve his or her English?

3 **The gerund versus the *to*-infinitive**
a Decide whether you need the gerund or the *to*-infinitive in the following sentences. (In two instances, you can use either.) Be prepared to explain your choices.
1 (clean) a river bank every spring is really worth (do) because it helps the wildlife.
2 Personally, I'm tired of (see) other people's rubbish all over my neighbourhood.
3 Most people want (save) the earth, but they find it hard (fit) it into their lifestyle.
4 It's time (do) something constructive about (save) the planet.
5 I'm not old enough (remember) the time before our town started (collect) rubbish in separate containers.
6 I can't imagine (live) in a place where people don't care about these issues.

b Make sentences to show that you understand the difference between the following pairs.
1 remember to do / remember doing
2 forget to do / forget doing
3 go on to do / go on doing
4 stop to do / stop doing

c Write four sentences in German using the infinitive with *zu*. Two should translate to use the *to*-infinitive in English, two the gerund. Now exchange sentences with a partner. Can each of you translate the other's sentences into English correctly?

Has this page pointed out any areas of difficulty for you that you had not yet noticed? If so, they should be added to your self-assessment 'plan of action' (cf. Workbook).

2

ECONOMY

1

3

⚠ **Trouble spot**
the economy = *Wirtschaft*
economy = *Sparsamkeit*

➤ Using a Monolingual Dictionary (p. 234)

1 In the pictures you can see various people who are in one way or another part of the economy. The boxes on the right contain words and expressions that could be used to describe their roles in the economy.

a Make sure you understand all the words. You may have to use a dictionary to check the meaning or pronunciation.

b The following verbs are taken from the boxes: 'purchase', 'consume', 'distribute', 'exploit', 'invest', 'represent', 'sell', 'trade'. Form nouns and adjectives from them where possible.

c Match the boxes and the pictures and say what each person's part in the economy is, using as many words from the boxes as possible.

A sales rep(resentative) • sell merchandise to retailers/distributors • secure a contract • take/receive orders for goods and services • advise sb. • distribute samples

B stockbroker • buy and sell shares • stockmarket • trade (sth.) • on behalf of shareholders • rise and fall of share prices • profitability of a company • economic trends • boom • slump • take advantage of currency exchange rates

C customer • purchase/buy sth. • retail outlet • consume sth. • product • be influenced by advertising • spend money on sth • create a demand for sth. • on the market

5

4

ECONOMY

2 It is often said that what one person in an economic system does always has some effect on everyone else. Choose two of the people from task 1 and explain how the action of one participant influences the others.

3 Money makes the world go round, some people say, and as it does so, it changes hands frequently. Imagine 'a week in the life of a dollar note' and tell its story (Whose pocket did it start in? Who was it given to then? What was it exchanged for after that? etc.).

4 Describe and analyse the cartoon below.

➤ Working with Cartoons (p. 225)

D plantation worker/labourer • agriculture • economy of third-world countries • cheap labour • exploit sth. • import/export sth. • in debt • depend on sth. • raw materials • price on the world market • live in poverty • give aid

E employee • sell your labour • earn a living • make a living by sth. • receive/get a salary • work for a firm • unprofitable area • labour costs • invest in sth. • make sb. redundant • cut jobs/wages • be/go on strike • unemployed • live on benefits • support a family

1 Business Is Business Arthur Miller

The following scene is taken from Arthur Miller's 1949 play *Death of a Salesman*. Willy Loman has spent his life as a travelling salesman; he is now old and tired, but he still needs to work in order to earn money. He asks Howard, his young boss, for an office job.

Arthur Miller.

HOWARD: Say, aren't you supposed to be in Boston?

WILLY: That's what I want to talk to you about, Howard. You got a minute? [*He draws a chair in from the wing.*]

HOWARD: What happened? What're you doing here?

WILLY: Well ...

HOWARD: You didn't crack up again, did you?

WILLY: Oh, no. No ...

HOWARD: Geez, you had me worried there for a minute. What's the trouble?

WILLY: Well, tell you the truth, Howard. I've come to the decision that I'd rather not travel any more.

HOWARD: Not travel! Well, what'll you do?

WILLY: Remember, Christmas-time, when you had the party here? You said you'd try to think of some spot for me here in town.

HOWARD: With us?

WILLY: Well, sure.

HOWARD: Oh, yeah, yeah. I remember. Well, I couldn't think of anything for you, Willy.

WILLY: I tell ya, Howard. The kids are all grown up, y'know. I don't need much any more. If I could take home – well, sixty-five dollars a week, I could swing it.

HOWARD: Yeah, but Willy, see I –

WILLY: I tell ya why, Howard. Speaking frankly and between the two of us, y'know – I'm just a little tired.

HOWARD: Oh, I could understand that, Willy. But you're a road man, Willy, and we do a road business. We've only got a half-dozen salesmen on the floor here.

WILLY: God knows, Howard, I never asked a favour of any man. But I was with the firm when your father used to carry you in here in his arms.

HOWARD: I know that, Willy, but –

WILLY: Your father came to me the day you were born and asked me what I thought of the name of Howard, may he rest in peace.

HOWARD: I appreciate that, Willy, but there just is no spot here for you. If I had a spot I'd slam you right in, but I just don't have a single solitary spot. [*He looks for his lighter, Willy has picked it up and gives it to him. Pause.*]

WILLY [*with increasing anger*]: Howard, all I need to set my table is fifty dollars a week.

HOWARD: But where am I going to put you, kid?

WILLY: Look, it isn't a question of whether I can sell merchandise, is it?

HOWARD: No, but it's a business, kid, and everybody's gotta pull his own weight.

WILLY [*desperately*]: Just let me tell you a story, Howard –

HOWARD: 'Cause you gotta admit, business is business.

WILLY [*angrily*]: Business is definitely business, but just listen for a minute. You don't understand this. When I was a boy – eighteen, nineteen – I was already on

■ salesman *person who travels around trying to sell his company's goods* **19** swing it (infml) *(here) get by, survive* **36** merchandise *things that are sold* **43** yearning (n) *Sehnsucht* **48** self-reliance *independence, autonomy* **52** drum sth. *(here) sell sth.* **60** smoker *(here) the smoking carriage in a train* **65** gratitude *thankfulness* **65** it's all cut and dried *es gibt keinen Spielraum* **72** Al Smith (1873–1944) *Democratic politician who was nominated as a presidential candidate in 1928* **81** commission *Provision* the road. And there was a question in my mind as to whether selling had a future for me. Because in those days I had a yearning to go to Alaska. See, there were three gold strikes in one month in Alaska, and I felt like going out. Just for the ride, you might say.

HOWARD [*barely interested*]: Don't say.

WILLY : Oh, yeah, my father lived many years in Alaska. He was an adventurous man. We've got quite a little streak of self-reliance in our family. I thought I'd go out with my older brother and try to locate him, and maybe settle in the North with the old man. And I was almost decided to go, when I met a salesman in the Parker House. His name was Dave Singleman. And he was eighty-four years old, and he'd drummed merchandise in thirty-one states. And old Dave, he'd go up to his room, y'understand, put on his green velvet slippers – I'll never forget – and pick up his phone and call the buyers, and without ever leaving his room, at the age of eighty-four, he made his living. And when I saw that, I realized that selling was the greatest career a man could want. 'Cause what could be more satisfying than to be able to go, at the age of eighty-four, into twenty or thirty different cities, and pick up a phone, and be remembered and loved and helped by so many different people? Do you know? when he died – and by the way he died the death of a salesman, in his green velvet slippers in the smoker of the New York, New Haven, and Hartford, going into Boston – when he died, hundreds of salesmen and buyers were at his funeral. Things were said on a lotta trains for months after that. [*He stands up. Howard has not looked at him.*] In those days there was personality in it, Howard. There was respect, and comradeship, and gratitude in it. Today, it's all cut and dried, and there's no chance for bringing friendship to bear – or personality. You see what I mean? They don't know me any more.

HOWARD [*moving away, toward the right*]: That's just the thing, Willy.

WILLY : If I had forty dollars a week – that's all I'd need. Forty dollars, Howard.

HOWARD : Kid, I can't take blood from a stone, I –

WILLY [*desperation is on him now*]: Howard, the year Al Smith was nominated, your father came to me and –

HOWARD [*starting to go off*]: I've got to see some people, kid.

WILLY [*stopping him*]: I'm talking about your father! There were promises made across this desk! You mustn't tell me you've got people to see – I put thirty-four years into this firm, Howard, and now I can't pay my insurance! You can't eat the orange and throw the peel away – a man is not a piece of fruit! [*After a pause*] Now pay attention. Your father – in 1928 I had a big year. I averaged a hundred and seventy dollars a week in commissions.

HOWARD [*impatiently*]: Now, Willy, you never averaged –

WILLY [*banging his hand on the desk*]: I averaged a hundred and seventy dollars a week in the year of 1928! And your father came to me – or rather, I was in the office here – it was right over this desk – and he put his hand on my shoulder –

HOWARD [*getting up*]: You'll have to excuse me, Willy, I gotta see some people. Pull yourself together. [*Going out*] I'll be back in a little while.

Dustin Hoffman as Willy Loman in the 1985 film version of the drama.

'There were promises made across this desk!'

■ 116 sample *(hier)* Warenmuster

[Howard returns after five minutes]

HOWARD *[rolling up the cord]*: Willy, look ...

WILLY : I'll go to Boston.

HOWARD : Willy, you can't go to Boston for us.

WILLY : Why can't I go?

HOWARD: I don't want you to represent us. I've been meaning to tell you for a long time now.

WILLY: Howard, are you firing me?

HOWARD: I think you need a good long rest, Willy.

WILLY: Howard –

HOWARD: And when you feel better, come back, and we'll see if we can work something out.

WILLY: But I gotta earn money, Howard. I'm in no position to –

HOWARD: Where are your sons? Why don't your sons give you a hand?

WILLY: They're working on a very big deal.

HOWARD: This is no time for false pride, Willy. You go to your sons and you tell them that you're tired. You've got two great boys, haven't you?

WILLY: Oh, no question, no question, but in the meantime ...

HOWARD: Then that's that, heh?

WILLY: All right, I'll go to Boston tomorrow.

HOWARD: No, no.

WILLY: I can't throw myself on my sons. I'm not a cripple!

HOWARD: Look, kid, I'm busy this morning.

WILLY *[grasping Howard's arm]*: Howard, you've got to let me go to Boston!

HOWARD *[hard, keeping himself under control]*: I've got a line of people to see this morning. Sit down, take five minutes, and pull yourself together, and then go home, will ya? [...] Oh, yeah. Whenever you can this week, stop by and drop off the samples. You'll feel better, Willy, and then come back and we'll talk. Pull yourself together, kid, there's people outside.

(From: *Death of a Salesman*, 1949)

➤ Glossary: Imagery (p. 268)

1 **a** State in one sentence what the conflict between the two men is about.

b Both Howard and Willy use images to illustrate their situation: 'I can't take blood from a stone' (Howard, l. 71) – 'You can't eat the orange and throw the peel away' (Willy, l. 78). Explain these images.

c Carefully study each man's position in this conflict. Collect characteristic expressions (like those in **b**) and summarize each man's case in your own words.

d Trace the development of the conflict. Who loses and why?

Useful words and phrases

address sb. as sth. • admit sth. (to sb.) • appeal to sb. • back down • confront sb. with sth. • offer (sb.) sth. • persuade sb. • refuse sb. sth. • remind sb. of sth.

➤ Glossary: Drama, Tragedy (p. 257)

2 Is this scene merely sad or could we call it tragic? If you are uncertain what makes a drama tragic, check the glossary. Then explain your opinion.

3 **Role play.** Imagine Howard and Willy tell their wives about the conversation when they get home that night. What do they say? With a partner, choose one couple, makes notes on what they say and act out the dialogue in front of the class.

2 Down and Out – and Up?

In every economy there are 'winners' and 'losers', with the latter often living in poverty. Before you read the following two texts try to define what poverty is.

A Poverty Is Relative Mari Marcel Thekaekara

Mari Marcel Thekaekara is one of the founders of ACCORD, an Indian organization working with the poor. Her idea of what it meant to be poor changed when she visited Glasgow.

Years ago I heard a Frenchman say 'I'd rather be poor in India'. And I thought: 'What utter crap.' How typical. Romanticizing India, poverty and all.

Then, in 1994, as part of a North-South exchange, my husband Stan and I came to Britain, to visit housing estates in inner-city England and Scotland. The idea was to bring over ideas about social change in India and also to reverse the usual stereotypical image of a Northern aid worker coming to help the Third World.

We were told that Easterhouse housing estate in Glasgow is considered Europe's worst slum. We thought this was ludicrous. These people had assured housing, electricity, hot and cold water, refrigerators, gas or electric cooking ranges. By Indian standards this was middle-class luxury. At the back of my mind, I could see anaemic, emaciated adivasi women carrying water in pots from half-a-kilometre away. Huts without electricity. Women searching for firewood every day, thankful if they had a kilo of rice to feed their families every evening. But then, suddenly, it hit us. Most of the men in Easterhouse hadn't had a job in 20 years. They were dispirited, depressed, often alcoholic. Their self-esteem had gone. Emotionally and mentally they were far worse off than the poor where we lived, even though the physical trappings of poverty were less stark.

■ **2** crap (vulg sl) *nonsense* **4** housing estate *housing area, esp. one for people with low incomes* **8** ludicrous *ridiculous* **8** assured *guaranteed* **11** anaemic [ə'ni:mɪk] *pale and weak due to lack of red blood cells* **11** emaciated [ɪ'meɪʃieɪtɪd] *thin and hungry* **11** adivasi (adj) *belonging to one of the adivasi communities (i.e. people in India living in archaic and primitive conditions)* **15** dispirited *resigned* **15** self-esteem *self-respect* **16** be worse off *schlechter dran sein* **17** stark *obvious*

20 deprivation *Benachteiligung*
21 scrabble *search around*
22 rags *Lumpen*

We'd fallen into the trap of looking at poverty only from the point of view of material benefits. The Easterhouse people looked better off than the Asian poor. In reality they suffered as much social deprivation. The Easterhouse men who'd been jobless for 20 years felt far more hopeless than people in India who scrabbled in garbage heaps to sell scrap metal, paper and rags to feed their kids, though both groups were at the bottom of society.

(From: 'Calvin Klein and the Teapickers', *The New Internationalist*, March 1999)

1 Describe what poverty is from the writer's point of view a) before she visits Glasgow, and b) after her experiences in Glasgow.
2 Compare your idea of what poverty is with the writer's.

B 'I Have to Keep the Hot Water for the Kids' Bob Holman

1 Cash may be less important than respect but it dominates your life when you don't have enough. Erica lives on the Easterhouse estate in Glasgow, Scotland with her husband Ivor and children Charlotte, Deirdre, Gilbert and Mary. She keeps a diary.

The Easterhouse estate in Glasgow.

9 child benefit *money the government gives to families for each child* **15** gas token *metal disk that you pay for and that is needed to turn the gas on for heating, etc.*

Monday I get up and get the kids dressed for school and give them some tea and toast.

Charlotte goes to the Post Office to collect the child benefit. I give Deirdre £2.80 for two days' bus fares to school and back. Go to shop and spend money like this:
0.69 potatoes
0.69 loaf of bread
5.00 gas token
5.03 cigarettes
0.60 two tins beans
0.22 soap
0.49 washing-up liquid

When they come home from school, Gilbert and Mary need money for school Christmas trips but I don't have it to give to them. I can't even start thinking about Christmas presents for the kids. I am still in debt paying for last Christmas. I am still paying for the kids' clothes. Sometimes you have to borrow to eat. Once I borrowed from a man and put down my child benefit book. I worked out he took £450 to lend me £220. It was robbery but I had no other option. We watch some TV and then we all go to bed.

Tuesday Get the kids up and to school.
Spend money on:
0.69 potatoes
0.60 two tins beans
0.69 bread
5.03 cigarettes
0.73 sugar
1.98 soap powder
1.77 two packets of toilet towels

0.67 packet of toilet rolls
1.40 bus fare for Deidre tomorrow.

I am left with £1.00. I get a letter from the Water Board. They say they are going to cut me off. I keep the £1.00 for the kids so they can get some sweets from the shops. It is not much but it will keep them happy for a little while. Make the tea, watch TV, then we all go to bed early. [...]

Saturday Get up as usual but my head hurts bad. The kids are running about mad so I have to shout at them so they are not pleased with me at all. Make them some toast. I have to send for bread plus some cigs. Must have my cigs or I can't get through the day. I hate it that people say that because you are on social security you shouldn't smoke. But it's like Valium, it calms me. I wish I could give it up. I've tried and failed.
0.69 bread
2.93 cigs
5.00 electric token.

I have £5.75 left. I have asked the kids to help clean up for me. They moaned but they did it. We all sit and watch TV. The TV set is on its last legs and I don't know what I'd do without it.

The kids ask for some bread. I can only give them one slice each because it is all that is left. Ivor has not got up today. Kids and I have a game of cards and I win. The kids go to bed. I want to go for a bath but I have to keep the hot water for Sunday for the kids.

(From: *Faith in the Poor*, Lion Publishing, Oxford, 1998)

1 Look at the things Erica purchases and comment on her choices. What is missing?
2 Mari Marcel Thekaekara senses that the Easterhouse people have lost their 'self-esteem' and are suffering 'social deprivation'. Find evidence for this in the text.
3 **Project work.** Find out how much money the family of a German unemployed worker who is married and has two children receives each week. Then draw up a budget showing what that money might have to buy.

➤ Doing Research (p. 230)

C Starting Your Own Business

In recent years, the young and the unemployed have been encouraged not to rely on others to provide employment, but to become self-employed. What do you think of this advice? Would you consider starting your own business? Explain your answer.
In Britain, there is an organization called Street (UK), which assists people who are trying to set up their own businesses. Here are two examples of the types of clients it helps.

1 **Sarah** – On her own and with two young children to look after, Sarah needs work which would allow her to collect her youngest from school and give her the flexibility she needs in the holiday times. Eventually she hits upon the idea of setting up a sandwich-making business from home and supplying businesses on the local industrial estate. Her sandwiches are a hit straight away; the only problem is that she is never able to carry enough to satisfy the demand or generate sufficient profit to develop the business and move off benefits. With an assistant and some form of transport Sarah feels she could make a proper living from the activity.

Leroy – Leroy is a painter/decorator and has been hovering between employment and unemployment for several years. When he is not in work he tops up his benefits by undertaking work for family and friends. He knows this is illegal and is afraid of being caught. In fact he only works one or two days a week to reduce the chance he is spotted. Leroy does a good job and the number of people willing to hire him has grown so that sometimes he has a waiting list. Leroy would love to become fully self-employed and legitimize his business but has no bank account, lives in rented accommodation and does not believe he will be able to raise enough finance to buy a van and build up his business to the level that compensates for the loss of his benefits.

(From: The website of *Street [UK]*)

1 **a** Look at the phrases below. If you are unsure of their meaning, check them in a dictionary. Make a table in which you assign phrases to either Sarah or Leroy, or to both.

start-up with no track record or collateral • a more established entrepreneur • develop a fledgling business • a single parent • unable to secure the credit he/she needs to ... • operate in the grey market • risk losing your benefits • become self-employed

b In not more than six sentences, describe Sarah's and Leroy's problems. Use some of the phrases from **1a**.

2 **a** In small groups, discuss what Sarah and Leroy could do to improve their situation. List their options.

Useful words and phrases

debt [det] • in debt • go deeper into debt • become self-employed
borrow/lend money • borrow on credit cards • be creditworthy
apply for / qualify for / receive a loan • approve/offer/grant a loan • repay a loan • a loan at a low/high/commercial interest rate

⚠ **Trouble spot**

borrow sth. from sb. = *von jdm. etwas (aus)leihen*
lend sb. sth. = *jdm. etwas (ver)leihen*

b Decide on what you think is their best course of action. Present your advice in class; the others should comment on it ('If Sarah/Leroy did what you suggest, I think they would ...').

➤ Doing Research on the Internet (p. 231)
➤ Giving a Talk or Presentation (p. 254)

3 **Project work**. Find out more about Street (UK) and the microcredit system. Make notes on a) how the microcredit system works; b) who runs it; c) the history of the microcredit movement and what it seeks to achieve. Then present your findings to the class.

4 **Creative writing**. Imagine you are either Sarah or Leroy. Write an e-mail to a close friend outlining how your life developed and changed after you received a loan from Street UK. Do not forget to mention how you feel about the changes.

5 What do you consider to be the opportunities and the limits involved in the microcredit system?

CONTEXT BOX

Towards a Global Economy

When the centrally planned economy of the Soviet Union collapsed in the early 1990s, the Western market economy based on free trade and enterprise was largely left unchallenged. Especially in the Anglo-American world, economists and politicians followed neo-liberal policies, i.e. governments tried to influence the economy as little as possible, leaving it to be determined by market forces. As a consequence, state-owned enterprises like transport, water, power and telecommunications were privatized. Social services such as health, education and welfare benefits (e.g. jobless benefits) were cut back. Labour laws were changed to allow more part-time and temporary work and greater flexibility for firms hiring and firing workers. These measures were intended to maximize efficiency and profits in an increasingly global economy.

Economic globalization was seen as both inevitable and beneficial, bringing prosperity to more and more people. In the process of globalization, companies in developed countries have often merged and moved their operations to countries where the wage level is lower. They have cut costs in order to be competitive in the global market. Developing countries have been able to profit from globalization through the emergence of new jobs, e.g. in local branches of multinational companies, and through capital inflow.

Demonstrators in Los Angeles in 2000.

In recent years, however, critics have argued that free trade is not working for the majority of the world. Trade unions find it increasingly difficult to represent workers' interests in a multinational business environment, in which shareholders' interests are often more important than social concerns. There is worry that the economic power of these multinationals is greater than that of many nations in the world, and yet they are not accountable to any elected government. Critics also point out that since the 1960s, inequality has worsened both internationally and within countries. The policies of the World Bank, the World Trade Organization (WTO) and the International Monetary Fund (IMF) have opened up nations to foreign investment and thereby made it easier for production to go to places where labour is cheapest and environmental protection is low. While this trend has brought new opportunities to developing countries, it also means that they have become more and more dependent on foreign investment. However, local economies can be devastated if foreign investors suddenly decide to pull out their capital. According to critics, the World Bank and IMF have been responsible for increasing unemployment in the developing world by demanding that governments reduce public spending and lay off workers.

1 Trace the development of the global economy since the 1990s.
2 Make a list of collocations (i.e. words that are commonly used together) that have to do with economics, e.g. 'an increasingly global economy', 'follow neo-liberal policies'.
3 **a** Define 'economic globalization' and give examples illustrating the definition. You may start like this: 'Economic globalization is a/the process that ... '
b Compare and contrast the benefits and disadvantages of economic globalization, using as many of the highlighted phrases as possible.
4 Explain how globalization affects your life. You may refer to economic, cultural, political and environmental aspects.

GETTING ALONG IN ENGLISH

Going Shopping

Going shopping abroad involves you in situations in which you need to ask questions and negotiate. You can gain confidence in these areas by working through this page.

1 All of the following responses are in answer to certain questions that have been asked. Check unknown words in a dictionary, then write down the questions. There is usually more than one correct solution.

No, sorry, only what's on that shelf.
Yes, sir, you'll find some in stationery opposite the escalator.
Of course, I'll fetch it for you, give me one moment to get my key.
Yes, madam, the ladies' changing rooms are over there.
Oh no, sorry, you can only get that at the off-licence.
Well, there's an ATM near the main entrance.
You need a DIY store, dear.

2 When you get to the checkout or cash desk, the following topics can be of importance: wrapping, options of payment, using a coupon, signing a receipt, using a credit card, having a bonus card.

CD

a Copy the above topics onto a sheet of paper. Now listen to the dialogue on the CD and number the topics in the order in which they appear.
b Each of the following phrases contains an error. Listen to the CD again and correct them.

1 I like to use this voucher, please.
2 And if you can sign the receipt here.
3 I wonder if you could possible wrap it as a present?
4 I can only give you a carry bag.
5 Not you worry.

3 Test your command of shopping phrases with this role play for three people: One of you finds a sweater that you try on after asking where the changing rooms are. The assistant fetches you the same in red. You ask where you pay and are directed to the cash desk. You ask to pay in cash. The cashier wraps the sweater according to your wishes but forgets the receipt. Remember always to be polite when dealing with each other – the words in the box below will help you.

could you ... • I wonder if ... • well, I don't know • is it alright if I ... ? •
I'm afraid ... • that's fine

CD

4 The customers in the final two recordings are not happy with their purchases. Listen first to find out where the problems lie. While listening again, write down all the 'fillers' and 'softeners' that help to make a difficult piece of communication work, e.g. 'excuse me', 'let's have a look', etc.

3 As Basic as the Screwdriver Stephen Baker et al.

Antonio Sanz might as well have won the lottery. In 1965, when the small, curly-haired Spaniard was 10, an American professor asked his parents if she might take the boy to the U.S. and enroll him in public school. They agreed. America seemed to offer a brighter future than the dairy farms where his father worked in the foothills north of Madrid. Sanz left, but came back to Spain every summer with stories from Philadelphia and boxes of New World artifacts: Super Balls, baseball cards, and Bob Dylan records.

His real prize, though, was English. [...]

Sanz, now 46 and a father of three, employs his Philadelphia English as an executive at Vodafone PLC in Madrid. But something funny has happened to his second language. These days, English is no longer special, or odd, or even foreign. In Paris, Düsseldorf, Madrid [...], English has put down roots. 'What else can we all speak?' Sanz asks.

Basic tool. No surprise there. English is firmly entrenched nearly everywhere as the international language of business, finance, and technology. But in Europe, it's spreading far beyond the elites. Indeed, English is becoming the binding agent of a continent, linking Finns to French and Portuguese as they move toward political and economic unification. A common language is crucial, says Tito Boeri, a business professor at Bocconi University in Milan, 'to take advantage of Europe's integrated labor market.'

English, in short, is Europe's language. And while some adults are slow to embrace this, it's clear as day for European children. 'If I want to speak to a French person, I have to speak in English,' says Ivo Rowekamp, an 11-year-old in Heidelberg, Germany.

The implications for business are enormous. It's no longer just top execs who need to speak English. Everyone in the corporate food chain is feeling the pressure to learn a common tongue as companies globalize and democratize. These days in formerly national companies such as Renault and BMW, managers, engineers, even leading blue-collar workers are constantly calling and e-mailing colleagues and customers in Europe, the U.S. and Japan. The language usually is English, an industrial tool now as basic as the screwdriver. [...]

How much is English worth? In jobs from offices to the factory floor, recruiters say that workers who speak English often command salaries 25% to 35% above those who don't.

(From: 'The Great English Divide', *Business Week*, 13 August, 2001)

1 List all the advantages of English as a global language mentioned in the text.

2 'English is Europe's language' (cf. l. 21). Discuss what this means for other European languages.

3 Discuss to what extent a global economy could exist without a global language.

4 Listen to the two interviews.

a Explain and analyse the metaphor Braj Kachru uses in the first interview.

b What reasons does David Crystal give for the worldwide spread of English?

'New World artifacts': baseball cards.

[6] artifact (AE) = (BE) artefact ['ɑːtɪfækt] *object of special cultural interest* [6-7] Super Ball *ball that bounces especially high and was popular in the 1960s* [7] baseball card *card with a picture of a famous baseball player, often collected and traded* [10] executive *leading manager of a company* [12] put down roots *Wurzeln schlagen* [26] corporate food chain *Nahrungskette der Geschäftswelt* [29] blue-collar worker *worker in a factory (as compared to a white-collar worker, who works in an office)*

CD

➤ Glossary: Metaphor (p. 268)

4 Freedom and Opportunity

Most people would agree that freedom is a good thing, but is this also true in economic affairs? Before you read two texts by the US economists Milton and Rose Friedman and the British journalist Will Hutton, try to define what economic freedom and economic regulation mean.

Useful words and phrases

market forces • free trade • supply and demand • consumer needs • meet sb.'s demands • prosper • state interference • centrally planned economy • regulate sth. • raise money from import taxes/tariffs • social programmes

A Political and Economic Freedom Milton and Rose Friedman

Adam Smith (1723–1790), Scottish economist and philosopher.

Ever since the first settlement of Europeans in the New World – at Jamestown in 1607 and at Plymouth in 1620 – America has been a magnet for people seeking adventure, fleeing from a tyranny, or simply trying to make a better life for themselves and their children.

An initial trickle swelled after the American Revolution and the establishment of the United States of America and became a flood in the nineteenth century, when millions of people streamed across the Atlantic, and a smaller number across the Pacific, driven by misery and tyranny, and attracted by the promise of freedom and affluence.

When they arrived, they did not find streets paved with gold; they did not find an easy life. They did find freedom and an opportunity to make the most of their talents. Through hard work, ingenuity, thrift, and luck, most of them succeeded in realizing enough of their hopes and dreams to encourage friends and relatives to join them.

The story of the United States is the story of an economic miracle and a political miracle that was made possible by the translation into practice of two sets of ideas – both, by a curious coincidence, formulated in documents published in the same year, 1776.

One set of ideas was embodied in *The Wealth of Nations*, the masterpiece that established the Scotsman Adam Smith as the father of modern economics. It analyzed the way in which a market system could combine the freedom of individuals to pursue their own objectives with the extensive cooperation and collaboration needed in the economic field to produce our food, our clothing, our housing. Adam Smith's key insight was that both parties to an exchange can benefit and that, *so long as cooperation is strictly voluntary*, no exchange will take place unless both parties do benefit. No external force, no coercion, no violation of freedom is necessary to produce cooperation among individuals all of whom can benefit. That is why, as Adam Smith put it, an individual who 'intends only his own gain' is led by an invisible hand to promote an end which was no part of his intention. [...] By pursuing his own interest he frequently promotes that of the society more effectually than when he really intends to promote it. 'I have never known much good done by those who affected to trade for the public good.'

The second set of ideas was embodied in the Declaration of Independence,

■ **5** trickle *small flow (usu. of liquid)* **9** affluence *wealth* **12** ingenuity [ˌɪndʒəˈnjuːəti] *ability to find solutions to problems* **12** thrift *careful spending of money* **26** coercion *use of force or threats* **29** end *(here) aim, goal* **32** affect *(here) pretend* **37** endow sb. with sth. [ɪnˈdaʊ] *equip sb. with sth., give sth. to sb.* **38** unalienable right (fml) *a right that cannot be taken away* **45** requisite [ˈrekwɪzɪt] (fml) *thing that is needed for a purpose* **47** disperse sth. (fml) *spread or share sth.* **48** offset (n) *Gegengewicht* drafted by Thomas Jefferson to express the general sense of his fellow countrymen. It proclaimed a new nation, the first in history established on the principle that every person is entitled to pursue his own values: 'We hold these truths to be self-evident, that all men are created equal, that they are endowed by their Creator with certain unalienable Rights; that among these are Life, Liberty, and the pursuit of Happiness.' [...]

Much of the history of the United States revolves about the attempt to translate the principles of the Declaration of Independence into practice – from the struggle over slavery, finally settled by a bloody civil war, to the subsequent attempt to promote equality of opportunity, to the more recent attempt to achieve equality of results.

Economic freedom is an essential requisite for political freedom. By enabling people to cooperate with one another without coercion or central direction, it reduces the area over which political power is exercised. In addition, by dispersing power, the free market provides an off-set to whatever concentration of political power may arise. The combination of economic and political *power* in the same hands is a sure recipe for tyranny.

(From: *Free to Choose*, Harcourt Brace Jovanovitch, New York, 1980)

The beginning of an economic miracle: The Mayflower bringing English settlers in search of a better life to America in 1620.

1 The Friedmans mention several key events from American history. Name them and say what they have got to do with economics.
2 What have Adam Smith and Thomas Jefferson got in common?
3 In the text, the Friedmans give what might be viewed as their version of the American Dream. Sum up this version in about 120 words.

B **The Fair Society** Will Hutton

The European conception of the fair society comprehends a larger, integrative role for the state as actively conciliating social partners, providing public services, and regulating business and society. It is not conceived as a mere night watchman or umpire; it is an actor, ensuring that risk and reward are fairly distributed [...]. A powerful system of collective insurance underwrites the risks of poor health, disablement or unemployment. Worker rights are supported and entrenched. Risks and rewards are not allocated by chance and the market forces; rather, their final balance is settled by an activist state, expressing and enforcing the choices made by the community.

(From: *The World We're In*, Little, Brown and Company, London, 2002)

■ 1 comprehend sth. *(hier) etwas umfassen* 2 conciliate sb. [kən'sɪlieɪt] *jdn. versöhnen* 3 conceive sth. as sth. else *imagine sth. as sth. else* 4 umpire ['ʌmpaɪə] *person who makes sure that no rules are broken e.g. in a football match* 4 actor *person who makes sth. happen or does sth.* 5 underwrite sth. *etwas absichern* 7 entrench sth. *guarantee sth.* 7 allocate sth. *etwas verteilen*

1 Will Hutton mentions several tasks which European governments generally fulfil. Name them and say where you can see them at work in Germany.

British phone boxes – before and after privatization.

2 What do the Friedmans and Hutton agree about, and what do they disagree about?
3 Liberal and neo-liberal economists like Adam Smith and the Friedmans are sceptical of government intervention in the economy. Other economists believe that governments should have a much more active role. In small groups, discuss the following statements and decide where you stand on each issue. Then present your views to the class.

It is the government's job to ...
- ensure that everyone has sufficient food, decent clothing and adequate health care;
- establish production levels and set prices for goods;
- impose tariffs and import quotas to protect the domestic economy;
- promote economic growth by supporting small businesses;
- make sure that those who enjoy the benefits of selling and consuming a product pay all the costs of producing and consuming it;
- establish and protect the right to private property;
- curb monopoly power;
- impose taxes to curb pollution;
- subsidize the arts.

CD

C NPWA Billy Bragg and the Blokes

The English singer-songwriter Billy Bragg (cf. photos) is well-known for his personal commitment to political and social issues.

➤ Doing Research (p. 230)

1 Before you listen to the song, find out what these institutions do: the World Bank, the International Monetary Fund (IMF) and the World Trade Organization (WTO). Why are they criticized for the role they play in the global economy? (The Context Box on p. 99 provides some help on this.)
2 **a** While listening to the song take notes on the following topics:
- the speaker, his background and his present situation;
- the slogan 'NPWA' and its meaning;
- the possible addressee of the song;
- the tone of the singer.

b Now sum up your findings: What social, economic and political problems does the song deal with? What do you think is its message?

➤ Glossary: Tone (p. 265)

⚠ **Trouble spot**
economic = *Wirtschafts-, wirtschaftlich*
economical = *sparsam*

WATCH YOUR LANGUAGE

1 Look at this text and put in the definite article where necessary.

> Where # conditions are right, # liberal trade is not only about # prosperity and # greater freedom of # choice but also about # fairness. It's about # fairness which ensures that a concern for # welfare of all # citizens is set above # special interests. # P/profits of # liberalization must be distributed more equally, both within and between # countries. This is why # politics matter.

2 Identify the places where the German translation would use the article but the English does not.

3 Where do the following rules apply in the text?
- We do not use 'the' with plural nouns and abstract nouns.
- 'The' is used when the meaning is specified by a relative clause or an *of*-phrase.
- An adjective before such nouns does not mean that 'the' must be used.

4 Look through the text 'Political and Economic Freedom' (p. 102) and find more examples for each of the rules.

5 'Competition is usually good for the consumer, but the competition between mobile phone companies is just making phoning more complicated than it needs to be.' Make similar sentences in which you use the following words twice, once in a general sense without the definite article, and once in a specific sense with the article.

debt • growth • prices • taxation • training • worker

6 Collocations

a When you use a word in a sentence you need to know its collocations, i.e. the words that are commonly used together with that word. Take the noun 'profit': Which of the following words and phrases would you say is not a collocation in English? You may need to use a German-English dictionary to find the error and correct it.

make a profit • share the profit • profits decline • guarantee profits • sell sth. with profit • an enormous profit

b Find out how your monolingual English dictionary lists collocations. Then use it to put together a list of collocations for the nouns in the box on the right.

➤ Using a Monolingual Dictionary (p. 234)

7 Imagine you have set up a small computer firm and you are celebrating the first year of its existence with parents and friends, who have invested money in your company. Use some of the collocations you have collected to write your speech:
'Dear Mum and Dad, dear friends and investors,
You will be pleased and possibly surprised to hear that the demand for our products is increasing every day and ...'

Vocabulary box
business • competition • supply • demand • industry • money • production • wages

Has this page pointed out any areas of difficulty for you that you had not yet noticed? If so, they should be added to your self-assessment 'plan of action' (cf. Workbook).

➤ Working with Cartoons (p. 225)

1 a State which media are dealt with in the four cartoons and explain in no more than two sentences what the message of each is.

b Choose one of the cartoons, describe it in as much detail as necessary and analyse it.

Useful words and phrases

Describing

- **the scene in general**
  The cartoon shows ... standing/ ...
- **significant details**
  vending machine
  news stand
  news room
  The sign in his hand says ...
  He is / They are looking at / holding /...
- **the characters**
  bewildered/bemused/annoyed/excited
  The expression on his face shows ...
  Lines suggest that ... is/are moving.
  The ... is speaking / has a speech bubble.
- **caption**
  The caption reads ...

Explaining and interpreting

The cartoonist has targeted ...
The caption is a pun on ... / plays on the different meanings/spellings of ... in order to ...
The cartoonist wants to make a point about ...
The fact that the character ... shows that ...
The cartoon assumes that the reader knows ...
What makes the cartoon funny is ...

2 **a** Make a list of all the different media you are familiar with.
b Rank the media on your list, first from most to least important for keeping people informed, then from the ones you use most to the ones you use least. What conclusions can you draw?

3 **a** Explain why a cartoon might be a more effective way of putting across an opinion than a simple statement.
b Collect cartoons from German newspapers, magazines or websites and bring them to class. Explain the stylistic devices they use and the sorts of topics they deal with. Try translating the cartoons into English. Explain why this is more difficult with some than with others

➤ Glossary: Cartoon (p. 264)

➤ Glossary: Stylistic Devices (pp. 267ff.)

CONTEXT BOX

The Media: Friend or Foe?

In today's world of global commerce, conflicts and communications we rely heavily on all sorts of media. And as our information about the world usually comes to us via a medium and not directly, we need to question the source of that information because the source may give a slant to the facts and events it transmits: What political affiliations and commercial interests does a newspaper or TV station owner have? What products or ideas are sold by the owner of the website we have just visited? Is the advertising for a new film adaptation trying to get us to read the book or to buy the T-shirt, the video game and other merchandise?

It makes sense to exercise caution in approaching the media, but this should not lead to 'media bashing', i.e. blaming the media for events which they report, unearth or publicize, as if the media themselves were responsible for the event. There have been some cases where a journalist may have significantly altered an interview, or encouraged people in a demonstration to act in a violent manner, but on the whole the media provide us with the information we need to understand our world better. Moreover, they offer us the means to make our everyday lives more comfortable: travel is easier with timetables and delays posted on the Internet; the print media, whether tabloids (popular newspapers), broadsheets (the quality or more serious newspapers) or newsmagazines, summarize for us complex issues so that we can grasp them quickly over the breakfast table.

Information technology (IT) is a vital part of our lives today, but it is entertainment that is still most people's main point of contact with the media: whether it is your favourite soap on TV, or music you listen to on the radio or download onto your computer, you would be fairly unusual if you did not spend at least an hour a day using one of the electronic media – just for fun.

In the UK an ethical standard for broadcast media was set early on by the BBC's promise to 'inform, educate and entertain'. The electronic media have vastly extended the amount and the availability of materials covering these three areas, but they are often not able or willing to control the flow of information. This accounts for the ongoing debate on what should and should not be freely available through the various media and who, if anyone, should have the right or duty to limit or censor that flow.

1 **a** Check that you understand all the highlighted words and phrases.
b Starting with relevant words and phrases from the Context Box, make clusters of words relating to the media under different headings.
c Now make a mind map about the media. Add as many words, phrases and collocations as you can.

2 Using your mind map, write a short article on one medium of your choice, explaining what it does best and what it does less well.

1 'Read All about It!'

A Germans Destroy Wembley Martin Wallace

Demolition work finally started at Wembley yesterday – with a GERMAN bulldozer ripping the stadium apart.

The 130-ton machine called Goliath tore into the 80-year-old concrete home of English soccer.

But the monster excavator carried a St George flag – draped across the back by driver Gabriel Ford, an Arsenal fan from Leyton, East London.

It will take six months to flatten the historic arena.

Demolition finally got the go-ahead last week after plans for a replacement £757 million stadium were agreed after a seven-year saga.

The work started almost two years to the day since Germany's last demolition job at Wembley – beating England 1–0 in the venue's final international match.

In just thirty minutes yesterday the press centre and VIP area in the North Stand were reduced to rubble.

Goliath – which has a 35-metre arm with giant mechanical shears on the end – was built specially for the Wembley job.

As it rumbled into action yesterday, England 1966 World Cup winner George Cohen said: 'This is a sad day but we have to move on. She is an old lady forever etched in the memory of fans.'

Even the Twin Towers will go – too flimsy to be preserved. But three tons of rubble will be sold to fans.

After the site is cleared a new Wembley will be born. A 90,000 seat stadium, tipped to be the best in the world, will feature a soaring 133-metre high arch and a sliding roof.

It will take four years to complete before staging English matches and cup finals. Aussie firm Multiplex, who built the 110,000-seater Stadium Australia for the Sydney Olympics, designed the new Wembley.

It is being financed partly by the GERMAN bank West LB with a £433 million loan. The FA is paying £148 million and Sport England £120 million.

FA chief executive Adam Crozier said: 'Players and fans can look forward to enjoying facilities at what will be the best stadium in the world.'

The Germans may think they had the last laugh – but the old venue will forever remain the site of England's greatest triumph, beating Germany 4–2 in the 1966 final.

(From: *The Sun*, 1 October, 2002)

1 demolition *destruction which has been planned* **2** rip sth. apart *destroy sth. completely* **5** excavator *large machine for digging and moving earth* **11** venue *place where people meet for an organized event* **13** rubble *Schutt* **14** shears (pl) *instrument like enormous scissors* **18** etched in sb.'s memory *unforgettable for sb.* **19** flimsy *not strong* **22** soar *rise up very high* **23** sliding roof *Schiebedach* **28** FA (abbr) = *Football Association* **30** facilities (pl) *buildings, equipment and services*

1 a Consider why the *Sun* devotes so much space to the demolition of a football stadium.

b The article does not merely relate facts. Find examples in the text of other sorts of information.

2 List the verbs or phrases used with the word 'German' or 'Germany'. Discuss why the *Sun* used the words it did.

3 The *Sun* is a tabloid newspaper. Make notes about how the article might have been written in a more serious newspaper.

B Work Starts and Stops on Wembley Simon Burnton

At precisely 11.09 a.m. yesterday, five years and 287 days after it was decided to build a new stadium at Wembley, work finally began at the site. Thirteen minutes later, workmen removed their hard hats and called it a day.

John Corcoran of Multiplex, the Australian construction firm in charge of the project, made a short speech to mark the occasion. 'The spirit of Wembley owes more to the inspiring feats of a nation's sporting heroes than it does to bricks and mortar,' he said.

And with that, Goliath swung into action. Positioned between the famous twin towers, the specially-constructed 35-ton bulldozer punched nervously through a window in what was once the press room. At the controls an 'excited but nervous' Gabriel Ford, an Arsenal fan from Leyton, curled the neck of his crane into a triumphant arch. He bashed in a few more windows, ripped off some roofing, and then stopped.

Assuming they can step up the pace it will take around six months, and some £93m, to complete the demolition.

(From: *The Guardian*, 1 October, 2002)

1 List any facts and figures you get from this article that you did not get from the *Sun* article. Categorize them under two or three headings.

2 Look at your notes for p. 109, **3**. Were any of your ideas taken up in the *Guardian* report?

➤ Glossary: Stylistic Devices (pp. 267ff.)

3 **a** Describe the stylistic and lexical devices which are used in the articles from the *Sun* and the *Guardian* to try and involve readers emotionally. Think about elements such as images, connotations (i.e. the associations a word has), etc.

b Compare the two articles, paying special attention to the points each might be trying to make between the lines.

Useful words and phrases

The hidden agenda in ... reveals ...
The article seems biased because ...
The language is evocative/emotive/banal/objective/...
While the first article concentrates on ..., the second provides more ...
The facts and figures / interpretation of events / ... appeal more/less to the ... reader
The article is fair ... / manipulates...

4 **Creative writing.** Write a short article on an event in your school or town using either devices similar to those you found in **3a** or paying attention to factual detail.

■ **5-6** call it a day *stop working* **9** mark sth. *celebrate sth. (esp. a date) important* **11** feat [fiːt] *achievement that needs skill, courage, etc.* **12** bricks and mortar (infml) *just a building* **19** curl sth. *make sth. form the shape of a curve* **20-21** bash sth. in *break sth.* **23** step up the pace *speed up*

C The Sheep in Wolf's Clothing James Thurber

Not very long ago there were two sheep who put on wolf's clothing and went among the wolves as spies, to see what was going on. They arrived on a fete day, when all the wolves were singing in the taverns or dancing in the street. The first sheep said to his companion, 'Wolves are just like us, for they gambol and frisk. Every day is fete day in Wolfland.'

He made some notes on a piece of paper (which a spy should never do) and he headed them 'My Twenty-Four Hours in Wolfland', for he had decided not to be a spy any longer but to write a book on Wolfland and also some articles for the *Sheep's Home Companion*.

The other sheep guessed what he was planning to do, so he slipped away and began to write a book called 'My Ten Hours in Wolfland'. The first sheep suspected what was up when he found his friend had gone, so he wired a book to his publisher called 'My Five Hours in Wolfland', and it was announced for publication first.

The other sheep immediately sold his manuscript to a newspaper syndicate for serialization.

Both sheep gave the same message to their fellows: wolves were just like sheep, for they gambolled and frisked, and every day was fete day in Wolfland.

The citizens of Sheepland were convinced by all this, so they drew in their sentinels and they let down their barriers. When the wolves descended on them one night, howling and slavering, the sheep were as easy to kill as flies on a windowpane.

Moral: Don't get it right, just get it written.

(From: *Fables for Our Time*, Harper and Row, 1940)

■ **2** be going on *los sein* **2-3** fete day [feɪt] *holiday* **3** tavern (old-fashioned) *pub* **4** gambol *jump about* **5** frisk *(of animals) run and jump in a lively way* **7** head sth. *write a heading for sth.* **9** Home Companion *(here) a lifestyle magazine* **10** slip away *quietly disappear* **12** wire sth. (AE) *send sth. as a telegramme* **15** newspaper syndicate *company that sells a newspaper column to different papers* **16** serialization *the publishing of a story in parts* **19** convince sb. *persuade sb. that sth. is true* **19-20** draw in the sentinels *(here) remove the guards* **20** let down their barriers *take down fences, etc.; become less worried* **21** slaver ['slævə] *sabbern*

1 **a** How are the sheep depicted in Thurber's fable?
b Describe the human characteristics that the wolves have.

2 Give examples from the text of features that are typical of fables.

3 **a** Analyse the title.
b Now analyse the moral of the fable. Who does the moral apply to (i) in the story and (ii) in real life?
c Consider what relevance the fable has to contemporary journalism.

➤ Glossary: Fable (p. 255)

D Front Pages

DAILY EXPRESS

CRUSADING FOR A SAFER BRITAIN

The World's Greatest Newspaper

TUESDAY OCTOBER 29, 2002 20p

FREE HEALTH SECTION

Revealed: Miracle pill that helps you shed pounds

How to get a body like a celebrity

ONLY 20p TODAY

STARS SEE ULRIKA'S SEX GAME ON VIDEO

She wins court ban on romps with ex-lover

By Paul Broster

FALLEN football star Stan Collymore showed fellow players a video of himself having sex with Ulrika Jonsson, it was revealed yesterday.

The High Court heard how the former England international had pledged that the explicit film had now been destroyed, amid reports that he had attempted to sell it to a Sunday newspaper.

Ulrika, 35, who once described Collymore as a "monster", persuaded a judge to ban the video.

She started the legal action after Collymore's lawyer Jonathan Crystal offered to sell the film two weeks ago, saying: "There will be plenty of nudity and her behaving disgustingly. Stan has always kept the tape back as his get-out-of-jail

TURN TO PAGE 3, COLUMN 4

Divorce letter to William found at butler's home

DIANA TRIAL LATEST – PAGES 6&7

OPINION 12 DIARY 27 EXPRESS WOMAN 31-38 CROSSWORD 39 STARS 40 LETTERS 42 TV 43-46 OBITS 47 CITY 51-55 SPORT 59-72

➤ Glossary: Layout (p. 266)

1 Compare the two front pages, above and right, published on the same day. Look at the headlines and the presentation – photos, colour, size of headlines, etc.; then explain which newspaper you would trust more to give you important news.

Useful words and phrases

banner headlines • capital letters • bold type • the nature of the photos used • the choice of photos • more column inches / space are/is given to ... • contents of the rest of the paper/... are displayed discreetly/clearly/attractively • ... shows that it is less/more interested in serious news / gossip / ... • ... indicate that ... • ... points to this newspaper belonging to the quality/popular press

2 a Write out all the headlines, then turn each into a proper sentence. What do you notice?

b Write two or three headlines for this week's news – local, national or international. Swap your headlines with a partner and write out the headlines as sentences.

Britain's passion for home-made porn
Libby Brooks investigates

Richard Rogers
A Marshall plan for architecture
In G2

Adrian Searle
Gainsborough – the verdict
In G2

The task facing Charles Clarke
In Education
With 100s of jobs

55p
Tuesday
October 29 2002
Published in London
and Manchester
guardian.co.uk
* * * *

The Guardian

After the storm Round-the-world race begins on a still, clear day

The eight yachts competing in the Clipper 2002 race set off from Liverpool yesterday, after being delayed for a day by gale-force winds. Their 35,000-mile journey will take in five continents Photograph: Tony Kenwright

US weapons secrets exposed

Julian Borger in Washington

Respected scientists on both sides of the Atlantic warned yesterday that the US is developing a new generation of weapons that undermine and possibly violate international treaties on biological and chemical warfare.

The scientists, specialists in bio-warfare and chemical weapons, say the Pentagon, with the help of the British military, is also working on "non-lethal" weapons similar to the narcotic gas used by Russian forces to end last week's siege in Moscow.

They also point to the paradox of the US developing such weapons at a time when it is proposing military action against Iraq on the grounds that Saddam Hussein is breaking international treaties.

Malcolm Dando, professor of international security at the University of Bradford, and Mark Wheelis, a lecturer in microbiology at the University of California, say that the US is encouraging a breakdown in arms control by its research into biological cluster bombs, anthrax and non-lethal weapons for use against hostile crowds, and by the secrecy under which these programmes are being conducted.

"There can be disagreement over whether what the United States is doing represents violations of treaties," Mr Wheelis told the Guardian. "But what is happening is at least so close to the borderline as to be destabilising."

In a paper to be published soon in the scientific journal Bulletin of the Atomic Scientists, the two academics focus on recent US actions that have served to undermine the 1972 Biological Weapons Convention. In a move that stunned the international community last July, the US blocked an attempt to give the convention some teeth with inspections, so that member countries could check if others were keeping the agreement.

Mr Dando believes Washington's motive for torpedoing the deal, which had the support of its allies, was to maintain secrecy over US research work on biological weapons. He said that work includes:

- CIA efforts to copy a Soviet cluster bomb designed to disperse biological weapons
- A project by the Pentagon to build a bio-weapon plant from commercially available materials to prove that terrorists could do the same thing
- Research by the Defence Intelligence Agency into the possibility of genetically engineering a new strain of antibiotic-resistant anthrax
- A programme to produce dried and weaponised anthrax spores, officially for testing US bio-defences, but far more spores were allegedly produced than necessary for such purposes and it is unclear whether they have been destroyed or simply stored.

In each case, the US argued the research was being done for defensive purposes, but their legality under the BWC is questionable, the scientists argue.

For example, a clause in the biological weapons treaty forbids signatories from producing or developing "weapons, equipment or means of delivery designed to use such agents or toxins for hostile purposes or in armed conflict".

Furthermore, signatories agreed to make annual declarations about their biodefence programmes, but the US never mentioned any of those programmes in its reports. Instead, they emerged from leaks and press reporting.

The focus on Washington's biological and chemical weapons programme comes at an awkward time for the Bush administration, which is locked in negotiations at the UN for a tough resolution on arms inspections of Iraq. According to Mr Dando, British and US research into hallucinogenic weapons such as the gas BZ encouraged Iraq to look into similar agents. "We showed them the way," he said.

Mr Dando added that the US was currently working on "non-lethal" weapons similar to the gas Russian forces used to break the Moscow theatre siege. Those include "calmative" agents which are designed to knock people out without killing them.

"What happened in Moscow is a harbinger of what is to come," Mr Dando said. "There is a revolution in life sciences which could be applied in a major way to warfare. It's an early example of the mess we may be creating."

He added that Britain "is implicated as well", as the Pentagon's Joint Non-Lethal Weapons Directorate has worked with British officers on its research. The directorate refused to comment last night.

Jonathan Tucker, a chemical weapons expert at the US Institute for Peace in Washington, said much of the work on non-lethal weapons was being carried out by an institute under the US justice department but was funded by the Pentagon.

"They are trying to keep it at arm's length, but it is problematic especially for military purposes. The chemical weapons convention makes a very clear distinction between riot control and incapacitants," he said.

While Mr Tucker believes that such knock-out gases are explicitly banned under the treaty, Mr Dando and Mr Wheelis believe the Pentagon has exploited a loophole that allows for such weapons for "law enforcement purposes".

But by blurring the edges of the treaty, they argue the US is inviting other countries to do the same. The US, Mr Dando said, "runs the very real danger of leading the world down a pathway that will greatly reduce the security of all."

Austin

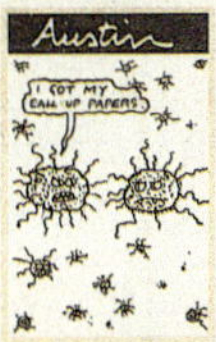

Inside

UN deadline nears, page 2
Moscow siege, page 4
Interactive guide and reports at guardian.co.uk/russia

Chirac cancels summit after row with 'very rude' Blair

Patrick Wintour and **Ian Black**

An enraged Jacques Chirac has cancelled the next Anglo-French summit after he accused Tony Blair of speaking to him with unprecedented rudeness over the future of the common agricultural policy and Africa.

It emerged yesterday that the French president delivered his snub on Friday afternoon at the EU enlargement summit in Brussels, as the two men rowed over their responsibilities to developing countries.

As the row flared – and with the Danish presidency backing the British – the French president told Mr Blair: "You have been very rude, and I have never been spoken to like this before." Mr Chirac then suggested the Anglo-French summit was off.

The two men apparently exchanged their harsh words in a mixture of French and English.

Mr Blair had bluntly told Mr Chirac that the oft-stated French concern for Africa would sound hollow if it blocked further CAP reform, keeping EU markets closed to developing countries and preventing an effective new round of World Trade Organisation talks at Doha.

Mr Blair passionately expressed his view that the west had a responsibility to open the developed markets of Europe, which would require major reform of the CAP and an end to production subsidies.

He pointed out that the EU had made a commitment to CAP reform at the world trade talks in Doha, and earlier at the Berlin EU summit on CAP reform in 1999.

The next Anglo-French summit had been due to be held in France by December, with the future of the EU stability and growth pact likely to be on the agenda.

Downing Street admitted that there were "vigorous exchanges" between the two men – official parlance for a row.

British officials admitted that Mr Blair had also been angered that Mr Chirac, prior to the summit, had revived plans to end the British CAP rebate which is guaranteed to 2008.

He had stitched up a deal on the future of CAP spending at a private meeting with the German chancellor Gerhard Schröder on the eve of the summit.

The meeting revived British fears that the Franco-German motor was once again going to begin to drive the European agenda, leaving other EU members to watch helplessly.

A separate Anglo-French row developed over draft proposals tabled yesterday by the former French ▸ Page 2

The two leaders at a photocall before Friday's meeting

Quick Index

9 770261 307927 44
CE ABFPRST

UK gives 400 tanks to Jordan

David Hencke
Westminster correspondent

A row broke out last night over a gift from Britain to Jordan's armed forces of more than 400 surplus Challenger tanks as Britain and the US prepare for a possible war against its neighbour, Iraq.

Senior backbench Labour MPs and the Liberal Democrat frontbench spokesman Menzies Campbell were last night demanding to know why Geoff Hoon, the defence secretary, had sneaked the deal through parliament during the recess.

They also said they were not satisfied that Jordan could guarantee that the secret of the tanks' reinforced armour would not leak across the border to Saddam Hussein. Jordan was named in the Scott report on arms sales to Iraq as a country where sensitive technology leaked to Iraq.

The gift has emerged in an obscure memorandum deposited in the Commons library by the Ministry of Defence. In it, ministers apologise for not giving parliament a chance to debate what is described as an "unusual gift" of tanks with a book value of £385,000 each. The tanks were last used in action during the Gulf war to invade Iraq.

According to the document, a deal was reached two years ago to present 288 tanks and 112 support vehicles to back up the foreign policy of King Abdullah, the new king of Jordan. Just before the parliamentary recess, Mr Hoon decided to give Jordan another 114 main battle tanks and 19 training tanks.

The document says: "In the interests of making the most efficient use of public funds, it was particularly desirable for parliamentary clearance to be achieved by the middle of October. Early clearance would help to maximise workshop efficiency by allowing transition, without a break, to the preparation of the proposed package of Challenger 1s after the preparation of the first batch of 288 tanks was completed in the third week of October.

It adds: "The department apologises that it did not prove possible to offer MPs 14 sitting days' notice."

Last night Mr Campbell said: "This is a particularly weak explanation for not telling parliament. I shall be pressing for an explanation from the Foreign Office of the impact of these extra tanks in the present Middle East situation."

Ann Clwyd, Labour MP for Cynon Valley and a campaigner for more openness on defence orders, said: "This is outrageous. Here we have a case where parliament was supposed to be consulted on this gift and they provide lame excuses why they didn't."

E A Letter to the Editor

Look at the photo and caption from the British newspaper *The Independent*.

McQueen's Parisian love story
ALEXANDER MCQUEEN said that the inspiration for his Spring/Summer 2003 show, the high point of the weekend at the Paris collections, was *Romeo and Juliet*.

(From: *The Independent*, 7 October, 2002)

Now read the letter to the editor that appeared the following day.

McQueen Mystery
Sir: The caption of your front page picture of 7 October asserts that 'Alexander McQueen looked to Shakespeare's *Romeo and Juliet* for inspiration'. I have thoroughly checked my volume of the complete works of Shakespeare, but cannot find the stage direction 'Enter Juliet, stage left, with her head up a parrot's backside'.
David Collins
Kidderminster, Worcestershire

➤ Glossary: Letter, Letter to the Editor (p. 264)
➤ Writing Letters (p.250)

➤ Glossary: Non-fictional Texts (pp. 262–264), Layout (p. 266)

1 Compare the opening and closing of this letter to the editor to an ordinary letter. Then write one yourself, either reacting to the articles on pp. 109–110 or to an article you have recently read in a newspaper.

2 **Project work.** Using what you have learned in this section, create a newspaper page in class.

a Discuss what you want the articles and reports for your newspaper to cover (e.g. politics, crime, fashion, films, sport) and what sort of style you wish to adopt.

b Choose one editor and then form different groups to be responsible for different aspects of the page (e.g. articles, photos, ads). In your group, choose a sub-editor and work to a tight deadline.

c When all the elements have been collected, the editor and sub-editors decide on the layout for the page and on the headlines. Display the page in your class.

2 The Role of Television

Warner Brother Studios in Los Angeles: a major film and TV studio.

A TV Is Big Business

The California sun is searing and the palm trees are tilting in the breeze, but the workers on the back lot are touching up icicles and snowdrifts. This is the set of *ER*, a medical drama for television, and the far corner of the lot at Warner Brothers is doubling for Chicago. Just across the way, past the peanut-butter-coloured walls of the vast studio sound stages, beckons the dazzling white entrance to the White House. Off the set, an improbably tanned actor, Rob Lowe, is shooting basketballs into a hoop. This set is Washington, DC, home to *The West Wing*, a drama about an American president. Round the corner, they are dressing the interior set for *Friends*, another hugely successful TV show, set in New York.

These are just three of America's most popular TV shows, set in three different corners of the country and exported around the globe. But they are all shot by one studio, on one lot, in the shadow of the Hollywood Hills. The bulk of the stuff that fills prime-time television screens in America is filmed between two valleys in Los Angeles, and is in the grip of a handful of production companies belonging to large media conglomerates. Over the past decade the country's television industry has enjoyed a bonanza that has brought millions of dollars, an ice-cool attitude and an air of entitlement to this West Coast city. The men in black T-shirts picking at salads in the smarter Beverly Hills restaurants – writers, producers, TV executives, actors and agents – have been the beneficiaries of the most sustained boom anyone in the business can recall. Movies may still have the edge for glamour, but as a business television dwarfs feature films, even in America: with a total turnover of $100 billion, it is around six times bigger.

2 back lot *outdoor part of a film studio* **2** touch sth. up *make small corrections to sth.* **16** bonanza *situation in which sb. can make lots of money* **17** air of entitlement *attitude of superiority* **20-21** have the edge for glamour *in Sachen Glamour führen*

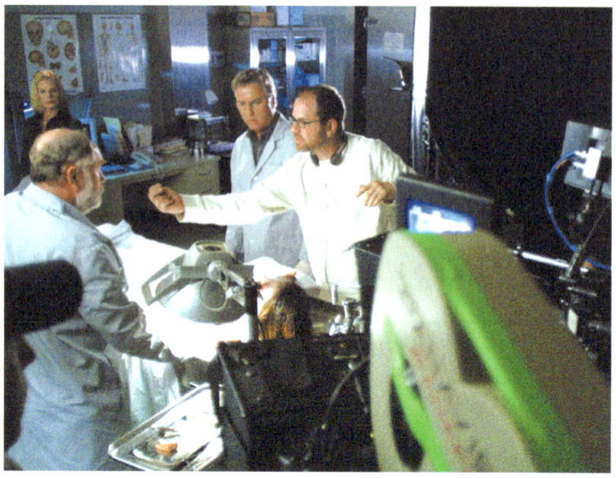

On the set of the TV series C.S.I.

Despite the formidable array of new gadgets – electronic games, computers, portable MP3-players, mobile telephony – that is now rivalling the television set for attention, the flickering image of the 75-year-old box still captivates people. The average American spends four hours a day watching television, and keeps the set turned on longer than that. [...] Watching TV was the single most popular way to spend an evening, Americans said in a recent Gallup poll: three times more so than seeing their friends. And according to research by MTV, a music-video channel owned by Viacom, an American media giant, even the widespread use of the Internet has not eaten significantly into TV time. 'In most cases,' says Betsy Frank, head of research and planning at MTV Networks, 'what TV viewers do less of, now that they are spending more time on the Internet, is sleeping, talking and personal hygiene.'

(From: 'Power in Your Hand', *The Economist*, 13 April, 2002)

■ **31** Gallup *organization that conducts market and opinion research* **34-35** eat into sth. *take away from sth.*

1 Devise headlines that capture the main theme for each of the three paragraphs.

2 Find words or expressions in ll. 10–22 that have strong connotations (i.e. the associations a word has beyond its literal or dictionary meaning). Explain the connotations and what they tell you about the writer's opinions on the subject. Example: 'The bulk of the stuff' (l. 12): 'bulk' is normally used to talk about cheap goods being sold in large quantities, showing that the writer probably thinks that this is exactly what Hollywood productions are.

3 **a** What reasons can you think of why American TV shows are 'exported around the globe' (l. 11)?

b Debate the following motion: 'There should be more European and fewer American programmes on German TV.'

➤ Debating (p. 252)

B Rather than Talking about the Weather Jo Croft

On average, people in Britain spend 230.6 minutes watching the television or video every day, which is more than in any other European country. These days, rather than talking about the weather, it is probably more accurate to say that television programmes provide a favourite topic of conversation for British people (according to market research, 46 per cent of the UK population discuss television programmes with their friends or family). In many ways, television now seems to be at the hub of 'the British way of life', offering a structure and rhythm around which people may shape their leisure time. Nowadays, the success or otherwise of major national holidays such as Christmas and Easter is less likely to be talked about in terms of the quality of church services, than about the quality of programmes on television. [...]

A traditional British Christmas has been characterised (or caricatured) through images of the family (ranging across three generations) sitting in front of the television after Christmas dinner, watching the Queen's Speech at 3 p.m. and then a classic film such as *The Sound of Music* or *The Wizard of Oz*. It is important not to underestimate the status of these televisual myths in relation to the attitudes which British people themselves express about national identity, and as a corollary of this, it is often the case that anxieties about social decline are most readily articulated in terms of 'falling standards' on television. The concept of family viewing is a central stake in debates about the role of the BBC, a public-owned institution known to the country as Auntie (suggesting its cosy, nanny-like persona [...]). It is often deplored in the press that current American or American-inspired television shows, such as *Baywatch*, *Blind Date* and *Gladiators*, are usually the most popular programmes, shown in the prime time family viewing slots on early Saturday evenings. In effect, programmes that are associated both with youth and American culture often seem to be regarded as anathema as far as British family values are concerned.

(From: Mike Storry and Peter Childs, eds., *British Cultural Identities*, Routledge, London, 1997)

14 the Queen's Speech *annual Christmas speech by the Queen broadcast on TV and radio* **17-18** corollary [kəˈrɒləri ☆ ˈkɔːrəleri] (fml) *result* **18** social decline *lowering of standards of behaviour in society* **20** central stake *(hier) Fixpunkt* **26** anathema [əˈnæθəmə] (fml) *thing that is hated*

1 Explain in your own words the ways in which television defines 'the British way of life' (l. 7).

2 Speculate on what is meant by 'American-inspired television shows' (ll. 22–23).

3 Compare the 'caricature' (cf. l. 12) of a traditional British Christmas with its German counterpart. What conclusions can you draw?

4 **Project work.** In groups, devise a questionnaire to determine the TV viewing habits of students in your year at school. Include questions which will allow you to make comparisons with claims made in this and the previous text. Combine the best from the different groups' questionnaires, then carry out the survey. Report your findings to the class.

C How to Get on TV

VIDEO

The two most talked about television genres in the UK in the last few years have been 'nasty host' shows (usually quizzes and talent-spotting shows) and reality shows. On the video you will find extracts from two of each.

1 Watch each of the extracts and say whether or not you think this statement from 'Rather than Talking about the Weather' (cf. above) applies to them: 'It is often the case that anxieties about social decline are most readily articulated in terms of "falling standards" on television' (ll. 18–19). Explain your answers.

2 Watch the extracts again. Pick two of the four and

a explain the popularity of each show;

b give your own opinion on what the producers' motives might be and whether you think they are fair on (i) the participants and (ii) the audience.

3 What trends do you see in German TV programming? What do you think of them?

4 Would you want to be a participant in any of the shows you have seen or discussed? Explain your answer.

3 I Saw It on the Internet ... so it's got to be true

A Nobody Knows You're a Dog

'On the Internet, nobody knows you're a dog.'

1 Describe the cartoon on the left in three sentences or less.

2 a In groups of four or five, discuss the relevance of the cartoon's message with regard to one of the following:

- chatting on the Internet;
- using the Internet for making purchases;
- doing research on the Internet.

b Now do a brainstorming on how you can try and safeguard yourself from the dangers of finding a 'dog' on the Internet. Report your ideas to the class.

B The Reliability of Internet Information

Judging the reliability of sources found on the Internet is crucial because there is no regulating body that monitors the reliability of what is on the Internet. Although there is so much information on the Internet that it can seem like a university library, it is actually more like a huge open-air market. In one corner there might be reliable sources from whom you can obtain valuable information. But over in another corner there might be weirdos, whackos, and eccentrics, from whom anything you obtain is, at best, questionable. The problem is that on the Internet there is no way to tell the difference. Someone who wants to turn *Moby Dick* into a glorification of bloodsports or an animal rights tract can post a rewritten version with no indication of its differences from Melville's original. There's a saying in Latin, *caveat emptor*, or 'let the buyer beware'. When it comes to doing your research on the Internet, the saying should be *caveat internauta*, or 'let the surfer beware'.

Here is a list of points to consider when you are trying to judge the reliability of information you find on the Internet:

- Who is the author or sponsor of the page?
- Are there obvious reasons for bias?
- Is contact information provided?
- Is this page a 'zombie', or one considered 'walking dead' because the person who posted it no longer maintains or updates it?
- What is the purpose of the page?
- How well organized is the page?
- Can you verify the information on the Web page some other way?

(From: 'How to Judge the Reliability of Internet Information', the website of *McGraw-Hill Higher Education*)

■ **1** crucial ['kru:ʃl] *extremely important* **6** whacko (sl) *crazy person* **8-9** 'Moby Dick' *classic 1851 novel by Herman Melville about a man's search for a great white whale* **17** bias ['baɪəs] *strong feeling for or against sth.* **23** verify sth. *check whether sth. is true*

1 This extract from the website of an academic publisher implies there is a difference between printed material and material on the Internet. List some of the differences.

2 Search the Internet for sites that fail one or more of the test questions given. Present one of them to the class, explaining why the site failed your test.

GETTING ALONG IN ENGLISH

Using the Phone to Get Information

These days getting information over the telephone may involve one of two techniques:

- old-fashioned question and answer, or
- touch-tone responses.

For the latter you may need to brush up your listening skills, for the former you have to be able to put across what you need as well as to understand the information you're being given. Working through this page should increase your confidence in both areas.

1 **a** You are meeting up with American friends for a holiday in Florida. From your hotel in Orlando you phone the airline to check when their flight, the 10.30 flight from Chicago, is due. Listen carefully to the recorded message and note down the numbers you would have pressed and the answers you would have given at each stage in order to get the information you require. CD

b Compare your list with a partner's. Listen again and check any discrepancies that came to light.

2 Lisa is youth hostelling in Cornwall. She has lost a filling and has terrible toothache. Listen to her first attempts to get help. CD

a What did Lisa do wrong? Note down as many points as you can.

b List some phrases you would use if you were trying to get information about medical services over the phone.

c Listen to Lisa's second attempt. Check whether her technique has improved. Add any useful words and phrases to your list. CD

3 Put the words and phrases you already know, have listed above or remember from the conversations in the following categories:

- starting a phone conversation;
- explaining what information/help you need;
- checking the information you are given;
- ending a phone conversation.

Remember, you are more likely to get the information you want if your questions are clear and your approach is polite.

4 **a** Now listen to Bernd, who is on holiday in New York, as he tries to get in touch with a German friend who is working there. Analyse his success in getting what he wants. Add any new words or phrases to your four categories. CD

b Here are some American words and phrases from Bernd's dialogues which often occur in the context of telephoning:

directory assistance • party • please hold • the line is busy • cell phone • phone booth

List the British equivalents, using a dictionary where necessary. Can you add more?

5 With a partner, decide on a situation in which you need to get some information over the phone. Plan a telephone dialogue – one of you prepares phrases for the information seeker, the other for the information giver. Perform the dialogue for the class. Listen to the class's analysis.

4 You Can Sell Anything

A We Are Speaking of Art Steven Millhauser

In the following extract from a recent novel which is set in New York at the beginning of the 20th century, Martin Dressler, an American entrepreneur, has gone to meet Harwinton, who runs an ad agency, to discuss advertising his latest hotel.

'Imagine two stones,' Harwinton said. 'Gray, smooth, flattish: small enough to hold comfortably in your hand. There is nothing interesting about these stones. Now, imagine that I single out one of them. Either one will do. I describe the pleasing feel of the stone in my hand. I compare its color to the color of an exotic animal. I admire its remarkable shape. I say that this stone fills me with well-being and confidence. Then I tell you that you may have either of the two stones. Which one are you more likely to choose? That's advertising.'

'But suppose one stone is really superior to the other?' Martin said.

'That's an interesting fact. It may even be a useful fact, a fact we can use. But it has nothing to do with the art of advertising.'

A grand hotel: not much different from a cake of soap?

As Harwinton spoke, Martin was struck again by his extreme youthfulness: with his short sandy hair combed neatly to one side in the manner of a schoolboy, his light-blue blond lashed eyes, and his small neat teeth, he looked no older than seventeen. In fact he was twenty-eight and reputed to be one of the best in the business. Harwinton had grown up in Indiana and attended the University of Minnesota, where a popular professor of psychology had given a series of lectures on the psychology of advertising, with special emphasis on the role of association in making ads memorable. He had made them read *The Principles of Psychology* by William James. Did Martin know the book? As Harwinton put it, his eyes were opened: advertising was a science, a system of measurable strategies for awakening and securing the attention of buyers. A study conducted by a professor at Northwestern University in Evanston, Illinois, had demonstrated that the right-hand pages of a magazine held the attention of readers more than the left-hand pages. Experiments aimed at gathering information about the attention value of particular kinds of space had shown that a full-page ad was more than twice as effective as a half-page ad. But size alone was only part of it: there was also the question of seizing the attention forcibly by an imaginative but experimentally verifiable use of words and pictures. One test showed that of fifty people who were asked to look through a magazine, immediately close it, and name all advertisements remembered, twenty-three mentioned In-er-Seal, but only sixteen of those twenty-three knew that In-er-Seal was used for wrapping a biscuit, whereas all twenty of the people who remembered the Pears advertisement knew that Pears was a kind of soap. Harwinton had come to New York to work in one of the new ad agencies, where he had devised a successful campaign for a new kind of pink soap powder produced by a company determined to seize a portion of the market controlled by cleansers in cake form. A year later he had begun his own agency, with a staff of artists and copywriters and a specially trained band of researchers who prepared questionnaires, conducted scientifically controlled tests, and studied the effectiveness of particular ads on particular social and economic groups.

'At least you admit,' Martin said, 'that there's a difference between a cake of soap and an eighteen-story hotel.'

'Only a very small one. Let me explain something, Mr. Dressler. The world sits there. It may have a meaning. As a private citizen, I am entitled to believe that it does. But as an advertiser, I train myself to experience the world as an immense blankness. It's my job to provide that blankness with meaning.'

'I'll grant you the point. Still, you have to admit –'

'A man comes to me with a cake of scouring soap. He wants me to sell it for him. I see a white lump. It's my job to make this white lump, which has no meaning, except in the most limited and practical sense, the most important thing in the world. I create a meaning for it. I create desire. To have this soap is to have what Aristotle says all men desire: happiness.'

When Harwinton spoke, in his cool and precise way, he looked directly at Martin with his light-blue eyes, never once averting his gaze; and Martin noticed that when he spoke he never moved his long, well-manicured hands or his erect body.

'And you yourself don't believe a word of it?'

'Belief has nothing to do with it. I present it. I create an illusion. We are speaking of art, Mr. Dressler.'

(From: *Martin Dressler*, Crown Publishers, New York, 1996)

■ **1** flattish *somewhat flat* **16** blond-lashed (adj) *mit blonden Wimpern* **19** be reputed to be [rɪ'pju:tɪd] *have a reputation for being* **45** verifiable ['verɪfaɪəbl] *able to be proved* **53** cleanser ['klenzə] *chemical substance used to clean things* **53** in cake form *in fester Form* **54** copywriter *person who writes advertising texts* **64** grant sb. a point *admit that sb. is right about sth.* **65** scouring soap *Scheuermittel* **66** lump *piece of sth. hard* **71** avert your gaze [ə'vɜ:t] *turn your eyes away (from sb./sth.)*

1 List Harwinton's claims about the nature of advertising and discuss them. Consider whether they are still true today.

2 Analyse how Harwinton is characterized in the extract.

3 **a** Identify the mode of presentation used in this passage and evaluate its effectiveness.

b State what changes would be necessary to convert the extract into a film script.

4 Advertising – an art or a science? State and justify your opinion.

➤ Glossary: Character and Characterization (p. 260)
➤ Glossary: Mode of Presentation (p. 259)

B AIDA Kevin Needham

➤ Glossary: Advertisement (p. 264)

Today advertisers still look for a scientific basis to help sell their products or messages. They develop formulas such as 'AIDA', explained here by a publisher of advice for online marketers.

■ [2] ad copy *advertising texts* [4] conceal sth. [kən'si:l] *hide sth.* [9] heaps *lots* [10] iron clad *(here) unbreakable*

Run the AIDA formula against all your sales literature and you will soon be creating winning ad copy.

A = Attention Make sure your headline catches your readers' attention. It must excite them just by seeing it. Make sure your headline either reveals or conceals a common interest. Consider a concern that a large percentage of your target market has and use that as the theme of your headline. [...]

I = Interest Interest is created by giving your potential customer multiple benefits that will enhance their life. Remember, customers buy on benefits not on features.

D = Desire You can build desire by making your offer irresistible. Include heaps of free bonuses (they can keep even if they return your product). Include an iron clad, no risk guarantee. Also it is important to build urgency into every offer. For example: 'Order now in the next 72 hours and you will get this free bonus.'

A = Action Last but most important, your sales piece must have a call to action. You must ask your customer to buy. If you have captured their attention, overwhelmed them with benefits and created an undeniable desire through free bonuses and the best guarantee, you must ask them to buy. You also must make it so easy for them to buy (as many payment methods as possible) that they will feel left out or disappointed if they don't.

(From: 'The Aida Formula', the website of *Danex Export Marketing Resources*)

■ trafficking *buying or selling sth. illegally* • assault and battery [ə'sɔ:lt] *crime of attacking another person* • extortion *making sb. give you money, etc. by threatening them* • apprehend sb. *arrest sb.*

1 Explain each of the four parts of the AIDA formula in your own words. Illustrate them with examples that you have thought up.

2 **a** Discuss why it might be effective if a headline 'reveals or conceals a common interest' (ll. 4–5).
b Explain what is meant by the statement that 'customers buy on benefits not on features' (l. 8).

3 Look at the ad on the left.
a Explain what it is trying to 'sell'.
b Evaluate it according to the AIDA formula.
c State your own opinion on its effectiveness. Does your judgment differ from your evaluation in **b**? Explain why or why not.

4 Bring magazine ads to class (or choose other adverts in this book) that you consider effective. Try to identify additional criteria for effective advertising not covered by the AIDA Formula.

5 **Project work.** Using the principles set down by Harwinton in 'We Are Speaking of Art' (p. 120) and in the AIDA formula, write an advert for your particular copy of this coursebook which makes it seem superior to all other copies.

WATCH YOUR LANGUAGE

Look at these mistakes, collected from student presentations on the media. Note that some sentences contain more than one mistake.

1. *Most young people take too much time watching TV.*
2. *I hardly ever watch anything on the first or second programmes. I prefer to watch the private canals.*
3. *There is too much violence in television.*
4. *You can have sent the news to your handy, which means your informations are always actual.*
5. *A lot of these new medias are in their very early stadiums of development.*
6. *Digital television makes use of relatively new technique which engineers originally developed for the military.*
7. *People can complain by the Ethics Commission if they believe they have been handled unfairly by the media.*
8. *A lot of people buy a product simply because they have seen it in a spot on TV.*

1 a Try to identify and correct the mistakes in the sentences above without consulting a dictionary or grammar book.

b With a partner, look at the sentences you were unsure of and decide where to look for help. Then make the necessary corrections.

➤ Using a Monolingual Dictionary (p. 234), Using a Grammar Book (p. 235)

2 Look again at the mistakes in the sentences above. What areas do the students need to study more closely? What might they do to improve their English?

3 Interference

a Give the German for the following English words and the English for the German ones. (Use your dictionary if necessary.) Make sentences with the English expressions to show that you understand the difference.

1 self-conscious – *selbstbewusst*
2 sympathetic – *sympathisch*
3 billion – *Billion*
4 meaning – *Meinung*
5 critic – *Kritik*
6 warehouse – *Warenhaus*
7 formula – *Formular*
8 pregnant – *prägnant*

b Explain the difference between the pairs below and use them in sentences.

1 have done sth. – have sth. done
2 let sb. do sth. – leave sb. to do sth.
3 must not do sth. – need not do sth.
4 stop doing sth. – stop to do sth.
5 oversee sth. – overlook sth.
6 take a photo of sb. – take a photo from sb.

c Explain and correct the mistakes the translator has made:

1 My mother is a successful undertaker.
– *Meine Mutter ist eine erfolgreiche Unternehmerin.*
2 She overheard Tom telling Pat a secret.
– *Sie überhörte, wie Tom Pat ein Geheimnis erzählte.*
3 She needed to go to the restroom. – *Sie brauchte den Ruheraum.*

Has this page pointed out any areas of difficulty for you that you had not yet noticed? If so, they should be added to your self-assessment 'plan of action' (cf. Workbook).

TURNING CONFLICT INTO ART

'Liberation'
by Ben Shahn (1945).

The arts presented in this chapter deal with one and the same theme – conflict, especially war. As you go through the chapter try and see how each art form has its own particular way of approaching this topic.

➤ Working with Pictures (p. 223)

1 Look at the painting 'Liberation' in silence for a few minutes, and then write down a few notes on the atmosphere and how it makes you feel. Try to explain why you feel this way.

Useful words and phrases

The atmosphere is depressing/cheerful/upsetting/... because (of) ...
The painting creates an atmosphere of ...

2 a Describe how the picture is composed.

Useful words and phrases

In the foreground/background/centre ...
On the right/left ...
The painting is static / seems to convey the feeling of movement.
The painting is colourful ... / The colours are bright/sombre/pale ...

b Discuss with a partner how the atmosphere you described was influenced by the composition of the picture. Present your findings to the class

3 Choose one of the children in the painting and put yourself in her position. Write an interior monologue about what is going on in your mind at that moment.

4 Why do you think Shahn painted this painting? When answering the question, bear in mind the subject matter, the atmosphere, the title and the date of composition.

5 **a** List some of the functions that you believe art has.
b Which of these functions does 'Liberation' fulfil?

6 **a** Most people surround themselves with things they like, some of which (e.g. posters, photos) may be art. Which art forms play an important role in your life?
b Bring one of your favourite examples of art (e.g. a photo, cartoon, poem or song) to class and share it with your classmates. Describe what it is about and say why you like it and what it means to you.

Now read this text from a novel by a contemporary British writer.

How do you turn catastrophe into art?

Nowadays the process is automatic. A nuclear plant explodes? We'll have a play on the London stage within a year. A President is assassinated. You can have the book or the film or the filmed book or the booked film. War? Send in the novelists. A series of gruesome murders? Listen for the tramp of the poets. We have to understand it, of course, this catastrophe; to understand it, we have to imagine it, so we need the imaginative arts. But we also need to justify it and forgive it, this catastrophe, however minimally. Why did it happen, this mad act of Nature, this crazed human moment?

(From: Julian Barnes, *A History of the World in 10 1/2 Chapters*, Jonathan Cape, London, 1989)

1 **a** List the examples Barnes gives of catastrophes and say how they can be turned into art.
b How does Barnes explain the fact that catastrophes are turned into art?

2 In groups, think of some examples of plays, books, films, poems or other forms of art, which have been 'inspired' by war and other catastrophes. Compare your findings with other groups.

3 Have another look at the painting 'Liberation'. Do you think what Barnes says applies to this painting? Explain why, or why not.

CONTEXT BOX

Art in Society

Art is considered an essential part of human achievement, and some of its many, varied creators are ranked among the most celebrated citizens of the world. In the general sense of the word, art involves both skill and creative imagination in a musical, literary, visual or performance context. Art provides the person or people who produce it and the community that observes it with an experience that might be aesthetic, emotional, intellectual, or a combination of these qualities. In a more limited sense of the word, art refers to painting, drawing or sculpture. In the plural, it refers to what is also known as the fine arts.

A traditional system of classification of the fine arts establishes categories like the visual arts (i.e. the graphic arts, e.g. drawing, the plastic arts, e.g. sculpture, and the decorative arts, e.g. carpets and glass), the performing arts (e.g. theatre, dance, music, film), literature (including poetry, narrative fiction, etc.), and architecture (often including interior design).

An artist's medium affects the style of his work: a sculptor must treat stone differently from wood, the painter uses watercolours differently from oil paints and a composer achieves different effects with trumpets than with flutes. An actor may be successful in films, but fail on the stage.

Industrialization, mass-production, technology and the popularity of museums have facilitated the public's access to art, so that fine art – created to be beautiful rather than useful – is no longer a luxury to be appreciated by a few. Art in all its forms attracts people because of the choice of medium, the function it might fulfil, because it is controversial, or even because it is an investment.

But the arts can only prosper if they are supported by public or private funds, and many young artists often rely on public grants or private sponsorship from patrons. Since the early 1980s in Britain, corporate (i.e. business) sponsorship has become increasingly important. However, especially in times of recession, art organizations find it increasingly difficult to attract business support.

In the USA artistic activities are financed primarily through private donations, business sponsorship and ticket sales, and there is a long tradition of wealthy businessmen donating their art collections to museums.

1 Choose one of the following aspects mentioned in the text:
a a definition of art and art forms;
b a particular medium;
c the role of art today.
Collect as many of the highlighted words and expressions as possible which belong to the aspect you choose and organize them in a mind map. Add any other words and phrases you already know.

2 How do the arts address or attract people? Write a short text, using as many suitable words from those highlighted in the text as possible. Use a dictionary to check you know the meaning of the words you choose and how they are used.

3 Do one of the following, in each case using as many words from the Context Box as possible:
a Devise a text for a brochure describing a famous work of art in your town or the area you live in. The brochure should aim to attract English-speaking tourists who are interested in art to visit your town.
b Work in groups to compile a brochure: each of you writes about one particular aspect of the arts.

1 Prose: Transforming Misery into Words

During the Spanish Civil War the American novelist and short-story writer Ernest Hemingway worked as a war correspondent. Here is an extract from one of his dispatches.

Europe, 1938: Spanish refugees.

A The Flight of Refugees (April 3, 1938) Ernest Hemingway

Soon we began passing carts loaded with refugees. An old woman was driving, crying and sobbing while she swung a whip. She was the only woman I saw crying all day. There were eight children following another cart and one little boy pushed on a wheel as they came up a difficult grade. Bedding, sewing machines, blankets, cooking utensils and mattresses wrapped in mats, sacks of grain for the horses and mules were piled in the carts and goats and sheep were tethered to the tailboards. There was no panic, they were just plodding along.

On a mule piled high with bedding rode a woman holding a still freshly red-faced baby that could not have been two days old. The mother's head swung steadily up and down with the motion of the beast she rode, and the baby's jet-black hair was drifted gray with the dust. A man led the mule forward, looking back over his shoulder and then looking forward at the road.

'When was the baby born?' I asked him, as our car swung alongside. 'Yesterday,' he said proudly, and the car was past. But all these people, no matter where else they looked as they walked or rode, all looked up to watch the sky. [...]

As we went on, the road choked and swelled with this migration, until, finally, it was not just the road, but streaming alongside the road by all the old paths for driving cattle came the civilian population and the troops. There was no panic at all, only a steady movement, and many of the people seemed cheerful. But perhaps it was the day. The day was so lovely that it seemed ridiculous that anyone should ever die.

(From: William White, ed., *By-Line: Ernest Hemingway*, Touchstone, New York, 1998)

■ **2** sob (v) *schluchzen* **2** whip (n) *Peitsche* **4** grade *slope* **4** bedding *bedclothes, sheets, blankets, etc.* **6** mule *Maultier* **6** tethered *tied* **7** plod along *walk slowly and tiredly* **10-11** jet-black *very black* **16** choked and swelled *became fuller and more crowded*

B Old Man at the Bridge Ernest Hemingway

Later, Hemingway wrote the following short story based on his experience of watching the flight of Spanish refugees.

An old man with steel rimmed spectacles and very dusty clothes sat by the side of the road. There was a pontoon bridge across the river and carts, trucks, and men, women and children were crossing it. The mule-drawn carts staggered up the steep bank from the bridge with soldiers helping push against the spokes of the wheels. The trucks ground up and away heading out of it all and the peasants plodded along in the ankle deep dust. But the old man sat there without moving. He was too tired to go any farther.

It was my business to cross the bridge, explore the bridgehead beyond and find out to what point the enemy had advanced. I did this and returned over the bridge. There were not so many carts now and very few people on foot, but the old man was still there.

'Where do you come from?' I asked him.

'From San Carlos,' he said, and smiled.

That was his native town and it gave him pleasure to mention it and he smiled.

'I was taking care of animals,' he explained.

'Oh,' I said, not quite understanding.

'Yes,' he said, 'I stayed, you see, taking care of animals. I was the last one to leave the town of San Carlos.'

He did not look like a shepherd nor a herdsman and I looked at his black dusty clothes and his gray dusty face and his steel rimmed spectacles and said, 'What animals were they?'

'Various animals,' he said, and shook his head. 'I had to leave them.'

I was watching the bridge and the African looking country of the Ebro Delta and wondering how long now it would be before we would see the enemy, and listening all the while for the first noises that would signal that ever mysterious event called contact, and the old man still sat there.

'What animals were they?' I asked.

'There were three animals altogether,' he explained. 'There were two goats and a cat and then there were four pairs of pigeons.'

'And you had to leave them?' I asked.

'Yes. Because of the artillery. The captain told me to go because of the artillery.'

'And you have no family?' I asked, watching the far end of the bridge where a few last carts were hurrying down the slope of the bank. 'No,' he said, 'only the animals I stated. The cat, of course, will be all right. A cat can look out for itself, but I cannot think what will become of the others.'

'What politics have you?' I asked.

'I am without politics,' he said. 'I am seventy-six years old. I have come twelve kilometres now and I think now I can go no farther.'

'This is not a good place to stop,' I said. 'If you can make it, there are trucks up the road where it forks for Tortosa.'

'I will wait a while,' he said, 'and then I will go. Where do the trucks go?'

'Towards Barcelona,' I told him.

1 steel rimmed spectacles (old-fashioned) *Nickelbrille* **4** spoke *Speiche* **19** shepherd *man who takes care of sheep* **19** herdsman *man who takes care of cattle* **29** pigeon *Taube* **45** blankly *with no expression* **56** dove *small pigeon* **66** low ceiling *low clouds covering the whole sky*

'I know of no one in that direction,' he said, 'but thank you very much. Thank you again very much.'

He looked at me blankly and tiredly, then said, having to share his worry with someone, 'The cat will be all right, I am sure. There is no need to be unquiet about the cat. But the others. Now what do you think about the others?'

'Why, they'll probably come through it all right.'

'You think so?'

'Why not?' I said, watching the far bank where from now there were no carts.

'But what will they do under the artillery when I was told to leave because of the artillery?'

'Did you leave the dove cage unlocked?' I asked.

'Yes.' – 'Then they'll fly.'

'Yes, certainly they'll fly. But the others. It's better not to think about the others,' he said.

Europe, 1994: Bosnian refugees.

'If you are rested I would go,' I urged. 'Get up and try and walk now.'

'Thank you,' he said and got to his feet, swayed from side to side and then sat down backwards in the dust.

'I was only taking care of animals,' he said dully, but no longer to me. 'I was only taking care of animals.'

There was nothing to do about him. It was Easter Sunday and the Fascists were advancing toward the Ebro. It was a gray overcast day with a low ceiling so their planes were not up. That and the fact that cats know how to look after themselves was all the good luck that old man would ever have.

(From: *The First Forty-Nine Stories*, 1938)

1 Note down as many differences as you can find between the dispatch and the short story and discuss them in class.

➤ Glossary: News Story (p. 262), Short Story (p. 255)

2 Describe the old man in the short story and his situation. Say what the war means for him as an individual.

3 Discuss with your classmates which of the two texts is more convincing in demonstrating the horrors of war and how they affect 'ordinary' human beings.

4 Creative writing.

a In small groups, choose one of the people described in the dispatch and map out a possible short story, bearing the following in mind:
- their situation before they were forced to flee;
- their personal troubles;
- what you think might happen to them in the further course of events.

b In your group, write a short story along the lines of 'Old Man at the Bridge'. You can either each write one part, or write the whole thing together. Whichever way you do it, correct each other's work and make suggestions for improvement.

➤ The Stages of Writing (p. 244)

c Read your stories to the class, or copy and hand them out to your classmates.

5 Now that you have examined both non-fiction and fiction and used a news story as a basis for writing a short story, summarize the differences between a non-fictional and a fictional text.

2 Poetry: Soothing the Soul?

A The Ultimate Pain Relief

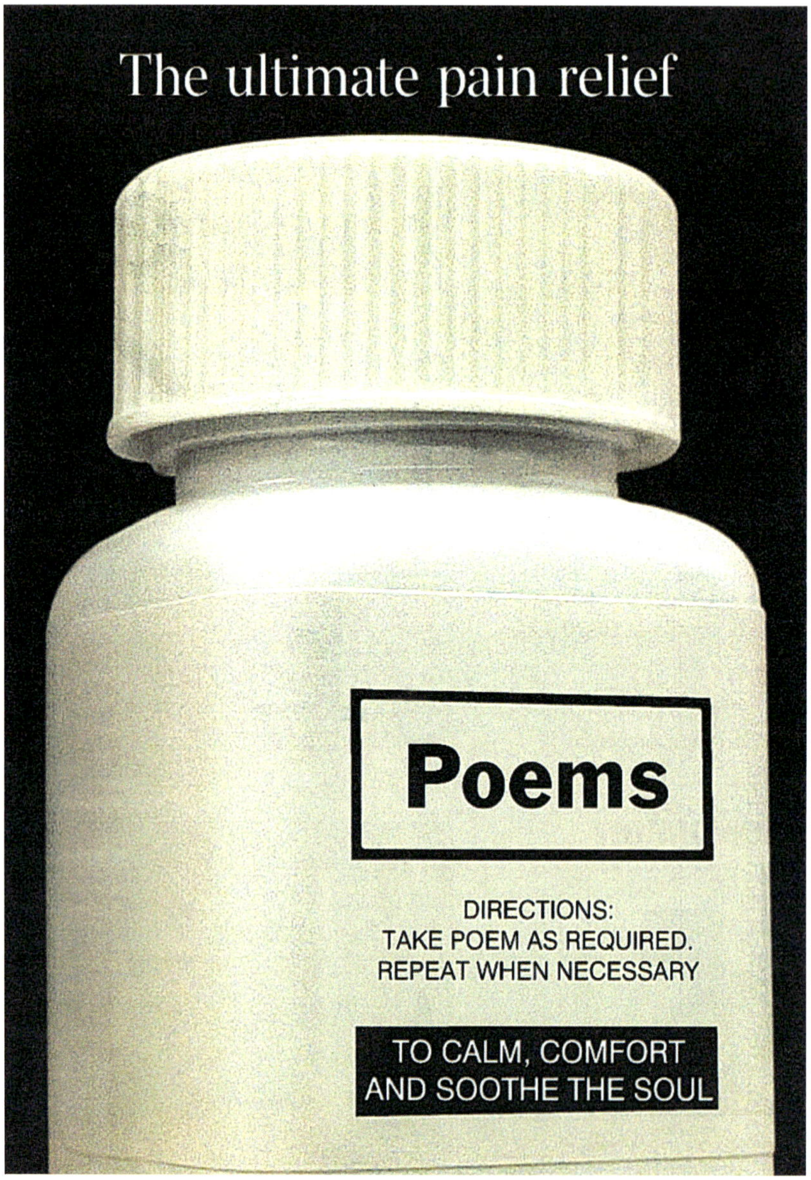

➤ Glossary: Advertisement (p. 264)

1 This photograph was used as the first page of a newspaper section dealing with poetry. It was intended to encourage people to read on. What elements of an advertisement can you identify in the picture?
2 Compare this 'advertisement' with other advertisements you have seen in newspapers and magazines.
3 Evaluate the effectiveness of the photograph.
4 Do you have a poem (or the lyrics of a song) that you find calming or soothing? Bring one to class and explain why it appeals to you.

B **In Flanders Fields** John McCrae

In Flanders fields the poppies blow
Between the crosses, row on row,
That mark our place; and in the sky
The larks, still bravely singing, fly
Scarce heard amid the guns below.

We are the Dead. Short days ago
We lived, felt dawn, saw sunset glow,
Loved and were loved, and now we lie
In Flanders fields.

Take up our quarrel with the foe:
To you from failing hands we throw
The torch; be yours to hold it high.
If ye break faith with us who die
We shall not sleep, though poppies grow
In Flanders fields.

(From: *Punch*, 1915)

C **Grass** Carl Sandburg

Pile the bodies high at Austerlitz and Waterloo.
Shovel them under and let me work –
  I am the grass; I cover all.

And pile them high at Gettysburg
And pile them high at Ypres and Verdun.
Shovel them under and let me work.
Two years, ten years, and passengers ask the conductor:
  What place is this?
  Where are we now?

  I am the grass.
  Let me work.

(From: *Cornhuskers*, 1918)

1 Identify the speakers in the two poems.

2 Interpret the poem 'Flanders Fields', paying special attention to the rhyme scheme, metre and imagery.

3 Read the poem 'Grass' again.
  a Say what Austerlitz, Waterloo, Gettysburg, Ypres and Verdun stand for.
  b Explain who or what the grass, the passengers and the conductor represent.

4 Compare the two poems, saying what attitude towards war they present. Decide which poem is more effective in conveying its message.

5 With regard to the advert on p. 130, say whether you find these two poems soothing or not. Explain your answer.

6 Which of these two poems do you prefer, and why?

7 Find another poem dealing with war or other conflicts. Present it to the class.

➤ Reading Poetry (p. 241), Glossary: Poetry (p. 256)

■ **B:** 1 poppy *Mohnblume* 4 lark *Lerche* 5 scarce *hardly* 11 failing *dying* 12 torch *Fackel*
■ **C:** 1 pile sth. *lay sth. on top of each other* 2 shovel sth. *etwas schaufeln*

3 Theatre: A Battle on a Stage

A A Shakespearian Performance

VIDEO

Watch the excerpt from the film *Shakespeare in Love*, which gives a good idea of what the theatre was like in Shakespeare's time.

➤ Reading/Watching Drama (p. 240)
➤ Viewing Skills (p. 227)

1 List all the problems that productions at the time posed.
2 What techniques does the director use to make *Romeo and Juliet*, which is a long play, fit into a short period of time while keeping the interest of the audience?

B *Henry V:* Prologue William Shakespeare

VIDEO

Now read this extract from the prologue to the history play *Henry V* (ca. 1599). (If you wish to watch how Laurence Olivier introduced the play in his 1944 film, you can watch the segment on the video.)

Chorus: [...] Can this cockpit hold
The vasty fields of France? Or may we cram
Within this wooden O the very casques
That did affright the air at Agincourt? [...]
And let us, ciphers to this great account,
On your imaginary forces work.
Suppose within the girdle of these walls
Are now confin'd two mighty monarchies,
Whose high upreared and abutting fronts
The perilous narrow ocean parts asunder.
Piece out our imperfections with your thoughts.
Into a thousand parts divide one man,
And make imaginary puissance.
Think when we talk of horses that you can see them
Printing their proud hooves i'th' receiving earth,
For 'tis your thoughts that now must deck our kings,
Carry them here and there, jumping o'er times,
Turning th'accomplishment of many years
Into an hour-glass.

(From: *Henry V*, Oxford University Press, Oxford, 2001)

■ 1 cockpit *(here) theatre*
3 casque *helmet*
5 account *(here) story*
7 girdle *(here) circular form*
9 high upreared and abutting fronts *high cliffs facing each other*
10 part sth. asunder *divide sth.*
11 piece sth. out *add to and complete sth.*
13 puissance *army*
16 deck sb. *dress, equip sb.*

1 Using what you have found out about the Shakespearean theatre from the extract from *Shakespeare in Love* (and perhaps the Olivier version of *Henry V*), summarize the demands the Chorus makes of the audience.
2 The Chorus mentions the Battle of Agincourt. What other elements might be used to make an audience believe they are experiencing a battle?
3 To what extent are audiences of today faced with the same conditions?

C Battle of Agincourt William Shakespeare

The following two extracts from *Henry V* concern the historic Battle of Agincourt between the English and French. Before you read the scene, imagine you had to stage a battle scene with a limited number of actors, and few props and special effects. In groups, discuss how it might be done. Act IV, Scene iii is set shortly before the battle commences, while Act IV, Scene vii is set towards the end of the battle.

Act IV, Scene iii

Enter Gloucester, Bedford, Exeter, Erpingham *with all his host;* Salisbury, *and* Westmorland.
Gloucester: Where is the King?
Bedford: The King himself is rode to view their battle.
Westmorland: Of fighting men they have full threescore thousand.
Exeter: There's five to one. Besides, they all are fresh.
Salisbury: God's arm strike with us! 'Tis a fearful odds.
God be wi' you, princes all. I'll to my charge.
If we no more meet till we meet in heaven,
Then joyfully, my noble lord of Bedford,
My dear lord Gloucester and my good lord Exeter,
And my kind kinsman, warriors all, adieu.
Bedford: Farewell, good Salisbury, and good luck go with thee! [...]
Enter the King.
Westmorland: O that we now had here
But one ten thousand of those men in England
That do no work today.
King Henry: What's he that wishes so?
My cousin Westmorland. No, my fair cousin.
If we are mark'd to die, we are enough
To do our country loss. And if to live,
The fewer men, the greater share of honour.
God's will, I pray thee wish not one man more.
By Jove, I am not covetous for gold,
Nor care I who doth feed upon my cost.
It yearns me not if men my garments wear.
Such outward things dwell not in my desires.
But if it be a sin to covet honour,
I am the most offending soul alive. [...]

Act IV, Scene vii

Enter King Henry, Exeter, Gloucester, Warwick [...]. *Enter* Montjoy.
Montjoy: [...] I come to thee for charitable licence,
That we may wander o'er this bloody field
To book our dead, and then to bury them,
To sort our nobles from our common men,
For many of our princes – woe the while –
Lie drown'd and soak'd in mercenary blood,
So do our vulgar drench their peasant limbs
In blood of princes, while the wounded steeds

5 threescore *three times twenty* **8** charge *men under his command* **24** be covetous for sth. *desire sth. strongly* **26** yearn sb. *make sb. sad* **31** Montjoy *French herald* **32** charitable license *kind permission* **37** mercenary *of soldiers who fight for money* **38** vulgar *common people*

40 fetlock *ankle* 41 yerk sth. *kick sth.* 46 if the day be ours *whether we have won the battle* 47 peer *appear* 54 the day of Crispin Crispianus *25th October*

Fret fetlock deep in gore, and with wild rage
Yerk out their armed heels at their dead masters,
Killing them twice. O, give us leave, great king,
To view the field in safety, and dispose
Of their dead bodies!
King Henry: I tell thee truly, herald,
I know not if the day be ours or no,
For yet a-many of your horsemen peer
And gallop o'er the field.
Montjoy: The day is yours.
King Henry: Praised be God, and not our strength, for it.
What is this castle call'd that stands hard by?
Montjoy: They call it Agincourt.
King Henry: Then call we this the field of Agincourt,
Fought on the day of Crispin Crispianus.

(From: *Henry V*, Oxford University Press, Oxford, 2001)

1 a Describe the situation facing the English army in Act IV, Scene iii.
b How do Salisbury, Westmorland and King Henry react to the situation?
2 Rewrite the last lines of King Henry's speech in Scene iii (ll. 21–29) in modern English.
3 What is the outcome of the battle?
4 Compare King Henry's reactions in Scene vii with his reactions in Scene iii.
5 Try and imagine some of the reasons for the English victory.
6 **Project work.** Imagine you belong to a group of actors in Shakespeare's time and are putting on a performance of *Henry V*. At the moment you are working on Act IV, which deals with the Battle of Agincourt.
a In groups, decide which scene you are going to rehearse and who is going to play which part. Then read through your parts and:
– identify the overall emotions in your speeches as well as where emotions change;
– decide how these emotions could be shown via facial and vocal expression, gestures and body language;
– think about how the audience's attention can be held by varying the pace;
– do a reading of the scene in your group; you can always change your notes;
– together, decide on any other effects you want to include.
b Now decide how to stage the battle, keeping in mind the limitations of the theatre. The script is unimportant, and you can make up any lines you think are necessary. Together, discuss how to do it, and then rehearse as often as you have to.
c Now give your own performance of Act IV with the two scenes here and the battle.

VIDEO

D Two Performances of *Henry V*

Watch two versions of Scenes iii and vii; one is a BBC TV version, the other a film version.

1 Comment on the performance of the actors. Is it what you expected?
2 Write a review of one of the versions. Compare it to the other version and say whether you found it more or less effective than the other.
3 Analyse the use of camera work in one of the two versions.

➤ Writing Reports and Reviews (p. 251)
➤ Viewing Skills (p. 227)

4 Music: Offering Hope

A Extracts from the *Resurrection Symphony* Gustav Mahler

CD

You are going to listen to music from Gustav Mahler's *Resurrection Symphony*.

1 Before you listen, read through the following instructions, and look up or ask the meaning of any words you do not understand:
- Listen for instruments you know.
- Be aware of what is going through your mind while you listen.
- Think how the music makes you feel.

Useful words and phrases

wind/brass/string instruments • percussion
The music reminded me of ... • The music took me ... • I could imagine ... •
evoke sth. • pictures • memories • associations
overwhelmed/overcome/awed/(un)inspired/bored • have a lump in your throat / tears in your eyes • nothing special • glad when it was over

Keep these instructions in mind while listening, and – when the music is over – make some notes.

2 What do you think Mahler wanted to convey in the *Resurrection Symphony*?

B An Infinitely Hopeful Message Martin Goldsmith

In his book *The Inextinguishable Symphony* Martin Goldsmith tells the story of his parents, Günther and Rosemarie Goldschmidt, who were members of the orchestra of the *Jüdische Kulturbund* in Berlin from 1938 to 1941. The *Jüdische Kulturbund* was set up by the Nazis to give German Jews, who were excluded from all German institutions of art, music, etc., some form of creative outlet and to show to the world that Jews were still able to pursue artistic activities. This excerpt deals with the performance of Gustav Mahler's *Resurrection Symphony*, which took place on the day the Goldschmidts received their immigration visas for the USA.

By five minutes past three o'clock, the massive orchestra and chorus were in place. Then the two soloists, soprano Henrietta Huth and alto Adelheid Müller, walked out on stage, followed closely by Rudolf Schwarz. He asked all his artists to stand, then turned to face the members of the audience, who rose and applauded a full minute before settling back into whatever resting place they had managed to squeeze into. Schwarz then turned back to face his musicians, swept his eye across the stage, smiled grimly, and gave the down beat to begin.

For the next hour and twenty-five minutes, Gustav Mahler's *Resurrection Symphony* took possession of the theatre, of the musicians, the audience. No one, either on stage or in the hall, was conscious of time passing, just of an immense sound and an equally immense spirit moving among them. Rosemarie, whose practical mind did not usually acknowledge such phenomena, was dimly aware of someone or something in addition to Rudolf Schwarz directing the proceedings.

■ 7 down beat (n) *Auftakt* 12 acknowledge sth. *accept sth. as true*

A concert by the Jüdische Kulturbund.

There were virtually no sounds – coughs or sneezes or rustling with coats, hats – coming from the crowd. More than a thousand people, men and women who had come to know danger and pain and hurt and humiliation on an almost daily basis for more than eight years, heard from a valiant ensemble of artists who had struggled along with them a vibrant musical account of their difficulties and then the infinitely hopeful message that they had not lived and suffered in vain and that from these depths they would rise again.

The final few measures of Mahler's magnificent vision of being borne upward through struggle are a wondrous clangor of open chords sounded by the strings, winds and brass of the orchestra, undergirded by the rumbling strength of the organ and augmented by crashing percussion and pealing bells. In those last lingering moments Günther and Rosemarie both experienced an awe they had previously known only in the presence of an incandescent sunset, a tumultuous thunderstorm or some similarly splendid composition of nature.

And then Rudolf Schwarz, his face radiant and dripping with sweat, his arms aloft urging the ultimate effort from his artists, gave the final beat and the symphony was over, the resurrection complete. For a moment there was only charged silence. Many members of the audience could only sit stunned and open-mouthed at what they had just experienced. And then, almost as one, the people rose and began to applaud and cheer and stamp their feet. Many of them wept. On stage, the chorus clapped their hands, the string players rapped their stands with their bows, and Rudolf Schwarz responded to the cheers of the crowd holding the score of Mahler's symphony high above his head where it, too, could receive its share of adulation. Pandemonium reigned in the theatre for a full fifteen minutes. Of all the emotional and spiritual peaks achieved by the Kulturbund since 1933, this one afternoon, given the external circumstances, the available resources, and the magnitude of the endeavor, may well have been its loftiest.

(From: *The Inextinguishable Symphony*, John Wiley & Sons, Hoboken/NJ, 2000)

■ **17** humiliation *Erniedrigung* **19** valiant *brave, courageous* **20** vibrant ['vaɪbrənt] *loud and powerful* **26** clangor *loud ringing* **27** undergird sth. *underline sth.* **28** augment sth. *add to sth.* **28** percussion *drums, cymbals, etc.* **29** linger ['lɪŋgə] *nachklingen* **30** incandescent *creating strong emotions* **31** tumultuous ['tjuː'mʌltʃuəs ☆ tuː-] *extremely loud* **32** radiant *strahlend* **33** aloft *high in the air* **35** charged *spannungsgeladen* **35** stunned *benommen* **38** rap sth. *tap sth.* **41** adulation *admiration* **41** pandemonium *situation in which there is a lot of noise, activity and confusion* **44** magnitude *greatness* **44** endeavor (BE: endeavour) *undertaking* **44** lofty *impressive, great, high*

1 a Explain what is so special about this performance for Rosemarie and Günther in particular and the musicians and the audience in general.

b Examine the role and effect of music as displayed in the excerpt.

2 Compare the reactions described in the text with your own experience of the music.

3 **Creative writing.** Imagine that ten years later the Goldschmidts, who emigrated to the USA, discover that Rudolf Schwarz survived the war and is living in London. They decide to write him a letter, going over the experiences at the concert again, and telling him about their own lives. Write this letter.

4 Do you have any piece of music which has a special effect on you, perhaps because you associate it with a certain situation, experience or feeling? Think about why the music could have this effect: Is it because of the instruments, the melodies or the motifs? Either present a recording to the class or write about it.

5 Architecture: Rising from the Ashes

Before you look at the pictures below, think of towns, buildings or monuments which were destroyed through war or other conflicts. Discuss whether they should be:

a) rebuilt as a symbol of reconciliation and forgiveness;
b) left as rubble to remind people of past horrors; or
c) replaced with something completely different.

Note down the pros and cons.

A Coventry: Destruction and Reconciliation

The importance of the city of Coventry as an industrial centre made it a target during the Second World War. On the night of 14th November, 1940, the Germans launched the worst bombing raid of the war up to that point. Much of the medieval city, including its cathedral, was destroyed. The day after the raid, it was decided to build a new cathedral close to the ruins of the old. The new cathedral was completed in 1962. Since then it has been a centre of forgiveness and reconciliation. On the video you can get information about the bombing and renewal of Coventry. VIDEO

The ruins of Coventry Cathedral (above) and the new and old cathedrals (right).

1 **a** Say why you think the architect chose to integrate the ruins of the old cathedral into the new building.
b Outline the effect the combination of old and new might have on visitors.

2 Below are two statues in Coventry Cathedral: 'Reconciliation' (left) by Josefina Vasconcellos and 'St Michael Subduing the Devil' (right) by Sir Jacob Epstein. Choose one of them and explain what you think it symbolizes.

B Dresden: Obliteration and Rebirth

In 1945 the city of Dresden was almost wiped out by allied bombing. One of the famous landmarks destroyed was the *Frauenkirche*. Following the reunification of Germany it was decided to rebuild the church using as much of the old material as possible.

1 a Role play. In groups, devise and act out a role-play in which two English tourists from Coventry are visiting the rebuilt *Frauenkirche* in Dresden. One thinks that rebuilding it just as it was is a good idea, while the other thinks a new, modern church should have replaced it.
Choose two people from your group to perform the role play.
b Having listened to the role plays, say what your opinion is.

The eight-metre-high gilded orb and cross (right) was made in London by goldsmiths Grant Macdonald, where one of the craftsmen, Alan Smith, is the son of a British pilot who was involved in the 1945 Dresden raid. It will replace the one destroyed in the bombing of Dresden, as a symbol of suffering, reconciliation and rebirth.

The Frauenkirche in 1953 (below) and 2004 (left).

2 **Project work.** In groups, research the partnership between Coventry and Dresden and present your findings to the class.

➤ Doing Research (p. 230)

3 Write a text on some other famous piece of architecture, sculpture or religious art you know of, describing its symbolism, the architect's or artist's intention (if possible) and the feelings it creates in the observer. Use pictures to illustrate your text.

➤ The Stages of Writing (p. 244)

GETTING ALONG IN ENGLISH

Talking about the Arts

Finding out what a certain place has to offer in the way of culture, buying a book or making intelligent comments at an art show can be worrying – especially in a foreign language. If you want to be able to cope with situations like these, work through this page and you should feel more confident.

CD

1 **a** Sandra and Michael have been touring the Midlands in an old Morris. However, their car breaks down and is towed to nearby Coventry, where they are told that they will have to wait a day for a spare part. They decide to go to the Tourist Information to find out how they could spend the day in the city.
While listening, take notes on the following:
- What is Michael interested in?
- Does Sandra share his interests?
- What do you learn about Coventry?
- What does Ansley have to offer in the way of 'art'?
- What expressions are used for the following:
  (i) you don't have to pay to get in;
  (ii) a brochure that tells you what is going on;
  (iii) there are no more tickets.

b Using as many expressions from the dialogue as possible, write a similar dialogue between someone visiting your town for a short period, and a person from the tourist information office.

CD

2 **a** Michael and Sandra decided to go to a film instead of to the pub. Before you listen to the dialogue, think about what things you might say about a film if a) you liked it; b) you disliked it. What features might you praise or criticize? Now listen to their conversation as they leave the cinema.
b Write down phrases which Michael and Sandra use to show their reactions to the film and the characters.
c Using the information from the recording and adding anything you feel necessary, write a similar dialogue and act it out in front of the class.

CD

3 Anita is working for a local newspaper, the *Kentish Express*, in Canterbury as part of a work experience programme. She has been assigned the task of reporting on the opening of an exhibition of local art. She has made it clear to her boss that she knows very little about art, but he has told her that, as it is a Friday night, no one else is available.
a Take notes of the comments she makes.
b From your notes, find out how Anita expresses that:
- she finds the watercolour very trivial;
- she does not really know what John is trying to express in his paintings;
- she just sees a mess of paint;

c Imagine you are going to the opening of a friend's exhibition of paintings and do not really know much about painting. What expressions might you use to hide your lack of knowledge?

WATCH YOUR LANGUAGE

Look at this paragraph from a book review a student has handed in. The teacher has marked the mistakes.

> The novel 'The Quiet American' is set in Vietnam in the 1950s, when the French were fighting the Vietminh. Fowler is a British reporter. He and the young Phuong are a couple which could not get married, as Fowler was already married. One day a young American with the name of Pyle turned up. Fowler suspected that he was involved with a shadowy organization which represented a third way, e.g. neither pro-Communist nor pro-French but supposedly pro-Democratic. This organization began to lay bombs in Saigon. Things reached a crisis point when Pyle took Phuong away from Fowler. This one, already angered by Pyle's involvement with terrorism, decided to take action, and betrayed Pyle to the Vietminh.

⚠ **Trouble spot**
review ≠ criticism
critic ≠ *Kritik*

Tenses

1 There is a difference between narrating a story and reviewing a book, film or play: it is important to use the correct sequence of tenses.

a Copy the chart below into your exercise book and fill in the correct tenses.

	Referring to what happens	Referring to what happened in the past	Referring to what will happen in the future
Telling a story	Simple Past or Past Progressive		
Writing a review, book report, etc.	Simple Present or Present Progressive		

b Rewrite the student's review and correct the mistakes.

2 a The following sentences tell the true story of Günther and Rosemarie (the main characters of *The Inextinguishable Symphony* by Martin Goldsmith). Put the verbs in brackets into the correct tense:

1. During rehearsals in Frankfurt Günther Goldschmidt (meet) the dazzling nineteen-year-old violist Rosemarie Gumpert – a woman who (change) the course of his life.
2. He (flee) to Sweden, but (return) six months later to the woman he (not / can) forget – and to the perilous country where hatred and brutality (begin) to flourish.
3. In the United States the two (make) a new life for themselves that, however, (remain) overshadowed by the fate of their families.

b Now imagine you are writing a review of *The Inextinguishable Symphony*, in which you wish to use the sentences above. How would you write them?

3 Choose a book, film or play and write a short summary of the contents for a review.

Has this page pointed out any areas of difficulty for you that you had not yet noticed? If so, they should be added to your self-assessment 'plan of action' (cf. Workbook).

THE UK – REDEFINING A NATION?

1 What do you associate with Britain? In small groups, collect words and phrases – the collage on these two pages will help you get started. Collect the class's results on the board in a structured way.

2 The following are reactions of people from the UK who were asked to define what Britain and Britishness mean to them.

a Read through the quotes and collect words you find useful for talking about Britishness.

A 'We're a people of innovation, on a permanent nostalgia trip.' *Tim Staddon*

B 'If someone asks me where I come from I would tell them the city I live in, I would never say my nation. I don't feel a sense of patriotic pride. I certainly wouldn't fall over myself for the monarchy despite all that is said, but nor do I think they are the worst thing happening this century. Mind you, I do think that at times British fashion rocks and we do a mean fish and chips, and a good pint.' *Mel*

C 'This country is epitomised by surprise – nothing is as you expect it to be. Unlike a police state, there is a tradition of allowing eccentricity and variety in Britain. The language is terribly important. Of course they speak English elsewhere, but it does not have the same reverberations. That, for a writer, is one of the most important aspects.' *UA Fanthorpe, poet*

D 'Britain's not a country, it's like a bundle of countries. If I was from Wales I'd say I was Welsh, I wouldn't say I was British. So 'cause I'm from Scotland I say I'm Scottish.' *A student from Scotland*

UK

E 'Being British is being able to moan about anything and everything, and not truly appreciate anything. The weather, the NHS, the roads, the schools, the crime levels – no one can be satisfied with anything. Oh yeah, and there's the monarchy. Everyone seems up for ousting them, but I think for once we ought to be proud and more than content with our royal family. They are British – a unified family with moral values.'

Shahid Hussain

F 'Three lions on the shirt!' *Eddie*

G 'Isn't every country a melting pot of sorts? France is just as "melted" as us, but I bet we have a strong idea of what it means to be French. Therefore, maybe we should ask those outside of Britain what it is to be British.' *RB*

(A, B, E, F, G from: 'What Makes You British?', the website of *BBC News* • 21.11.2002;
C from: 'Who Do We Think We Are?', *The Guardian*, 20 January, 1999;
D from: James Oliver, 'Young People on Being British and European: Some Scottish Identities', the website of *The University of Sheffield*)

b In a first reaction, say which of the statements surprised or confused you or which appealed to you most. Try to explain why.

3 After working through these two pages, try to draw together a general idea of what it is to be British. Comment on this picture of Britishness.

4 Imagine you had to portray Germany abroad, e.g. for a penfriend. Make a collage of six or seven pictures you find typical or describe pictures you would want to include.

1 What It Means to Be British

A Chicken Tikka Massala Robin Cook

⚠ **Trouble spot**
give/make/deliver a speech
Not: ~~hold a speech~~

The following is an extract from a speech given by Robin Cook on 19 April, 2001. At the time he was the British Foreign Secretary.

Robin Cook (born 1946), British Foreign Secretary (1997–2001).

The first element in the debate about the future of Britishness is the changing ethnic composition of the British people themselves. The British are not a race, but a gathering of countless different races and communities, the vast majority of which were not indigenous to these islands.

In the pre-industrial era, when transport and communications were often easier by sea than by land, Britain was unusually open to external influence; first through foreign invasion, then, after Britain achieved naval supremacy, through commerce and imperial expansion. It is not their purity that makes the British unique, but the sheer pluralism of their ancestry.

London was first established as the capital of a Celtic Britain by Romans from Italy. They were in turn driven out by Saxons and Angles from Germany. The great cathedrals of this land were built mostly by Norman Bishops, but the religion practised in them was secured by the succession of a Dutch Prince. Outside our Parliament, Richard the Lionheart proudly sits astride his steed. A symbol of British courage and defiance. Yet he spoke French much of his life and depended on the Jewish community of England to put up the ransom that freed him from prison.

The idea that Britain was a 'pure' Anglo-Saxon society before the arrival of communities from the Caribbean, Asia and Africa is fantasy. But if this view of British identity is false to our past, it is false to our future too. The global era has produced population movements of a breadth and richness without parallel in history.

Today's London is a perfect hub of the globe. It is home to over 30 ethnic communities of at least 10,000 residents each. In this city tonight, over 300 languages will be spoken by families over their evening meal at home.

This pluralism is not a burden we must reluctantly accept. It is an immense asset that contributes to the cultural and economic vitality of our nation.

Legitimate immigration is the necessary and unavoidable result of economic success, which generates a demand for labour faster than can be met by the birth-rate of a modern developed country. Every country needs firm but fair immigration laws. There is no more evil business than trafficking in human beings and nothing corrodes social cohesion worse than a furtive underground of illegal migrants beyond legal protection against exploitation. But we must also create an open and inclusive society that welcomes incomers for their contribution to our growth and prosperity. Our measures to attract specialists in information technology is a good example.

Our cultural diversity is one of the reasons why Britain continues to be the preferred location for multinational companies setting up in Europe. The national airline of a major European country has recently relocated its booking operation to London precisely because of the linguistic variety of the staff whom it can recruit here.

■ Foreign Secretary *Außenminister/in*
4 indigenous to sth. (fml) *belonging to sth. (esp. a particular place)* **7** naval *connected with the navy*
8 imperial *referring to the Empire* **14** steed *horse*
16 ransom *Lösegeld*
22 hub *centre, most important place* **26** asset *thing of value* **30** traffic in sth. *buy and sell sth. illegally* **31** corrode sth. *destroy sth. slowly*
31 cohesion *Zusammenhalt* **52** implication *possible effect*

And it isn't just our economy that has been enriched by the arrival of new communities. Our lifestyles and cultural horizons have also been broadened in the process. This point is perhaps more readily understood by young Britons, who are more open to new influences and more likely to have been educated in a multi-ethnic environment. But it reaches into every aspect of our national life.

Chicken Tikka Massala is now a true British national dish, not only because it is the most popular, but because it is a perfect illustration of the way Britain absorbs and adapts external influences. Chicken Tikka is an Indian dish. The Massala sauce was added to satisfy the desire of British people to have their meat served in gravy.

Coming to terms with multiculturalism as a positive force for our economy and society will have significant implications for our understanding of Britishness.

(From: 'Robin Cook's Chicken Tikka Massala Speech', *The Guardian*, 19 April, 2001)

1 Cook's speech deals with different aspects of British society. Divide the text into sections and find a heading for each section.

2 Summarize Cook's definition of the British as 'a race'.

3 Analyse how British lifestyle has been affected by multi-ethnicity.

4 Write an editorial (of about 100–150 words) in which you comment on the speech. First summarize what Cook says, then give your opinion.

5 **Project work.** Using the information in the text and from other sources, make a timeline that illustrates how British 'pluralism' (ll. 9, 25) developed.

➤ Glossary: Editorial (p. 263)

➤ Doing Research (p. 230)

B **Golden Jubilee Speech to Parliament** Queen Elizabeth II

CD

On the occasion of her Golden Jubilee in 2002, Queen Elizabeth II travelled throughout Britain meeting many people and giving many speeches. Perhaps the most important speech she gave was to Parliament on 30th April, 2002. Read task **1** below and make notes while you listen. Then answer tasks **1 a–d**.

1 **a** How does the Queen describe the past 50 years of her reign?
b How does she define the British people?
c What aspect of community life is emphasized in the speech?
d How does the Queen end her speech?
In groups of three, compare your answers and add anything you missed.

2 Decide which member of your group will deal with which of the following topics: 'Changing Times', 'National Identity' and 'The Tradition of Service'. Listen to the speech again and collect as much information as possible on your particular topic. Tell the others in your group what you have noted down.

3 Copy and then fill in the following chart comparing what Robin Cook and Queen Elizabeth say on each of the three topics:

	Robin Cook	Queen Elizabeth II
History		
Identity		
Change		

⚠ **Trouble spot**
much information
Not: ~~many informations~~
a piece of information
Not: ~~an information~~

2 The Great Immigrant Experiment

Zadie Smith

The following text is an excerpt from Zadie Smith's (cf. p. 196) best-selling novel *White Teeth*, which tells the stories of three families from three different cultures living in London. The narrator describes the effect immigration and multiculturalism can have on people's identities. The diagrams on the left show the important characters mentioned in the text and their individual backgrounds.

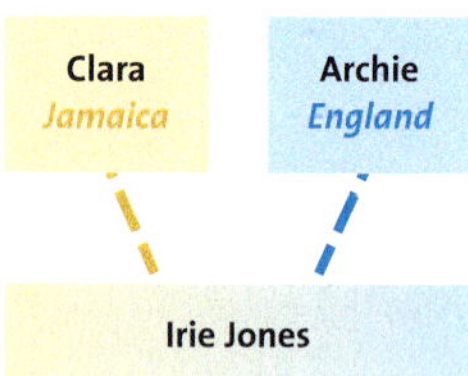

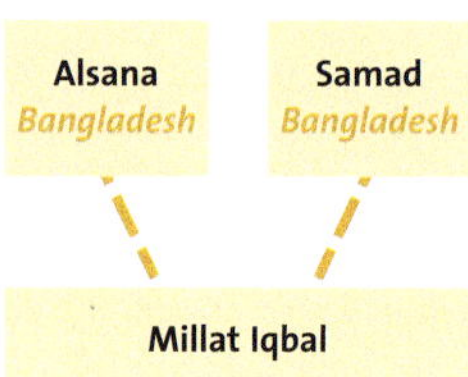

This has been the century of strangers, brown, yellow and white. This has been the century of the great immigrant experiment. It is only this late in the day that you can walk into a playground and find Isaac Leung by the fish pond, Danny Rahman in the football cage, Quang O'Rourke bouncing a basketball, and Irie Jones humming a tune. Children with first and last names on a direct collision course. Names that secrete within them mass exodus, cramped boats and planes, cold arrivals, medical checks. It is only this late in the day, and possibly only in Willesden, that you can find best friends Sita and Sharon, constantly mistaken for each other because Sita is white (her mother liked the name) and Sharon is Pakistani (her mother thought it best – less trouble). Yet, despite all the mixing up, despite the fact that we have finally slipped into each other's lives with reasonable comfort (like a man returning to his lover's bed after a midnight walk), despite all this, it is still hard to admit that there is no one more English than the Indian, no one more Indian than the English. There are still young white men who are *angry* about that; who will roll out at closing time into the poorly lit streets with a kitchen knife wrapped in a tight fist.

But it makes an immigrant laugh to hear the fears of the nationalist, scared of infection, penetration, miscegenation, when this is small fry, *peanuts*, compared to what the immigrant fears – dissolution, *disappearance*. Even the unflappable Alsana Iqbal would regularly wake up in a puddle of her own sweat after a night visited by visions of Millat (genetically *BB*; where *B* stands for Bengali-ness) marrying someone called Sarah (aa where 'a' stands for Aryan), resulting in a child called Michael (*B*a), who in turn marries somebody called Lucy (aa) leaving Alsana with a legacy of unrecognisable great-grandchildren (Aaaaaaa!), their Bengali-ness thoroughly diluted, genotype hidden by phenotype. It is both the most irrational and natural feeling in the world. [...]

[In] the Iqbal house the lines of battle were clearly drawn. When Millat brought an Emily or a Lucy back home, Alsana quietly wept in the kitchen, Samad went into the garden to attack the coriander. The next morning was a waiting game, a furious biting of tongues until the Emily or Lucy left the house and the war of words could begin. But with Irie and Clara the issue was mostly unspoken, for Clara knew she was not in a position to preach. Still, she made no attempt to disguise her disappointment or the aching sadness. From Irie's bedroom shrine of green-eyed Hollywood idols to the gaggle of white friends who regularly trooped in and out of her bedroom, Clara saw an ocean of pink skins surrounding her daughter and she feared the tide that would take her away.

It was partly for this reason that Irie didn't mention the Chalfens to her parents. It wasn't that she intended to *mate* with the Chalfens ... but the instinct was the same. She had a nebulous fifteen-year-old's passion for them, overwhelming, yet with no real direction or object. She just wanted to, well, kind of, *merge* with them. She wanted their Englishness. Their Chalfishness. The *purity* of it. It didn't occur to her that the Chalfens were, after a fashion, immigrants too (third generation, by way of Germany and Poland, née Chalfenovsky), or that they might be as needy of her as she was of them. To Irie, the Chalfens were more English than the English. When Irie stepped over the threshold of the Chalfen house, she felt an illicit thrill, like a Jew munching a sausage or a Hindu grabbing a Big Mac. She was crossing borders, sneaking into England; it felt like some terribly mutinous act, wearing somebody else's uniform or somebody else's skin.

She just said that she had netball on Tuesday evenings and left it at that.

(From: *White Teeth*, Hamish Hamilton, London, 2000)

1 Explain what the names in ll. 3–10 illustrate.

2 Compare the fears of some 'young white men' (l. 14) and those of immigrants.

3 **a** Describe Alsana's worries and concerns. How are they increased by Millat's behaviour?

b Explain the consequences Clara's anxiety has for Irie.

4 Find the terms in the text which express the following:
- contradicting each other (ll. 1–16);
- hide (ll. 1–16);
- not worth mentioning (ll. 17–26);
- not speaking although one really wants to (ll. 27–36);
- mix or unite with sb. (ll. 37–49);
- in a way (ll. 37–49).

5 Describe the narrative technique used in this extract and the effect it has.

➤ Glossary: Narrator and Point of View (p. 258)

6 **Role play.** In groups, choose one of the following situations, prepare a role play and act out the scene in front of the class:

a Millat's new English girlfriend Victoria has just left Millat's house after spending the night in Millat's room. Samad and Alsana are shocked, and try to convince Millat that he should choose a girlfriend from his own ethnic group.

b Clara confronts Irie and wants to know why she has been lying about where she goes on Tuesday evenings. Irie tries to explain why she likes going to the Chalfens's.

c Clara decides to visit Mrs Chalfen. Each mother explains her position concerning Irie's and Marcus's friendship.

6 secrete sth. *hide sth.* **15** closing time *time when the pubs close* **18** miscegenation [ˌmɪsɪdʒəˈneɪʃn] (fml) *fact of children being born to parents from different races* **18** small fry *unimportant things* **19** dissolution *process of disappearing slowly* **19** unflappable *not easily excited* **25** dilute sth. *weaken sth.* **25** genotype *information about an organism which is encoded in its genes* **25** phenotype *outward physical manifestation of your genetic make-up* **33** shrine *place where objects of great spiritual value are kept* **34** gaggle *noisy crowd* **36** tide *flood* **38** mate with sb. *have children with sb.* **39** nebulous *unclear* **45** threshold *Schwelle* **46** illicit *forbidden* **48** mutinous act [mjuː-] *act of disobedience*

3 On Tour in the UK

Project work. Imagine the following situation:
Together with two friends you are planning a week's trip to a certain region of the UK. You need another person to make up a travel group of four.
In a team of three, put together a display notice in A4 format to attract a fourth member for your travel group. Give precise details of your travel plans, so that the fourth person knows exactly what is involved.

Follow these steps to complete the project:

1 Choose an area to visit, for instance Cornwall, Wales, the Highlands, Northern Ireland, the Lake District, the Yorkshire Moors, some Scottish islands, the Peak District, etc.

➤ Doing Research on the Internet (p. 231)

2 Do research on the Internet to gain a general impression of your chosen area: what sort of countryside are you going to find, what are the areas and points of interest there, what sort of activities do they offer? The following sites may help to start off with: www.visitbritain.com and www.uktheguide.com.

3 From the variety of opportunities open to you as a visitor, focus on a small number which you want to follow up.

4 Work out a detailed tour plan to include:
- travel to and from the region you have chosen;
- the route you intend taking while there, the mode of transport and its prices;
- accommodation available together with prices;
- activities you are planning.

Make sure you use definite dates and times and take note of exact costs from the webpages.

➤ The Stages of Writing (p. 244)
➤ Giving a Talk or Presentation (p. 254)

5 Put together your itinerary in an attractive way with illustrations to appeal to the fourth person.

6 Make a classroom display of your finished notices. When you present them to the others, you might add your impressions of the places you have visited virtually. Try to convince your listeners to join you.

7 When you have finished, each student should choose which trip he or she would like to join.

GETTING ALONG IN ENGLISH

Finding a Place to Stay

1 Look through these different types of accommodation from around the UK. What sort of places are they and what differences would you expect in the facilities and services they offer?

Antrim Bay (N.Ireland) – YHA
157 Antrim Bay Road, Ballintoy, Ballycastle, County Antrim, BT54 6HN, N.Ireland
Tel. 44-28-65721715

Beds	**Age 05–17:**	**£9**
	Age 18+:	**£11.50**

The ideal base to explore Scotland's unique North East
SCOTLAND – UNIVERSITY OF ABERDEEN
STUDENT SELF-CATERING ACCOMMODATION
minimum 2 days at £16.00 per night
B&B £22.00 no minimum stay
e-mail m.duncan@admin.abdn.ac.uk
Telephone 0044 1224 272664

RAMSEY HOTEL
Single from £39, double from £47, triple from £64. One minute walk from Earls Court Tube Station. Open 24 hrs, most rooms with private showers. All rooms colour TV, sky movies & sports channels and telephone.
30 Hogarth St, Earls Court, London SW5 OPU
Tel. 0171 370 1425
e-mail ramsey@rasool.demon.co.uk

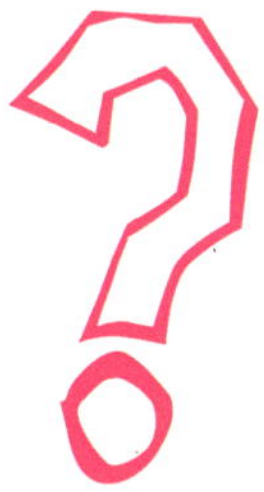

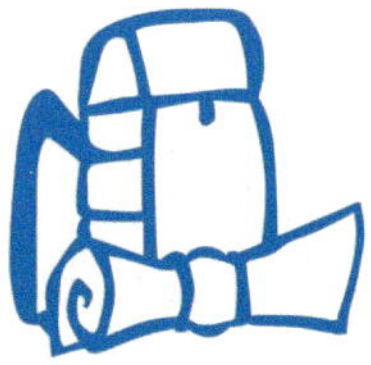

2 Start to make a list of words and phrases that will be useful when talking about accommodation: 'self-catering', 'minimum stay', etc. Check their meaning if necessary.

3 Marc and his friends from Halle want to tour the UK. Listen to Marc's phone call to Antrim Bay Youth Hostel to reserve accommodation.

CD

a Before he phoned, Marc made a list of points he wanted to enquire about. Listen again and draw up the list he might have had in front of him.

b Add more useful words and phrases to your collection.

4 Here is the e-mail sent in reply to Marc's enquiry about accommodation in Aberdeen. Use the information in the reply to reconstruct the original e-mail Marc sent.

Dear Marc,
Thanks for your request for accommodation at the University. We would be happy to offer you two rooms on campus for three nights from Wednesday, August 17th. Regret we do not have doubles available for the dates requested. Breakfast is full English breakfast taken in the refectory, and yes, you do have access to the University's Sports Hall and Swimming Pool.
There is a frequent bus service into town and we are served by late-night buses, too. We do not have a curfew.
If you wish to confirm the booking, we would need a deposit of one night's accommodation (£44). A credit card number would also secure your reservation.
Yours sincerely
Maggie Duncan, Accommodation Centre

4 The Parts of the Whole

■ devolution *Regionalisierung, Dezentralisierung*
[1] act *law passed by a parliament* [3] Secretary of State *minister in the government (here: responsible for Wales)*
[10] tax-varying (adj) *able to make changes to the system of taxation*

A Devolution in the UK

In recent years, Scotland, Wales and Northern Ireland were given greater autonomy within the United Kingdom. The following information about the process of devolution in Wales gives an idea of what this change involves.

The Government of Wales Act 1998 provides for the establishment of the National Assembly of Wales, to be located in Cardiff. The Assembly takes over virtually all the Secretary of State's functions: Welsh language, water, arts and heritage, industry, education and training, economic development, social services, agriculture and fisheries, environment, housing, health, highways, local government, town and country planning, and tourism. The UK Government retains responsibility for non-devolved areas of overall economic policy, defence and the armed forces, foreign policy (including EU matters), the justice system and prisons, police and fire services, broadcasting and sport. The Assembly does not have tax-varying powers.

(From: The website of the *Foreign and Commonwealth Office, London* • 6.2000)

1 Make a list of words and phrases that will help you to talk about devolution, e.g. 'be located in', 'take over sb.'s functions', etc.

2 Work with a partner. Partner B: Go to p. 153.
Partner A: Copy out the following table.

Partner A

■ voter turnout *Wahlbeteiligung* • seat *(here) place, esp. a city, where a government is located*

Country:	Wales	Northern Ireland	Scotland
Population:	2.94 million	1.7 million	
Year of referendum:	1997	1998	
Voter turnout:	50%	81%	
Name of parliament:		Northern Ireland Assembly	
Seat:		Belfast	
Powers:		legislative & executive powers in areas like agriculture, arts,education, economic policy	

a Complete the table for Wales and compare the results with your partner.
b With the help of your list of words from task 1 and the information in the table, tell your partner what you know about devolution in Northern Ireland. Then listen to what your partner tells you about Scotland and complete your table.

3 Study the completed table and compare each country's status. Explain the differences.

➤ Doing Research (p. 230)

4 Devolution or de-centralization is new to Britain, but not to Germany. Do research on the system of regional and central government in Germany and the UK. Then compare the two systems.

Useful words and phrases

two levels of government • elect sb. (to sth.) • the *Länder* • be represented in sth. • the *Landtag* • control matters like ... • send representatives to the *Bundesrat* • the central government in ... • the German *Bundestag* • two chambers of Parliament • involved in the legislative process • federal system

1

2

3

4

B A New Flag for a Changing Country?

Many people in the UK feel a new flag should be introduced that reflects the changing times. Here are some suggestions for designs which readers sent to the *Guardian* newspaper. Which of them appeals to you most?

1 Describe the Union Jack (cf. flag on p. 150) and the flags above and say
  a what the Union Jack symbolizes;
  b what the flags above might symbolize.

Useful words and phrases

straight/diagonal/wavy • stripe • rectangle • rectangular • field of ... (a colour) swirl (of colours) • pattern consisting of ... • multi-coloured • miniature

2 Now read extracts from what the designers said about their sketches. Match the flags to the explanations. To what extent do they change your opinion of the flags?

A This design represents more cultures, more colours. The union has spun out of control and colonialism is an embarrassing and painful memory that needs throttling.
B The brown and black areas represent West Indian, Indian and Pakistani British citizens, while the darker purple is taken from the West Indian cricketing flag. The blank blue ensign signifies Britain's long colonial history; the pink stripe is a mischievous historical reference to the pink bits on the map. The light green, red and yellow stripes are a reminder of Britain's history in Africa, Asia and other parts of the world, while the darker green and orange stripes are specific references to Ireland and India.
C The lion is a strong symbol of British unity, especially for sporting teams. The four stars represent the home nations: Wales (red), Scotland (blue), Northern Ireland (green) and England (white). The background uses the colours of the Union Jack in a pattern of waves representing the UK's close links with the sea.
D The negative connotations of the Union Jack have been well documented. Better to adopt the colours as used by dozens of countries throughout the world, from Lithuania to Bolivia, Mali, Guyana and so many more. The significance of the colours may vary slightly, but I believe the common interpretation is: red = the blood of the people (and the struggle towards independence); gold = the sun (the giver of life); green = the earth (the abundance of nature). The flag will recognise and acknowledge the multicultural society which we live in, placing the UK firmly within global society. So much more relevant to UK2000.
(From: 'Redesign the Union Jack', the website of *The Guardian*)

■ [3] throttle sth. *(here) put an end to sth.* [6] ensign ['ensən] *ship's flag; (here) single-coloured flag with a small Union Jack in the upper left* [7] mischievous ['mɪstʃɪvəs] *frech* [7] pink bits *reference to old maps of the Empire on which British colonies were coloured pink or red (cf. p. 159)*

1 uniform *einheitlich*
2 bunch (infml) *group*
6 prosperous *wealthy*
8 intermarriage *marriage between two ethnic groups*
15 prospects *Aussichten*
18 estate *housing area, esp. one for people with low incomes*
22 ward *(Wahl-) Bezirk*
26 no riots *reference to the race riots in various English cities in 2001*
29 Treasury *Finanzministerium*
30 concede sth. *etwas einräumen*
31, 37 gap, gulf *difference between two situations, amounts, groups of people, etc.*
38 composite measure *measure combining different criteria*
39 density *Dichte*

C Down in the North

Can the United Kingdom stay 'united'? In the following extract from an article the writer looks at the relationship between race, regions and riches in Britain. Before you read it, discuss the following statements:

1 Ethnic minorities are basically all in the same situation in Britain.
2 Indians and Pakistanis in Britain are more integrated than blacks.
3 In racially mixed areas, unemployment rates for ethnic minorities will always be higher than for whites.
4 In time, economic inequalities between a nation's regions decline.

British society is not uniformly segregated, any more than immigrants are a uniform bunch. West Indians came to Britain in the 1950s and 1960s, mostly to work in public services such as the health service and the buses. Pakistanis and Bangladeshis were imported as low-skilled workers for the textile industry. East African Asians were thrown out of Uganda and Kenya because they were so prosperous, and many re-created their prosperity in Britain. These different communities all behave differently.

If intermarriage is the highest expression of integration, some immigrants are highly integrated. You can see it on the streets of south London, where the babies are many shades of brown. Among West Indian-origin men born in Britain, half marry a white woman, and 30% of West Indian-origin women born in Britain marry a white man. Among Indians and East African-origin Asians, 19% of British-born men and 10% of British-born women marry white partners. Hardly any Pakistanis and Bangladeshis do.

The economic prospects for the Pakistanis and Bangladeshis are different to those of other groups, too. They are less qualified, and less employed, than any other ethnic group. In fact, the people they have most in common with are the people from whom they are so sharply divided – the poor whites on the estates next door.

In Glodwick in Oldham, a mainly Asian area, unemployment is 40%. In Manningham in Bradford, which also has a high Asian population, it is 38%. But there's nothing particularly Asian about this. Poor white wards have levels nearly as high. And, further south, in Leicester, the British city with the highest proportion of Asian-origin people, the ward with the highest unemployment rate (12.3%) is 97% white, while the ward with the highest Asian population (67%) has 6.7% unemployed. There were no riots in Leicester.

If poverty is the breeding ground for racial tension, then the signs are bad for northern England. A recent Treasury report conceded that the wealth gap between the rich south-east and the poor north was larger than the regional divide in any other European country. [...]

The prosperity gulf seems to be getting wider. Robert Huggins, who runs an economic consultancy in Cardiff, says that on a composite measure of wealth creation, incomes, employment, and business density, the gap between Britain's three richest regions – London, the south-east and East Anglia – and the three poorest – the north-east, Wales, Yorkshire and Humberside – has grown by 30% since 1997. [...]

Lots of poor people live in social housing. Social housing is in short supply in high-growth areas. For people who rely on social housing, moving from a depressed area to a prosperous one is hard.

Nor does the private housing market make it easy. Britain's economy is highly centralised on London and the south-east. High house prices in those areas make it virtually impossible for poor people from other regions to move there, even if they own their own property. The price of a house in some areas of Bradford won't buy you a garage in the better bits of London.

(From: 'Down and Out Up North', *The Economist*, 15 December, 2001)

1 State what the text says about:
  a the divisions in British society;
  b the economic situation of the different groups;
  c the regional distribution of prosperity and poverty.

2 Explain the meaning of the sentence 'In fact, the people they have most in common with are the people from whom they are so sharply divided' (ll. 17–18).

3 Has the article changed your position on the statements you discussed before reading the text? Explain.

4 Write a comment of 200–300 words on the role of one of the following in present-day European society: 'immigration', 'intermarriage', 'unemployment'. Go beyond the article and draw on your own knowledge and experience.

➤ Writing a Comment (p. 249)

Partner B

A Devolution in the UK

2 Copy out the following table.

Country:	Wales	Scotland	Northern Ireland
Population:	2.94 million	5.1 million	
Year of referendum:	1997	1997	
Voter turnout:	50%	60%	
Name of parliament:		The Scottish Parliament	
Location:		Edinburgh	
Powers:		Wide range of powers in areas like health, education, social services, environment, law-making, economic development, income tax.	

a Complete the table for Wales and compare the results with your partner.

b Listen to what your partner tells you about Northern Ireland and complete your table. Then, with the help of your list of words from task **1** and the information in the table, tell your partner what you know about devolution in Scotland.

Now go back to p. 150 and task **3**.

5 This England

A This Sceptred Isle William Shakespeare

The following passage is taken from Shakespeare's play *Richard II* (ca. 1595). On his deathbed John of Gaunt, Duke of Lancaster and uncle to King Richard II, praises England.

■ sceptred *(here) royal*
2 Mars *Roman god of war*
3 demi-paradise *like paradise* 8 office *function*
9 moat *Wassergraben*
11 plot *piece of land*
11 realm [relm] *(fml) country*

This royal throne of kings, this sceptred isle,
This earth of majesty, this seat of Mars,
This other Eden, demi-paradise,
This fortress built by Nature for herself
Against infection and the hand of war,
This happy breed of men, this little world,
This precious stone set in the silver sea
Which serves it in the office of a wall,
Or as a moat defensive to a house
Against the envy of less happier lands,
This blessed plot, this earth, this realm, this England, [...]

(From: *Richard II*, Oxford University Press, Oxford, 1998)

1 What general impression of England does this description create?
2 In the first three lines of this passage England is referred to as a 'royal throne of kings', the 'seat of Mars', and a 'demi-paradise'. Using these mini-quotes as headings, make lists of words and expressions from the passage which fit the headings.
3 Select three metaphors from the passage and explain where they come from, why they are used here and what effect they have.

➤ Glossary: Metaphor (p. 268)

B Chocolate Box Englishness

The artist John Constable (1776–1837) is famous for his paintings of the landscape in southern Suffolk, which is now often referred to as 'Constable Country'. Suffolk attracts many tourists due to Constable's paintings.

'The Hay Wain' by John Constable (1821).

➤ Working with Pictures (p. 223)

1 Look at the picture for a while. How does it make you feel?
2 Imagine you could be in the picture: Where would you like to be? What would you be doing, hearing, seeing, feeling, thinking?
3 Read the following quote:
Twenty miles down the road from Lavenham is Flatford Mill – a classic chocolate box image of Englishness. This rustic tranquil place is where John Constable painted the famous 'Hay Wain'. Flatford Mill gets very busy in summer, so it's best to time your visit carefully.
(From: The website of the *BBC*)

   a What do you think is meant by 'chocolate box image of Englishness'?
   b What might people be looking for when they visit Flatford Mill?
4 Which picture or pictures would you choose to present a typical image of (i) England or Britain, (ii) your region or Germany?

4 boil sth. down to sth. *reduce sth. to sth. more simplistic* **6** dispenser (fml) *person who manages or organizes sth. fairly and in a correct way* **12** soberside (infml) *controlled and rational person* **15** madcappery (infml) *crazy behaviour*

Legoland England.

C Those Wild and Crazy English Julian Barnes

The following is an extract from an interview with the English writer Julian Barnes, who in his novel *England, England* (1999) tried to convey his idea of Englishness. In the following interview about his book, he talks about the English.

Trouble spot
the English = *die Engländer*
an Englishman [ˈɪŋɡlɪʃmən] = *ein Engländer*
an Englishwoman = *eine Engländerin*

Every time I drive down the M4, there is a wonderful moment of confirmation of the book. Beyond Heathrow there's one of those brown Heritage signposts saying 'Turn off here: to Windsor Castle, Legoland and Royal Ascot'. This is one sort of essence of England that the nation is being boiled down to … The way we see ourselves as English people is very different from how we are seen. At a very simple level, we see ourselves as peaceable dispensers of good government, an example to others of the civilised life. People abroad see us as much madder than that, and not just in terms of soccer hooliganism.

The English, and to a lesser extent the British, are considered wild and crazy. If you read Madame De Stael on the English, she writes about a tendency to suicide, a tendency to violence and the madness brought on by eating too much meat. We haven't been, and aren't seen as the sort of sobersides that we seem to ourselves. And maybe that's why Lewis Carroll often seems an eccentric sort of Englishman to the English, whereas to the French, say, he seems typical of what seems to them the sort of madcappery that ends up with Monty Python. We think of Python as parodying something essentially English, which is the norm, and they look at Python as an example of the norm.

(From: 'He's Turned Towards Python', *The Observer*, 30 August, 1998)

1 Describe how, according to Barnes, the English see themselves and how others see the English.

VIDEO

2 It is often said that the English have a special kind of humour and that the comedy team Monty Python is an example of this kind of humour. Visit Monty Python's Argument Clinic. Do not worry if you miss some words while listening for the first time – comedy often depends on the speed of dialogue.
   a Name the therapy rooms the patient enters and say what happens in each.
   b Describe your reaction to the sketch and try to explain it.

3 **Creative writing.** Try to imagine a new clinic. How about a Flirting Clinic, Indifference Clinic, etc.? Team up with a partner and develop a few lines of dialogue to read out.

CONTEXT BOX

The UK at the Beginning of the New Millennium

In 2001 the British television presenter Jeremy Paxman singled out four main forces responsible for shaping Britain today. The four elements he saw were: the end of Empire, the pressures for Britain to become more a part of Europe, the uncontrollability of international business, and divisions within the United Kingdom.

The British Empire in the 19th century spanned the globe and included a large number of colonies that were important for Britain's trade; among these were Trinidad, India, Hong Kong, Australia, Nigeria and Egypt. In the course of the 20th century, virtually all of the colonies gained independence, but many kept up their ties with Britain by joining the Commonwealth. Today this free association is made up of 54 member countries (with 1.7 billion people) which recognize the Queen as the Head of the Commonwealth. Member states co-operate in trade and meet to solve political conflicts. The Commonwealth Games (athletics and team sports) are held every four years.

Members of the former Empire were able to immigrate to Britain as British citizens, and, especially in the 1950s and early 1960s, the 'mother country' welcomed large numbers of immigrants from the Caribbean and South Asia (India, Pakistan, Bangladesh) to join the workforce in postwar reconstruction. They were later joined by South Asians from Uganda and Chinese from Hong Kong. The immigrants settled mainly in London, the industrial Midlands and the north of England, leaving a permanent imprint on British culture and society.

With the decline in industry and the economic crises of the 1970s, unrest grew among workers faced with unemployment. The government of Prime Minister Margaret Thatcher (1979–1990), the so-called 'Iron Lady', pushed through a programme of modernization, which cut social benefits and relied on free market forces to create wealth and employment. The open markets of the 1980s led to an increase in wealth for some of the population, especially in the south-east, but many others felt left out of the boom.

Like many British Prime Ministers, Thatcher sought a 'special relationship' with the USA and mistrusted the European Union. The UK joined the EU in 1973, but many British people still find it difficult to accept their nation giving up power to a European government. Tony Blair's Labour government, which was first elected in 1997, seems to be in favour of introducing the Euro in Britain, but the issue is sensitive and the government is waiting for a good time to hold a referendum on it.

Within the UK, the process of devolution means that the people of Scotland, Wales and Northern Ireland are moving away from central control by the Parliament in Westminster, and have more say in their own affairs. At the same time the central Parliament itself is facing democratic reform: many voices are calling for the non-elective chamber, the House of Lords, to be abolished; others would like to see Members of Parliament (MPs) in the House of Commons elected by proportional representation rather than by simple majority (the first-past-the-post system).

1 Briefly state how the four forces mentioned by Paxman influenced Britain.

2 **a** Define the highlighted words and phrases, using a dictionary if necessary.
b Note down two collocations for each word or phrase.
c Write ten sentences about the present-day situation in Germany using some of the collocations.

3 In groups, do research on one of the following topics, then give a three-minute talk on it:
- the British Empire;
- the monarchy since 1990;
- Britain and Europe;
- the peace process in Northern Ireland;
- the election system in Britain.

6 Pride in Our Past, Confidence in Our Future

Queen Elizabeth II's words 'pride in our past, confidence in our future' (cf. 'Golden Jubilee Speech to Parliament', p. 145) sum up the feelings of many Britons. This section looks at aspects of that 'past' and 'future'.

A Old Empire Niall Ferguson

The following extracts are taken from a book called *Empire: How Britain Made the Modern World*. What kind of book does the title lead you to expect?

■ 4 bar none *without exception* 7 address sth. *look at or think about sth. (esp. a problem or situation)* 9 on balance *looking at both sides*

(i) Introducing the Empire

Once there was an Empire that governed roughly a quarter of the world's population, covered about the same proportion of the earth's land surface and dominated nearly all its oceans. The British Empire was the biggest Empire ever, bar none. How an archipelago of rainy islands off the northwest coast of Europe came to rule the world is one of the fundamental questions not just of British but of world history. It is one of the questions this book seeks to answer. The second and perhaps more difficult question it addresses is simply whether the Empire was a good or bad thing.

It is nowadays quite conventional to think that, on balance, it was bad.

The Victoria Memorial, Calcutta.

1 What are the two fundamental questions Ferguson poses in this extract?
2 What might be good and bad about empires? Illustrate your answers from what you know about history, politics and economics.

Map from 1927 showing the British Empire.

(ii) The Raj

The Victoria Memorial in the centre of Calcutta was intended by the British to be their answer to the Taj Mahal, a timeless expression of imperial grandeur that would awe those over whom they ruled. Today, however, the statue of Queen Victoria, gazing wearily out over the Maidan, looks more like a symbol of the transient nature of British rule. Splendid though it looks, the memorial is a solitary white island in the sea of Bengalis who inhabit every available corner of this miasmic metropolis. The astounding thing is that for the better part of two centuries not just Bengal but the whole of India was ruled by just a few thousand Britons. As someone remarked, the government of India was 'a gigantic machine for managing the entire public business of one-fifth of the inhabitants of the earth without their leave and without their help'.

The British were also able to use India to control an entire hemisphere, stretching from Malta all the way to Hong Kong. It was the foundation on which the entire mid-Victorian Empire stood.

Yet behind the marble facade, the Raj was the conundrum at the very heart of the British Empire. How on earth did 900 British civil servants and 70,000 British soldiers manage to govern upwards of 250 million Indians?

■ Raj [rɑːdʒ] *Hindi name given to Britain's rule over India (1858–1947)* **2** imperial grandeur ['grændʒə] *der Glanz des Reichs* **3** awe sb. *make sb. feel respect and fear* **3-4** Queen Victoria (1819–1901) *queen of the United Kingdom (1837–1901) and empress of India (1876–1901)* **4** Maidan *park in Calcutta* **5** transient ['trænziənt ☆ -ʃnt] *vergänglich* **7** for the better part of sth. *for most of sth.* **11** leave (n) (fml) *permission* **15** conundrum *confusing and difficult question or problem*

1 Explain the difference between the intended meaning of the Victoria Memorial and its meaning as Ferguson sees it today.
2 Explain the metaphor in ll. 5–6. How does it relate to British imperial rule as a whole?

➤ Glossary: Metaphor (p. 268)

■ 1 flotsam and jetsam *rubbish floating in the sea* 2 supremacy [suːˈpreməsi] *Vorherrschaft* 4 bound to do sth. *certain to do sth.* 4 crumble *break up* 4 buckle *collapse* 10 dwindle *become less* 18 acknowledge sth. [əkˈnɒlɪdʒ ☆ -ˈnɑːl-] *admit sth.* 21 discernible [dɪˈsɜːnəbl] (adj) *recognizable*

(iii) The End of Empire

The British Empire is long dead; only flotsam and jetsam now remain. What had been based on Britain's commercial and financial supremacy in the seventeenth and eighteenth centuries and her industrial supremacy in the nineteenth was bound to crumble once the British economy buckled under the accumulated burdens of two world wars. The great creditor became a debtor. In the same way, the great movements of population that had once driven British imperial expansion changed their direction in the 1950s. Emigration from Britain gave way to immigration into Britain. As for the missionary impulse that had sent thousands of young men and women around the world preaching Christianity and the gospel of cleanliness, that too dwindled, along with public attendance at church. Christianity today is stronger in many of her former colonies than in Britain itself. [...]

Without the influence of British imperial rule, it is hard to believe that the institutions of parliamentary democracy would have been adopted by the majority of states in the world, as they are today. India, the world's largest democracy, owes more than it is fashionable to acknowledge to British rule. Its elite schools, its universities, its civil service, its army, its press and its parliamentary system all still have discernibly British models. Finally, there is the English language itself, perhaps the most important single export of the last 300 years.

(From: *Empire. How Britain Made the Modern World*, Allen Lane, London, 2003)

A remnant of British rule: the Indian Parliament building in Delhi.

1 What benefits did the Empire bring Great Britain? Use examples from this and the other two excerpts to illustrate your answer.

2 Discuss possible reasons why Ferguson considers the export of the English language so important. Do you agree with him? Give reasons.

B A Book Review: 'Sweet Taste of Empire' Michael Brunton

The following text is taken from a review of Niall Ferguson's book *Empire. How Britain Made the Modern World*, which appeared in *Time* magazine.

■ 2 lay claim to sth. *take sth. over* 4 glowing (adj) *enthusiastic* 5 decry sb./sth. (fml) *strongly criticize sb./sth.* 7 asset *thing of value* 9 emergent *developing* 9 be hooked on sth. (infml) *need to have sth.*

In *Empire* (and an accompanying six-part series on Britain's Channel Four), [Ferguson] charts how, over a span of 300 years, Britain laid claim to a quarter of the planet's land surface and its people. The tale he tells is astonishing – but what really astounds is Ferguson's glowing praise. Contemporary historians routinely decry the Empire's sins; Ferguson celebrates it for dragging the world into the modern age.

As an economist, Ferguson is particularly good at explaining how the assets seized by Elizabethan buccaneers fed, in the 18th century, the habits of an emergent consumer society hooked then as now on sugar, coffee and tobacco;

how Britain evolved a system of national debt to build a vast navy; how the East India Company's ports and forts seeded a global system of trade – which he dubs Anglobalization – that still thrums today.

But Ferguson's Empire balance sheets show some creative accounting. Though he dutifully frowns on the horrors of slavery or, say, the Battle of Omdurman, Sudan, in 1898 (in which 10,000 Muslims were annihilated in five hours by Lord Kitchener's Maxim guns), few such moments make it into the debit column. 'The question is not whether British imperialism was without blemish,' Ferguson writes. 'It was not. The question is whether there could have been a less bloody path to modernity.' There might have been, he admits, but he clearly doubts it.

Of all the benefits bestowed on the colonies, Ferguson prizes the English language and 'the idea of liberty' most.

(From: 'A Sweet Taste of Empire', *Time Europe*, 20 January, 2003)

■ **12** thrum *(here) be full of life* **13** balance sheet *Bilanz* **13** creative *(here) questionable* **13** accounting (n) *Buchhaltung* **15** annihilate sb./sth. [ə'naɪəleɪt] *destroy sb./sth. completely* **16** make it into sth. *succeed in getting into sth.* **20** bestow sth. on sb. (fml) *give sb. sth.* **20** prize sth. *value sth. highly*

1 What does the reviewer criticize about Ferguson's account of the British Empire? Give examples from the text.

2 Find lines in the extracts on pp. 158–160 to illustrate at least two points Brunton makes.

➤ Scanning (p. 236)

3 Explain how you think 'the English language and "the idea of liberty" ' (ll. 20–21) might have been beneficial to the colonies.

4 Do research on one country in Asia, Africa or North America and draw up a 'balance sheet' for British colonial rule there. Discuss your findings in class.

➤ Doing Research (p. 230)

C New Empire: The Triumph of English

It is everywhere. Some 380m people speak it as their first language and perhaps two-thirds as many again as their second. A billion are learning it, about a third of the world's population are in some sense exposed to it and by 2050, it is predicted, half the world will be more or less proficient in it. It is the language of globalisation – of international business, politics and diplomacy. It is the language of computers and the Internet. You'll see it on posters in Côte d'Ivoire, you'll hear it in pop songs in Tokyo, you'll read it in official documents in Phnom Penh.

■ **3** be exposed to sth. *have contact with sth.* **6** Côte d'Ivoire (the Ivory Coast) *country in West Africa, and a former French colony* **7** Phnom Penh *capital of Cambodia*

Deutsche Welle broadcasts in it. Bjork, an Icelander, sings in it. French business schools teach in it. It is the medium of expression in cabinet meetings in Bolivia. Truly, the tongue spoken back in the 1300s only by the 'low people' of England, as Robert of Gloucester put it at the time, has come a long way. It is now the global language. [...]

It was not always so. In the eastern half of the Roman empire, Greek remained the language of commerce, and of Christians such as St Paul and the Jews of the diaspora, long after Greek political supremacy had come to an end. Latin continued to be the language of the church, and therefore of any West European of learning, long after Rome had declined and fallen. But Greek and Latin (despite being twisted in the Middle Ages to describe many non-Roman concepts and things) were fixed languages with rigid rules that failed to adapt naturally. As Edmund Waller wrote in the 17th century,

Poets that lasting marble seek,
Must carve in Latin or in Greek.
We write in sand, our language grows,
And like the tide, our work o'erflows.

English, in other words, moved with the times, and by the 19th century the times were such that it had spread across an empire on which the sun never set (that word again). It thus began its rise as a global language.

That could be seen not just by the use of English in Britain's colonies, but also by its usefulness much farther afield. When, for instance, Germany and Japan were negotiating their alliance against America and Britain in 1940, their two foreign ministers, Joachim von Ribbentrop and Yosuke Matsuoka, held their discussions in English. But however accommodating English might be, and however much of the map was once painted red, the real reason for the latter-day triumph of English is the triumph of the English-speaking United States as a world power.

(From: 'A World Empire by Other Means', *The Economist*, 19 December, 2001)

■ **9** medium of expression *language used* **10** tongue [tʌŋ] *language* **11** Robert of Gloucester ['glɒstə ☆ 'glɑːstər] (1260–1300) *chronicler of English history* **12** come a long way *make a lot of progress* **18-19** of learning *having knowledge gained from reading and studying* **20** twist sth. *change or adapt sth.* **21** rigid ['rɪdʒɪd] *unchanging* **27** o'erflows (old-fashioned) *overflows* **28** move with the times *sich den Zeiten anpassen* **32** farther afield *further away; (here) in unlikely contexts* **35** accommodating (adj) *able to adapt* **36** painted red *on British maps of the Empire all countries belonging to the Empire were red (or pink)*

1 Based on the information in the text, make a timeline which shows under which conditions or for what purposes English was used in the past. Also include possible future events.
2 'A third of the world's population are in some sense exposed to it' (ll. 2–3). List as many forms of exposure to English around the world as you can.
3 Explain in your own words the meaning of the poem in ll. 24–27.
4 Using the information you gained from this section and your own knowledge, explain how the following are responsible for the 'triumph of English' (l. 37): a) the British Empire (cf. also the map on p. 159); b) the Commonwealth; c) the USA.
5 Speculate on what things bind Britain to mainland Europe and what things keep it apart from Europe. Consider the role of Britain's imperial past when answering this question.

WATCH YOUR LANGUAGE

Read the following text about a visit to Britain and see if you can find the mistakes:

My host family in Britain lived in a beautiful built cottage. Although my host father obviously didn't have a high paid job, the house was good equipped with all the latest gadgets. Clear, they felt very proudly of it.

When we talked together, I found that I could express myself more easier than I could understand what they said. It was only after I had asked them to talk more slow that I was able to follow.

They often spoke to me funnily, and not much they said was meant to be taken total serious. They often appeared seriously while they were speaking, but they were joking all the same.

At the weekends, my host family went usually to the pub and let me meet their friends. I will be eternal grateful for their generous hospitality.

1 **a** Correct as many mistakes as you can without consulting a grammar book.
b With a partner, find the rules in a grammar book where you are unsure.
c Look at the mistakes again and try to identify the areas where speakers of German are likely to make mistakes in English.

➤ Using a Grammar Book: (p. 235)

2 **Adjectives and Adverbs**
a Compare different things you do, using adverbs in the comparative and superlative form.
Example: 'I write more carefully with a pen than when I'm using the computer.'
b Think of what adjectives you could put after the following adverbs:

extremely • highly • surprisingly • well • strictly • truly • naturally

Make one sentence for each adverb–adjective combination.
Example: 'It's extremely difficult to pass your driving test the first time.'
c Take a look around where you are at the moment and use 'look', 'feel', 'smell', 'sound', 'taste' or 'seem' to describe impressions you have of different things or people.
d Tell the class or your partner about how you got to school this morning, using as many adverbs as you can.
Example: 'Obviously, I needed my alarm to wake me up because I was sleeping soundly. I slouched off lazily to the bathroom ...'

Has this page pointed out any areas of difficulty for you that you had not yet noticed? If so, they should be added to your self-assessment 'plan of action' (cf. Workbook).

➤ Glossary: Symbol (p. 268)

1 a Identify the symbols and symbolic acts depicted in the photos on these two pages. Explain their significance.
b How do the New York firefighters and the demonstrators differ in their attitude to the American flag and what it stands for?

2 a What comes to mind when you hear the words 'United States of America'? Do your impressions come from books, films, TV, articles or your own experience?
b Make a collage of things that symbolize the United States and the American way of life for you.
c Explain your ideas to the class.

Useful words and phrases
stand for / symbolize / be a symbol of ... • honour/desecrate/protect/raise/display/wave the flag • show/demand respect for the flag • ruins/rubble • aircraft carrier

⚠ **Trouble spot**
a symbol of sth.
Not: ~~a symbol for sth.~~

3 Read the following short extract from Paul Auster's *Leviathan*.

All in all, there are some one hundred and thirty scale-model replicas of the Statue of Liberty standing in public places across America. They can be found in city parks, in front of town halls, on the tops of buildings. Unlike the flag, which tends to divide people as much as it brings them together, the statue is a symbol that causes no controversy. If many Americans are proud of their flag, there are many others who feel ashamed of it, and for every person who regards it as a holy object, there is another who would like to spit on it, or burn it, or drag it through the mud. The Statue of Liberty is immune from these conflicts. For the past hundred years, it has transcended politics and ideology, standing at the threshold of our country as an emblem of all that is good within us. It represents hope rather than reality, faith rather than facts, and one would be hard-pressed to find a single person willing to denounce the things it stands for: democracy, freedom, equality under the law. It is the best of what America has to offer the world, and however pained one might be by America's failure to live up to those ideals, the ideals themselves are not in question. They have given comfort to millions. They have instilled the hope in all of us that we might one day live in a better world.

(From: Paul Auster, *Leviathan*, Viking Penguin, New York, 1992)

a Summarize the different views people have towards the Statue of Liberty and the American flag.

b Collect all the words and phrases in the extract that have to do with symbols or the role they play or the effect they have.

4 Describe your thoughts and feelings when you see:
a) the American flag, b) the German flag, c) the European flag.
Explain the reasons for your reactions.

5 Considering how large and varied the USA is, it is not surprising that many people have mixed feelings about the United States. Write two paragraphs of about 120 words each, one of which begins 'The USA at its best ...', the other of which begins 'The USA at its worst ...', and try and show your own feelings towards the USA.

⚠ **Trouble spot**
The USA is ...
Not: ~~The USA are~~ ...

1 American Dreams

Here are extracts from four poems or songs, all of which offer a different view of the USA.

A America the Beautiful Katherine Lee Bates

CD

'America the Beautiful' is one of the most popular American patriotic songs. It has often been suggested as a replacement for 'The Star-Spangled Banner' as the national anthem. Study the first stanza and reconstruct stanzas 2–4 from the worksheet that your teacher will give you. Then compare your version with the one on the CD.

O beautiful for spacious skies,
For amber waves of grain,
For purple mountain majesties
Above the fruited plain!
America! America!
God shed His grace on thee,
And crown thy good with brotherhood
From sea to shining sea!
(From: 'America the Beautiful', 1893)

■ **2** amber *bern-stein(farben)* **6** shed sth *(here) pour sth.* **6, 7** shed, crown *these are the subjunctive forms of the verbs* **6** grace *(hier) Gunst, Wohlwollen* **6** thee (old-fashioned) *you* **7** thy (old-fashioned) *your*

B The New Colossus Emma Lazarus

The poem 'The New Colossus' is inscribed at the bottom of the Statue of Liberty.

Here at our sea-washed, sunset gates shall stand
A mighty woman with a torch, whose flame
Is the imprisoned lightning, and her name
Mother of Exiles. From her beacon-hand
Glows world-wide welcome; [...]
'Give me your tired, your poor,
Your huddled masses, yearning to breathe free,
The wretched refuse of your teeming shore.
Send these, the homeless, tempest-tost to me,
I lift my lamp beside the golden door!'
(From: 'The New Colossus', 1883)

■ **1** sunset *(here) western* **4** beacon-hand *(here) hand holding a beacon (= Leuchtfeuer)* **7** huddle *be crowded close together* **8** refuse ['refju:s] *waste material* **8** teeming (adj) *full, crowded* **9** tost (old-fashioned) = tossed *thrown about*

C Dirty Blvd. Lou Reed

This room cost 2,000 dollars a month, you can believe it man it's true
Somewhere a landlord's laughing till he wets his pants
No one here dreams of being a doctor or a lawyer or anything
they dream of dealing on the dirty boulevard

Give me your hungry, your tired your poor I'll piss on 'em
That's what the Statue of Bigotry says
Your poor huddled masses, let's club 'em to death
and get it over with and just dump 'em on the boulevard

Going to end up, on the dirty boulevard
Going out, to the dirty boulevard
He's going down, on the dirty boulevard
Going out

(From: 'Dirty Blvd.', *New York*, Sire Records, 1989)

■ [6] bigotry *intolerant behaviour or beliefs* [7] club sb. *hit sb.* [8] dump sb./sth. *unload sb./sth. and leave them/it there*

D American Dream Bad Religion

I hate my family, hate my school, speed limits and the golden rule.
Hate people who aren't what they seem, more than anything else, American Dream.
American Dream's gonna swallow you whole, it's bursting at the seam,
it'll sweep you away, so enjoy it today, tomorrow you'll be old thus useless.
American Dream ... American Dream ...
American Dream, that's ok, 'cause no one dare give you away.

(From: 'American Dream', *How Could Hell Be Any Worse?*, Epitaph Records, 1982)

■ [1] golden rule *'In everything do to others as you would have them do to you'* [3] swallow sth. *etwas verschlingen* [3] burst at the seam (*usu.* seams) *aus allen Nähten platzen*

1 Compare the attitudes towards the 'American Dream' presented in the extracts above.

2 Discuss the views presented in 'Dirty Blvd.' in the light of **a** Lazarus's 'The New Colossus' and **b** the excerpt from Auster's *Leviathan* (cf. p. 165).

3 Analyse Bad Religion's view of the American Dream.

4 Choose either 'Dirty Blvd.' or 'American Dream' and ask your teacher for the complete lyrics. Or bring your own song about the USA to class.
Compare the song you have chosen with 'America the Beautiful'. Take their content, tone, language, style and music into consideration.

➤ Glossary: Style and Language (pp. 265ff.)

Useful words and phrases

The tone of the song is angry/bitter/critical/ironic/optimistic/patriotic/playful/scornful/serious/solemn/...
The choice of words implies that the singer is ... / wants to create a mood of ...

CONTEXT BOX

American Dreams, American Nightmares

What is it that has lured tens of millions of people from every nation to the shores of the United States? This question was asked by the historian James Truslow Adams in the 1930s. His answer was the American Dream – 'that dream of a land in which life should be better and richer and fuller for every man, with opportunity for each according to his ability and achievement.' It is not merely the dream of the land of plenty but a dream of a social order in which men and women are able to realize their full potential, regardless of their socio-economic and ethnic background.

If you ask Americans today how they understand the American Dream, you will get many different responses. Some see it as a thing of the past. Others claim that it is alive and well and feel that Americans should make it a reality for all. For some it is the dream of decent and affordable housing. For others it is the dream of racial equality and justice for all, while some see it as the dream of upward social mobility, of success through education and hard work. Most Americans still emphasize the importance of self-reliance and are sceptical of government interference. For them the American Dream has to do with individual freedom and the opportunity to make a better life for yourself. But all Americans will agree that the American Dream has been central to American beliefs and behaviour.

Historically, the American Dream was a dream of the West and the frontier, i.e. the moving borderline between civilization and wilderness. When the westward movement reached the Pacific coast in the second half of the 19th century, there was no more open space to be conquered. Unlimited expansion had come to an end, and Americans had to seek new frontiers and challenges in science and technology, in space exploration, in social and political reform, in foreign aid and global commitment.

While patriotism, positive thinking, optimism about the future, pragmatism, and a can-do attitude are characteristic of many Americans, there has always been a self-critical awareness that America has failed to live up to its ideals and that for many the promise of America has not come true. The United States has not become the New Jerusalem that the Puritans hoped for; rather it has become a society which faces a host of social, economic and ecological problems. Some even fear that the American Dream has turned into a nightmare. The United States, they say, has become a wasteful consumer society of lonely individuals, with a government that does not do enough to close the growing gap between the rich and the poor.

1 Write a short fact sheet explaining the historical background to the American Dream.
2 Look at John Gast's painting 'Manifest Destiny' (1872) on the left. How does it capture the 19th-century American belief that the USA was chosen by God to settle most of North America?
3 Find synonyms in the text for the following words and phrases: dubious of; act of depending on oneself; typical of.
4 Start an A–Z of terms relating to the American way of life. In it you should define and explain terms such as 'the American Dream', 'frontier', 'Manifest Destiny' and 'Puritans'. Add to your A–Z as you work through this chapter.

2 God Bless America

A Inaugural Speech George W. Bush

VIDEO

Every four years, the newly elected president of the United States is sworn into office at a ceremony called the 'inauguration'. The president takes the oath of office on the steps of the Capitol and addresses the American people.

On 20 January, 2001, George W. Bush was sworn in as 43rd president. Before you watch and listen to an excerpt of Bush's inaugural address, speculate on the kinds of things a newly elected president might say in an inaugural address.

While you listen, make notes on the main points of Bush's speech.

⚠ **Trouble spot**
give/make/deliver a speech
Not: ~~hold a speech~~

1 a Did what Bush said reflect what you had expected?
b Describe Bush's vision of America at its best.

2 Study the extracts your teacher will give you from Bush's speech.
a Identify the recurring themes in this speech.
b Analyse the stylistic devices he uses.

➤ Glossary: Stylistic Devices (pp. 267ff.)

3 a What is your personal reaction to this inaugural address? Do you find it moving, stirring, brilliant, hypocritical, hollow, cynical, etc.? Explain in some detail.
b From what you know about the USA and its history, background and attitudes, list and analyse the elements that you would consider typically American.

4 Project work. Bush became president in January 2001. Find out more about his term as president by examining his domestic and foreign policies. Then compare what he said in his speech with what he actually did.

➤ Doing Research (p. 230)

B Facts and Figures

Look at the following figures. Then do the tasks below them.

Income Inequality:

Country	Year	Gini*
Sweden	1995	0.222
Luxembourg	1994	0.235
Netherlands	1994	0.282
Canada	1994	0.286
Germany	1994	0.300
Australia	1994	0.317
United Kingdom	1995	0.346
United States	1997	0.375

* The Gini index is a measure of income inequality ranging from 0 (absolute equality) to 1 (one household has all the society's income).
(From: *Working Paper No 252*, Luxembourg Income Study, March 2000)

Children Below Poverty Level in the United States:

Year	Percent below poverty level				
	All races	White	Black	Asian and Pacific Islander	Hispanic
1970	14.9	10.5	41.5	(NA)	(NA)
1980	17.9	13.4	42.1	(NA)	33.0
1990	19.9	15.1	44.2	17.0	37.7
1999	16.3	12.9	32.7	11.5	29.9

NA Not available.

State and Federal Prisoners in the United States:

1980	329,821
1990	773,919
1998	1,366,721

(Source: *Statistical Abstract of the United States*, US Census Bureau, 2001)

1 **a** What do these statistics reveal about the United States?
b How do they support or contradict what President Bush said about the United States in his inaugural address (cf. p. 169)?

➤ Working with Numbers (p. 226)

2 Choose one of these tables and present the data in a more visual way, e.g. as a line graph, bar chart or pie chart.

3 Having listened to Bush's inaugural address and examined the facts and figures on this page, say what the photos above reveal about American society and attitudes.

3 America in the Eyes of the World

As the only remaining superpower since the collapse of the Soviet Union in 1991, the United States evokes strong feelings among non-Americans. The first two texts are British views on the USA, while the third examines how the world views the USA.

A America Triumphant

It is a terrible memory. A memory of four plane-loads of people setting off on a beautiful morning but then hijacked to their deaths. A memory of thousands of innocent, unsuspecting civilians, of many nationalities, slaughtered when three planes hit the twin towers of the World Trade Centre and one side of the Pentagon; and of many more, lucky to survive but living ever since with the nightmare of that day. [...]

A year later, much more has changed, and mostly for the better. An America that Osama bin Laden and his al-Qaeda terrorists wanted to frighten, proving the world's greatest power was actually weak, vulnerable and cowardly, has shown a remarkable resolve. [...] Afghanistan was liberated from the Taliban, al-Qaeda's bases and forces there were destroyed or scattered, and that war-torn country managed to choose its own provisional government. An astonishingly broad alliance backed America in that war, and the two old superpower foes – Russia and China – were respectively supportive and acquiescent.

(From: 'Remember', *The Economist*, 7 September, 2002)

■ [8] Osama bin Laden *leader of the al-Qaeda network that carried out the attacks on New York and Washington on 11 September, 2001*
[9] vulnerable *weak and easily hurt* [13] foe *enemy*
[14] respectively *in the order in which things are listed*
[14] acquiescent [ˌækwiˈesnt] *willing to do what sb. else wants*

B Imperial Power George Monbiot

The United States [...] behaves like any other imperial power. Imperial powers expand their empires until they meet with overwhelming resistance. [...]

We can resist the United States neither by military nor economic means, but we can resist it diplomatically. The only safe and sensible response to American power is a policy of non-cooperation. Britain and the rest of Europe should impede, at the diplomatic level, all U.S. attempts to act unilaterally. [...]

Only when the United States can accept its role as a nation whose interests must be balanced with those of all other nations can we resume a friendship that was once, if briefly, founded upon the principles of justice.

(From: 'The Logic of Empire', *The Guardian*, 6 August, 2002)

American soldier patrolling in Afghanistan, 2002.

■ [6] impede sth. *try to stop sth.*

C A Growing Dislike of the USA

A major survey of global public opinion has found increasing anti-Americanism.

The trend is most dramatic in Muslim societies, and some of the strongest anti-Americanism is in Egypt and Pakistan, according to the study by the US-based Pew Research Center.

After 38,000 interviews in 44 countries, researchers concluded that in the past two years discontent had also grown in countries considered traditional US allies.

But the survey also revealed that opinions about the US were 'complicated and contradictory', with people at the same time embracing American things and decrying US influence on their societies.

Most people in most countries liked American television, films and music, and thought the spread of American science and technology was beneficial, the survey found.

President George Bush said the results partly reflected the work of foreign 'propaganda machines' which painted the US in a bad light, the Reuters news agency reported.

Former US Secretary of State Madeleine Albright, who headed the survey, said its results should not be interpreted as a criticism of the Bush administration.

She described the survey as a 'snapshot of the way the world is viewed at a very complicated time'.

'In many ways it is still in the US national interest to understand what others think of us,' Ms Albright said.

The survey concludes that:

- While there is growing dislike of the US, people in 35 out of 42 nations hold a generally favourable view of America.
- In Russia, US popularity has enjoyed a surge – 61% of Russians have pro-US attitudes compared to 37% in 2000.
- Dislike of America is concentrated in the Muslim nations of the Middle East and Central Asia.
- America's war on terror enjoys support outside the Muslim world.
- People in Canada, Germany and France – traditional American allies – are more critical about US policy and business practices than people in Africa and Asia.

(From: 'Global Anger at US "Growing" ', the website of *BBC News*, 5 December, 2002)

■ **8** embrace sth. (fml) *accept sth.* **9** decry sth. (fml) *strongly criticize sth.* **11** beneficial *helpful and useful* **25** surge (n) *sudden and large increase*

1 Using information from all three texts, describe and explain the emotions evoked by the United States among non-Americans.

2 Make a display of pictures that illustrate the USA's role in the world. Write captions for the pictures and explain your choices.

3 Choose a current foreign policy issue and discuss the roles played by the United States and Europe with regard to this issue.

➤ Writing Letters (p. 250)

4 Write a letter to an American friend explaining attitudes to the USA in your own country. Before you do this, look at 'Getting Along in English' (cf. p. 175).

Useful words and phrases

intervene/interfere in sth. • disregard multilateral agreements / world opinion • pursue your own interests unilaterally / at the expense of others • hegemony • superpower • launch a pre-emptive attack • defend/promote freedom/democracy

4 An American Quilt

A Bound by a Common Thread Jesse Jackson

Jesse Jackson, one of the leading black politicians in the USA since the time of the Civil Rights movement, gave the following speech to the Democratic Party Convention in 1988.

America is not a blanket woven from one thread, one color, one cloth. When I was a child growing up in Greenville, South Carolina, my grandmother could not afford a blanket; she didn't complain and we did not freeze. Instead, she took pieces of old cloth – patches, wool, silk, gabardine, crockersack – only patches, barely good enough to wipe off your shoes with. But they didn't stay that way very long. With sturdy hands and a strong cord, she sewed them together into a quilt, a thing of beauty and power and culture.

Now, Democrats, we must build such a quilt. Farmers, you seek fair prices and you are right, but you cannot stand alone. Your patch is not big enough. Workers, you fight for fair wages. You are right – but your patch is not big enough. Women, you seek comparable worth and pay equity. You are right – but your patch is not big enough. Women, mothers, who seek Head Start and day care and prenatal care on the front side of life, rather than jail care and welfare on the back side of life, you are right, but your patch is not big enough. Students, you seek scholarships. You are right. But your patch is not big enough. Blacks and Hispanics, when we fight for civil rights, we are right, but our patch is not big enough. Gays and lesbians, when you fight against discrimination and a cure for AIDS, you are right, but your patch is not big enough. Conservatives and progressives, when you fight for what you believe, right wing, left wing, hawk, dove – you are right, from your point of view, but your point of view is not enough.

But don't despair. Be as wise as my grandmama. Pool the patches and the pieces together, bound by a common thread. When we form a great quilt of unity and common ground, we'll have the power to bring about health care and housing and jobs and education and hope to our nation.

(From: The website of *PBS*)

■ **4** patch *Flicken* **4** gabardine, crockersack *types of material* **11** equity *fairness, equality* **12** Head Start *(in the USA) pre-school programme for children from disadvantaged families to prepare them for school* **19** hawk *Falke* **19** dove *Taube*

1 Identify the patches in Jackson's American quilt.

2 Briefly state what kind of America Jackson dreams of.

3 Examine how Jackson uses language to convince his audience of his vision of America.

4 A wide range of metaphors has been used to describe American society, e.g. 'melting pot', 'salad bowl', 'rainbow', 'pizza' and 'quilt'. Compare these concepts and state which you think is the best metaphor to describe America today.

➤ Glossary: Style and Language (pp. 265ff.)

➤ Glossary: Metaphor (p. 268)

Useful words and phrases

fair/just/multicultural/multi-ethnic/inclusive society • integrate/assimilate minorities • melt/blend people of different ethnic and religious backgrounds into a single nationality • retain your identity

5 **Project work.** In small groups, design an American quilt. Describe it in detail (you might want to draw it or make a photo collage of it) and explain the ideas behind it.

B Lifeblood of the Nation T. Coraghessan Boyle

The following excerpt is from T. Coraghessan Boyle's novel *The Tortilla Curtain*. Delaney and Kyra Mossbacher are liberal white Americans who live an idyllic life in Los Angeles with their young son Jordan until one day Delaney hits a poor illegal immigrant from Mexico with his car, seriously injuring him. In this extract Jack Jardine, a friend and neighbour, is talking to Delaney in a supermarket, where they have met by accident.

'Did you know that the U.S. accepted more immigrants last year than all the other countries of the world *combined* – and that half of them settled in California? And that's *legal* immigrants, people with skills, money, education. The ones coming through the Tortilla Curtain down there, those are the ones that are killing us. They're peasants, my friend. No education, no resources, no skills – and all they've got to offer is a strong back, and the irony is we need fewer and fewer strong backs every day because we've got robotics and computers and farm machinery that can do the labor of a hundred men at a fraction of the cost.' He dropped his hand in dismissal. 'It's old news.'

Delaney set the milk down on the floor. He was in a hurry, dinner on the stove, Jordan in the car, Kyra about to walk in the door, but in the heat of the moment he forgot all about it. 'I can't believe you,' he said, and he couldn't seem to control his free arm, waving it in an expanding loop. 'Do you realize what you are saying? Immigrants are the lifeblood of this country – we're a nation of immigrants – and neither of us would be standing here today if it wasn't.'

'Clichés. There's a point of saturation. Besides which, the Jardines fought in the Revolutionary War – you could hardly call us immigrants.'

'Everybody's an immigrant from somewhere. My grandfather came over from Bremen and my grandmother was Irish – does that make me any less a citizen than the Jardines?'

A woman with frosted hair and a face drawn tight as a drumskin ducked between them for a jar of olives. Jack worked a little grit into his voice: 'That's not the point. Times have changed, my friend. Radically. Do you have any idea what these people are costing us, and not just in terms of crime, but in real tax dollars for social services? No? Well, you ought to. You must have seen that thing in the *Times* a couple of weeks ago, about the San Diego study?'

■ 16 point of saturation *Sättigungspunkt* 21 drumskin *Fell einer Trommel* 21 duck (v) *lower your head quickly* 22 grit *courage and determination* 34-35 bear down on sb. *move quickly and threateningly towards sb.*

Delaney shook his head. He felt his stomach sink. [...]

'Look, Delaney,' Jack went on, cool, reasonable, his voice in full song now, 'It's a simple equation, so much in, so much out. The illegals in San Diego County contributed seventy million in tax revenues and at the same time they used up two hundred and forty million in services – welfare, emergency care, schooling and the like. You want to pay for that? And for the crime that comes with it? You want another crazy Mexican throwing himself under your wheels hoping for insurance payoff? Or worse, you want one of *them* behind the wheel bearing down on you, no insurance, no brakes, no nothing?'

Delaney was trying to organize his thoughts. He wanted to tell Jack that he was wrong, that everyone deserved a chance in life and that the Mexicans would assimilate just like the Poles, Italians, Germans, Irish and Chinese and that besides which we'd stolen California from them in the first place, but he didn't get the chance.

(From: *The Tortilla Curtain*, Viking, New York, 1995)

1 State the issue dealt with in this excerpt.

2 Explain what Jack means when he talks about 'the Tortilla Curtain' (l. 4)?

3 **a** Make notes on the positions taken by Jack and Delaney.

b How does Jack argue his case?

c Using your notes, summarize this passage in about 130 words.

➤ Summary Writing (p. 248)

4 Discuss Jack's and Delaney's positions. Which do you find more convincing? Explain your answer.

5 Identify the mode of presentation used in this passage and evaluate its effectiveness. (It might help you to consider how else this scene might have been presented.)

➤ Glossary: Mode of Presentation (p. 259)

➤ Viewing Skills (p. 227)

6 State what changes would be necessary to convert this passage (or an extract from it) into a film script. You might want to act it out in class.

C Assimilation, American-style Robert J. Samuelson

The latest census seems to have been a consciousness-raising exercise [...]. The nation's population increased from 249 million in 1990 to 281 million in 2000. Those numbers – and the numbers of new immigrants in the United States – turned out to be much higher than expected. There's no doubt immigration has had a huge impact. Already, a fifth of school-age children come from immigrant families.

As a society, America's central interest lies in assimilating these families. This means more than having them join the economic mainstream. It also means that they think of themselves primarily as Americans. If the United States simply becomes a collection of self-designated 'minorities', then the country will have changed for the worse.

Americans first need to admit that assimilation is desirable. The term has fallen into disrepute because it's viewed 'by its antagonists as a means of imposing cultural conformity on America's minority groups,' as Peter Salins recently wrote in his book *Assimilation, American Style*. To those who worship 'multiculturalism' and 'diversity', assimilation is dated and detestable.

American assimilation never demanded this sort of rigid cultural conformity,

■ **5** impact (n) *powerful effect* **12-13** fall into disrepute *get a bad reputation* **13-14** impose sth. on sb. *force sth. on sb.* **16** detestable *that deserves to be hated* **17** rigid *starr*

18 retain sth. *keep sth.* 21 embrace sth. *(here) accept sth.* 22 self-reliant *not needing help from others* 25 updraft *Aufwind* 26 temptation *Versuchung* 36 backlash *strong negative and often violent reaction to a situation* 41 odds *chances, probability* 43 neglect (n) *lack of care and attention* 44 benign [bɪ'naɪn] (fml) *kind, not causing any harm*

said Salins. People could retain ethnic traditions and affections. But assimilation did require three things he argued. First, immigrant families had to adopt English as the national language. Second, they had 'to take pride in their American identity' and the country's democratic principles. And, finally, they had to embrace the so-called Protestant ethic – 'to be self-reliant, hardworking and morally upright.'

Assimilation is mostly a spontaneous process, driven by the economy, popular culture and the belief in individual opportunity. People are caught in an updraft of activity, new ideas and temptations. A *Washington Post* survey last year asked Latinos the language of their TV programs. Among the first generation, 31 percent watched mainly Spanish programs and 42 percent watched 'equally' in Spanish and English; by the third generation, 88 percent watched English programs. On many issues, the attitudes of third-generation Latinos mirrored those of other Americans. But assimilation has never been easy for immigrants or Americans already here.

That's true now. About 30 percent of immigrant children are in poverty, says a report from the Urban Institute; in 1999 wages for immigrant Hispanic men were only 68 percent that of U.S.-born workers. Meanwhile, there's always a danger of an anti-immigrant backlash, particularly if there's a recession. [...]

Americans may face a paradox. To benefit from immigration, they may need a little less of it. People need time to adjust. American institutions (schools, hospitals) and sensibilities can be overwhelmed by too many newcomers – a reality ignored in the recent economic boom. America may also need to favor skilled over unskilled immigrants, further improving the odds for assimilation. Of course, all these controversial propositions pose difficult philosophical and practical problems. But Americans aren't debating them. This is neglect – and not benign.

(From: 'Can America Assimilate?', *Newsweek*, 9 April, 2001)

New citizens of the USA at a swearing-in ceremony.

1 **a** Compare the different definitions of the term 'assimilation' referred to in the text.
b Collect all the words and phrases that have to do with assimilation and arrange them in a visually interesting way.

2 Compare Samuelson's views on immigration with those expressed by Jack and Delaney in the text 'Lifeblood of the Nation' (p. 172).

3 In your view, does cultural diversity enrich or endanger a society? Illustrate your view with examples from your own experience, from texts you have read, etc.

4 Write a text entitled 'Assimilation, German-style'.

➤ The Stages of Writing (p. 244)

Useful words and phrases

ethnic Germans • people of German/Turkish/... ancestry/descent/origin • be granted/given (automatic) citizenship (at birth) • acquire/receive German citizenship • apply for German citizenship • choose between Germany and your homeland • have dual citizenship/nationality • keep / give up / renounce your citizenship • opt for German citizenship or that of your country of origin • grant/deny sb. asylum • economic/political refugees • bogus refugees • blame foreigners for sth.

GETTING ALONG IN ENGLISH

Avoiding Bluntness

Germans are often considered rude because they tend to be rather direct when they express criticism – even when they are guests or visitors. In most social situations Americans (and other English-speaking people) prefer a more indirect, less confrontational approach. This page will help you develop strategies and teach you phrases that you can use when discussing sensitive issues with Americans, e.g. US foreign policy, capital punishment, gun control or energy consumption.

1 Listen to the conversation which takes place on a bus trip. CD
- Find out who is talking.
- Trace how the conversation develops.

2 Now match the strategies and phrases below:

Strategies

1 Say you do not understand and ask for clarification.
2 Refer to your German background and ask for a comment from an American perspective.
3 Say something positive before touching on a sensitive issue.
4 Present your criticism as a personal concern.
5 Present your criticism as something others have said or might say and ask for a comment.

Phrases

a I really like ..., but there's one thing I've noticed ...
b I have heard it said that ... . How do you feel about that?
c In Germany we hear a lot about ... . What do you think about that?
d I'm a bit confused. Are you saying that ...?
e I'm having trouble with ...

3 Explain how these strategies can help you talk about sensitive issues.

4 Imagine you are travelling on a Greyhound bus. After a while, the woman sitting next to you asks you where you are going. When she finds out that you are from Germany, she wants to know where you live in Germany (her brother was in the army in Bad Kreuznach) and how long you are staying in the USA . Then she asks, 'How do you like it here?' How do you react? Do you:

a) follow the rule 'If you cannot say something positive, do not say anything'?
b) talk about the differences between Germany and the USA (as you perceive them)?
c) start with a positive remark, e.g. about the beauty of Yellowstone National Park?
d) give your honest opinion about something you find irritating, e.g. the low temperatures in air-conditioned buildings?

With a partner, write down the conversation on the bus and act it out in front of the class. Then, in class, discuss which of the dialogues would probably lead to a friendly and interesting conversation between you and an American.

5 The American Way of Life

A The Magic of Baseball Doris Kearns Goodwin

What is your favourite sport, and why? How did you become interested in it? Is it a sport that is popular throughout the world?
Now find out how Doris Kearns Goodwin became 'crazily committed' to a game that, in her childhood, was played only by men and boys.

The game of baseball has always been linked in my mind with the mystic texture of childhood, with the sounds and smells of summer nights and with the memories of my father.

My love for baseball was born on the first day my father took me to Ebbets Field in Brooklyn. Riding in the trolley car, he seemed as excited as I was, and he never stopped talking; now describing for me the street in Brooklyn where he had grown up, now recalling the first game he had been taken to by his own father, now recapturing for me his favorite memories from the Dodgers of his youth – the Dodgers of Casey Stengel, Zach Wheat, and Jimmy Johnston.

In the evenings, when my dad came home from work, we would sit together on our porch and relive the events of that afternoon's game which I had so carefully preserved in the large, red scorebook I'd been given for my seventh birthday. I can still remember how proud I was to have mastered all those strange and wonderful symbols that permitted me to recapture, in miniature form, the every movement of Jackie Robinson and Pee Wee Reese, Duke Snider and Gil Hodges. But the real power of that scorebook lay in the responsibility it entailed. For all through my childhood, my father kept from me the knowledge that the daily papers printed daily box scores, allowing me to believe that without my personal renderings of all those games he missed while he was at work, he would be unable to follow our team in the only proper way a team should be followed, day by day, inning by inning. In other words, without me, his love for baseball would be forever incomplete. [...]

So the seasons of my childhood passed until that miserable summer when the Dodgers were taken away to Los Angeles by the unforgivable O'Malley, leaving all our rash hopes and dreams of glory behind. And then came a summer of still deeper sadness when my father died. Suddenly my feelings for baseball seemed an aspect of my departing youth, along with my childhood freckles and my favorite childhood haunts, to be left behind when I went away to college and never came back.

Then one September day, having settled into teaching at Harvard, I agreed, half reluctantly, to go to Fenway Park. There it was again: the cozy ballfield scaled to human dimensions so that every word of encouragement and every scornful yell could be heard on the field; the fervent crowd that could, with equal passion, curse a player for today's failures after cheering his heroics the day before; the team that always seemed to break your heart in the last week of the season. It took only a matter of minutes before I found myself directing all my old intensities toward my new team – the Boston Red Sox.

I am often teased by my women friends about my obsession, but just as often, in the most unexpected places – in academic conferences, in literary discussions,

■ **5** trolley car (AE) *tram* **16** entail sth. *result in sth.* **20** inning *one of nine periods of a baseball game in which each team has a turn at batting* **27** haunt (n) *place which a person visits often* **30** Fenway Park *home ground of the Boston Red Sox* at the most elegant dinner parties – I find other women just as crazily committed to baseball as I am, and the discovery creates an instant bond between us. All at once, we are in deep conversation, mingling together the past and the present, as if the history of the Red Sox had been our history too. [...]

Perhaps I have circled back to my childhood, but if this is so, I am certain that my journey through time is connected in some fundamental way to the fact that I am now a parent myself, anxious to share with my three sons the same ritual I once shared with my father.

For in this linkage between the generations rests the magic of baseball, a game that has defied the ravages of modern life, a game that is still played today by the same basic rules and at the same pace as it was played 100 years ago. There is something deeply satisfying in the knowledge of this continuity.

And there is something else as well which I have experienced sitting in Fenway Park with my small boys on a warm summer's day. If I close my eyes against the sun, all at once I am back at Ebbets Field, a young girl once more in the presence of my father, watching the players of my youth on the grassy field below. There is magic in this moment, for when I open my eyes and see my sons in the place where my father once sat, I feel an invisible bond between our three generations, an anchor of loyalty linking my sons to the grandfather whose face they never saw but whose person they have already come to know through this most timeless of all sports, the game of baseball.

(From: 'From Father. With Love', *The Boston Globe*, 6 October, 1986)

1 When Kearns Goodwin speaks of her love for baseball, she mentions her 'journey through time' (l. 44). Trace that journey and explain how she changed over the years.

2 'Journey through time' is a metaphor. Find at least one more metaphor in this text and explain what associations it evokes.

➤ Glossary: Metaphor (p. 268)

3 What are the factors that make Kearns Goodwin 'crazily committed' (l. 39) to baseball, even as an adult? Which of them seems to be the single most important?

4 The United States is a sports-loving nation, with baseball, American football and basketball attracting huge audiences. This love of sport is reflected in American speech. Use your dictionary and find out the meaning of the following expressions. Which sports do they come from? Are there other English expressions you know that come from the world of sport?

play hardball
quarterback (v)
touch base (with sb./sth.)
ballpark
way off base
in a league of your own
out of your league
not in sb.'s league
throw sb. a curve
the ball is in your court
not to get to first base
in a different league

B A Sedentary Nation Bill Bryson

Bill Bryson is an American who lived for many years in England. After moving back to the USA, he started to write a column for the British newspaper the *Daily Mail*.

I'll tell you this, but you have to promise that it will get no further. Not long after we moved here we had the people next door round for dinner and – I swear this is true – they drove.

I was astounded (I recall asking them jokingly if they used a light aircraft to get to the supermarket, which simply drew blank looks and the mental scratching of my name from all future invitation lists), but I have since come to realize that there was nothing especially odd in their driving less than a couple of hundred feet to visit us. Nobody walks anywhere in America nowadays.

A researcher at the University of California at Berkeley recently made a study of the nation's walking habits and concluded that 85 per cent of people in the United States are 'totally' sedentary. The average American walks less than 75 miles a year – about 1.4 miles a week, barely 350 yards a day. I'm no stranger to sloth myself, but that's appallingly little. I rack up more mileage than that just looking for the channel changer.

One of the things we wanted when we moved to America was to live in a town within walking distance of shops. Hanover, where we settled, is a small, typical New England college town, pleasant, sedate and compact. It has a broad green, an old-fashioned Main Street, nice college buildings with big lawns, and leafy residential streets. It is, in short, an agreeable, easy place to stroll. Nearly everyone in town is within a level five-minute walk of the shops, and yet as far as I can tell virtually no one does.

I walk to town nearly every day when I am at home. I go to the post office or library or the local bookshop, and sometimes, if I am feeling particularly debonair, I stop at Rosey Jekes Café for a cappuccino. Every few weeks or so I call in at the barbershop and let one of the guys there do something rash and lively with my hair. All this is a big part of my life and I wouldn't dream of doing it other than on foot. People have got used to this curious and eccentric behaviour now, but several times in the early days passing neighbours would slow by the kerb and ask if I wanted a lift.

'But I'm going your way,' they would insist when I politely declined. 'Really, it's no bother.'

'Honestly, I enjoy walking.'

'Well, if you're absolutely sure,' they would say and depart reluctantly, even guiltily, as if they felt they were leaving the scene of an accident.

People have become so habituated to using the car for everything that it would never occur to them to unfurl their legs and see what they can do. Sometimes it's almost ludicrous. The other day I was in a little nearby town called Etna waiting to bring home one of my children from a piano lesson when a car stopped outside the local post office and a man about my age popped out and dashed inside (and left the motor running – something else that exercises me inordinately). He was inside for about three or four minutes, then came out, got in the car and drove exactly 16 feet (I had nothing better to do so I paced it off) to the general store next door, and popped in again, engine still running.

And the thing is this man looked really fit. I'm sure he jogs extravagant distances and plays squash and does all kinds of exuberantly healthful things, but I am just as sure that he drives to each of these undertakings. It's crazy. An acquaintance of ours was complaining the other day about the difficulty of finding a place to park outside the local gymnasium. She goes there several times a week to walk on a treadmill. The gymnasium is, at most, a six-minute walk from her front door. I asked her why she didn't walk to the gym and do six minutes less on the treadmill.

She looked at me as if I were tragically simple-minded and said, 'But I have a programme for the treadmill. It records my distance and speed, and I can adjust it for degree of difficulty.' It had not occurred to me how thoughtlessly deficient nature is in this regard.

According to a concerned and faintly horrified recent editorial in the *Boston Globe*, the United States spends less than 1 percent of its $25 billion-a-year roads budget on facilities for pedestrians. Actually, I'm surprised it's that much. Go to almost any suburb developed in the last thirty years – and there are thousands to choose from – and you will not find a pavement anywhere. Often you won't find a single pedestrian-crossing. I am not exaggerating. [...]

The fact is, Americans not only don't walk anywhere, they won't walk anywhere, and woe to anyone who tries to make them, as a town here in New Hampshire called Laconia discovered to its cost. A few years ago Laconia spent $5 million pedestrianizing its town centre, to make it a pleasant shopping environment. Aesthetically it was a triumph – urban planners came from all over to coo and take photos – but commercially it was a disaster. Forced to walk one whole block from a car park, shoppers abandoned downtown Laconia for suburban malls.

In 1994 Laconia dug up its pretty brick paving, took away the benches and tubs of geraniums and decorative trees, and put the street back to the way it had been in the first place. Now people can park right in front of the shops again and downtown Laconia thrives anew. And if that isn't sad, I don't know what is.

(From: 'Why No One Walks', *The Daily Mail*, 18 May, 1997)

■ sedentary ['sedntri ☆ -teri] *spending a lot of time sitting down or not moving* **4** astound sb. *surprise or shock sb.* **5** draw sth. *produce sth. (esp. a reaction)* **5** blank (adj) *showing no understanding* **12** sloth [sləʊθ ☆ sloʊθ] *laziness* **13** rack sth. up *collect sth.* **17** sedate [- '-] *slow, calm, relaxing* **17** green (n) *grassy area of public land* **23** debonair (old-fashioned) *fashionable, elegant and confident* **26** other than *except* **36** unfurl sth. *(here) stretch out sth.* **40** exercise sb. *occupy sb's thoughts (esp. in a negative way)* **62** woe to sb. *there will be trouble for sb.* **66** coo (infml) *make noises expressing admiration, etc.*

1 Compare the writer's lifestyle with that of his neighbours.

2 Show how Bryson uses humour to criticize the American love of cars.

➤ Glossary: Humour (p. 265)

3 **a** Find all the verbs of movement in the ll. 1–21 and 35–50. With the help of a monolingual dictionary explain the differences in meaning and usage.

b Now add other verbs of movement you know to the list.

➤ Using a Monolingual Dictionary (p. 234)

4 To what extent do you think there is a difference in public perception of transportation between Europe and the USA?

CD

C Car Culture and the Shopping Mall

Listen to the following excerpt from a BBC radio documentary about American global influence.

1 Explain the global popularity of shopping malls.
2 How does the layout of malls influence consumer behaviour?
3 How popular are malls in your area of Germany?

VIDEO

D The American Way of Life as Reflected on TV

American TV shows reflect and shape American lifestyles. Broadcast around the world, they also have a huge impact on the way the rest of the world sees the United States. Watch the following excerpt from the TV series *The Sopranos*.

1 List all the aspects in the excerpt that you would consider typical of the USA, its lifestyles, attitudes and culture.
2 Name American TV shows that are popular in Germany and say how they differ from German shows.
3 In small groups, prepare a summary of an American TV show of your choice.
   a Write a comment on what you like or dislike about the show.
   b Discuss what you have learned about the American way of life from the show.

The Cosby Show

Friends

Married with Children

Dawson's Creek

WATCH YOUR LANGUAGE

Look at these paragraphs from a student's paper about the United States. The teacher has marked the mistakes.

Americans are people, which believe in freedom and individual opportunity. To most Americans, freedom of choice is more important than social equality, what is understandable in the light of American history. Fleeing from persecution and poverty in their birth lands, America has always been a land of liberty and opportunity for millions of immigrants. Many Americans see the United States as a 'city upon a hill', i.e. a country, that has a mission in the world: to offer opportunities for those, who are seeking a better life and to bring democracy and prosperity to other parts of the world.

One lasting feature of American democracy is the election of the president of the USA every four years. Elected in November, the president's inauguration does not take place until the following January. In their inaugural addresses, American presidents have traditionally called for national unity and emphasized that what all Americans believe in.

1 a Correct as many of the mistakes in the paragraphs above as you can without consulting a dictionary or grammar book.

b With a partner, look at the mistakes you were not able to correct and use a dictionary or grammar book to correct them.

c Look again at the mistakes in the paragraphs above. What area does the student need to study more closely? How might he or she improve his or her English?

➤ Using a Monolingual Dictionary (p. 234), Using a Grammar Book (p. 235)

2 Sentence variety

Rewrite this paragraph on quiltmaking to improve the style. You can use connectors, participles, conjunctions, etc.

➤ Linking Ideas (p. 246)

In the old days quilts were made. They served as warm bedcovers. During this time the tasks of caring for their homes and family filled up many hours for women. Most of them had little leisure time. They could not express their creativity. Many of them channeled their inventive talent and imagination into quiltmaking. Hundreds of hours were spent composing quilts from bits of fabrics. The makers had accumulated the bits of fabric and kept them in scrap bags. One piece might be from a favourite dress. Another piece might be from a child's bonnet. They were reminders of the past. It was in the past that these pieces were worn. A twentieth-century writer (she writes on quilts) quotes her great-grandmother. The great-grandmother said, 'My whole life is in that quilt. It scares me sometimes when I look at it. All my joys and all my sorrows are stitched into those little pieces.'

(Adapted from: Cynthia V.A. Schaffer, *Discovering American Folk Art*, Museum of American Folk Art, New York, 1991)

Has this page pointed out any areas of difficulty for you that you had not yet noticed? If so, they should be added to your self-assessment 'plan of action' (cf. Workbook).

Below are snippets from young people's answers to the question 'Who am I?'. Read through them, making sure you understand all the words they use.

a) I come from a working-class background, so everybody's always assumed I'd grow up to work in a factory like my dad. But here I am, studying for a degree in business.

b) I was pretty quiet and withdrawn when I was at school, but since university I've become more outgoing. That doesn't mean I've completely overcome my insecurities, though!

c) My parents would have a fit if I brought my boyfriend home with me. They claim to be liberal, but I don't think they would approve of inter-racial dating.

d) I guess I'm pretty happy with who I am.

e) I suppose it was in the fifth form, when all the other kids were starting to show an interest in the opposite sex, that I first realized I was different.

f) I suppose you'd have to say my parents are middle class because my mum's a solicitor and my dad's a doctor, but I've never really thought about it.

g) My faith is important to me. I can't imagine marrying outside my religion.

h) Yes, I have friends from different races, but I feel more comfortable around people from my own ethnic group.

i) Being tolerated isn't enough. I want respect!

j) Yes, I'm quite religious – not a fanatic or anything, but I pray and attend church regularly.

k) I really admire people who are self-confident. I'll never be like that. I know I need to be more assertive, but that isn't me.

l) I'd like to have children, but I want to wait till I've established myself in my career.

m) If I had to describe myself in a word, it would be 'easy-going'. I don't get upset often, I just sort of go with the flow.

n) I'm still not sure what I want to do with my life. Yeah, I want to earn good money, but I'd like to find fulfilment at work, too.

o) It's the lack of social mobility in this country that turned me into a socialist.

A

D

E

1 Now look at the people in the photos and allocate at least two of the statements to each person. Make sure that the statements are consistent.

2 **a** Discuss the matches you made with a partner. Be prepared to explain your choices – were your matches based on how the individuals look, or did you have other reasons?

B

F

Useful words and phrases

I thought he/she looks as if he/she might be ...
He/she reminds me of someone I used to know who ...
The way he/she ... makes me think he/she ...
Anybody who ... would probably ...
Just because ... doesn't mean that ...
Not all ... are ..., you know.
... a clichéd/stereotypical view of ...

b Collect words that are useful for describing different aspects of people's identities: background, attitudes, personality traits, etc. Make lists or a mind map. Continue collecting words as you work through the chapter and add them to your lists or mind map.

➤ Mind Mapping (p. 222)

C

3 **Creative writing.** Choose one of the people from the picture and write your character's complete answer to the question 'Who am I?'. Try to imagine their background, their beliefs, their worries and interests, etc.

➤ The Stages of Writing (p. 244)

1 Origami Susan K. Ito

Try to imagine situations in which a person's ethnic identity plays a role. Then read the following short story by the Japanese-American writer Susan K. Ito.

I take my place, hesitantly, among the group of Japanese women, smile back at the ones who look up from their task to nod at me. Their words float around me like alphabet soup, familiar, comforting, but nothing that I clearly understand. The long cafeteria table blooms with folded paper birds of all colors: royal purple, light gray, a small shimmering silver one. They're weaving an origami wreath for Sunday's memorial service, a thousand cranes for the souls of those who died at Tule Lake's internment camp.

I spread the square of sky-blue paper flat under my hands, then fold it in half. So far, this is easy. I'm going to follow all the directions. It's going to be a perfect crane, *tsuru*, flying from my palm. Fold again, then flip that side of the triangle under to make a box. Oh no. What? I didn't get that. I'm lost. The women around me keep creasing, folding, spreading, their fingers moving with easy grace. My thumbs are huge, thick, in the way of these paper wings that are trying to unfold but can't.

My heart rises and flutters, beating against its cage in panic, in confusion. I try to retrace my steps, turn the paper upside down, in reverse. It's not working. I want to crumple the paper into a blue ball, an origami rock.

But instead I unfold the paper with damp, shaking fingers. I persevere. *Gambaro*. Don't give up. I'm going to make this crane if it kills me. I'm going to prove that I can do this thing, this Japanese skill. I'm going to pull the coordination out of my blood, make it flow into my fingers. I have to.

But what if I can't? Then it only proves the thing that I fear the most, don't want to believe. That I'm not really Japanese. That I'm just an impostor, a fake, a watered-down, inauthentic K-mart version of the real thing.

I remember the summer when I was nineteen years old. Waitressing at the Gasho restaurant in upstate New York, the centuries-old farmhouse brought over, beam by beam, from Japan. It took over forty-five minutes to dress for work each day, from the white Japanese underthings, pure snowy cotton, to the stiff red and gold obi. My mother helped me, turning me around in front of the mirror, her pride making her tall as she fussed over me. I put up my hair, an elegant round sculpture full of air, with red lacquered chopsticks holding it all together. I shuffled around the house in my wooden *geta* clogs, practicing small dainty bows toward the dog, my parents, various pieces of furniture.

It didn't matter that I was making less than minimum wage, that I was putting in more time getting dressed and commuting up the New York Thruway than I was actually working. I was proud.

I still remember that one July night, the frogs singing in the garden behind the restaurant, the moonlight shining like wetness on the stone lantern. I stood in the back doorway of the kitchen, listening to the chefs shouting in Japanese, the dishwashers howling in Spanish. The smell of miso soup and green onions floated in the steam of the kitchen.

I passed through the swinging dining room doors and called out to the next party on the waiting list. 'Harrison?'

A short woman with champagne-colored curls waved enthusiastically in my direction. I greeted the group of eight people as they milled around the bar, clinking glasses of emerald green. Midori on ice. I led them to the horseshoe-shaped table with the flat steel grill in the middle, handed them each a steaming towel.

'Good evening,' I said, smiling. 'Welcome to Gasho.'

The customers took the towels, pressed them into their faces, wiped their hands. They made small sounds of pleasure as the steam softened their skin. One man, wearing a beige polyester jacket, did not unroll his towel. He stared at me with reddened eyes and chewed on the end of a toothpick.

'Wait a minute,' he said.

'Yes? Is there something wrong?' Sometimes a towel came out of the steamer cold, or not moist enough.

'You're not Japanese, are you?' The man looked up and down, craned his neck to look at the back of me.

'Pardon?' I faltered.

'This is supposedly a Japanese restaurant.' He swept his arm up in a wide circle, and I could see a ring of perspiration soaked into his shirt. 'I read that brochure in the bar. It's supposed to be an antique farmhouse that was built in Japan.'

'The farmhouse is authentic,' I murmured. My face was getting hot. 'It was shipped here directly from Osaka.'

'And what about you?' he demanded. 'Where were *you* shipped from?'

I felt the blush draining out of my face, and my fear became so intense I thought my body would fail me. I imagined the blood pooling at my feet and then completely seeping out of my soles, leaving me standing in a puddle of my own blood, my half-authentic, tainted blood.

I nearly lost my balance. I stood there, holding the tray of heaped-up towels, tottering on my *geta*. 'I'm half-Japanese.' Just a whisper.

'Half?' he scoffed. 'Hey. I come to a Japanese restaurant, I expect to have a Japanese waitress.' He gestured toward petite, silky-haired Kimi passing out bowls of rice at the next table. He didn't have a clue, and I didn't tell him, that she was from Korea, and no more Japanese than he was.

He shook his head in disgust. 'No, sir, if I wanted to be served my dinner by someone like you ...' he looked me up and down again, 'I'd have gone to McDonald's.'

I stop, unfold everything, smooth the paper out on the table, take a deep breath, start again. My sweat is starting to make the paper all slick and even more unmanageable.

It must be those paternal genes that make me so klutzy, I tell myself. I take stock of all the ways his shadow marks my body. The dark hair that pushes up, unwanted, through the skin of my forearms, my legs, sometimes my belly, or worse, under my chin. No Japanese has to deal with this. I long for the smooth gold skin of my Nisei adoptive parents, the way they tan like caramels under the sun. My skin reddens to a dusky burnt color, and I know it's those delicate European genes that can't take the heat. Then there are the freckles. The huge flat feet, the bushy eyebrows. I blame him and his ancestors for all the parts of me that I hate.

5 wreath [ri:θ] *small circle of flowers, etc. placed on graves, etc.*
6 crane *Kranich* **7** Tule Lake internment camp ['tu:li] *place in northern California where Japanese-Americans were imprisoned during World War II*
18 persevere [ˌpɜ:sɪ'vɪə] *durchhalten* **23** impostor *person who pretends to be sb. else* **24** K-mart *name of a chain of US discount stores* **29** obi *wide belt traditionally worn by Japanese women*
32 bow [baʊ] (n) *Verneigung* **46** midori *melon-flavoured Japanese liqueur*
56 crane your neck *stretch your neck (like a crane) in order to see better*
58 falter ['fɔ:ltə] *say weakly*
68 tainted *impure*
81 paternal *coming from the father* **81** klutzy ['klʌtsi] (AE sl) *ungeschickt, ungelenk*
81-82 take stock of sth. *think carefully about sth.*
85 Nisei *person born in the USA to Japanese parents*
87 freckles *Sommersprossen*

■ **89** lineage ['lɪnɪɪdʒ] (fml) *series of family members living before you* **92** defiant [dɪ'faɪənt] *trotzig* **99** would-be *Möchtegern-* **99** scar sth./sb. *injure sth./sb., leaving behind a mark on the skin* **102** oba-san *(Japanese) title of respect for sb. else's aunt or an elderly woman* **104** knotty ['nɒti] *(here) bigger than normal because of arthritis*

People ponder my lineage. What *are* you, anyway? they ask. They've guessed my roots to be Puerto Rican, Jewish, Italian, Hawaiian, Irish (the freckles). My pencil hovers over the forms that say, *check one for Ethnicity*. One? I mark Asian, defiantly, and then feel guilty, humiliated. It's a lie. A half lie, anyway.

I'm ready to give up. Hundreds of origami birds are piled into a mountain of color, spiky wings and beaks poking out like hatching newborns. What difference will it make if I don't complete this one? There are more than plenty for the memorial service.

I look down once again at the failed sculpture in my hands. There are so many folds in the blue paper, the color is starting to wear away at the creases. My would-be crane, still an awkward triangle, is scarred with white lines. I fold it again and again, over into itself, until finally something squat and deformed finally emerges. I shove it into my pocket and get up from the table when I notice the little *oba-san* sitting next to me. Her gray-white head, with its round rice-bowl haircut, the kind little children have, barely reaches my shoulder.

Her knotty, bent fingers are working a piece of pale butter-yellow paper. The folds she makes are gross, awkward, and her eyes are huge with concentration behind her spectacles. She doesn't seem to be having much more success than me, but I know it's not for lack of experience.

Finally she places her lopsided product in front of her and sighs. 'This is no *tsuru*,' she mutters. 'Looks more like sick chicken.'

I take my crane out of my pocket and sit it down next to hers. They make a sort of clumsy, humble symmetry on the table. *Oba-san* looks up at me with a tiny hint of smile behind her round glasses. She reaches for my sleeve, sways a little bit, and I help her to her feet. She and I walk slowly to the kitchen. It's time for tea.

(From: Diane Glancy and C.W. Truesdale, eds., *Two Worlds Walking*, New Rivers Press, Minneapolis, 1994)

1 **a** Collect as much information about the narrator as possible and group it under headings: 'background', 'appearance', 'identity', etc. Use the information to write a brief description of the narrator and her personality.

b What words and images does the narrator use to refer to her feelings about herself and her ethnic identity?

➤ Glossary: Imagery (p. 268)

c Describe how the narrator's attitude towards her identity has changed at the end.

2 What impression do we get of the man in the restaurant (ll. 50–77)? How is this achieved?

3 Analyse the structure of the short story and explain why the author used this structure.

➤ Glossary: Short Story (p. 255), Flashback (p. 262)

4 **a** Find all the words the author uses to introduce direct speech in ll. 53–77 and in ll. 108–109. Rank them on a scale of self-confidence.

b What is the effect of using so many different expressions, rather than just 'say'?

5 There are lots of expressions in the story that could be useful to you in your everyday speech. Find how to say:

a) alle Anweisungen befolgen (ll. 1–24);
b) etwas (immer) weiter machen (ll. 1–24);
c) keine Ahnung haben (ll. 59–77);
d) jdm. die Schuld an etwas geben (ll. 78–92);
e) Es liegt nicht an mangelnder Erfahrung (ll. 97–113).

CONTEXT BOX

Personal Identity

Self-awareness seems to be one of the things that sets human beings apart from other members of the animal kingdom. Many factors go into shaping an individual's personality. Some of these are hereditary, while other influences come from the environment. For example, the colour of a person's skin is something they are born with; the way a person with a particular skin colour is treated is largely determined by the society that person lives in.

No one can say for certain which personality traits we inherit and which are learned from our environment. But, just as each of us is born with a unique set of DNA and has a unique background and upbringing, so everyone's personality is also unique.

Some aspects of identity are our racial, ethnic, national, regional and class identities: who we are is largely a question of background and the values and attitudes that go with that background. Our religious identity, which includes both our religious background and the faith and beliefs we identify with later, also determine our moral code in life.

Gender identity (how we feel towards our identity as a man or a woman) should not be confused with sexual identity (who we are interested in sexually). No one knows whether sexual orientation is in-born or learned, but who we love may make a significant difference in our personalities. Do we find members of the opposite sex attractive, i.e. are we 'straight' (heterosexual)? Or are we attracted to our own sex, i.e. are we 'gay' (homosexual)? Or do we feel sexual attraction towards both sexes, making us bisexual?

Doubts about any aspect of our identity can lead to an identity crisis. Such self-doubts can be very destructive and prevent us from realizing our full potential in life. Our success in achieving our goals has a lot to do with how we perceive ourselves and whether we feel happy and fulfilled. That explains why so many self-help books and courses deal with 'empowering oneself'.

In any discussion of the topic of 'identity' it is important to remember two things. Firstly, identity is not constant – many aspects of our personalities can change over the course of a lifetime. Secondly, no one can be reduced to just one trait or feature: to say someone is 'a Hispanic' or 'a lesbian' is to ignore all the other aspects of that person's personality that make him or her a unique and valuable individual.

'The English Condition' by Liz Wright (1993).

1 a Draw a diagram to show different influences on personality. Try to think of others rather than just using ones from the text above.

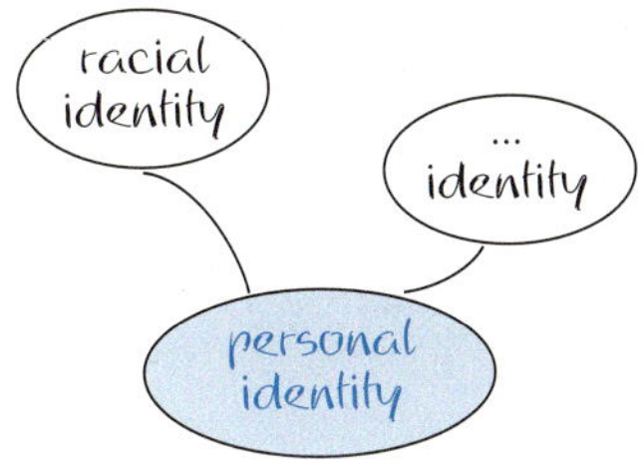

b Now make another diagram showing aspects of a person's life that are affected by their personal identity.

2 Make a list of the kinds of self-doubt that can lead to an identity crisis. Then explain the items on your list to a partner, giving concrete examples. Try to use as many expressions from the Context Box as you can.

2 I'm Not Lying Any More Paul Berges et al.

Jess and Tony in Bend It Like Beckham.

David Beckham and his wife Victoria.

Here is a scene from the screenplay of the film *Bend It Like Beckham* (2002). Set in England, it tells the story of Jesminder (Jess), a teenage Indian girl who has a passion for football. She plays in the park with the boys, including her cousin Tony until, one day, she is talent scouted for a women's football team. Because of her parents' disapproval she has to play secretly. In this extract she has come to the park to talk to Tony.

A Beckham Is the Best

95. EXT. PARK BENCH. DAY.

JESS *looks sad.*

TONY Hey, don't mind them ... you're better than the lot of them – and they know it.

TONY *puts his arm around her.* JESS *suddenly leans forward and kisses* TONY.

What're you doing Jess?

JESS *pulls away.*

JESS Sorry ... do you fancy me, Tony?

TONY I like you but ...

JESS Good, maybe we can go out then.

TONY Jess, what's wrong with you ...

JESS You're not shagging Bubbly or Monica are you?

TONY No way ...

JESS I'm sorry Tony ... I just think I need an Indian boyfriend ...

TONY What's going on Jess? You're acting all weird.

JESS *(tentative)* Sorry ... you know my coach ...

TONY *nods.*

I ... I nearly kissed him in Germany ...

JESS *goes red.*

TONY Wow ... and that's why you need an Indian boyfriend?

JESS Jules likes him too and now she hates me ...

TONY You can't choose who you fall for Jess, it just happens ... Look at Posh and Becks.

JESS *grins.* TONY *smiles.*

JESS Beckham is the best.

TONY I really like Beckham too.

JESS Of course you do – no one can cross a ball or bend it like Beckham ...

TONY No Jess I really like him.

The penny suddenly drops for JESS, *her eyes widen.*

JESS You mean ...

TONY *nods his head.*

But you're Indian?

TONY I know ... I haven't told anyone ...

JESS God ... what're your mum and dad going to say?

TONY *shrugs his shoulders.* JESS *takes in the enormity of his disclosure.*

My sister thinks you're mad about me.

TONY I am ... but I don't want to marry you.

She punches him playfully. JESS looks from him to the BOYS playing.

JESS God, just imagine what all those tossers would say if they knew ...

TONY You won't tell anyone Jess ...

JESS Of course not ... it's okay Tony ... I mean it's okay with me ...

TONY Well you liking your gora coach is cool with me ... he is kinda fit ...

JESS *(smiling)* I don't get one thing though ... why do you hang out with all these wankers here, they're so backwards ...

TONY Where else am I gonna get to see Indian boys without their shirts on?

(From: *Bend It Like Beckham. The Screenplay*. Courtesy of BILB productions, Ltd., 2002)

■ bend a ball *einen Ball mit Effet kicken* **1** ext. *(in stage directions) exterior, outside* **8** fancy sb. *be attracted to sb.* **12** shag sb. (vulg sl) *have sex with sb.* **21** Jules *Jess's friend who also plays in her team* **22-23** Posh and Becks *footballer David Beckham and his wife Victoria (formerly 'Posh Spice' of the group 'Spice Girls')* **27** cross a ball *einen Ball flanken* **39** tosser (sl) *stupid or unpleasant person* **42** gora (Indian) *English* **42** kinda (non-standard) *kind of* **44** wanker (vulg sl) *Wichser*

1 a Which aspects of personal identity does the scene deal with? Which parts of the dialogue reveal these aspects?

b How do their families influence Jess and Tony in these areas? Illustrate your answers from the text.

c Jess and Tony do not talk directly about issues. Name the issues they touch on here and explain what they leave unsaid.

2 The screenplay gives little indication in the stage directions of how the characters feel.

a Imagine you are the director. Write notes about what the characters are feeling during this dialogue and how you think they should deliver their lines.

b Now watch the scene on the video. Did the actors play the scene according to your directions?

c Explain how the camera work and editing developed or changed the script. Why do you think the director of the film has made these changes?

VIDEO

➤ Viewing Skills (p. 227)

Useful words and phrases

When Jess/Tony looks down / ... it tells you / shows that she is/he is ...
The close-up/medium long shot at the point where Tony/Jess says ... emphasizes ...
The fact that you can see ... in the background/foreground means that ...
Because the camera zooms/tracks / is so static it helps to underline ...

B We Have Something to Tell You

VIDEO

In *Bend It Like Beckham*, Jess's dad wants her to go to university and study law, but her passion for football continues. Later in the film, on her sister's wedding day, Jess's team wins the cup and she is offered a football scholarship to an American university. Watch the second segment of the film and then answer the questions on it.

1 a Why does Tony make his announcement? Is the action consistent with his character as shown in the first extract? Explain.

b 'If I can't tell you now what I really want now then I'll never be happy whatever I do.' Do you think Jess is brave or stupid to make this speech? Explain.

c Describe how Jess's character has developed between the first extract you saw (cf. 'Beckham Is the Best', **2b** above) and this scene.

2 Watch the scene once more. Then, with a partner, choose a short part of the scene and write the script for it, including stage directions as well as dialogue. Finally add the camera directions.

➤ Viewing Skills (p. 227)

3 My Region, Myself

CD

A Four English Accents

1 In the UK accents are an important aspect of a person's identity – they say something both about the place he or she comes from and about his or her social status. Is there a German regional accent that you laugh at, that you think sounds less educated than yours, or that tells you the speaker is 'posh' (upper class)?

2 Listen to the CD. The four people each speak with a different English accent: Received Pronunciation, Estuary (spoken in and around London), Midlands and Yorkshire. Which is easiest and which is the most difficult to understand?

B A Question of Accent Rose George

The following extract will give you an idea of how emotionally British people often react to accents.

Claire Lemon. I've always wanted to put her name in print, and if I could remember her brother's name, I'd publish that, too. Claire Lemon and her brother, in their self-built house up the road, tied me to a radiator 20 years ago and told me to 'Stop speaking posh, you snobby cow.'

Admittedly, I was speaking with a Hertfordshire accent in Yorkshire, so such treatment could conceivably fall within the acceptable parameters of childhood cruelty. [...]

Scratch an accent, and childhood linguistic trauma usually crawls out from underneath.

According to my friend Tom: 'I said raspberry [with a long 'a'] on a school trip and from that moment on I was doomed. Three years of unrelenting grief every time I forgot my new school accent and did a long 'a' instead of a short one. I remember a total panic one day when I had to say aunt and couldn't work out whether the local accent was ant or arent. Oh, and the first girl to notice it was Sally Parker and I hope she's burning in hell.'

My mother, even more surprisingly, said: 'I went to this posh school and, coming from a common background, I felt like a pariah. The first week there I was told by Miss Crout to stand up and read. As I started she said: 'Stop.' And then said coldly: 'Don't ever read in my class again until you learn not to drop your aitches and to speak correctly.' All the girls (upmarket Surrey girls whose fathers worked in the City) giggled and I remember feeling so humiliated.'

Surprising, because the southern, 'posh' accent of my southern-educated, northern-based mother has always been a household feature. Last Christmas, it sparked a new family game, whereby a young nephew was asked to choose between two pronunciations (he chose southern 'car' and northern 'bus', for the record). It was good timing; linguistic experts have learnt that children start distinguishing between accents at the age of three and a half (about the same time they give their toys different voices). In England, though, they probably develop perfect accent pitch in the womb. Nowhere, not even the most rigid of Hindu caste systems, is as obsessed by accent as this small island. Or part of it – the Scottish and Welsh were too busy (fighting the English, probably) to develop as complex and damning an accent hierarchy as ours. Only here do so few words reveal so much – background, gender, sexuality, schooling – and generate such contempt so concisely.

(From: 'Money Where Your Mouth Is', *The Independent Magazine*, 6 April, 2002)

■ **4** posh *upper class* **4** snobby *hochnäsig* **5** Hertfordshire ['hɑːtfədʃə] *county in southern England* **5** Yorkshire *county in northern England* **10** with a long 'a' *with an 'a' sound as in 'car'* [kɑː] **11** doomed *certain to suffer* **11** grief *great sadness* **12** a short one *a short 'a' as in 'ant'* [ænt] **25** pariah [pə'raɪə] *person who is considered not acceptable by society* **31** drop your aitches *not pronounce the 'h' at the beginning of a word (which is considered uneducated)* **32** Surrey *county in south-east England* **32** the City *business district in London* **35** household (adj) *(here) typical of her family* **36** spark sth. *lead to sth.* **41** perfect accent pitch *ability to recognize any accent* **41** womb [wuːm] *Gebärmutter*

1 What are the traumas (l. 8) George refers to in her article? Give examples from her text.
2 Which accent is associated with being 'posh'?
3 What makes English accents 'complex and damning' (l. 44)? Think of regions and social class as you look for answers in the article.

C Why Can't the English? Alan Jay Lerner

CD

In the successful musical *My Fair Lady*, which is based on George Bernard Shaw's play *Pygmalion*, Professor Higgins, a professor of phonetics, encounters a poor girl selling flowers when he leaves the opera with his friend Colonel Pickering. Her way of speaking English prompts a song from Higgins.

1 a Listen to the song. List all the people whose English upsets the professor. Listen again to confirm and expand your list.
b Higgins speaks of a 'verbal class distinction'. What does he mean by this and what examples does he give?
2 Compare the attitudes towards accents expressed in the song and in 'A Question of Accent' (p. 192).

A scene from the film musical My Fair Lady *(1964).*

GETTING ALONG IN ENGLISH

Being Interviewed

When you travel or live in an English-speaking country or in a country where your only means of communication is English, you will come across lots of interview situations.

'I'm Kurt ... this brochure will explain the rest.'

Here are just a few:

- an interview for a part-time job or a course;
- a market-researcher wanting your opinion on a product or service;
- a local newspaper wanting to know about your country, the reasons for your trip, etc.;
- a host family or school class, etc. wanting to know more about where you come from.

People will judge you by how you react in these situations, and how you feel will be influenced by the way people respond to your reactions. Work through this page, and you won't be caught unawares!

1 a Try to add at least two situations to the list above.
b Think about the kinds of questions you might be asked in the situations you have listed. Begin to collect words, phrases and sentences with which to answer them and keep them for further reference.

CD
2 Listen to the first set of dialogues.
a Describe the situation of each of the dialogues.
b Rank the dialogues from 1 (formal) to 4 (very informal). Explain your rankings.
c Listen again. Note down words, phrases and general features that made you think the interview situation was formal or informal – listen out for the forms of address, the way questions are phrased, typical words and expressions used, etc.

CD
3 Listen to the second set of dialogues. What mistakes, in your opinion, does each interviewee make?

4 Use your list to devise an 'interview code' for yourself – with appropriate words and phrases for each stage. Remember to distinguish between formal and informal situations, e.g.:

Interview code

Formal situations (e.g. job interview)	Informal situations (e.g. school class asking you about Germany)
1 Greet formally (Good morning, How do you do?, etc.)	1 Greet informally (Hi!, Hello!, etc.)
2 State full name clearly	2 Use only ...

5 With a partner, choose a situation and prepare a short interview to record or act out for the class. (Use the phrases you collected in **1b** and those which you remember from the recordings). Describe the situation: is it formal or informal?
After listening to other students' dialogues, comment on them. Did the language fit the formality of the situation?

4 Believing in Me: Goals and Ambitions

A Aim Higher

1 Look at this advert, which appeared regularly as two full pages, one behind the other, in UK teenage magazines.

a Describe the advert.

b Who issued the advert? What might be the reasons for it?

c What message do you get from the advert?

d **Project work.** Prepare adverts along the same lines as the *Vogue* ad, but for boys. Display them and discuss your reactions to them.

(From: *Sugar*, February, 2002)

Zadie Smith at an awards ceremony in 2000.

B I Have an Ambition ... Simon Hattenstone

Collect words to describe your goals in life and your ideas on how to achieve them. Then read the article about writer Zadie Smith (cf. p. 146) and add any other words to this list.

It has been an extraordinary year for Zadie Smith. Last Christmas she was an unknown 24-year-old living in Willesden. Then her novel, *White Teeth*, was published to great acclaim, and the spotlight has been on her ever since. So how has the winner of last week's *Guardian* first book award been affected by her fame? SIMON HATTENSTONE found out.

It can't be easy being Zadie Smith. She has become so much more famous than her celebrated first novel because she had the fortune, or misfortune, to be the perfect demographic. Young, attractive, black, female – and very talented. She is everything the media hankers after, the ideal head and shoulders to parade on a newspaper's masthead. [...]

It's too easy to reduce Smith to a victim of fame. She seems to have spent much of her life preparing for celebrity. She was five or six when she started writing poems and stories. A few years later she was writing pastiches of Agatha Christie. Her photographer dad and psychotherapist mum sent her to the local comprehensive in Willesden. Was she swotty? 'Was I swotty? Yes, I was very swotty,' she echoes in her deep singsong voice. At 14, Sadie changed her name to Zadie – it seemed right, exotic, different, while still true to herself. She always knew that there was more to a person than body and soul. There was image.

She spent much of her childhood watching Fred Astaire and Ginger Rogers and the great old movie musicals and saying to herself, 'One day that's going to be me'. Eventually she realised she was fooling herself. She probably wouldn't make the grade, and anyway she was a child out of time – they had stopped making those movies decades ago. So she decided on Cambridge University. 'I wanted to be an academic, and all the writers I loved went there.'

She seems to have mapped out her future rigorously. At 18, she was reading up about the working methods of her favourite authors. 'The worst thing is to be terrorised by the way other people write, if you hear that so and so wakes up at eight in the morning, walks the dog for two hours, then stands on his head, then writes 15,000 words, you think, like, shit, why don't I do that, but I've stopped thinking that way.' At Cambridge she received a £250,000 advance for two novels.

Smith says she sees naked ambition all around her, and it terrifies her. But she must have been ambitious? 'I have an ambition to write a great book, but that's really a competition with myself. I've noticed that a lot of young writers, people in all media, want to be famous but they don't really want to do anything. I can't think of anything less worth striving for than fame.'

(From: 'White Knuckle Ride', *The Guardian*, 11 December, 2000)

3 acclaim (n) *praise* **8** demographic (n) *representative of a group in the population* **9** hanker after sth. *want sth. very much* **10** masthead *banner at the top of the front page of a newspaper* **13** pastiche [pæ'stiːʃ] *piece of writing deliberately written in the style of another writer* **15** swotty (BE infml) *studying very hard* **18** there is more to sth. than sth. else *sth. consists of more than just sth. else* **19** Fred Astaire, Ginger Rogers *stars of film musicals of the 1930s and 40s* **25-26** read up about sth. *get information about sth. by reading a lot* **30** advance (n) *Vorschuss*

1 How did Zadie Smith 'prepare for celebrity' (cf. l. 12)?

2 Discuss the difference between Smith's ambition (cf. ll. 32–35) and what she calls 'naked ambition' (l. 31). Comment on this distinction.

3 With the help of the words you collected before you read the text, write a short text about your goals and ambitions and how you plan to achieve them.

C Find Your Hidden Strengths Marty Nemko

Skim the following feature on careers that appeared in the US teen magazine *Cosmo Girl*. Then sum up the contents of the feature in not more than three sentences.

➤ Skimming (p. 236)

Some people (maybe even your best friend) have always known what their dream job is. Others have an obvious talent that makes them perfect for a certain career. But for most people, deciding what they want to spend their life doing is harder. The key? Find your hidden strengths, and then look for careers where you can use them! Don't freak out if you have no idea where to begin. After reading this you'll be on your way. Really!

Marty Nemko, Ph.D., is an Oakland, CA, career counselor and radio talk-show host. [...]

Clue Yourself In!

These four questions may make you say, 'Eureka! I know what I'd be great at!' If not, they'll still point you toward a few types of careers you just might love. (Use a separate sheet of paper if you need more room for your brilliant answers!)

What do you have a knack for? Are you good at fixing things? Writing expressively? If you don't know, ask your parents, a friend, or a teacher you like.

Write your knack(s) here:

____

Think of something you've endured in your life. Like, have you been able to succeed in school, despite having dyslexia? Did your dad go blind when he was young? These could point to a career for you – maybe you'd want to work with dyslexic kids or develop a device that will reverse blindness.

Write about a problem you have struggled with:

____

Are there any tools you really love to use? It could be a computer, a sewing machine, a microscope – even books can be considered tools.

Write your favorite tool(s) here:

____

Is there an unusual subject that you love or talk a lot about? There could be a career related to it. Do you find insects fascinating? Israeli art? (Can't think of anything? Ask someone you trust to help.)

Write your favorite unusual topic here:

____

(From: *Cosmo Girl*, February 2002)

⚠ **Trouble spot**

career – *(erfolgreiche) Karriere* / *berufliche Laufbahn*

1 Now read the article through carefully.

a On a separate piece of paper write your own responses to the four 'Clue Yourself In' sections.

b Swap your paper with a partner. On the basis of your responses discuss together what jobs you think would be suitable for you.

Useful words and phrases

The area of ... offers a wide range of jobs.
People who are good with words / their hands / ... would be particularly suited to this job.
If you're the sort of person who ... / ... then you might think about this field of work.
You need to be an outgoing/thoughtful/careful/... sort of person for this job.
If your temperament/abilities/... doesn't/don't fit you for ..., you could try ...

6 Ph.D. = doctor of philosophy *highest university degree* **9** Eureka! [ju'rikə] *exclamation expressing joy esp. after finding the solution to a problem* **14** have a knack for sth. *have a special talent for doing sth.* **21** dyslexia [dɪs'leksiə] *Legasthenie, Lese- und Rechtschreibschwäche*

CD

The Road Not Taken:
[1] diverge [daɪ'vɜːdʒ ☆ də-] *go in two different ways* [5] undergrowth *bushes growing wild* [8] want sth. *be in need of sth.* [8] wear (n) *sign that sth. has been used* [9] as for that *was das betrifft* [12] tread – trod – trodden sth. black [tred] *make sth. black by walking on it* [17] hence (fml) *(here) from now*
Ships?: [4] float *stay on the surface of sth. (esp. water)*

D The Road Not Taken Robert Frost

Two roads diverged in a yellow wood,
And sorry I could not travel both
And be one traveler, long I stood
And looked down one as far as I could
To where it bent in the undergrowth;

Then took the other, as just as fair,
And having perhaps the better claim,
Because it was grassy and wanted wear;
Though as for that the passing there
Had worn them really about the same,

And both that morning equally lay
In leaves no step had trodden black.
Oh, I kept the first for another day!
Yet knowing how way leads on to way,
I doubted if I should ever come back.

I shall be telling this with a sigh
Somewhere ages and ages hence:
Two roads diverged in a wood, and I,
I took the one less traveled by,
And that has made all the difference.

(From: *The Atlantic Monthly*, 1915)

E Ships? Maya Angelou

Ships?
Sure I'll sail them.
Show me the boat,
If it'll float
I'll sail it.

Men?
Yes I'll love them.
If they've got the style,
To make me smile,
I'll love them.

Life?
'Course I'll live it.
Let me have breath,
Just to my death,
And I'll live it.

Failure?
I'm not ashamed to tell it,
I never learned to spell it.
Not Failure.

(From: *Complete Collected Poems*, Little, Brown and Company, London 1994)

➤ Reading Poetry (p. 241), Glossary: Symbol (p. 268)

1 How would you interpret the symbol of the 'two roads' in 'The Road Not Taken'? Try to give an example from your own experience.

2 **a** How and why is the last stanza of 'Ships?' different from the previous ones?
b State in one sentence what the message of the poem is. Do you agree with it? Give reasons.

3 Describe the outlook on life the speakers of the poems seem to have. Can you identify with either of them? Explain your answer.

➤ Glossary: Imagery (p. 261), Rhyme (p. 249)

4 In which poem do you find:
a) the images more effective?, b) the language more expressive?,
c) the rhyme scheme most appropriate to the content?
Explain, quoting from the poems where appropriate.

5 Which poem do you like better? Explain your choice.

6 What do the two poems have in common with 'Aim Higher' (p. 195) and 'Find Your Hidden Strengths' (p. 197)?

WATCH YOUR LANGUAGE

Look at this list of 'favourite' mistakes (some sentences contain more than one), which a teacher has gathered from her *Abitur* class.

1. **The school has a course in cross-cultural studies since three months.**
2. **'I help you,' is what Sharon always says when she sees someone with a problem.**
3. **Matthew works in the job he dreamed of since 2001.**
4. **Tom isn't the same since his mother has died last year.**
5. **Sharon took a shower when her girlfriend rang, so she cannot come to the phone.**
6. **They meet after work tonight to talk about their problems.**
7. **Ginny was seeming somewhat depressed lately.**
8. **An important decision has been reached at the conference yesterday.**

1 a Correct as many of the mistakes in the list above as you can without consulting a dictionary or grammar book.

b With a partner, look at the mistakes you were not able to correct and decide where to look up the correct forms. Then make the necessary corrections.

➤ Using a Monolingual Dictionary (p. 234), Using a Grammar Book (p. 235)

2 Look again at the mistakes in the list above. What areas does the class need to study more closely? What might they do to improve their English?

3 Mixed tenses

a Revise the rules for the present perfect and the simple past, then complete the following:

1 The family (live) in Britain longer than I can remember. They'll never leave.
2 We first (meet) back in 1999, and since then we (only/see) each other twice.
3 They (know) they (must) come to a decision before last night's press conference.

b Revise the different ways of expressing future time. Then decide what tense you need to express the following and make three examples for each:

1 something you and someone else have agreed to do later;
2 something you intend to do sometime in the future;
3 something that is scheduled or timetabled for later;
4 something you offer or promise to do right away;
5 something you expect to happen later.

c Translate the sentences into English. Be prepared to explain your choice of tenses.

1 Morgen kostet die Kamera schon mehr. – OK, dann nehme ich sie.
2 Die Projektgruppe trifft sich heute abend, um die Präsentation vorzubereiten.
3 Daniel weiß seit seiner Kindheit, dass er schwul ist. Irgendwann wird er es seinen Eltern sagen. Er glaubt, dass sie damit Probleme haben werden.

Has this page pointed out any areas of difficulty for you that you had not yet noticed? If so, they should be added to your self-assessment 'plan of action' (cf. Workbook).

'Untitled', Bruce Davidson (1965).

➤ Working with Pictures (p. 223)

1 a What do you think the girl in the photo is doing? Where do you suppose the picture was taken? Explain.

b Describe and analyse the photo.

Useful words and phrases

Because the photo is black and white, it ...
The background/foreground is / is not in focus/lit/..., so ...
The graininess / blurred background / ... of the photo has the effect of making/... you ...
Because the girl is not looking directly into the lens/camera, you ...
The fact that the light falls on ... / the ... is in the centre of the frame / ... directs your attention toward ...
She looks sad/dazed/tired/bored/..., which indicates that she ...

➤ Glossary: Mode of Presentation (p. 259)

c Write a short interior monologue for the girl.

OUT

2 **Hot-seat activity.** Choose one person to sit in the hot seat; this person must imagine that he or she is the girl in the photo. Everyone in the class has the chance to ask the girl a question. Repeat the activity with a different person in the hot seat who gives his or her own interpretation of the girl's thoughts in answer to more questions (which can be the same or different).

3 Collect all the words and phrases you know that have to do with your future. Group them under these headings: qualifications, education after school, careers, special interests, a place to live, hopes, fears. Add to the groups as you go through the chapter.

4 List reasons which you think might cause someone to leave home. You can include thoughts about young people in other parts of the world (e.g. a young person from Somalia might leave home to seek refuge in a safer country, an Indian IT graduate might leave home to ..., etc.).

5 **A Fantasy Journey** CD

a Listen to the recording, which will take you on a fantasy trip to ...

b Add any words and phrases that you remember from the recording to those you gathered in task **3** above. Then write a brief account of your journey, using as many of the words from your lists as you can.

c In groups of no more than five, describe to each other what you plan to do when you finish school. The group can ask questions about each person's plans.

1 Leaving Home

A The Road to London Laurie Lee

The English writer Laurie Lee (1914–1997) is perhaps best known for his autobiographical trilogy – *Cider with Rosie* (1959), *As I Walked Out One Midsummer Morning* (1969) and *A Moment of War* (1991). This extract is from the second of these books, in which he describes leaving his home in the country to seek his fortune and see the world. Before you read the extract, list the aspects of home you look forward to leaving and those you think you will miss.

The stooping figure of my mother, waist-deep in the grass and caught there like a piece of sheep's wool, was the last I saw of my country home as I left it to discover the world. She stood old and bent at the top of the bank, silently watching me go, one gnarled red hand raised in farewell and blessing, not questioning why I went. At the bend of the road I looked back again and saw the gold light die behind her; then I turned the corner, passed the village school, and closed that part of my life for ever.

It was a bright Sunday morning in early June, the right time to be leaving home. My three sisters and a brother had already gone before me; two other brothers had yet to make up their minds. They were still sleeping that morning, but my mother had got up early and cooked me a heavy breakfast, had stood wordlessly while I ate it, her hand on my chair, and had then helped me pack up my few belongings. There had been no fuss, no appeals, no attempts at advice or persuasion, only a long and searching look. Then, with my bags on my back, I'd gone out into the early sunshine and climbed through the long wet grass to the road.

It was 1934. I was nineteen years old, still soft at the edges, but with a confident belief in good fortune. I carried a small rolled-up tent, a violin in a blanket, a change of clothes, a tin of treacle biscuits, and some cheese. I was excited, vainglorious, knowing I had far to go; but not, as yet, how far. As I left home that morning and walked away from the sleeping village, it never occurred to me that others had done this before me.

I was propelled, of course, by the traditional forces that had sent many generations along this road – by the small tight valley closing in around one, stifling the breath with its mossy mouth, the cottage walls narrowing like the arms of an iron maiden, the local girls whispering, 'Marry, and settle down.' Months of restless unease, leading to this inevitable moment, had been spent wandering about the hills, mournfully whistling, and watching the high open fields stepping away eastwards under gigantic clouds ...

And now I was on my journey, in a pair of thick boots and with a hazel stick in my hand. Naturally, I was going to London, which lay a hundred miles to the east; and it seemed equally obvious that I should go on foot. But first, as I'd never yet seen the sea, I thought I'd walk to the coast and find it. This would add another hundred miles to my journey, going by way of Southampton. But I had all the summer and all time to spend.

That first day alone – and now I was really alone at last – steadily declined in excitement and vigour. As I tramped through the dust towards the Wiltshire

■ **1** stooping (adj) *bending over (usu. because of age)* **4** gnarled [nɑːld] (adj) *twisted because of age* **14** searching (adj) *bohrend* **18-19** vainglorious *overconfident* **20** occur to sb. *(of an idea or a thought) come into sb.'s mind* **22** propel sb./sth. [- '-] *push or force sb./sth. to move in a particular direction* **23** stifle sth. ['staɪfl] *prevent sth. from happening* **24-25** iron maiden *Foltergerät* **27** mournful *very sad* **35** steady (adj) *happening in a way that is constant* **35** decline (v) *become smaller, fewer, weaker, etc.* **36** vigour (BE) = (AE) vigor *energy* **36** tramp (v) *walk with heavy steps, esp. for a long time* **36-37** Wiltshire Downs ['wɪltʃə] *low hills in southern England*

Downs a growing reluctance weighed me down. White elder-blossom and dog-roses hung in the hedges, blank as unwritten paper, and the hot empty road – there were few motor cars then – reflected Sunday's waste and indifference. High sulky summer sucked me towards it, and I offered no resistance at all. Through the solitary morning and afternoon I found myself longing for some opposition or rescue, for the sound of hurrying footsteps coming after me and family voices calling me back.

None came. I was free. I was affronted by freedom. The day's silence said, Go where you will. It's all yours. You asked for it. It's up to you now. You're on your own, and nobody's going to stop you. As I walked, I was taunted by echoes of home, by the tinkling sounds of the kitchen, shafts of sun from the windows falling across the familiar furniture, across the bedroom and the bed I had left.

When I judged it to be tea-time I sat on an old stone wall and opened my tin of treacle biscuits. As I ate them I could hear mother banging the kettle on the hob and my brothers rattling their tea-cups. The biscuits tasted sweetly of the honeyed squalor of home – still only a dozen miles away.

I might have turned back then if it hadn't been for my brothers, but I couldn't have borne the look on their faces. So I got off the wall and went on my way.

(From: *As I Walked Out One Midsummer Morning*, André Deutsch, London, 1969)

37 weigh sb. down [weɪ] *jdn. bedrücken* **37** elder-blossom *type of flower* **40** suck sb./sth. *pull sb./sth. (in a certain direction)* **41** long for sb./sth. *sich nach jdm./etwas sehnen* **44** affront sb./sth. (fml) *treat sb./sth. without respect* **45** will (old-fashioned) *want, like* **52** squalor [ˈskwɒlə ☆ ˈskwɑː-] *dirty conditions* **54** bear sth. – bore – borne *etwas aushalten/ertragen*

1 Describe the things that made Lee set out on the road to London.

2 Analyse the relationship between mother and son as portrayed in ll. 1–15.

3 List the images and the emotive words and phrases which Lee uses to express his different moods as he walks along the road. Explain how each is intended to affect the reader.

➤ Glossary: Imagery (p. 268)

4 'Naturally, I was going to London' (l. 30). Try to explain this statement in the context of the extract. Discuss comparable attitudes to big cities today.

5 **Creative writing.** Write a short account of how you might feel or how you felt on your first day away from home. Try to find images and words that help your reader really understand your feelings.

➤ The Stages of Writing (p. 244)

■ Gemma ['dʒemə] [3] malcontent ['- - -] (n) *person who is not happy with a situation* [8] wits (pl) *brains* [10] abduct sb. *kidnap sb.* [11] pervert ['- -] *Perverser* [11] be at sb. (infml) *attack sb. physically* [12] binliner (BE) *Müllsack* [14] of sb.'s own accord *by sb.'s own choice* [14] copper (BE infml) *police officer* [14-15] on your tail (infml) *following you* [17] rag (infml, derog) *low-quality newspaper* [20] no hard feelings *nehmt es mir nicht übel* [24] undermine sth. *make sth. weaker or less effective* [24] credibility *Glaubwürdigkeit*

B **Running Away** Melvin Burgess

If you were planning to leave home secretly, what preparations would you make? Melvin Burgess's novel *Junk* (1996) tells the story of Gemma, a middle-class English girl who runs away from home and nearly ends up as a homeless drug addict. In this extract Gemma plots her departure.

GEMMA BROGAN'S
PRACTICAL HANDBOOK TO RUNNING AWAY FROM HOME
A step-by-step guide for radical malcontents

1 You will need: Clothes – woolly vest, long underwear, plenty of keep-warm stuff. Plenty of underwear and other personal items. A waterproof coat. A sleeping bag.
A pencil and paper. Money. Your father's bank card and pin number.
2 Your wits. You'll need 'em.
3 Think about it. What are your mum and dad going to do? Try to get you back, of course. It'll be police. It'll be, Oh my God, my little girl has been abducted. It'll be, Maybe some dreadful pervert is at her right now. Maybe she's lying murdered in a binliner in the town rubbish tip THIS VERY SECOND! It never occurs to them that little Lucinda got so fed up with Mumsy and Dadsy that she actually left of her own accord. So ... if you don't want every copper in the land on your tail and pictures of little you shining out of all the national newspapers, you tell your mum and dad exactly what you're doing. (Of course, maybe you want your piccy in the local rag. Not me. I was leaving home.)
4 This is where the pencil and paper comes in. You write them a note explaining that you're going away so that they can expect to see very little of you in the immediate future. Wish them luck, tell them no hard feelings and that you hope they will understand. Alternatively you can ask them how they can bear to live with themselves after they've made your young life so unbearable that you've had to go away into the hard world, etc. etc. But beware! This will undermine your credibility.
5 Book your coach ticket using your father's Visa card.
6 Take the money and run.

(From: *Junk*, Andersen Press, London, 1996)

1 Comment on Gemma's advice to would-be runaways.
2 Do you think Gemma is worried about her parents or not? Illustrate your answer with examples from the text.

C **Free!** Lauren Krugel

The end of a school career opens up all sorts of new possibilities, as one school-leaver describes in this article from the website of Canada's *Young People's Press.*

I will be finished with high school in exactly five days. That's seven if you include weekends and twelve if you include exams. After that I'm free – no looking back – sayonara, adios, au revoir, and good riddance. I can hardly wait! I am eighteen and have everything to live for. For the seven months before I go (preferably away) to university I'll have more time on my hands than I'll know what to do with. Maybe I'll 'find myself' in Europe. Or perhaps I can tear through America in the back of an old beat up convertible just like Jack Kerouac in *On the Road*. If I choose, I can stuff my face with bon-bons and watch soaps all day long. The possibilities are endless!

I told my parents I wanted to see Vancouver, Alaska, Afghanistan and Tibet. I want to see oceans and mountains – jungles and deserts. I told them I wanted to buy an old, beat up car, stuff some of my friends in it and mindlessly 'look for America' (à la Simon and Garfunkel). My father flat-out laughed in my face and my mother said 'fine' so long as I didn't mind being raped and murdered. The world isn't the same as it used to be, she said (she always has to be so dramatic!) And then I began to resent the fact that I missed the sixties by three and a half decades. Freedom just ain't what it's cracked up to be, it seems.

■ **3** good riddance *unkind way of saying you are glad sb./sth. has gone* **6** tear [teə] *move quickly* **7** convertible *Cabrio* **7** Jack Kerouac (1922–1969) *US cult author* **8** stuff your face (infml) *eat a lot* **12-13** 'look for America' *quote from a song by the singers Simon and Garfunkel* **16** resent sth. [rɪ'zent] *feel angry about sth.* **17** ain't what it's cracked up to be *isn't as good as people say it is*

■ **18** hobo-itis [ˌhəʊbəʊˈaɪtɪs ☆ ˌhoʊboʊ-] *desire to travel without plans or possessions, like a hobo (= Penner/in, Wanderarbeiter/in)* **20** hit sth. (infml) *set out on sth. (esp. the road)* **21** bite your thumb at sb./sth. (old-fashioned) *jdn. verspotten* **29** Palm Springs *town in Southern California where many retired people live* **32** Jean-Paul Sartre (1905–1980) *French philosopher and writer* **36** OAC (abbr) = Ontario Academic Credit *(in Canada) final qualification; similar to A-levels in the UK* **37** honor roll *list of the best students* **38** catch sb.'s drift (sl) *understand sb.* **48** have a point *be right* **48** a.k.a. (abbr) = also known as

We teenagers are all suffering from a mass epidemic of hobo-itis (a brilliant term that Chrissy Hynde used in an interview I watched recently on *Much More Music*). We early graduates are itchy and restless to get away – to hit the highway, bite our thumbs at authority and grow old knowing that we didn't waste our youth planning for retirement. We vow to never, ever become like our parents.

This is it! This is the real thing – and I'm not going to waste my life planning for something bigger and better that I'm not even sure will come along. It seems like everything is a preparation for something else. You go to elementary school to prepare for high school. You go to high school to prepare for university. You go to university to prepare for ... what will we be preparing for again? Oh yeah – to learn how to make as much money as quickly as possible so that we can retire in Palm Springs at 65 and play golf and bridge all day. I refuse to look back on my life and say, 'all those years of back-breaking, mindless labor – and look where I am now!'

But as Jean-Paul Sartre put it, we are all condemned to be free. With freedom comes responsibility and with responsibility comes the drudgery and tedium that we teenagers try so very hard to avoid (and the funny thing is, I'm not even trying to be pretentious by quoting my good buddy Sartre. It's just that I've been studying so hard for my philosophy exam which will hopefully raise my OAC average which will hopefully get me on honor roll which will hopefully get me into my university of choice which will ... you catch my drift. Ultimately I'll end up in Palm Springs playing bridge, is what I'm saying ...)

Now, back to the issue at hand. After the laughter had subsided, my father then calmly asked me where I intended to get the money for university once I've peed it all away on 'frivolous' journeys and expeditions. And if I didn't decide to go to university (which according to my father would be an absolute travesty because I have so much potential), how would I get a job, raise a family, retire? Money doesn't simply, 'grow on trees', you know!

'Details ... details ...' I scoffed but it occurred to me then that I hadn't really thought my life-plans through. This is when Sartre came to mind. I mean, the guy does have a point. And Jack Kerouac, a.k.a. 'Mr. Reckless Freedom', died of alcoholism at the age of forty-seven, didn't he? Freedom, really, really ain't what it's cracked out to be.

So here's my proposition: plan for the future – but plan for only what makes you happy. Not your parents, nor society, not your friends or the audience who will adore your books only after you've died an untimely death. Travel, indulge, explore. Be purposeless and random and creative and free – but make it mean something. Find your own rhythm in the madness so that when you're retired and old and gray you'll be able to say 'Look where I am now! Boy, was the journey ever worth it.'

(From: The website of *Young People's Press*, 2001)

1 'Freedom just ain't what it's cracked up to be, it seems' (l. 17). List Krugel's reasons for coming to this conclusion.
2 Do you share Krugel's views as expressed in the last paragraph? Explain.
3 Look at ll. 3, 10–11 and 25–29. Describe the stylistic devices the writer uses and explain their effect on the reader.

➤ Glossary: Stylistic Devices (pp. 267ff.)

D So I Have a New Name – Refugee Ruvimbo Bungwe

CD

Strange that a name should take away from me
My past, my personality and hope
Strange refugee this
So many seem to share this name – refugee
Yet we share so many differences.

I find no comfort in my new name
I long to share my past, restore my pride,
To show, I too, in time, will offer more
Than I have borrowed
For now the comfort that I seek
Resides on the old yet new name
I would choose – friend.

(From: *Credit to the Nation*, The Refugee Council, London, 2002)

1 Compare the name which the speaker in the poem has been given with the one he or she would like. List the associations which each word has, then analyse the reasons for the speaker's preference.

2 **a** What do you think the speaker means by the paradox in l. 7?

b List as many 'differences' (l. 7) as you can think of.

3 What might be the speaker's reason for leaving home? Compare and contrast it with the reasons of the other three people in texts A–C of this section. Write one sentence for each person about why he or she chose / might have chosen / might choose to leave home.

CONTEXT BOX

Moving Out

When we are very young we are dependent on adults – in most cases our parents – to take care of us. Throughout our youth we grow increasingly independent until, eventually, we can get along on our own.

The desire for independence usually sets in with adolescence and gets stronger during our teen years. At some point, normally after we have left school, we move out of our childhood home and set out on our own. Perhaps it's for a gap year – whether doing volunteer work in a hospital in Peru or backpacking round Australia with a friend – to give us time to decide what we want to do with our lives. Or maybe it's to go to college or university. Some young people, especially in rural areas, rush into marriage simply to get away from their parents and to have a bit of freedom and privacy. Leaving home is an essential rite of passage in our society.

Besides this usual path, quite a few adolescents try running away from home, often in the belief that life will be better elsewhere. Most runaways return home after a short time, but those who stay away often find themselves the victims of exploitation by a different set of adults. All too many of these young people end up living on the streets, taking drugs and supporting themselves with petty crime, prostitution, or by begging.

Whatever the reasons, every 'moving out' is also, initially, a 'moving in' somewhere. Student housing is a cheap alternative for those attending college or university. Some people move in with partners, others with friends or even total strangers in a flat-share arrangement. Whatever place they choose, most young people consider the first 'place of one's own' to be quite a landmark in their lives.

When their children have left the house, many parents go through a period of depression. They suffer from what is known as 'empty nest syndrome'. But an increasing number of parents do not know this feeling because their children never leave or because they return after a time away.

Often young people stay at home or return because of the cost of living in a place of their own: rents in towns and cities are high, and utility bills for gas and electricity are more than many young people starting out in life can afford. Sometimes they just miss home cooking and having someone to do their washing for them. Whatever the reason for this development – which, for example, has led to more than one in four Americans between the ages of 18 and 34 living at home – sociologists see it as a sign that the family is alive and well.

1 **a** Check your understanding of the words and phrases that have been highlighted.
  b Group these words and phrases, putting the ones with similar meanings together. Use one expression from each group in a sentence.

2 Using words and phrases from the Context Box, discuss the claim that the trend towards staying in one's parental home longer – or returning there – is a sign that the family is 'alive and well'.

2 Choices

A Career Plan

Finding a job is not the only problem for most young people. Finding out what sort of job they want can be just as difficult, as this online advice column for US teens shows.

➤ Glossary: Column (p. 263)

What do you want to be?
With all career possibilities available, how do you make a decision? Once you know what career path you want to follow, how do you get there?
One way to answer questions about your future career is to develop a career plan. A career plan outlines the steps you need to take to reach your career goal.

Steps to developing a career plan
Develop a career plan to determine your interests and skills. Thinking about your skills and interests can help you find a satisfying career.

1 To determine your interests, think about what you like to do. Think about experiences you have enjoyed. Evaluate what you liked, what you found challenging, and what you may have learned from those experiences. Make a list of activities you have enjoyed during the past few years.
2 Make a list of skills you have. Your skills may include training you have gained through part-time or full-time jobs. Even if you haven't been employed before, you do have some skills which will help you find a job. For example, you may have skills you learned through volunteer work or through social activities. Evaluate those skills and interests you have listed. Are there similar activities on the two lists? Are there any experiences that could turn into a career? For instance, if you volunteered at a hospital and enjoyed the experience, you may want to consider a medical career.
3 Find out about the types of careers available to you. If you don't research careers, you may not know about the best occupations to fit your interests and skills.
It's also important to decide if the career you are considering is really what you expect and whether it offers the salary and benefits you want. One good way to learn about a career is to intern in the position. (Internships are also a great way to gain experience in your selected career field.) Another good way to find out about a job is to network – talk to someone who is in the career now.
4 Once you have determined what career path you want to follow, assess what you need to do to prepare for that career. Do you need special training? If so, research the schools that offer the kind of training you need. What kinds of experience will you need to be successful in the career? Consider an internship as a way to get work experience in the career field.

By developing a career plan, you can focus on what you want to do and how to get there. And when you are ready to write your resumé for your job search, you will have a better understanding of your skills and experiences to discuss with potential employers.

(From: The website of *Mapping Your Future*)

■ **26** intern (v) (AE) *work as an intern, i.e. a person getting practical experience in a job, often for little or no pay*
28 network (v) *meet people who can help you*
35 resumé ['rezjumeɪ ☆ 'rezə-] (AE) = (BE) curriculum vitae (CV) *Lebenslauf*

Notes on the Curriculum Vitae:

1 Do not use special German letters (e.g. 'ä', 'ß') in your address.

2 For the UK, your CV might read: 'Abitur (similar to A-levels)'. For the USA: 'Abitur (similar to high school diploma)'.

3 Your interests need not be relevant to the job you are applying for.

'When did you say you left school?'

1 In no more than three sentences, explain what a career plan is and why it is important to develop one.

2 Comment on how useful this advice is for German teenagers. If you think certain changes would make it more useful, point out what you would change and how.

3 **a** Identify the dominant grammatical form in the text and explain why it is used so often in this sort of text.
b Examine why the writer often uses questions.

4 When applying for a job – or even for a place at a college or university – you may need to write a resumé/CV. Study this sample, then write your own.

CURRICULUM VITAE

NAME	Stevens, Samuel John
ADDRESS[1]	16, Rose Street Camborne Cornwall TR6 9FJ
DATE OF BIRTH	5 September 1985
NATIONALITY	British
EDUCATION	
1990–1996	St. Peter's Primary School, Camborne
1996–2001	Sir Henry Davy Comprehensive School, Penzance
2001–2003	Penwith Sixth Form College, Penzance
QUALIFICATIONS[2]	A-levels in Chemistry (Grade B), Maths (A) and German (B)
LANGUAGES	German and French
EXPERIENCE	two years volunteer work at West Cornwall Hospital, Penzance
INTERESTS[3]	Sailing, travel, computers (web design)

5 **a** Develop your own career plan to work out what sort of internship would be suitable for you and which organizations in Britain or the USA you might apply to.
b Write a covering letter to one of the companies or institutions you have chosen. Be sure to give all the reasons why they might want to take *you* on for an internship. Use standard expressions from the box below where appropriate.

➤ Writing Letters (p. 250)

Useful words and phrases

I read your advertisement in ... and would like to apply for the position of / a job as ...
As a student of ..., I would like to enquire whether you would consider taking me on as a trainee / an intern / ...
As you will see from the attached/enclosed resumé/CV, I have already ...
As my grades in ... reflect, I am interested in / rather good at ...
Because of my interest in ..., I would appreciate the opportunity to ...
I look forward to hearing from you soon / to your early reply.
Thank you for your consideration / considering my application.

⚠ **Trouble spot**
look forward to ... + ing
Not: ~~look forward to hear~~

B Doomsday

Every year in mid-August, British sixth-form students receive the results of their A-level examinations. Their grades determine what universities will accept them as well as what courses they may take. In this extract from a newspaper feature a girl describes her feelings waiting for the big day.

Name Emma Prest
Age 18
Home town north London
Subjects A-levels: Spanish, Chemistry, Geography; (AS-level History of art and Maths)
Uni/college applied for and course UCAS (American Studies), but dropped out after reconsidering and will reapply in September

My friends and I refer to 15 August as Doomsday. I try not to think about it, as I'm very scared. I had 14 exams over May and June and it was hell. A month before, I thought to myself, 'Oh no, I'd better start revising – stop the social life and work as hard as I can.' Why did I leave it till the last minute? I got away with the minimum amount of work in my GCSEs but it's not the same in A-levels. You can't bullshit your way through science. My parents are worried. They're planning to book me into a crammer. Their expectations (mainly As and Bs) are higher than mine. Being realistic, it may be ABC. I want to work for a charity, such as Amnesty International; it doesn't matter too much what my degree is in. But there is a possibility of retaking, which I really don't want. I am dreading going in and all my friends getting straight As. After this build-up of tension, I guess we'll all go out and have a good time – whatever our results. Then I am taking a gap year. I'm going to California and Belize in February. Until then I need to get a job. What I save will be for university. But my parents will pay the main bill.

(From: 'The Students Awaiting Their Fate', *The Independent*, 14 August, 2002)

■ doomsday *der Jüngste Tag* **4** AS-level (abbr) = Advanced Subsidiary level *(in the UK) qualification equivalent to one-half of an A-level, taken after one year of study* **6** UCAS ['ju:kæs] (abbr) = Universities and Colleges Admissions Service *UK organization which admits and places student applicants in universities* **6** drop out (of sth.) *no longer take part in sth.* **12** bullshit (v) (sl) *bluff* **14** crammer (BE infml) *Paukschule* **18** straight As *grade A in all exams* **19** gap year (BE) *year between school and university*

1 Explain why sixth-formers in general, and Emma Prest in particular, view 15 August as 'Doomsday' (l. 8).

2 List Emma's options after she leaves school, as mentioned in the text. Then state what she intends to do and in what order.

3 **Project work.**

a In groups, make a diagram showing either the British or the American school system with its exams up to university or college. Use information from the text, from what you can remember and from any research you find necessary.

➤ Doing Research (p. 230)

b Present your diagrams to the class. Then discuss the differences between the two systems, considering the advantages and disadvantages of each as compared with the German system.

➤ Giving a Talk or Presentation (p. 254)

4 State whether the British A-level exams or the German *Abitur* seems to be more rigorous. Explain.

C Applying to a US University

Even state-run universities and colleges in the USA are highly competitive: those institutions with the best reputations take only the best students. Part of the application procedure involves writing a 'personal statement', as described in this explanation for applicants to the University of California at Berkeley. As in a job application, candidates use the personal statement to present themselves in the best possible light.

Why is the personal statement so important?
It is a *vital* part of your application and may be reviewed by either the Admissions or Scholarship offices on many of the campuses to which you apply.

At Berkeley we use the personal statement to discover and evaluate distinctions among applicants whose academic records are often very similar. Your personal statement, when reviewed along with your academic record, accomplishments and activities, helps us to gain insight into your level of academic, personal and extracurricular achievement. It also affords you the opportunity to provide the Undergraduate Admissions Office with information that may not be evident in other parts of your application.

What does Berkeley look for in my personal statement?
We consider all achievement, both academic and non-academic, in the context of the opportunities you have had and the ways in which you have responded to them. Within that frame of reference, we seek the following personal characteristics: creativity; intellectual curiosity and achievement; exceptional personal or academic recognition; unusual talent or ability; initiative; motivation; leadership; persistence; service to others; special potential; substantial experience with other cultures; and your ability to overcome or manage significant challenges.

You need not address all of the personal statement prompts listed in the application; you may wish to focus on one or two aspects of your life as a student, for example, your participation in an outreach program or internship, or the hours you must work in order to help your family. You may also write about the way in which an activity or experience changed an attitude, crystallized a conviction, or helped you to establish a goal. We look for essays in which the quality of an individual's character emerges. No matter what you choose to write about, remember that this statement should tell us *who you are*, what you do, and give us

⚠ **Trouble spot**
vital ≠ *vilul*
vital *(English) = necessary or essential*
vital *(German) = very active, energetic*

■ **2-3** Admissions Office *office at a university that decides which applicants will be accepted to study there* **3** Scholarship Office *office at a university that gives financial assistance to students* **5** academic record *(here) school grades and test scores* **8** afford sb. sth. (fml) *offer, give sb. sth.* **21** outreach program *(in the USA) nationwide scheme in which high-school students take on work-related activities in their communities to gain knowledge and experience* **23** crystallize sth. *make sth. clearer or firmer* a sense of your background, intellectual vitality and level of achievement. We are interested not only in what you've done, but also in the choices you have made and what you have gained as a result of those choices.

What makes an effective personal statement?

A carefully composed, reflective personal statement that tells us about you is much more likely to be effective than a hastily-written one. Because of its autobiographical nature, allow time for reflection, thoughtful preparation, and several revisions, if necessary! We do not evaluate your writing ability; however, correct grammar, spelling and sentence structure contribute to an effective personal statement. After we have read your personal statement, we will ask the question, 'What do we know about this individual?' If we have learned very little about you, your personal statement has not been successful.

(From: 'The Personal Statement for Freshman Applicants', the website of *UC Berkeley Office of Undergraduate Admissions*, August 2002)

1 According to the text, what sort of student has the best chance of being accepted at Berkeley? What reasons are given for the university's preferences?

2 **a** Write your own personal statement of no more than 500 words.

b Exchange personal statements with a partner. Read your partner's statement and make suggestions for improving it. Listen to your partner's ideas and revise your statement accordingly.

➤ The Stages of Writing (p. 244)

3 **a** List as many noun–verb or verb–noun collocations from the text as you can find; be sure to include any prepositions that go with them. Examples:
review an application, the quality of a person's character emerges, ...

b Choose ten collocations that you find particularly useful and write sentences with them.

4 Study the chart below. What reasons can you think of to explain the different budgets for living on or off campus or living at home?

Tuition and Fees – Student Budget for International Students
International students will need approximately $33,000 to cover expenses for one year at UC Berkeley. Tuition and fees are subject to change without notice.

Average resident student budget for the 2003–2004* academic year (mid-August to mid-May)

	Living on Campus	Living off Campus	Living at Home
Registration fees[1,2]	$5502	$5502	$5502
Housing, Food & Utilities	11,212[3]	8524	2318
Books and Supplies	1158	1158	1158
Personal Expenses	1208	1452	1300
Transportation	630	1038	1494
Total	**$19,710**	**$17,674**	**$11,772**

[1] Non-resident tuition add $13,009.
[2] Health insurance fee of $608 may be waived if proof of adequate coverage is presented.
[3] An additional fee is charged for selected residence halls.
* Subject to change

■ • tuition (fees) [tjuˈɪʃn ☆ tu-] *Studiengebühren* • international student *foreign student* • subject to change (adj) *Änderung vorbehalten* • resident student (in the USA) *student who comes from or lives in the state that runs a college or university*

5 Debate the following motion: 'Tuition fees should be introduced at German universities.'

➤ Debating (p. 252)

■ **6** petulant ['petjulənt ☆ 'petʃə-] *bad-tempered and unreasonable* **9-10** Torremolinos *coastal town in Spain which is popular with working-class British holidaymakers* **18** jack-in-the-box *figure of a clown that jumps out of a box when you open it* **40** debutante ['debjutɑ:nt] *upper-class girl who is being formally introduced into society* **43** BO (abbr) = body odour **48-51** Finsbury Park, Islington ['fɪnzbəri, 'ɪzlɪŋtən] *two areas within the London borough of Islington, the centre of which (Islington) is considered very elegant, the outer areas of which (e.g. Finsbury Park) are rather poor*

D **Victoria, not Vicky** Andrea Levy

The narrator of the following extract from Andrea Levy's novel *Never Far from Nowhere* (1996) is the child of poor immigrants from Jamaica. Despite the odds against her, she is able to leave home to attend art college in Canterbury.

The door was marked with a black three. Had I known that as soon as I opened it twenty pairs of students eyes, female and male, would turn and look at me, I would have patted my hair down and checked my mascara. It was not the entrance I had wanted to make, puffing, sweating and cursing, but I was late.

I'd struggled down from Canterbury station with my bag that was acting like a petulant child – wanting to go one way whilst I wanted to go the other. 'Put your bag down over there,' Miss Schwarz said. She was sitting on a table at the front of the room in tight jeans and a huge white shirt with the collar up. 'It's Vivien, isn't it?' I nodded and placed my bag in a corner, then turned it round so the Torremolinos sticker wasn't visible. 'Have a seat – you haven't missed much.' I looked up and around: everyone in the room was smiling at me. I took a seat.

'We were just about to introduce ourselves. So what I want you to do is turn to a neighbour and tell them three interesting things about yourself.' The room tittered collectively. 'Now come on,' Miss Schwarz laughed, 'you must be able to think of just three things.'

It was then I remembered that I hadn't put on any deodorant that morning. I'd packed it the night before and had had such trouble getting my bag shut that I feared opening it again in case everything sprung out like a jack-in-the-box. So I just sprinkled a handful of Johnson's baby talc under each arm. But since then I had sweated. I had really sweated. I slid my hand inside my T-shirt as discreetly as I could, rubbed it around my armpit and pulled it out. I was about to put my fingers to my nose when someone said 'Hello, I'm Victoria and that is Victoria, not Vicky.'

'Vivien,' I said.

'Vivien not Viv?'

'I don't mind.'

Victoria was a blond woman with one of those faces that was so pretty it was boring. The sort of faces that if you were asked to draw them you'd just have to put everything in perfect symmetry and it would be a good likeness. Petite, turned-up nose, blue eyes and straight, lifeless hair – they all looked the same to me.

'Number one,' she carried on, 'I'm from Northumberland.' I nodded while resting my fingers close to my nose.

'Number two – well, no, it's number three really, because number one should have been that my name's Victoria and not Vicky. I always insist on that.' I inhaled deeply.

'Number three, well, I suppose it's that I was debutante of the year a few years ago – no, don't say that, I don't want everyone staring at me, I haven't washed my hair today. Does it look an absolute fright? Go on – tell me the truth.' I stank of BO.

'No,' I said, moving away from her.

'Well, tell me about you. I know your name's Vivien but where are you from?'

'London.'

'Whereabouts?'

I was about to say Finsbury Park, but I looked at Victoria's immaculate red-painted fingernails, her tight, well-fitting jeans with a gold belt running through the loops, her soft pink shirt opening low down her breasts, the delicate gold chain round her neck and gold and pearl stud earrings and said 'Islington'.

(From: *Never Far from Nowhere*, Headline, London, 1996)

1 List the ways in which the narrator gets off to a bad start at her new college.
2 Explain how Victoria is characterized. How does this make the reader feel about her?
3 What is the effect of the narrator relating her 'BO' test over several paragraphs (cf. ll. 16–43)?
4 **Creative writing.** Retell the entire extract from Victoria's point of view.

➤ Glossary: Character and Characterization (p. 260)

➤ Glossary: Narrator and Point of View (p. 258)

E Off to College

VIDEO

Watch the excerpts from the first programme of the UK documentary series *College Girls* (2002). It follows three female students through their time at Oxford University.

1 Describe the different scenes and settings that are shown.
2 Why does Laura think it might be good for her to get away from her father?
3 Watch the sequence again in detail. List the different film techniques that you notice. Then discuss the effects these techniques have on the viewer and explain why you think they are or are not suited to a documentary film.
4 **Creative writing.** Choose one of the three girls – Laura, Afshan or Natasha – and write a diary entry for the end of her first day. Describe what it was like for her and what her hopes and fears are. Alternatively, write a few scenes for a film script for a glossy movie about a girl's first day away at college.

➤ Viewing Skills (p. 227)

GETTING ALONG IN ENGLISH

Finding a Place to Live

If you spend any length of time abroad – for a work placement, for instance – you will need to rent accommodation. In England this will mean looking at the *small ads* in a local newspaper. But will you know

- how to read them?
- how to interpret what is written?
- how to go about getting the flat or room you want?

This page will help you learn how to cope.

Small ads – words and phrases

BR *British Rail, i.e. main-line railway* • dble *double* • gdn *garden, i.e. ground floor or basement* • dep *deposit (usually one month's rent)* • mod cons *modern conveniences, e.g. kitchen and bathroom* • months dep *deposit of one month's rent* • n/s *non-smoking* • pad (infml) *flat* • pcm *per calendar month* • prof *professional person (not a labourer)* • p.w. *per week* • ref *reference* • req *required, needed* • suit *be good for* • tube (infml) *London underground system* • well-appointed *nice, well equipped*

1 Small ads, as their name suggests, are meant to take up very little space in the newspaper. So they are full of abbreviations. Look at the example below from a London newspaper. Before going through the legend on the left, see how many of the abbreviations you can turn into words. Then try to work out their meanings.

> **Islington** dble room in well-appointed gdn flat, all mod cons. Suit n/s female. Close BR and tube, months dep and ref req. £400 pcm.– ☎ 0207 222 5544

2 Now look at three more small ads below. Which room would interest you if you were a) a male nurse who has a difficult work schedule and smokes? b) a lively female secretary with lots of friends? c) an animal-loving female teacher who likes to get out of town at weekends? Explain.

> **Camden** Dble room in fabulous pad, very close tubes, buses, shops, pubs. Friendly fun flatmates, must view. £95 p.w. – ☎ 0207 268 5544

> **Hackney** Dble room in charming Victorian house, close 73 bus, sharing with student and nightclub waitress. Dep req. £380 pcm – ☎ 0208 954 231

> **Clapham** Bright semi-furnished room in flat share near BR. To share with two others and spaniel, would suit easy-going, n/s prof female. £460 pcm – ☎ 0207 775 4987

CD

3 Listen to the dialogues between would-be tenants and landlords/-ladies. In the context of the conversations, interpret the meaning of these phrases from the above ads: *very close, charming, semi-furnished.*

4 **a** On a piece of paper, write a small ad for a vacant room in an imaginary flat or house. Put all the papers in a box.
b Listen once more to the conversations.
c Then each student pulls out one piece of paper. Imagine you are desperate for a place to live. Devise a dialogue with a partner in which you persuade him or her (the landlord/landlady) that you are the right person for the flat advertised on your paper.
d Act out the dialogue. (It can be humorous.)

3 **Eveline** James Joyce

The short story collection *Dubliners* (1914) established James Joyce (1882–1941) as one of Ireland's leading authors of the 20th century. The following story of adolescence is taken from that collection.

James Joyce, 1919.

She sat at the window watching the evening invade the avenue. Her head was leaned against the window curtains and in her nostrils was the odour of dusty cretonne. She was tired.

Few people passed. The man out of the last house passed on his way home; she heard his footsteps clacking along the concrete pavement and afterwards crunching on the cinder path before the new red houses. One time there used to be a field there in which they used to play every evening with other people's children. Then a man from Belfast bought the field and built houses in it – not like their little brown houses, but bright brick houses with shining roofs. The children of the avenue used to play together in that field – the Devines, the Waters, the Dunns, little Keogh the cripple, she and her brothers and sisters. Ernest, however, never played: he was too grown up. Her father used often to hunt them in out of the field with his blackthorn stick; but usually little Keogh used to keep *nix* and call out when he saw her father coming. Still they seemed to have been rather happy then. Her father was not so bad then; and besides, her mother was alive. That was a long time ago; she and her brothers and sisters were all grown up; her mother was dead. Tizzie Dunn was dead, too, and the Waters had gone back to England. Everything changes. Now she was going to go away like the others, to leave her home.

Home! She looked round the room, reviewing all its familiar objects which she had dusted once a week for so many years, wondering where on earth all the dust

■ Eveline ['evlɪn, 'iːvlɪn]
3 cretonne [kre'tɒn ☆ krɪ'tɑːn] *heavy cloth, often used for curtains, etc.*
6 cinder ['sɪndə] *burnt coal or wood, crushed like sand*
11 Keogh ['kiːəʊ ☆ 'kiːoʊ]
13 blackthorn *bush with black branches and thorns and white flowers*
13 keep nix (IrE) *watch out for danger*

came from. Perhaps she would never see again those familiar objects from which she had never dreamed of being divided. And yet during all those years she had never found out the name of the priest whose yellowing photograph hung on the wall above the broken harmonium beside the coloured print of the promises made to Blessed Margaret Mary Alacoque. He had been a school friend of her father. Whenever he showed the photograph to a visitor her father used to pass it with a casual word:

—He is in Melbourne now.

She had consented to go away, to leave her home. Was that wise? She tried to weigh each side of the question. In her home anyway she had shelter and food; she had those whom she had known all her life about her. Of course she had to work hard, both in the house and at business. What would they say of her in the Stores when they found out that she had run away with a fellow? Say she was a fool, perhaps; and her place would be filled up by advertisement. Miss Gavan would be glad. She had always had an edge on her, especially whenever there were people listening.

—Miss Hill, don't you see these ladies are waiting?

—Look lively, Miss Hill, please.

She would not cry many tears at leaving the Stores.

But in her new home, in a distant unknown country, it would not be like that. Then she would be married – she, Eveline. People would treat her with respect then. She would not be treated as her mother had been. Even now, though she was over nineteen, she sometimes felt herself in danger of her father's violence. She knew it was that that had given her the palpitations. When they were growing up he had never gone for her, like he used to go for Harry and Ernest, because she was a girl; but latterly he had begun to threaten her and say what he would do to her only for her dead mother's sake. And now she had nobody to protect her, Ernest was dead and Harry, who was in the church decorating business, was nearly always down somewhere in the country. Besides, the invariable squabble for money on Saturday nights had begun to weary her unspeakably. She always gave her entire wages – seven shillings – and Harry always sent up what he could, but the trouble was to get any money from her father. He said she used to squander the money, that she had no head, that he wasn't going to give her his hard-earned money to throw about the streets, and much more, for he was usually fairly bad of a Saturday night. In the end he would give her the money and ask her had she any intention of buying Sunday's dinner. Then she had to rush out as quickly as she could and do her marketing, holding her black leather purse tightly in her hand as she elbowed her way through the crowds and returning home late under her load of provisions. She had hard work to keep the house together and to see that the two young children who had been left to her charge went to school regularly and got their meals regularly. It was hard work – a hard life – but now that she was about to leave it she did not find it a wholly undesirable life.

She was about to explore another life with Frank. Frank was very kind, manly, open-hearted. She was to go away with him by the night-boat to be his wife and to live with him in Buenos Ayres where he had a home waiting for her. How well she remembered the first time she had seen him; he was lodging in a house on the main road where she used to visit. It seemed a few weeks ago. He was

■ **26** Blessed Margaret Mary Alacoque ['blesɪd, 'æləkɒg ☆ -kɑːg] (1647–1690) *French saint to whom Christ is believed to have made twelve promises* **30** consent to sth. (fml) *agree to sth.* **36** have an edge on her *have an angry sharpness about her* **45** palpitations *Herzklopfen* **46** go for sb. (infml) *attack sb. physically* **47** latterly (fml) *lately, recently* **47-48** what he would do ... sake *what he would like to do but doesn't because of her dead mother* **50** squabble ['skwɒbl ☆ 'skwɑːbl] *argument about sth. unimportant* **51** weary sb. ['wɪəri ☆ 'wɪri] *make sb. tired or fed up* **52** shilling *former currency of Ireland* **61** leave sb. to sb. else's charge *leave sb. with sb. else so that person can look after him or her* standing at the gate, his peaked cap pushed back on his head and his hair tumbled forward over a face of bronze. Then they had come to know each other. He used to meet her outside the Stores every evening and see her home. He took her to see *The Bohemian Girl* and she felt elated as she sat in an unaccustomed part of the theatre with him. He was awfully fond of music and sang a little. People knew that they were courting, and, when he sang about the lass that loves a sailor, she always felt pleasantly confused. He used to call her Poppens out of fun. First of all it had been an excitement for her to have a fellow and then she had begun to like him. He had tales of distant countries. He had started as a deck boy at a pound a month on a ship of the Allan Line going out to Canada. He told her the names of the ships he had been on and the names of the different services. He had sailed through the Straits of Magellan and he told her stories of the terrible Patagonians. He had fallen on his feet in Buenos Ayres, he said, and had come over to the old country just for a holiday. Of course, her father had found out the affair and had forbidden her to have anything to say to him.

—I know these sailor chaps, he said.

One day he had quarrelled with Frank, and after that she had to meet her lover secretly.

The evening deepened in the avenue. The white of two letters in her lap grew indistinct. One was to Harry; the other was to her father. Ernest had been her favourite but she liked Harry too. Her father was becoming old lately, she noticed; he would miss her. Sometimes he could be very nice. Not long before, when she had been laid up for a day, he had read her out a ghost story and made toast for her at the fire. Another day, when their mother was alive, they had all gone for a picnic to the Hill of Howth. She remembered her father putting on her mother's bonnet to make the children laugh.

Her time was running out but she continued to sit by the window, leaning her head against the window curtain, inhaling the odour of dusty cretonne. Down far in the avenue she could hear a street organ playing. She knew the air. Strange that it should come that very night to remind her of the promise to her mother, her promise to keep the home together as long as she could. She remembered the last night of her mother's illness; she was again in the close dark room at the other side of the hall and outside she heard a melancholy air of Italy. The organ-player had been ordered to go away and given sixpence. She remembered her father strutting back into the sick-room saying:

—Damned Italians! coming over here!

As she mused the pitiful vision of her mother's life laid its spell on the very quick of her being – that life of commonplace sacrifices closing in final craziness. She trembled as she heard again her mother's voice saying constantly with foolish insistence:

—Derevaun Seraun! Derevaun Seraun!

She stood up in a sudden impulse of terror. Escape! She must escape! Frank would save her. He would give her life, perhaps love, too. But she wanted to live. Why should she be unhappy? She had a right to happiness. Frank would take her in his arms, fold her in his arms. He would save her.

■ **72** 'The Bohemian Girl' *Irish opera from 1843* **74** the lass that loves a sailor *reference to a patriotic English song of the same title* **77** deck boy *unskilled worker on a ship* **80** Straits of Magellan [mə'gelən ☆ mə'dʒelən] *channel between the mainland of South America and Tierra del Fuego* **80** Patagonian [ˌpætə'gəʊniən] *person from Patagonia, the southernmost region of Argentina* **81** fall on your feet *be lucky* **84** chap (BE infml) *man* **93** Howth [həʊθ] *place near Dublin* **94** bonnet *Haube* **97** air (old-fashioned) *tune* **105** muse sth. [mjuːz] *think carefully about sth. for a long time* **105** lay a spell *do magic* **105-106** the very quick *the most sensitive part* **109** Derevaun Seraun (corrupt Gaelic) *possibly: the end of pleasure is pain*

116 passage ['pæsɪdʒ] *journey by ship* **118** quay [kiː] *platform in a harbour where boats come in to load, etc.* **124** nausea ['nɔːziə] *feeling that one is going to be sick* **125** seize sb./sth. [siːz] *take hold of sb./sth. suddenly and with force*

She stood among the swaying crowd in the station at the North Wall. He held her hand and she knew that he was speaking to her, saying something about the passage over and over again. The station was full of soldiers with brown baggages. Through the wide doors of the sheds she caught a glimpse of the black mass of the boat, lying in beside the quay wall, with illumined portholes. She answered nothing. She felt her cheek pale and cold and, out of a maze of distress, she prayed to God to direct her, to show her what was her duty. The boat blew a long mournful whistle into the mist. If she went, to-morrow she would be on the sea with Frank, steaming towards Buenos Ayres. Their passage had been booked. Could she still draw back after all he had done for her? Her distress awoke a nausea in her body and she kept moving her lips in silent fervent prayer.

A bell clanged upon her heart. She felt him seize her hand:

—Come!

All the seas of the world tumbled about her heart. He was drawing her into them: he would drown her. She gripped with both hands at the iron railing.

—Come!

No! No! No! It was impossible. Her hands clutched the iron in frenzy. Amid the seas she sent a cry of anguish.

—Eveline! Evvy!

He rushed beyond the barrier and called to her to follow. He was shouted at to go on but he still called to her. She set her white face to him, passive, like a helpless animal. Her eyes gave him no sign of love or farewell or recognition.

(From: *Dubliners*, Grant Richards, London, 1914)

1 Trace Eveline's life from the earliest memories mentioned here to the time the story takes place.

2 **a** Gather as many facts as you can about Frank (cf. ll. 64–83). What impression do you get of him?

b State whether you think Eveline loves Frank. Be prepared to justify your answer, quoting from the story as necessary.

3 List as many reasons as you can find

a for Eveline to stay at home

b for her to leave home with Frank.

Compare your lists with those of a partner and together try to rank the reasons in each list in order of importance.

Which reason or reasons, in the end, do you think played a major role in her decision?

4 What sort of life does Eveline choose in the end? How might it be different after her experience with Frank?

➤ Glossary: Action and Plot (p. 261)

5 **a** How much of the story takes place in Eveline's head, and how much of it is external action?

b What is the effect of telling the story in this way?

➤ Glossary: Imagery (p. 268)

6 Identify images of being closed in and images of being free in 'Eveline'. What effects does the author achieve by using them as he does?

7 **a** **Creative writing.** Write a letter from Eveline to Frank or from Frank to Eveline explaining their feelings after the ship left for Buenos Aires.

b Do you think the character you chose will send his or her letter? Why or why not?

WATCH YOUR LANGUAGE

Look at these sentences from covering letters that students wrote to go with their CVs (cf. p. 210, **5b**). There is one mistake with the verb forms in each sentence.

1 I will get a job as a teacher after university.
2 I expect to be going to do an apprenticeship as a goldsmith.
3 I have had good marks in maths so far, so I shall get a '1' in my Abitur.
4 By then I have completed a course in economics and I believe I will be able to make myself useful.
5 I take a gap year first and will be available to work from 15 June the following year.
6 If you will hire me, I will do a good job, I can assure you.
7 Since I am about to finish school next year, I would appreciate an opportunity like this.
8 I am to do a gap year if I can, but military service could get in the way of those plans.

1 **a** Try to identify and correct the mistakes in the sentences above without consulting a dictionary or grammar book.
b With a partner, look at the sentences you are unsure of and decide where to look for help. Then make the necessary corrections.

➤ Using a Monolingual Dictionary (p. 234), Using a Grammar Book (p. 235)

2 Look again at the mistakes in the sentences above. What areas do these students need to study more closely? How might they improve their English?

3 **Expressing future time**
a With the help of your grammar book, write out the rules for using:
– the *will*-future – the *going to*-future – *shall* vs. *should*
– *be about to* – the future perfect – *expect/hope to*
Write at least two examples of each that show that you understand the differences.
b Complete the following paragraph with future forms from **a** above. (In some cases there is more than one right answer.)
In a little more than a year's time I ... (finish) school. But I ... (look) for something to do with my life before that. I ... (have) good grades in my Abitur, so I ... (not have) problems getting a place at university. The question is: What ... (I/do) until then? I ... (start) talking to people who have done volunteer work in developing countries soon – maybe that would be a good idea.
c Translate the following into English. Be careful how you express future time.
1 *Hoffentlich ist die Stelle in einem halben Jahr noch frei.*
2 *Bis dahin habe ich alle nötigen Kurse bestanden.*
3 *Mit meinem Jodel-Diplom und zwei Jahren Erfahrung kann ich mich dann überall bewerben. Ich gehe wahrscheinlich nach Amerika.*
4 *Dort wird man mich mit offenen Armen aufnehmen. Ich habe gelesen, dass man in den Staaten bis 2015 mindestens 10.000 Jodler braucht.*

Has this page pointed out any areas of difficulty for you that you had not yet noticed? If so, they should be added to your self-assessment 'plan of action' (cf. Workbook).

Skills Overview

Study and Language Skills

Mind Mapping

A skill which involves arranging all the information you have around a central word or phrase. It is particularly useful for brainstorming, trying to get a general or detailed view of a topic or planning a text or talk.

How to proceed:

Step 1: Start with an empty, unlined piece of paper and colour pens.

Step 2: Write the *topic word* or *phrase* in the middle of the paper.

Step 3: Using different colours, draw various *branches and sub-branches* out from the central word or phrase and along them write key words and phrases only, not whole sentences. Remember that you can add ideas at any stage.

➤ Giving a Talk or Presentation (p. 254)

Step 4: Add symbols, pictures and icons to emphasize the important points. They can help catch your eye if you are using the mind map as part of your notes for a talk.

Step 5: Finally, add numbers to the branches and sub-branches in order to give the ideas a logical order.

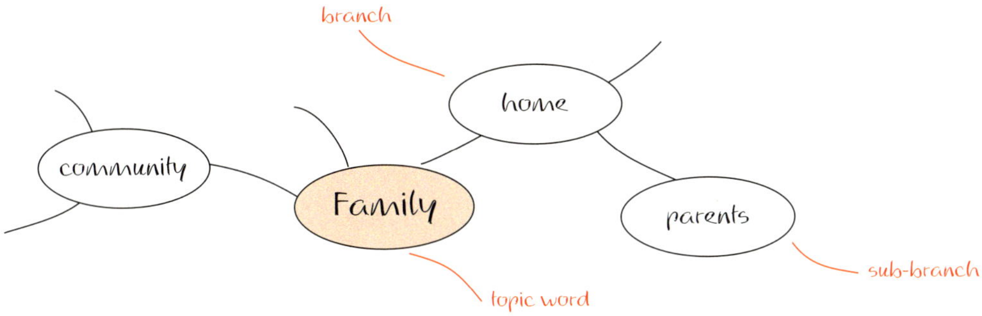

Working with Pictures

When you describe or analyse a picture you need a systematic approach and a set of useful phrases. These will help you to describe the contents of a picture to someone or to make a presentation involving pictures.

➤ Giving a Talk or Presentation (p. 254)

⚠ **Trouble spot**
in a picture
Not: ~~on a picture~~

Describing a picture:

Step 1: What's in the picture?

Look at the picture carefully, then choose one of these methods for describing it:

1) Start with the *main subject*, i.e. the dominant *foreground*, and describe it in detail. Then describe the *background*. This is a good method for a picture with one dominant image, e.g. a portrait, a seascape with one boat, a landscape with one castle, etc. The photo on p. 201 could be looked at in this way.

2) Start at the left of the picture and work across to the right. This is a good method for a picture where there is no marked difference between foreground and background or where there is a lot of activity (e.g 'Liberation' on p. 125)

3) Start at the top of the picture and work down to the bottom, or vice versa. This method is good for pictures with no marked difference between foreground and background, and for pictures where the interest tails off towards the top or bottom. 'The Lake at Petworth' on p. 76 could be looked at in this way.

➤ Note Making (p. 243)

When you have decided on your method, use it to make notes about the picture. Be sure that you show how the picture is structured.

Step 2: What techniques did the painter or photographer use?
Make notes on a few key technical features:
- *The artist used oils / water colours / light brush strokes / ...*
- *The photographer used colour / soft focus / slow film ...*

Analysing a picture:
Step 1: What can you find out about the context?
- Find out when the picture was created and see if the historical and social background gives you a better understanding of the picture.
- Find out if a person or company asked the artist or photographer to make (i.e. commissioned) the picture for them.
- Is there anything in the artist's or photographer's biography that might help you understand the picture?

Step 2: What do you think the artist was trying to say, and how did he or she say it? Was the artist or photographer trying to make a point? Answering this could help you to understand the message, if there is one.
- *I think the artist's/photographer's use of ... was intended to create ... / was aimed at making ... / conveys ...*
- *The dominance of ... / The way the light/shadows ... directs the viewer's attention to ...*
- *Because the foreground/background is ..., the impression given is that ...*

Step 3: What effect does the picture have on you?
Once you have looked carefully at all aspects of the picture, reflect on the effect the picture has on you, and be honest about your feelings.
- *Because of ..., the picture touches me .../ leaves me unmoved/cold/....*
- *I think the ... is a symbol of ...*
- *The ... helps to create a ... atmosphere, which forces you to / has the effect of ...*

Points to remember:
- *Describe the picture systematically* so that you do not leave out anything important. Do not jump around when describing the picture.
- Ask yourself the following questions when analysing a picture:
  What does it say?
  How does it say it? Or: *What effect does it have on the viewer?*
  What does it mean? Or: *Why was it made?*

Working with Cartoons

Cartoons are humorous or satirical drawings that often deal with a topical event. There are various ways of approaching a cartoon in order to understand the point it is making. In many ways the process of describing and analysing a cartoon is similar to that of describing a picture.

➤ Working with Pictures (p. 223)

Describing a cartoon:

Step 1: Name the source if you can.
Knowing the source of the cartoon (e.g. the newspaper or magazine in which it appears) can be helpful, as a conservative paper is more likely to be critical of a socialist politician than a liberal paper, and vice versa.

Step 2: Say who or what it is about or deals with (its theme or subject).
If the cartoon is a caricature of a well-known person, it is important to *say who it is.*
– *The cartoon shows the US president as a cowboy who …*

Step 3: Describe the important details in the cartoon.
You should only describe *details which contribute to the message of the cartoon*; they must represent something related to the central topic. Often they are symbols standing for something else.
– *The prime minister is wearing a crown, which is meant to show that he …*

➤ Glossary: Symbol (p. 268)

Step 4: Examine the words printed in the cartoon. Read the *labels, speech bubbles* or *captions* and make sure you understand them.

thought bubble ('speech bubble' – when the characters are talking)

caption **Justice vs Microsoft**

label

Analysing a cartoon:

Step 1: A cartoon is usually topical, so you will need to say *what it refers to*:
– *The cartoon has to do with the recent discussion of …*

Step 2: Are the figures presented in a positive or negative light? Be sure to say how this is done.

Step 3: Examine whether the cartoon uses irony, and if it does, what effect this has.

➤ Glossary: Irony (p. 269)

Step 4: Explain the *point* the cartoonist is trying to make by examining the source, the caption, speech bubbles and the picture together.

Points to remember:

- Cartoons are often critical of real people, current events or trends. It is important to recognize and identify them.
- Read all the words in a cartoon carefully, and examine all the symbols and be prepared to explain them.
- Be careful when trying to interpret the message of a cartoon, as it may be ironic.

Working with Numbers

Numbers can be presented in many different ways. It is important to examine whether the way you or someone else presents numbers leads to a clear and proper understanding of the numbers or whether the presentation (even if it is truthful) conveys a false impression.

Types of presentation:

There are various types of tables, graphs and charts. Which one you choose depends on what you are trying to show:

1990	2000
5	7,5
10	7,5

table

- Table

A table is an ordered and labeled list which can be used to present any kind of numbers. It is useful for giving 'raw' data but not for quick and easy orientation.

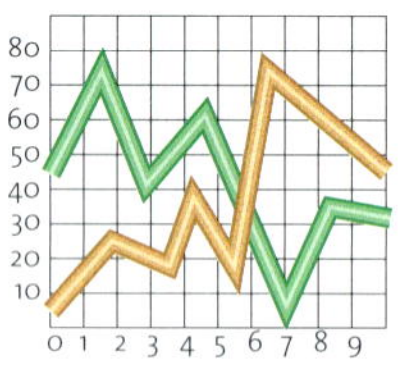

line graph

- Line graph

A line graph is mostly used to show the development of something over a period of time. It shows tendencies or trends very clearly, and it can be used to compare two or more different developments.

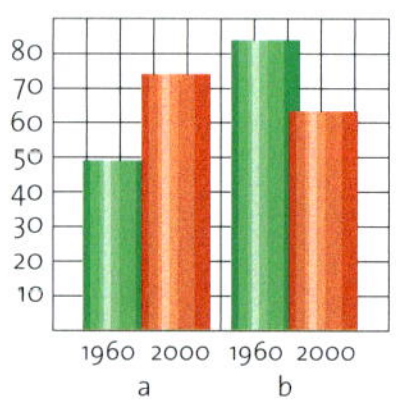

bar chart

- Bar chart

A bar chart is used to compare the amounts, quantities, sizes, etc. of two or more different things. It can also be used to show change from one point in time to another.

pie chart

- Pie chart

A pie chart consists of a circle (pie) divided into different sections/sectors/segments that represent parts of a whole – usually in the form of percentages. (Two or more pie charts are needed to show changes over time.)

Analysing how numbers are presented:

Step 1: When looking at numbers in any form, always consider their *source*: How reliable might the statistics be? Are the numbers up-to-date?

Step 2: Examine *how the numbers are presented*. Consider why the numbers were presented as a table or as a chart.

Step 3: Study the statistics and read all the information about a chart carefully. Are the numbers you see *absolute numbers* (e.g. 52.7 million) or *percentages* (e.g. 52%)? The title or the legend (i.e. the information next to the graph) will usually tell you this.

Step 4: When looking at visual presentations of numbers, check whether the numbers themselves have been given and verify that *they have been visualized accurately*: Are the amounts and time periods all the same size, or do they differ so that they are no longer trustworthy? Are proportions represented accurately? Be careful: visual impressions are often more powerful than numbers alone. Also check that the numbers have not been rounded up or down so much that they are meaningless.

Step 5: If conclusions are drawn from statistics, think carefully: Is the conclusion given really what the numbers suggest? Are there other possible interpretations?

Presenting numbers:

Step 1: Decide what form of presentation serves your purpose best: Do you want your audience to have access to exact figures? Then a table might be best. Or should they have a quick overview of your figures? Then some form of graph or chart is probably best.

Step 2: Explain briefly what the table or chart shows: topic, period of time covered, whether the figures represent absolute numbers or percentages, the source.

Step 3: Describe the relevant parts of your table or chart:
- relationships between numbers: *the vast majority of ...; a mere third of ...; over half of ...*
- changes over time: *a huge increase/decrease; a small/slight rise/dip; a sudden reversal; a brief recovery; experienced an increase / a drop in ...; showed steady growth; remained constant; ...*
- extremes (peaks, low points): *an all-time high/low; reached a peak of ...; ...*

Step 4: State what conclusions can be drawn from your numbers, and explain any background that might help your audience to understand them.

Points to remember:

- Choose the *form in which you present numbers* according to the kind of numbers you want to show.
- Use *reliable sources* for your information.
- Reach conclusions based on numbers carefully. Watch out for manipulation.
- Present numbers in *an easily understandable form* and explain clearly to your audience what the numbers show.
- Always be *sceptical* of statistics – remember these old sayings:
  - 'There are three kinds of lies: lies, damned lies and statistics.'
  - 'Never trust statistics unless you've manipulated them yourself.'

'That's the gist of what I want to say. Now get me some statistics to base it on.'

Viewing Skills

When you watch a film, video, documentary, etc., it is important to know how to extract information and analyse characters, the plot, camera work, etc. in order to understand what effect they have on the audience.

Developing viewing skills

Step 1: Preparation.
Prepare yourself for the viewing, i.e. talk/think about your expectations of what you are going to see, and collect words and phrases that might be useful.

Step 2: Watch for gist.
Watch the film or segment for gist, i.e. do not worry if you do not understand every word or cannot remember every scene.

Step 3: Use a viewing log.
Prepare a viewing log to help you to focus on the following aspects of content and film technique:
- storyline (Who?/What?/When?/Where? questions should help you here.)
- camera work (Words and phrases from the mini glossary below will help you.)
- editing (Cf. the mini glossary below.)

Watch the film segment again, then fill in a log like the one below. A viewing log will help you to talk about most aspects of a film or film segment.

scene	Who?	What?	When?	Where?	camera work	comments
2:30-3:30 mins	family	walking	daytime winter	park	establishing shot: long shot, then the camera zooms in on the family	why are they all smiling so much?

Step 4: Watch again for anything you have left out.
If you find out that you have neglected a component of the film, view it again, concentrating on that one component.

Film viewing – mini glossary:

Camera work – static shots:

1

2

3

4

long shot 1	A view of a situation from a distance. This gives an overall impression of the setting.
medium shot 2	A shot which shows one or two people from waist up. This allows the viewer to get an idea of the interaction between the characters.
close-up 3	A full screen shot of one person's face or one object. This allows the viewer to see clearly the emotions a character is experiencing or to consider the role of the object that is shown.
establishing shot	A long shot which is usually taken at the start of a scene, showing the location or setting for the scene to come.
point-of-view shot	A shot taken from the point of view of one character. This allows us to view the scene through the eyes of the character.
high-angle 4 / low-angle 5 shot	A shot which either looks down on or up at the subject (a person, a building, etc.).

Useful phrases:
The director uses a long shot of the scene so the viewer can see the group and the setting ...
There is a medium shot of the two characters so the viewer can see ...
The viewer sees the character in close-up / there is a close-up of the character ...
The establishing shot of the film shows ...
This scene is shot from X's point of view.
The director uses a high-angle shot of ... in order to ...

Camera work – moving shots:

pan shot **6**	A shot where the camera moves horizontally (pans) – left to right or right to left – from a static position
tilt shot **7**	A shot where the camera moves up or down (tilts) from a static position.
tracking shot **8**	A shot where the camera moves along tracks beside, behind or in front of a moving person or object.
zoom	A shot from a stationary camera in which the lens achieves the effect of moving towards (zoom in) or away from (zoom out) the subject.

Useful phrases:
The camera pans from left to right / tilts up/down ...
We first see X as the camera tilts from ... to ...
There is a tracking shot in this scene as the camera follows ...
The camera zooms in on ... in order to show ...
The camera zooms out to reveal ...

Editing terms:

cut	The point at which one shot changes (cuts) directly to another.
cross-cutting	The process of cutting several times directly between two different scenes.
jump cut	An abrupt and unexpected cut from one shot to another where, for example, an element of time or space has been left out.
fade-in/out	The gradual appearance (fade-in) or disappearance (fade-out) of a shot – usually at the beginning or end of a scene.
dissolve	Also known as 'cross-fade', this form of film editing brings the incoming shot (the fade-up) in under the outgoing shot (the fade-out) so that the images 'dissolve' into each other.

Useful phrases:
The director makes use of a lot of cuts in this scene ...
Cross-cutting is used to show X approaching the house, while Y is still asleep.
The scene gradually fades in to show ...
The director uses a fade-in in order to ...
The use of a dissolve between these two scenes makes the connection stronger / produces a ... effect ...

5

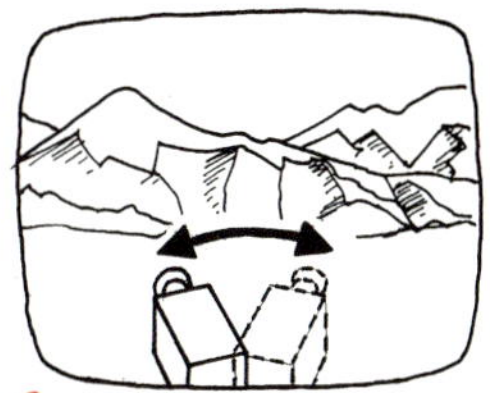
6

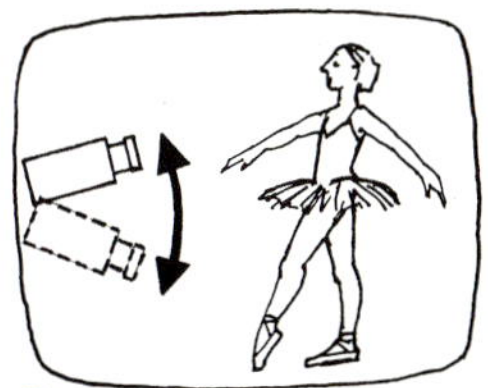
7

8

Doing Research

➤ Doing Research on the Internet (p. 231)

The first step in preparing a report, project or presentation is to do research in order to find good, solid information on which to base the report, etc.

How to proceed:

Step 1: Before starting your research, be clear exactly what it is you need to know. Formulate in one sentence what it is you are researching and then make lists of *key words* to search for; be as specific as possible.

Step 2: Use (where possible) only *sources in English*, as this will help you find useful vocabulary.

Step 3: Start with general *works of reference* such as encyclopedias to get an overview of your topic before you consult *specialized sources*.

Step 4: Examine the point of view of your source of information and decide how reliable, valid, objective or useful the information is. Obviously, it is best to use *reliable sources*. In order to find out how reliable the source is, it is always wise to look for more information about the writer or use various sources to check the information you have.

➤ Skimming (p. 236)
➤ Scanning (p. 236)

Step 5: *Skim* articles before reading them to find out whether they are relevant. If only parts of the article seem relevant, *scan* the article to find those parts quickly.

➤ Note Making (p. 243)
➤ Quoting (p. 232)

Step 6: Make thorough *notes*. Be sure to list your sources, especially when you might want to use information word for word. Use index cards.

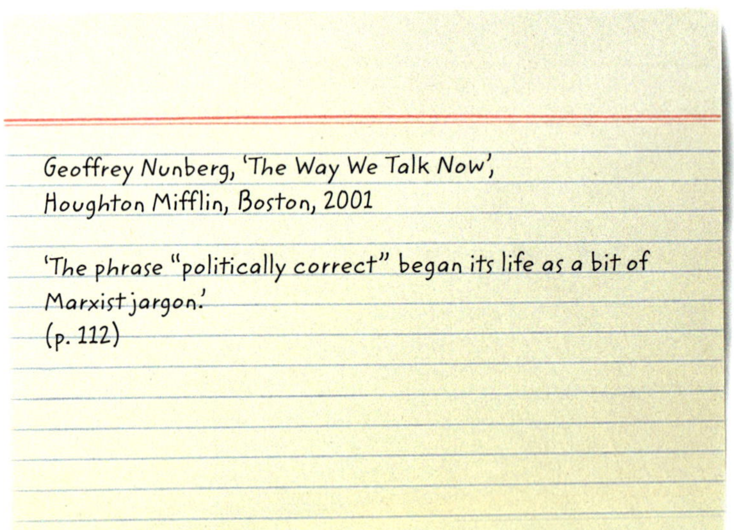

Doing Research on the Internet

➤ Doing Research (p. 230)

The Internet is a good source of information when preparing a project, essay or talk, but it is important to know how to find and retrieve the precise information you want.

How to proceed:

Step 1: Before starting your research, formulate in one sentence what it is you are researching and then make lists of *key words* to search for; be as specific as possible.

Step 2: Start your Internet research by consulting general works of reference, e.g. *online encyclopedias,* to get an overview of your topic.

Step 3: Use (or look for) a good and reliable *search engine*. Use all its features to find more material on your topic. Always type in as many words as possible related to the topic you are researching. For example, if you are looking for information about the Eden Project (cf. p. 84) type in the words 'Eden', 'Project' and 'Cornwall'.
If you do not find any useful information, try another search engine.

Eden Project - Welcome to the Eden Project...
Based in **Cornwall**, England. The **Eden Project** takes a fresh look at our world and our place in it, explores positive futures and shows what can be achieved when people work together. ...
Description: Ecological **project**, growing tropical and temperate plants in giant biomes. Information for visitors...
Category: Science > Institutions > Botanical Gardens and Arboreta
www.edenproject.com/ - 35k - 17 Mar 2003 - Cached - Similar pages

Keith's **Eden Project** site, Virtual Visit Latest Information
Keith's **Eden Project** web site, giving latest information, and photos, and tips when to visit and where to stay, by a local person. ... The **Eden Project Cornwall**. ...
www.eden-project.co.uk/ - 42k - 17 Mar 2003 - Cached - Similar pages

Organization responsible for the website. Which of the two is more likely to provide you with the information you need?

contents showing how the words (in bold [= *fett*] print) occur on the website

other websites that might be interesting to check out

Step 4: Use (where possible) only *articles and sources that are in English*.

Step 5: Use only *reliable sources*. The Internet is not a particularly reliable source of information, as anybody can set up a website and offer material and information. For this reason check who (e.g. a corporation, an institution, company, government or private person) is responsible for the contents of the website.

Step 6: *Skim* articles before reading them to find out whether they are relevant. If only parts of the article seem relevant, *scan* the article to find those parts quickly.

➤ Skimming (p. 236)
➤ Scanning (p. 236)

Step 7: Make thorough *notes*. Be sure to list your sources if:

➤ Note Making (p. 243)

a) you want to return to that site
b) you want to *quote* directly from the information on that site.

➤ Quoting (p. 232)

Quoting

When writing a text or giving a talk, it is important to cite original material from either primary literature (e.g. a short story that you are writing about) or secondary literature (e.g. somebody's opinion about or analysis of the short story). This shows your reader or listener that you have researched your topic well and that you are able to support your arguments. It is vital that you know how to quote correctly and know how to give the source from which you have quoted.

Introducing a quote:

- Try to work quotations into your own sentences as smoothly as possible.
- If you wish to say directly that you are using someone else's ideas, try to vary your introductory phrases and use proper punctuation, e.g.:
  - *According to Cahal Milmo, 'British teenagers of both sexes are ...'*
  - *The article goes on to say that more and more boys 'were also found to be ...'.*
  - *'It is disappointing,' Steve Bloomfield is quoted as saying, 'that ...'.*
- In writing, you can skip introductory phrases and name the source of your quote (cf. 'Citing sources' below) in a different way, e.g.:
  - *The problem discussed in the article is that teenagers are becoming 'increasingly fixated with their weight' (Milmo 2000).*
- When giving a talk, you can show your audience that you are using a quotation, e.g.:
  - directly, e.g.: *Cahal Milmo says in the article, and I quote, 'British teenagers of both sexes are increasingly fixated with their weight', end of quote.*
  - or indirectly. This is usually done by pausing briefly before reading out the quote.

Deleting from or adding to a quote:

- In general, quotes must be given *exactly as they appeared in the original text*. If it is necessary to shorten or expand on a quote, this must be clearly shown.
- If it is necessary to leave out part of a quote, this is shown by using ellipsis (often in square brackets): [...], e.g.
  - *Steve Bloomfield describes it as 'disappointing that the figures [...] should be so high'.*
- If part of a quote is unclear, you can add an explanation in square brackets, e.g.
  - *Some of the girls in the study were skipping meals 'despite the fact that fewer than one in eight females of that age [14 to 15] is clinically overweight' (Milmo 2000).*

Citing sources:

- When using someone else's words, you must *use quotation marks* and *state where the quote comes from*.
- In an essay on a literary text, it is usually enough to give the page and line numbers for your quote.
  For secondary literature, it is customary to *cite the source* both in the body of your essay (as a short reference in brackets or in footnotes) and in a bibliography.

- There are many different *conventions for proper citation*. One standard convention for printed sources is to put these items in the following order:
  author, title of text, publication, publisher, place published, year, e.g.
  – Nadia Wheatley, 'Land/scape', *The Night Tolkien Died*, Random House, Sydney, 1994
  For electronic sources, you should give the address of the website and date on which the material was put online or the date when you checked the information (as online sites rarely indicate when information was put online):
  – www.envirozine.org/article/3245.htm · 23.8.2003
  Your teacher may use a different convention, so check with him or her beforehand.

Points to remember:

- Quotes can *add authority* to a talk or paper, but *use them sparingly* and only *use short passages* that are particularly interesting or well-formulated. Too many quotes may confuse your readers or listeners, and it might look as if you have no original ideas.
- Quotes should fit into your words smoothly but be *clearly indicated* as someone else's thoughts.
- Any change you have to make to a quote must be clearly marked and must not change the meaning of the quote.

Dealing with Unknown Words

It is important for you to learn techniques to work out the meanings of unknown words in a foreign language when reading or listening so that you can understand the main point of a text or conversation.

Various techniques for dealing with unknown words:

- When reading a long, difficult text, whether for pleasure or for school or work, *you do not need to understand every word*. Make the effort only if a word seems to be central to the understanding of the text.

- Use *similarities* the unknown word may have with other words you already know to work out its meaning:
  – from the same word family in English (e.g. 'aggressor' from 'aggressive');
  – from an English stem you know with prefixes (e.g. *un-*, *de-*, *pre-*) or suffixes (e.g. *-less*, *-able or -ible*, *-ion*);
  – from your own language (e.g. 'initial' from German *Initialen*) or another language (e.g. 'embellishment' from French *belle*).

- Use the *context*:
  – It will help you to narrow down your search by telling you what word class (e.g. a noun, verb or adjective) you are looking for.
  – The sense of what it says around the unknown word will narrow your search down further. Often you will find that only one meaning really 'fits'.

- Use your *dictionary* only if you cannot work out the meaning by other means.

Using a Monolingual Dictionary

A monolingual dictionary is a useful tool to find out the meaning or pronunciation of words, to improve your vocabulary and to understand how to use a word in a sentence. A monolingual dictionary will also give you information about grammar and idioms.

How to proceed:

General

- Familiarize yourself with everything your dictionary has to offer. Besides vocabulary help, learner's dictionaries often give grammatical advice, collections of words in word families, pronunciation help with names, etc.
- Look at the words around the word you are looking up in order to expand your vocabulary to include entire *word families*.
- Study the full entry, especially the *example sentences*, to learn what words can be combined with the word you are looking up.

More information about the types of noun, verb grammar codes, etc. can be found on the Study Pages of the dictionary.

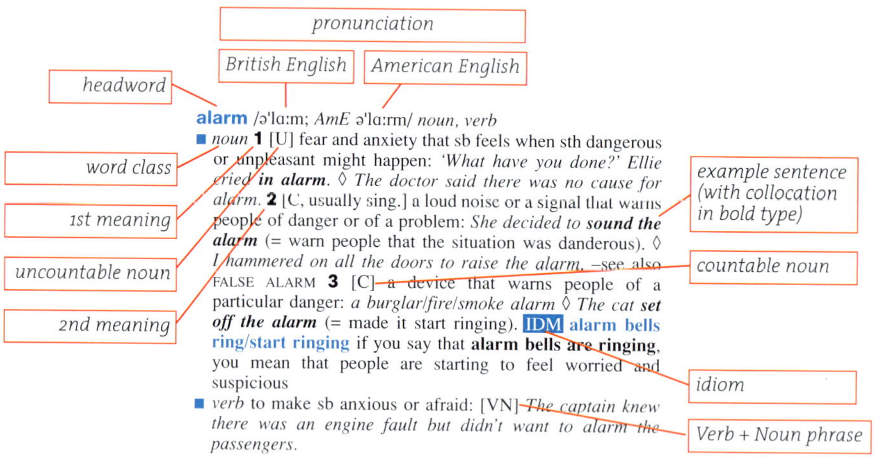

Reading

➤ Dealing with Unknown Words (p. 233)

When you are *reading*, only look up words if they are important to help you understand a text and you cannot work out their meanings in another way.

Pronunciation

In order to *check the pronunciation of a word*, you must understand the phonetic symbols. These are always explained in the dictionary, with examples of the sounds used with vocabulary you already know. Say the word you are checking out loud.

Writing

- Use your dictionary to check that you have *spelled difficult words correctly*.
- Find out *how a word is used* (e.g. in which context, what preposition goes with it, typical idioms and example sentences, etc.) so that the word is part of a well-constructed sentence.
- When you look up a word, do not just look for the definition you need – look at the *grammatical help* given (usually abbreviations or symbols). This will help you to use the word properly by telling you, for example, if a noun is countable or uncountable, a verb transitive or intransitive, etc.

Using a Grammar Book

To improve the correctness of your English, you have to know how to use a grammar book; this involves understanding how a grammar book is structured so that you can find the information you need quickly and efficiently.

How to proceed:

Step 1: Familiarize yourself with your grammar book. Find the most important parts (*table of contents*, *list of grammar terms*, and, above all, the *index* at the back of the book) and try to understand how they are organized.

Step 2: Read the tips on how to use the grammar book. These will tell you what features your grammar book has, e.g. what the symbols mean, what the different colours indicate, how bold (= *fett*) and italic (= *kursiv*) print are used.

Step 3: Try to learn the correct grammatical terms. If you are not certain of the right term, look at the table of contents and look for the terms in the appropriate section.

Step 4: To revise a problem area check the section of the grammar book that deals with it. If you want to check a specific point quickly, it is usually best to use the index to find the sections of the grammar book that deal with that point.

Step 5: Always *read rules together with the examples* which are given. Watch for hints about frequent mistakes or exceptions, often indicated with a warning triangle (⚠).

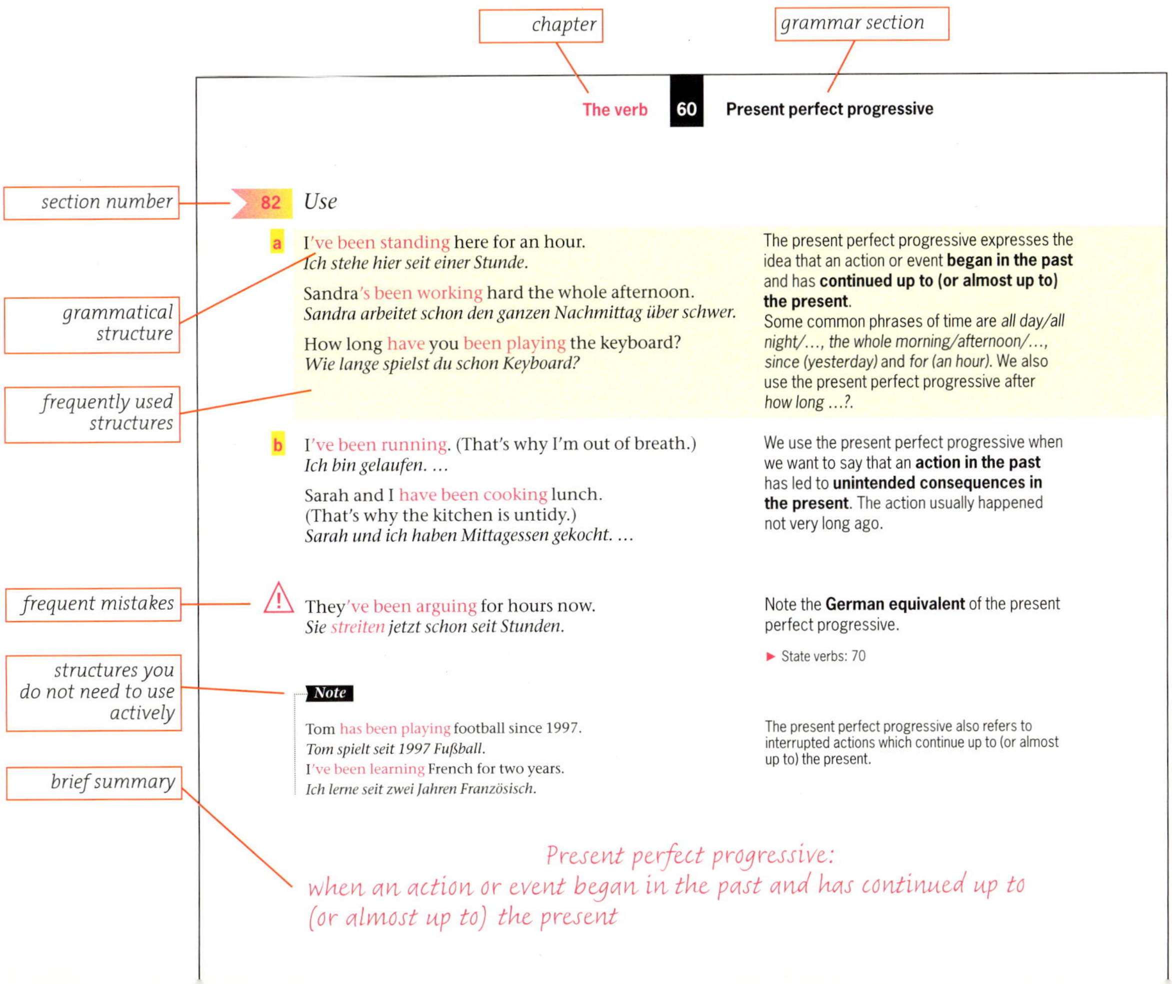

The verb **60** **Present perfect progressive**

82 *Use*

a I've been standing here for an hour.
Ich stehe hier seit einer Stunde.

Sandra's been working hard the whole afternoon.
Sandra arbeitet schon den ganzen Nachmittag über schwer.

How long have you been playing the keyboard?
Wie lange spielst du schon Keyboard?

The present perfect progressive expresses the idea that an action or event **began in the past** and has **continued up to (or almost up to) the present**.
Some common phrases of time are *all day/all night/…, the whole morning/afternoon/…, since (yesterday)* and *for (an hour)*. We also use the present perfect progressive after *how long …?*.

b I've been running. (That's why I'm out of breath.)
Ich bin gelaufen. …

Sarah and I have been cooking lunch.
(That's why the kitchen is untidy.)
Sarah und ich haben Mittagessen gekocht. …

We use the present perfect progressive when we want to say that an **action in the past** has led to **unintended consequences in the present**. The action usually happened not very long ago.

⚠ They've been arguing for hours now.
Sie streiten jetzt schon seit Stunden.

Note the **German equivalent** of the present perfect progressive.

▶ State verbs: 70

Note

Tom has been playing football since 1997.
Tom spielt seit 1997 Fußball.
I've been learning French for two years.
Ich lerne seit zwei Jahren Französisch.

The present perfect progressive also refers to interrupted actions which continue up to (or almost up to) the present.

Present perfect progressive:
when an action or event began in the past and has continued up to (or almost up to) the present

Reading Skills

Skimming

Skimming is the first step in reading a long text. When you skim a text, you look at it quickly and use any clues you can find to get an idea of what the text is about. Skimming a text will make it easier to understand when you read it in detail or, if the information is not relevant to your subject, will help you to decide quickly that the text can be struck off your list of sources.

How to proceed:

Step 1: Look first at *the title, the words in bold print, pictures and their captions*.

Step 2: Then look at the *first and last sentences* of each paragraph – one is usually the *topic sentence* (i.e the sentence that shows what aspect is being dealt with).

Step 3: *Do not read every sentence in detail*, run your eyes over the whole text and look for words that seem important. It may help to underline them.

- Skim the article on p. 237. Say in one sentence what it is about.

Scanning

➤ Skimming (p. 236)

A technique for finding specific information in a longer text. Use scanning to locate parts of a longer text that are relevant to you. ⚠ Do not confuse it with skimming.

How to proceed:

Step 1: Choose a *key word* or *key phrase* that will lead you to passages of a text that will be relevant to your purpose.

Step 2: Make a *mental picture* of the key word or phrase as it would appear on the page.

Step 3: Keeping your mental picture in mind, *move your eyes quickly* over the printed text. (You can use your finger to guide your eyes.) The word(s) that correspond to your mental picture will 'jump out at you'.

Step 4: After you have located relevant passages, read them for the information you need. You may have to *scan again* with the same keyword(s) or with new ones.

- Scan the article on p. 237. What are the keywords that tell you what is about?

Reading Non-fiction

When you read factual texts, you should have a set of methods to help you understand and remember better what you have to or want to read. These techniques are useful whenever you have to absorb a lot of information from non-fictional texts such as newspaper articles, articles from encyclopedias, extracts from non-fictional books, etc.

How to proceed:

Step 1: *Skim the text* to find out quickly what the text is about, whether you are interested in its topic or whether it is relevant to your research, e.g. for a presentation or an essay. In addition, it might help to write down a couple of sentences, e.g. in the text 'Sowing the Seeds of a Better Future' below, you could write the following:

➤ Skimming (p. 236)

- *It seems to be about genetic engineering and genetic modification.*
- *It mentions a Chinese institute and the decoding of the rice genome.*
- *It talks about the importance of certain crops.*

Sowing the seeds of a better future

Ignore the doubters. GM crops can help to feed the world.

Johnjoe McFadden

Only four years ago, the Beijing Genomics Institute was an empty brick building. But through the dynamism of its director, geneticist Yang Huanming, and with seed money from the state, Yang's hometown municipal government, and even loans from employees, family and friends, it became a world-class research institute. Soon, several hundred employees were working two 12-hour shifts to keep the sequencing machines running 24 hours a day. With little more than ping-pong to distract them from decoding the rice genome, science in the developing world took on multinational biotechnology, and won.

But the rice genome is far more than a David versus Goliath story. More than a billion people live on less than $1 a day and that usually buys rice. The crop is prone to many diseases and much of it ends up in the belly of an insect. An outbreak of brown plant-hoppers disease cost Java 70% of its rice crop in the 1970s. Climate change is a major worry in marginal lands. Droughts brought by the 1997-98 El Niño inflicted losses across Asia.

Genetic engineering to generate varieties resistant to disease, pests, drought or salinity could revolutionise third world farming. The release of the sequence will help researchers eager to improve crop yields.

Many aid organisations – often influenced by western green campaigns – say GM technology does little to address the real causes of world poverty and hunger. They said the same decades ago when famine was predicted to follow population explosion. The population explosion materialised but the famine didn't. While others argued for social reform, pioneering plant breeders, such as Norman Borlaug, developed high-yielding varieties of maize, wheat and rice. Global harvests soared and have continued to rise at a rate of 2% per year. The green revolution saved millions from starvation, but is grinding to a halt as plant breeders run out of natural genetic variation. To keep pace with population growth, breeders need to tinker with genes. That is why China spent $100m on GM technology in 1999.

(From: *The Guardian*, 24 April, 2002)

Step 2: *Examine the structure* of the text to see how the information is presented. Look at the layout: paragraphs (often with sub-headings) usually deal with different aspects of the topic. Scan the text for adverbs, connectors or conjunctions (e.g. 'only', 'but while', 'that is why', 'while ...') the writer uses to structure his or her arguments.

➤ Note Making (p. 243)

Step 3: *Extract information* by reading the text carefully and slowly. Look up any words you do not know or understand (but remember you can guess the meaning of a lot of words). Underline or copy out key words and expressions, e.g.

- *a world-class research institute*
- *decoding the rice genome*
- *more than a billion people live on ... rice*
- *the crop [rice] is prone to many diseases*

➤ Writing Outlines (p. 244)

➤ Mind Mapping (p. 222)

Step 4: *Organize your information* in a way that will help you to remember it. Look at what you have underlined or at the notes you have made. Can the information be structured or organized? Make headings – perhaps on index cards – and put key words and expressions under the appropriate headings (headings often correspond to the paragraphs in the text), or make a mind map. Now read through your information again – is anything missing; do you need to go back to the text for further details?

The Beijing Genetics Institute
- Now a world-class institute
- Decoded the rice genome

The importance of rice
- more than a billion people ...
- it is prone to diseases

➤ Giving a Talk or Presentation (p. 254)

Step 5: *Present your information* to inform others. You should now be able to use your notes to summarize the text, to talk about it or to include the information you have gained in an essay or talk.

- *This text deals with ...*
- *The writer puts forward the view /points out that ...*

Step 6: *React to the text* with your own opinion. State what your opinion on the topic was before you read the text. Explain whether the text has confirmed your opinion, made you rethink the issue or even changed your mind.

- *I always thought/believed/felt that ...*
- *I was unaware of the fact that ...*
- *It is worth considering that ...*

➤ Glossary: Narrative Prose (p. 255)

Reading Narrative Prose

Narrative prose is a fictional text in which an author presents actions, setting and characters in some kind of order. It is the reader's job to understand the 'signs' the author gives and to re-construct the meaning and the intention of the text.

➤ Glossary: Narrator and Point of View (p. 258)

The point of view (also called 'the narrative perspective')

It is important to find out which *perspective* or *point of view* the story is told from, but note that this may change during a story.

- The narrator may speak in the *first person*, as someone who is in some way involved in the events.
- The narrative may be presented in the *third person* by:
  a) an *omniscient narrator*, i.e. someone who seems to know everything about all the characters and the events; in this case we speak of an *unlimited point of view*
  b) someone who shows the events through the eyes of one or more of the characters; in this case we speak of a *limited point of view*.

- The narrative may give insights into what is going on in the characters' minds.
- The narrator may comment on the fact that he or she is telling a story.

Action and plot

➤ Glossary: Action and Plot (p. 261)

The story is presented as a set of events (the action) connected by cause and effect; this is called the plot. The structure of the plot creates *suspense*.
- The story may develop from start to finish in a *chronological order*, or involve two *interconnected stories* which take place on different levels of time, etc.
- The development of the story will be influenced by events. Examine which events are important for the development of the story.
- The story may have a *climax* and/or *turning point*. Analyse how these are achieved.
- The story may have an *open ending*, or a *surprise ending* or a *denouement/solution*. Explain what effect the ending has.

Characterization

➤ Glossary: Character and Characterization (p. 260)

The characters provide interest in a story.
- They can be complex (*round characters*), or presented through one or two characteristic features only (*flat characters*). If they are the former, they will probably develop in the course of a story; if the latter they may remain static.
- How much the narrator reveals about a character influences the reader's view of the character. It is noticeable that even unpleasant protagonists can win the sympathy of the reader.
- The characters may be presented through *explicit* or *implicit characterization* (cf. 'Telling and showing', below).

Telling and showing

➤ Glossary: Mode of Presentation (p. 259)

An author may present characters, setting, action and events either by *telling* about them or by *showing* them. Usually both these techniques are used in narrative fiction.
- If there are passages or direct comments from the narrator or other characters which present and describe the setting, etc. or the external features and internal qualities of the characters, we speak of 'telling'.
- If we learn about the characters by what they say, their actions and reactions, we speak of 'showing'.

Analysing fiction

Step 1: Make notes on all the points above while reading a fictional text.

Step 2: Make it clear that you are analysing a text and not talking about real life. Use expressions like:
- *The story is about ...*
- *In his short story / the text from ... the author deals with the theme/topic of ...*
- *Events/Characters are presented in a way / so that ...*
- *The author wants to convey ...*

Step 3: Never just name the narrative point of view or stylistic devices, but comment on the effect they have on the reader. Some helpful phrases could be:

➤ Glossary: Narrator and Point of View (p. 258), Stylistic Devices (pp. 267ff.)

- *The first-person narrator helps the reader to identify with him/her because (of) ...*
- *The author chose the perspective of the omniscient narrator in order to ...*

- *As the third-person narrator has a limited perspective, the reader must ...*
- *The open ending shows that ... / is intended to ...*

Step 4: Whatever opinion you are expressing, always give evidence from the text to support it:
- *X's behaviour when ... reveals that he/she is ...*
- *X's reactions to ... give the reader the impression that he/she is / seems to be ...*

➤ Glossary: Drama (p. 257)

⚠ **Trouble spot**
The *setting* is the time and place in which a novel or play is set.
The *set* in a drama is the scenery on the stage.

Reading/Watching Drama

A play is a fictional text in which a playwright presents actions, setting and characters to be performed in front of an audience. What looks like 'normal behaviour' or 'normal dialogue' is, in fact, planned. Moreover, plays are written to be performed, so when reading drama it is important to take this into consideration and to try and picture the stage, the characters and how they play their roles, and how the audience is involved.

Acts and scenes

- A play is normally divided into *acts* and *scenes*, except in the case of short one-act plays.
- These divisions usually correspond to changes in action, time, and/or place.

Language and dramatic dialogue

- The language usually mirrors the social status of the character(s) and may or may not be close to normal, everyday conversation. If not, it is worth considering what the playwright's intention is.
- The dialogue can be used to a) move the action forward, b) give information about the characters, which would otherwise remain unknown to the audience, c) describe the setting (when this is not clear from the set).

Stage directions

- Stage directions are useful when reading a play, as they give information about the playwright's intentions and how he or she imagined the setting, characters, etc.
- The stage directions may include special effects, such as sound and lighting, which may, for example, heighten the dramatic effect or influence the atmosphere.

The audience/reader

- It is important to ask whether anything has been left to the audience's/reader's imagination.
- There are situations in which the audience/reader knows more than a character in the play. The character's words may then have a different meaning for the audience than for the character. This is called *dramatic irony*. It often gets the audience/reader more involved, as they can sympathize with the unsuspecting character(s)

Analysing drama

Step 1: When analysing a play or an extract from a play, make it clear you are not talking about real life. Some helpful expressions could be
- *In his/her play the playwright is concerned with the topic/issue/subject of ...*
- *He/She has divided his/her play into ... acts, which correspond to ...*
- *The development of the action corresponds with the play's division into acts and scenes.*
- *He/She makes the social differences between the characters clear by ...*

Step 2: Do not just say what the play is about, but what the author's intention is, e.g.
- *In the play a conflict develops between ...and ..., who could be seen as representing / standing for ...*
- *The play has an open ending, which demonstrates that the playwright did not want to present solutions to the problems/conflicts.*

Step 3: When describing the characters remember to look not only at what they themselves say, but also how they are presented in the stage directions and what other characters say about them:
- *Although Y is described as a friendly character, the way he/she behaves towards Z shows us that ...*
- *Although he is described as being ..., Y's language reveals him/her to be ...*

Reading Poetry

➤ Glossary: Poetry (p. 256)

A poem is a piece of writing structured by lines and rhythm. Interpreting poetry means identifying the theme, the speaker, the formal elements and the use of language, and showing how they contribute to the overall effect of the poem and how effective they are in conveying the message or meaning of the poem to the reader.

Interpreting poetry

Step 1: Get a general understanding by reading the poem two or three times, or until you feel you have grasped it. It is often a good idea to read it out loud. Then state:
- what sort of poem it is. It may be descriptive, it may tell a story or relate a problem;
- the event or situation presented in the poem;
- the theme or topic of the poem;
- who the speaker is (if there is one), and who (if anybody) he or she is addressing; remember that the speaker [the 'I'] in a poem may not be identical with the poet;
- the intention of the poem;
- how the title is linked to the poem:

Step 2: Consider how the poem is composed by examining:
- how many stanzas the poem has and whether they make up a traditional form (e.g. a sonnet);
- the rhythm and a rhyme scheme (if relevant);
- the effect of the rhythm, rhyme scheme and form;
- whether any unexpected changes in rhythm or rhyme underline the importance of a particular line or passage.

➤ Glossary: Rhyme (p. 256)

➤ Glossary: Style and Language (pp. 265ff.), Stylistic Devices (pp. 267ff.)

Step 3: Examine the *language* in the poem, by analysing:
- whether the language is *simple* or *more elevated*;
- whether there are any *repetitions* or *contrasts*, and what effect they have:
- the use of *imagery* (e.g. similes, metaphors, symbols, etc) and its effect.

Step 4: Organize your findings and work out an interpretation, which should have an introduction, a main body and a conclusion.

a) *Introduction:* this should contain the title of the poem and the poet's name, and the theme of the poem, e.g.
- *The poem X by (the poet) Y was written in ... and deals with ...*
- *In his/her poem (the poet) Y describes / thinks about ...*

b) In the *main body* you must explain how the poem conveys its message by analysing in detail the *form, structure and language* of the poem. However, do not just identify or name the various devices but explain how and why you think they are used, e.g.
- *The poem is made up / composed of / written in ... which follow the rhyme scheme ... . This creates an impression of regularity/monotony/...*
- *Line 4 runs on into line 5, which underlines the ... / makes the reader ...*
- *The pause in line 4 underlines the ... / makes the reader ...*
- *The poet ignores the traditions of / traditional metre and rhyme in order to ...*
- *The poet speaks to the reader directly/indirectly / as if ...*
- *The language is simple/elevated, which underlines the feeling of ...*
- *The imagery suggests/conveys ...*
- *The poem contains a great deal of imagery / figures of speech, for example, ... These are used to ...*

c) In your *conclusion*, state whether you think the poem is successful and/or effective, and if asked, how you personally react to the poem, e.g.
- *All in all, / In general the rhythm, rhyme scheme and use of imagery contribute to ...*
- *The contrast between the traditional form and simple language ...*
- *What I like/dislike about the poem is ...*

Writing Skills

Note Making

This skill is useful when you are trying to remember information you have read or heard or for organizing information before writing or making a presentation.

Various techniques for making notes

- Notes that you make are very individual – it is not necessary for anyone else to understand them. You should feel free to develop your own style of making notes.
- Always give your notes a *title* to show the topic and source. For a lecture, for example, you could write 'Effects of genetic engineering on the environment – Speaker: Richard Steger, 14 March'.
- *Write clearly*, as you may have to refer to notes you have made long after making them. If you cannot write clearly, e.g. during a presentation or lecture, rewrite your notes as soon as possible.
- Write only *key words*, not whole sentences.
- Use your own *abbreviations and symbols*, but not too many as you will not be able to remember what they mean.

Common abbreviations and symbols

and so on, et cetera	…, etc.	not	ô
approximately, about	~	not the same as	≠
becomes	→	the same as, equal to	=
between	bet.	with	w., w/
for example	e.g.	without	w/o
important	impt.; !		

- Be an *active listener or reader*. Listen or watch for signals that show the structure of what you are reading or hearing. Your notes should reflect that structure:
  - show that points belong together. You can draw lines or leave an empty line to separate things that do not belong together, or you can indent all the points that belong together under a heading.
  - use the margins to mark the most important information and to show, for example, which part of the notes is on the introduction to the lecture, which show the development of ideas, and which the conclusion.

Writing Outlines

An outline is a special, more formal kind of note making. Writing an outline is useful when you are examining the structure of a text; it should reflect completely the structure of the text under consideration. It is also useful to prepare an outline of a talk or presentation you are making. If you hand out an outline or put it on an OHP (overhead projector), your audience will be able to follow what you say more easily.

The structure of an outline:

- An outline is set up as a kind of hierarchy:

  Title
  I. Main idea 1
    A. Important fact
      1. Supporting fact
      2. Supporting fact
        a. Example
        b. Example
    B. Important fact
  II. Main idea 2
  ...

- All 'Main ideas' are of more or less equal importance, as are the 'important facts' etc.
- The 'Main ideas' often correspond to a section of the text, the 'Important facts' to individual paragraphs.
- There are two major kinds of outline: topic and sentence outlines. Whichever one you decide on, you must be consistent throughout.
  – *Topic outline:* Use only individual words (usually nouns) or short phrases.
  – *Sentence outline:* Use simple, but complete sentences.

The Stages of Writing

It is vital to know how to produce well thought-through, interesting and correctly written texts as efficiently as possible. The different stages of writing involve many other skills, including techniques for gathering and organizing ideas, doing research, using reference works and proofreading.

Planning your written work

No matter what you intend to write, you should plan it well before you actually start writing. These steps will help you:

Step 1: *Define your topic.* You should know exactly what it is you want or have to write about. Be clear in your mind what your purpose is: do you want to inform, persuade or entertain your readers?

➤ Mind Mapping (p. 222)

Step 2: *Brainstorm your topic.* Collect on paper every aspect of the topic that you can think of. Some people find that simple lists are enough, others prefer to use a mind

map. Do not try to elaborate on or to organize these ideas yet, and do not think about which ideas are good and which are not so good.
If you are planning to write on a topic you do not know much about, you will have to do some research at this point to find out about different aspects of your topic.

➤ Doing Research (p. 230)

Step 3: *Organize your ideas.* Decide on an order in which you wish to present your information or arguments. Use a mind map (marked with numbers) or an outline – whatever works best for you.

➤ Mind Mapping (p. 222), Writing Outlines (p. 244)

The first draft

Once you have a plan, you can start the actual writing process.
Step 1: *Do your research.* Use your plan to identify areas you need to know more about. Look specifically for them, trying not to waste time with irrelevant matters. Be prepared, however, to refine the plan you have made for your text if you discover new aspects of the topic that you had not considered before.

Step 2: *Organize your material/information.* If you have done any research, order your notes so that they correspond with your mind map or outline. At the same time, mark your mind map or outline to show where you found the background material.

Step 3: *Write a first, rough draft.* Following your mind map or outline, write what you want to say. Do not waste a lot of time trying to get every formulation right, and feel free to put in a German expression when you cannot think of the English. Leave lots of room to add things and make corrections later.

Step 4: *Finish your first proper draft.* Read what you have written and make your first improvements. Use your dictionary to find the right English expressions where you have written something in German. Write your text again clearly, again leaving room to make additions and add corrections later.

➤ Using a Monolingual Dictionary (p. 234)

Step 5: Check that you have used enough *connectors to link your ideas and sentences.*

➤ Linking Ideas (p. 246)

Step 6: *Do something else.* Set your work aside for a while and get your mind off it. You will have a fresh perspective on what you have written after you return to it.

The revision stage

Always allow time to rewrite what you have written. Depending on how complex your written work is, you may have to do more than one rewrite.
Step 1: *Read your work.* Read what you have written from beginning to end without making any changes. Afterwards, consider whether it is logical, whether it says what you want and whether everything is in the right order. Make any necessary changes.

Step 2: *Proofread your work.* Check the content, style, grammar, spelling and punctuation. Consider whether the sentence structure is clear and simple, whether you can cut out any wordiness and whether the ideas in your text develop from paragraph to paragraph. Also check that you have quoted correctly from the text.

➤ Proofreading (p. 247)

Step 3: If possible, *give your text to a classmate* to check through. Have him or her check the content, style, grammar, spelling and punctuation, and get him or her to tell you what he or she thinks of how your ideas are organized and presented.

Step 4: *Rewrite your piece.* Make a clean copy of your work.

Points to remember:

- Whenever you have to write something, allow time for planning and revision.
- Always have a clear idea of what you want to write.
- When you write a first draft, do not waste time trying to get everything right – you will rewrite what you have written at least once.
- When preparing your final draft, keep your readers in mind. Ask yourself whether your piece gives them everything you want them to know and whether it is understandable for someone who has not done the same amount of research as you

Linking Ideas

Whenever you have to organize and present ideas, whether they are your own or you are referring to a text or a talk written or given by someone else, they must be structured in a way that the reader or listener can follow them easily. This can be done by means of certain conjunctions (e.g. 'however') and adverbs (e.g. 'probably'), which are called 'connectors', 'linking words' or 'linkers'.

Using connectors

➤ Mind Mapping (p. 222)

Step 1: Collect your ideas on the topic you have to deal with – a mind map is a great help here – and remember to number them in the order you want to present them in.

Step 2: Check through the list of types of connectors (cf. below) and decide where you can use them in your text.

Step 3: Use connectors as much as possible in every text you write.

Types of connectors

It is important to know how you want to link your ideas. Go through the examples below, and pay special attention to how the connectors are used in the sentence (e.g. in front position or mid-position, with clauses, nouns with -ing forms, followed by a comma or not).

- Organization:
  - *In her text 'Can Science Save Us from Ourselves?' Walter discusses many aspects of the controversial issue of cloning. Firstly, she states that ... Secondly,/Then she goes on to say that ... Another point she makes is that ... Finally, ...*
- Reason:
  - *Due to / because of / as a result of all the discussions about designer babies, the public ....*
  - *Designer babies have been talked about a lot. Therefore, the public ...*
  - *Designer babies have been talked about a lot, so the public ...*
- Addition:
  - *Natasha Walter states that people in the Western world now believe that life should be controllable. In addition, / Moreover, they believe that all babies should be perfect. / They also believe that ......*
  - *In addition to / Besides / As well as believing that life should be controllable, people in the Western World believe that ...*

- Contrast:
  - Although genetic engineering may save babies from their genetic heritage, babies in some countries still die from drinking dirty water.
  - In spite of the advantages of genetic engineering, babies in some countries ...
  - Whereas genetic engineering in the western world can save babies from ..., babies in the Third World ...
  - Genetic engineering may save babies ... .However, / But nevertheless, babies in some countries ...
  - On the one hand, genetic engineering can save babies ...; on the other hand, babies in some countires still die from ...

- Giving Examples:
  - The writer is of the opinion that we can rely on science to help us in certain areas, for example / for instance / such as / e.g. ...

- Result and consequence:
  - As a consequence, / All in all, / consequently, Natasha Walter thinks that ...
  - To sum up / To conclude, I would like to say ...

Points to remember:

- Practise using connectors in every text you write and every presentation you give; soon you will find that they help you to express yourself more precisely. Try out new ones all the time.
- Check every text you write to make sure you have used enough 'connectors'.
- When reading, looking out for connectors will help you to follow the structure of a text.

Proofreading

Whenever you write a text, it is important to check the correctness and style of the English you used and, where possible, improve the text. This goes not only for tests and essays, but also for quick e-mails to friends. Making unnecessary mistakes may not only cost you a good mark in school – it is also rather rude.

How to proceed:

Step 1: If possible, ask someone else to check your written work, or try to set it aside for a while before proofreading it.

Step 2: Keep a checklist of mistakes you have made in the past. (This could, for example, be based on your self-assessment sheets; cf. pp. 8–19.) When you read what you have written, look for these mistakes first. Train yourself to hear a warning bell in your head every time you see a certain word or phrase, e.g. *since* – should it be *since* or *for*?

Step 3: Plan to read your work several times, watching for different kinds of mistakes each time. In a test situation, always allow time at the end to read your work!

Step 4: Do not just look for spelling and grammar mistakes. Make sure you have used correct collocations, and watch for style (a topic sentence in each paragraph which states what aspect you are dealing with, varying sentence lengths, interesting use of connectors – not just *and* or *but*).

➤ Linking Ideas (p. 246)

Step 5: Be suspicious of anything that looks or sounds too German – it might be correct, but then again it might not.

Step 6: Read your work out loud; if that is not possible, 'vocalize' the text in your head. It is often easier to hear mistakes than to see them, especially problems like words you may have left out or errors in the logic of what you have written.

Step 7: If you are unsure of a spelling and cannot look it up, write down alternatives. The one that looks the least wrong is probably right.

Summary Writing

When trying to pass on briefly information you have read, seen or heard, you need to be able to reduce the information to the bare essentials.

How to proceed:

Step 1: Read, watch or listen to the text you are dealing with as often as possible.

Step 2: If, for example, you are dealing with an article or book you have read, say in *one or two sentences* what it is about. An example (based on the text on p. 237) might be:
- *This article is about genetic modification. It deals with the advantages it could bring to farming, especially in underdeveloped countries.*

Step 3: Decide what information your reader needs to know by asking yourself *Who? What? When? Where? Why?* questions, e.g.
- *Who: geneticist Yang Huanming*
- *What: decoded the rice genome*

➤ Note Making (p. 243)

➤ The Stages of Writing (p. 244)

Step 4: Write down *key words* and *make notes*.

Step 5: Write a first draft, using your own words as much as possible. Do not give your own opinion on the subject. Remember to change direct speech into indirect speech.

Step 6: Work on the draft. If the summary is part of an examination, it is best to work on the draft once you have dealt with all the other tasks on the text, as you will have a much clearer idea of what the text is about.

Step 7: If you have been told to use a certain number of words for your summary, count all the words, and then see if you need to add or remove words. If you need to cut down on the number of words, remember that the following are not essential in a summary:
- examples and illustrations;
- figurative language.

Other methods of cutting down the number of words include:
- using single words instead of long phrases;
- combining a series of short sentences into a long sentence;
- using conjunctions and clauses.

Step 8: When you reach a final draft it should contain *all the important points* and read well.

Writing a Comment

The aim of a comment is to demonstrate that you are able to present your opinion on a certain topic or issue in a coherent form. Writing a comment is often a requirement in both school-leaving and international language proficiency examinations. You usually have a time limit and must keep within a certain number of words.

How to proceed:

Step 1: Read the task(s) carefully and make sure you know what you have to do.

Step 2: Collect and group your ideas – either in a mind map or as an outline. This way you will have an overview of what you are going to say, and can plan your introduction.

➤ Mind Mapping (p. 222), Writing Outlines (p. 244)

Step 3: Make your introductory statement, in which you refer to the task. Suitable introductory phrases are:

- *In the following I shall be concerned with / deal with the problem/subject/issue of ...*
- *I would like to discuss ...*
- *I intend to present arguments in favour of ... and against ...*

Step 4: Devote one paragraph to each of the arguments you want to present. If you are weighing up the pros and cons of an issue, you can take the argumentative approach and deal with all the arguments in favour first, and then against. Alternatively, you can discuss one aspect at a time, presenting the ideas for and against.

Step 5: Make your concluding statement, in which you sum up your arguments. Useful phrases here are:

- *All in all, I think it can be said that ...*
- *In conclusion, I would like to say that ...*
- *I would like to conclude by saying that ...*

Points to remember:

- Present your arguments clearly and precisely, avoiding repetition.
- Illustrate your ideas with appropriate examples.
- Underline the structure of your text with connectors.
- Keep track of the number of words you write as you go along.
- Plan your time carefully, and make sure you have time left at the end to proofread your text and, if the use of a dictionary is permitted, to check spelling and proper use of words.

➤ Linking Ideas (p. 246)

➤ Proofreading (p. 247)

➤ Using a Monolingual Dictionary (p. 234)

Writing Letters

Knowing how to write a well-structured letter is equally important for work (e.g. applying for jobs and places on courses) and for pleasure (e.g. communicating with friends who live far away).

How to proceed:

Step 1: Decide whether your letter is *formal* or *informal.*

Step 2: Always write your *address at the top right* with the *date underneath.*

Step 3: If the letter is formal write the *name of the recipient on the left*, just above the start of the letter.

Step 4: Always *start with 'Dear...'*. For personal letters then use the first name of the recipient, for business letters the title (Mr, Mrs, Ms, Dr, etc.) and family name. For recipients whose name you do not know, use 'Sir or Madam'.

Step 5: *Always close a letter properly.* Close informal letters as personally as you want ('love', 'miss you' etc.); close formal letters with 'Yours sincerely' if you know the recipient's name, 'Yours faithfully' if you do not.

Step 6: If you are sending a formal, typed letter, you should *type your name under your signature* at the end.

Step 7: The only exception to these rules is a *letter to the editor* of a newspaper, which always begins simply with 'Sir:' or 'Madam:' and ends with just your name and address. E-mails follow the same rules as normal letters (except your address is normally given at the bottom of the e-mail, below your name).

Formal letter (letter of application)

Hermannstrasse 5
10000 Berlin
Germany

PLT Ltd.
Personnel Dept
5 Herbert St
London WC1 5NW
England

1 August 2003

Dear Sir or Madam,

I am writing to you to apply for the position of project manager, which was advertised in the Guardian of 31st July. Please find enclosed a copy of my CV.

I feel that I am qualified for the job because ...

I hope you will consider my application and look forward to hearing from you.

Yours sincerely

M. Kemps

Maria Kemps

Informal letter

Hermannstrasse 5
10000 Berlin
Germany

1 August 2003

Dear Julian,

I hope you are well. I'm fine, even though the weather is miserable here. It has been raining for the past week.

I'm just writing to tell you that I've just applied for a job in London. If they give me the job, I was wondering whether I could take up the offer you made last time we met, and rent one of your spare rooms. As I don't know anybody in London, it would be great to have a place to stay.

Let me know and don't forget to send me any news of you and your family.

Lots of love

Maria

Writing Reports and Reviews

Reports and reviews are written texts that aim to provide information so that it can be easily and quickly understood by the reader. Whereas a report presents events and factual information in an objective manner, a review (usually of a book, play or film) is intended to either recommend the work in question or discourage somebody from reading or seeing it. A review also serves to help a person form his or her own opinion.

How to proceed:

A report

Step 1: Prepare your information carefully.

➤ Reading Non-fiction (p. 237), Listening for Information (p. 252)

Step 2: *Concentrate on the facts* and avoid mentioning your own personal feelings and thoughts, although you are able to state your own opinion at the end.

Step 3: *Use formal language.*

Step 4: Illustrate your report with *diagrams and/or charts* if this makes the report clearer.

➤ Working with Numbers (p. 226)

Step 5: Use *quotes*, especially if you are writing a written report.

➤ Quoting (p. 232)

A review

Step 1: If you are reviewing a film, prepare yourself beforehand by considering the various elements that make up a film.

➤ Viewing Skills (p. 227)

Step 2: Say what your book (which may be a novel or a work of non-fiction), film or play is about, giving the title, the name of the writer, director, etc. and when it was written, made, etc.

➤ Reading Narrative Prose (p. 238), Reading/Watching Drama (p. 240)
➤ Watch Your Language (p. 140)

Step 3: Give background information on your book, film or play and on the author, director, playwright.

Step 4: Give specific information on what the book, play or film is about and a short summary, but try not to give the ending away (unless for some reason it is required).

Step 5: Present a short extract that is typical of the work you are reviewing.

Step 6: Finish your review with your own personal opinion, give reasons for it and say whether you would recommend it or not.

Listening and Speaking Skills

Listening for Information

In order to understand spoken English, e.g. personal conversations, telephone calls, interviews as well as lengthy talks and lectures, you should know how to prepare yourself for the situation (wherever possible) and how to separate essential information from 'padding' (i.e. non-essential words and phrases that contain no real information).

How to proceed:

Conversations, telephone calls and interviews

Step 1: Before going into a communicative situation, prepare questions you may want to ask.

Step 2: Then collect words and phrases relevant to your topic.

Step 3: While communicating, *ask for clarification* when necessary. If for any reason you do not understand the information you are being given, do not hesitate to ask the other person to repeat, spell out or explain a piece of information or to confirm that you have understood it correctly, e.g.

- *Excuse me, could you repeat that / what you just said?*
- *I'm not sure I understood you correctly. Could you please rephrase your question / what you just said?*

Lengthy talks and lectures

Step 1: Before attending a talk or lecture, write down *key words* that deal with the information you are looking for or expect to get.

Step 2: Collect *words and phrases relevant to the topic* you are going to hear about and check that you fully understand them.

➤ Note Making (p. 243)

Step 3: While listening to a talk or lecture, *note* down information you want in *key word* form.

➤ Dealing with Unknown Words (p. 233)

Step 4: Use the *context* of each section of the talk or lecture to help you to understand words you do not know.

Step 5: Look out for *signpost words* (e.g. 'however', 'in my view', 'in short', etc.) These will help you to follow the structure of the speech (e.g. when a new argument is introduced, a personal opinion is given, a summing up is offered, etc.)

Debating

A debate is a formal method of arguing for or against a specific motion (proposal), which involves the skills of collecting arguments, organizing them systematically and presenting them as convincingly as possible.

Organizing a debate

Step 1: Choose a *motion* and word it like this:
– *This house proposes that your student years are the best years of your life.*

Step 2: The class divides into roughly equal groups for and against the motion. (What you really think does not matter.) The groups must collect and research as many arguments for their side as they can.

➤ Doing Research (p. 230)

Step 3: List and rank the arguments you have in order of importance.

Step 4: Choose three speakers and a timekeeper.
– The first speaker *proposes* or *opposes* the motion.
– The second speaker *seconds* the motion or continues the case for the opposition.
– The third *speaks to the motion.*
– The timekeeper times each speech and intervenes if a speaker overruns his or her allotted time.

Step 5: Decide on the length of time (e.g. 5–8 minutes) to be allotted to each speaker.

Step 6: Allocate arguments to your group's speakers and help them prepare for the debate by making notes and looking up any necessary words or phrases. Use index cards.

➤ Note Making (p. 243)

During the debate – speakers:

- The speakers alternate as follows:
  – Speaker 1 (for) *proposes the motion*, defines it from his or her team's point of view and presents the most important argument(s) in favour of its acceptance.
  – Speaker 2 (against) *opposes the motion*, re-defines it (if necessary) from his or her team's viewpoint and then presents the most important argument(s) against it.
  – Speaker 3 (for) *seconds the motion*, responds to the previous speaker, trying to weaken the points made and then adds his or her team's remaining arguments.
  – Speaker 4 (against) responds to the previous speaker by trying to weaken the points made and goes on to present his or her team's remaining arguments against the motion.
  – Speaker 5 (for) answers the previous speaker, puts any remaining arguments, but – most importantly – sums up the debate from his or her team's point of view.
  – Speaker 6 (against) makes any remaining points and then sums up the debate from his or her team's point of view.
- Points of information: you can interrupt the other team's speakers if you have information that contradicts what they are saying. Stand up and say 'Point of information'. The speaker can refuse ('No, thank you'). If he or she accepts ('Yes, please'), he or she must react to it immediately.
- Support your arguments with facts, but hold your audience's attention by startling or amusing them. Try not to be distracted by your audience or opponents.
- Speak clearly and loudly enough for everyone to hear you; do not rush what you are saying, otherwise you may have difficulty speaking. Face the audience, keeping eye contact with them.
- Keep to the allocated time – if your speech is too short the audience might feel that you do not know enough about the subject or that you were not effective in putting across your argument. If it is too long, you will almost certainly be stopped by the time-keeper and you may bore your audience.

During the debate – audience:

➤ Listening for Information (p. 252)

- Try to follow the arguments – you will have to vote on them at the end. (Taking notes may help you.)

At the end of the debate:

- The house votes on the motion. (Remember: you are not voting on what you agree with, but on who made the better case.) When the votes have been counted, the time-keeper can announce the results, e.g.
  - *For the motion: .... Against the motion: .... I declare the motion carried/defeated by ... votes.*

Giving a Talk or Presentation

Informing an audience about a topic is an important skill to master and is one that will serve you well at school (for classroom lectures, etc.) and in later life (university, college, work, etc.).

How to proceed:

Before giving your talk or presentation

➤ Doing Research (p. 230)
➤ Note Making (p. 243)

Step 1: Research your subject thoroughly, making *notes in English*. If you are using notecards, *number them*.

➤ The Stages of Writing (p. 244), Using a Monolingual Dictionary (p. 234)

Step 2: *Check your English* and look up words that are difficult to pronounce in a dictionary.

Step 3: Think of ways to make the talk more interesting, e.g. by using *visuals, sound, jokes,* etc.

Step 4: Check that all the *equipment you need* is available.

Step 5: Practise your talk beforehand.

During your talk or presentation

Step 1: Start your presentation by *explaining your topic* and how your talk is structured.

Step 2: *Make things clear* for your audience – keep the talk simple, speak slowly and clearly.

Step 3: Use *visuals, handouts,* etc to hold your audience's interest. If you use an OHP (overhead projector) make sure that you do not overload your transparencies or pictures and that they can be read easily or seen by people in the back row.

Step 4: Pay attention to your body language: stand straight and face the audience, keeping eye contact with them. Speak clearly and loudly enough for everyone to hear you; do not rush what you are saying, otherwise you may have difficulty speaking.

Step 5: *Summarize the important points* at the end of your talk.

Step 6: Thank your audience for their attention and ask whether they have any questions.

Literary Texts

Fiction: A fictional text is an imaginative work in which an author creates his or her own world and/or presents an invented story. The reader is expected to accept this world or story as existing or true (this is called *suspension of disbelief*). Although fiction covers most literary texts, it is mostly used to refer to *narrative prose (e.g. *novels, *short stories).
Fiction usually comprises a variety of elements, such as *characters, *action and plot, *setting and *atmosphere. The *mode of presentation (scenic or panoramic) and the *point of view adopted (first-person or third-person, limited or unlimited, reliable or unreliable narrator) play a central role in how the reader reacts to the story.

*An asterisk indicates that the term has its own entry in the Glossary. For an **alphabetical list of terms** cf. p. 270. Words in the Glossary which are in italics are also to be found in the list.

Narrative Prose: A narrative prose text is a *fictional text which is told by a narrator (cf. *narration) and is written in prose. (Prose is writing that is formed by sentences in a continuous flow and is broken up only by paragraphs.) Typical examples of narrative prose are *novels and *short stories. Fiction can further be subdivided by aspects of content (e.g. *coming-of-age stories and *fables).

Genre

➤ Reading Narrative Prose (p. 238)

Novel: A novel is a long and complex fictional narrative text often divided into chapters. The storyline and structure of a novel are normally more complicated than those of shorter fictional works and, accordingly, there may be greater variety and a more detailed development of *characters and *setting (i.e. the time and the place). In every novel the author must decide from which *point of view the story will be told. In some cases there is more than one narrator (cf. *narration). No other art form can recreate life on the same scale as the novel with its almost unlimited possibilities.

⚠ **Trouble spot**
novel = *Roman*
Not: ~~*Novelle*~~

Short Story: There is no generally accepted definition of the short story that clearly separates it from other narrative texts like the *novel. However, there are some elements that can be regarded as characteristic. Most short stories can be read at one sitting and concentrate on one *character, situation, dilemma or problem. In a short story the characters, the situation, etc. are not fully developed (unlike in a novel); the focus is on one single aspect which undergoes a change in the course of the story. There are different types of short stories, e.g. the *coming-of-age story or the 'slice of life' story (which shows just one particular aspect of everyday life).

Sitzung

Fable: A fable is a short narrative text in which animals represent human types or act like human beings. Fables are usually didactic, since they intend to teach a moral lesson, make a satirical comment or illustrate some general truth. A moral may be understood from the text or there may be a moral (*epilogue*) at the end, which in modern fables is often ironic (cf. *irony).
Example: In 'The Sheep in Wolf's Clothing' (p. 111) the sheep and wolves represent human types or forms of behaviour, and there is an ironic moral at the end of the tale.

Coming-of-age Story: A coming-of-age story is a *short story or *novel in which the process of growing up is portrayed. Usually the protagonist (cf. *character) is a child or, more often, an adolescent who undergoes an experience which changes his or her

abbreviation of "compare"

durchmachen

Initiation: Einführung der Jugendlichen in den Kreis der Erwachsenen bei Naturvölkern, durch bestimmte Bräuche geregelt

outlook on life and marks an important stage in his or her development towards maturity and adulthood. The coming-of-age story is sometimes referred to as the 'story of initiation'.
Example: In 'Land/scape' (pp. 8–17) the protagonist has to confront his father in order to grow up and become an adult.

Frame Story: A frame story is a *novel or *short story which contains one or more quite independent stories within it. The main story provides the frame for the other stories. Often the main story consists of a *character in one *setting recounting another story in another setting.

Poetry:

Poetry: A poem is a piece of creative writing structured by *lines* and *rhythm* (the arrangement of stressed and unstressed syllables in a line). The lines of a poem are often arranged into groups called *stanzas*. To emphasize the structure and to create certain effects, traditional poets frequently make use of *rhyme. Modern poetry often uses *free verse*, which makes little use of rhyme. The poetry comes from *repetition, *imagery and the arrangement of words and stresses in the poem.
Poems are often *lyrical* (i.e. they express personal thoughts and feelings), but they can also be *narrative* (i.e. they tell a story).
The *speaker* is the voice in which a poem is spoken, especially when the personal pronoun 'I' is used. This speaker is not always identical with the voice of the poet.

Sonnet: A sonnet is a poem consisting of 14 lines. Sonnets became popular in England in the 17th century and were used mostly for love poetry, but later they came to embrace a wide number of themes. There are various types of sonnets: Shakespeare's sonnets comprised three *quatrains* (a quatrain consists of four lines with a shared *rhyme scheme) and a *couplet* (i.e. two successive lines which rhyme). As the couplet's rhyme scheme was different from the rest of the sonnet it was used to sum up or vary or change the theme of the sonnet.
Example: Sonnet 130 (p. 43)

Shape Poem: A shape poem (also called a *concrete poem*) is a poem in which the words form a shape or picture. The shape usually reflects the theme or contents of the poem.
Example: The poem 'If the Earth' (p. 74) has the shape of a circle, which reflects the spherical shape of the earth.

Rhyme: Rhyme is the similarity of sounds between certain words (especially stressed syllables), usually at the end of lines. When identifying the *rhyme scheme* (i.e. which words at the end of the lines rhyme), it is usual to use small letters to indicate that words share a rhyme. If the words 'abide', 'thee', 'wide' and 'see' occur respectively at the end of four successive lines, the rhyme scheme is written as a b a b (this pattern is called *alternate rhyme*). If 'abide', 'wide', 'thee' and 'see' occur respectively at the end of four successive lines, the rhyme scheme is written a a b b (this pattern is called *rhyming couplets*). Other letters are then used for other rhymes.

Metre: Metre is the regular rhythm of the words in a poem. Traditionally, this is achieved by the arrangement of stressed and unstressed syllables in the line of a poem. The most common metre in English is the *iambic pentameter*, which consists of a line of five feet (each *foot* consists of an unstressed syllable followed by a stressed syllable).

Example: This ró/yal thróne / of kíngs, / this scépt'/red ísle
foot — stressed syllable
(From: 'This Scept'red Isle', p. 154, l. 1)

Drama:

Drama: A drama or *play* is written to be performed by actors in a theatre, in a film, or on TV or on the radio. It is usually divided into several *acts* (in classical drama, there were usually five acts, but modern plays normally consist of three and sometimes of only one act). An act may be subdivided into *scenes*. A scene is a smaller unit of action in which there is no change of place or break in time. The actors take on roles of *characters, perform the *action and speak the *dialogue*. The actors' way of speaking, their appearance and their movements, as well as the *setting, the sound and lighting, etc. are often given in the *stage directions* – this helps an acting company perform a play.

➤ Reading/Watching Drama (p. 240)

Tragedy: A tragedy is a type of *drama in which the protagonist (cf. *character) passes through a series of misfortunes towards his or her downfall. Usually the downfall is brought about partly by the protagonist's own fault, e.g. through too much pride, weakness, uncertainty, etc.

Comedy: A comedy is a type of *drama which deals with a light topic or a more serious one in an amusing way. A comedy always has a happy ending.

Feature Film: A feature film is a full-length film that has a story and *characters who are played by actors. A feature film is based on a film script, which the director then turns into a film. Important elements in a film are the *dialogue*, the use of *camera techniques* and the acting.

➤ Viewing Skills (p. 227)

TV/Radio Series: A series is a regular programme on TV or radio about the lives and problems of a character or, more usually, a group of *characters. A series may centre on a couple or family life or a leading character's career, and some involve magic and/or fantasy. Each programme is self-contained, i.e. it deals with a particular issue or storyline which is concluded at the end of the programme. The lives of the characters evolve slowly over the course of a series.

Sitcom: A sitcom (situation comedy) is a comic *TV/radio series which usually centres around a *character or group of characters, who are often stereotypes as they do not evolve over the series. It may be filmed in front of a live audience or have canned laughter added to make the audience aware of or to reinforce the funny lines.

Soap: A soap (soap opera) is a regular TV or radio programme about the everyday lives of a group of people. The storyline of a soap, unlike that of a normal *TV/radio series, develops from programme to programme and may often end with a *cliffhanger* (an exciting situation so you want to know what will happen next) to encourage the audience to tune in to the next episode.

Analysing Fictional Texts

➤ Reading Narrative Prose (p. 238)

Narrator and Point of View

Narrator: The narrator is the voice or *character who tells the story and is part of the fictional world created by the author.
There are two types of narrator:

a *first-person narrator*	The narrator is a character in the story and refers to him- or herself as 'I'.
a *third-person narrator*	The narrator is not a character in the story and refers to the characters as 'he', 'she' or 'they' or by their names.

Point of view: The point of view is the perspective from which characters, events, etc. are presented in a fictional story. This has an important effect on the reader: for example, we tend to respond more sympathetically to a character whose mind we enter, as we experience for ourselves what the character goes through.
A fictional work can have several points of view (depending on the narrator):

a *first-person narrator*	can only have	a *limited point of view;* a character in fictional work does not know everything that occurs, therefore he or she imposes his or her understanding and interpretation on the action.
a *third-person narrator*	can have	a *limited point of view;* the narrator looks at the events and characters from the perspective of one of the characters or from the outside (as an *observer narrator*) and so does not have access to the thoughts and feelings of all of the characters.
	or	an *unlimited point of view;* the narrator can move freely in place and time and enter the minds of the characters at will (here we speak of an *omniscient narrator*).

Often, the point of view changes to make for more interesting reading.
A reader must ask him- or herself how reliable a narrator is. Often one cannot take everything in a fictional work at face value:

a *reliable narrator*	The reader may take everything the narrator tells at face value.
an *unreliable narrator*	the reader must find out just how much of what the narrator says can be accepted. First-person narrators are usually unreliable as they give only one perspective on the action and the characters.

Example of a first-person narrator: The Pilgrims gave thanks at Thanksgiving because the Native Americans saved their sorry butts from starving. I give thanks at Thanksgiving because my mother finally goes to work and my father orders pizza. (From: 'Giving Thanks', p. 31, ll. 1–3)
The use of 'I' and other first-person determiners indicates a first-person narrator. The reader must take care when reading the text, as only one person's point of view is given (the subjective nature of the narration is underlined by the comments about the Pilgrims).

Example of a third-person narrator: The rest of the passengers sighed, ostentatiously took out again the company reports that they'd stowed in their briefcases. Ant grinned. A short reprieve.
Ant was dreading the thought of five days with his father [...].
(From: 'Land/scape', p. 8, ll. 5–8)
In this example the narrator is a third-person narrator as the protagonist is referred to by his name ('Ant'). The story is, however, told from Ant's point of view (i.e. there is a limited point of view): 'A short reprieve', 'Ant was dreading'. As the reader experiences the action of the story from Ant's perspective and is shown only his feelings, the reader's sympathies are with Ant in his conflict with his father. As we are not shown the father's point of view, we cannot speak of a reliable narrator.

Mode of Presentation: The way a writer narrates events is known as mode of presentation. There are two modes of presentation, and usually a combination of both are used in a narrative text:

scenic presentation	If the author shows an event in detail as it occurs, using dialogue, depicting thoughts and emotions, describing a scene, etc., he or she uses scenic presentation (also known as '*showing*').
includes: *interior monologue*	This is a particular kind of scenic presentation in which the author depicts the thoughts and feelings passing through a character's mind. Often an interior monologue does not follow a chronological order, since, when people think, their thoughts jump from one subject to another. Interior monologues are normally narrated in the present tense. However, it is more common to find *reported thought*, in which the thoughts are presented as reported speech (i.e. in the past tense).
panoramic presentation	If the author tells the story as a condensed series of events, summarizing in a few sentences what happens over a longer period of time (e.g. an hour, a week, months), he or she uses panoramic presentation (also known as '*telling*').

Example of scenic presentation: 'This is Captain Klein speaking. Unfortunately there is a bit of a queue here at Tullamarine today, so we are entering a holding pattern. Our estimated arrival time will now be 2.10 pm ...'
The rest of the passengers sighed, tapped their watches, ostentatiously took out again the company reports that they'd stowed in their briefcases.
(From: 'Land/scape', p. 8, ll. 2–6)

Example of reported thought:

But think now.
Stay calm.
The ocean had to be on that side – didn't it?
And the river had to be over there – hadn't it?
And the car must be ...

(From: 'Land/scape', p. 14, ll. 194–198)

Example of panoramic presentation: It took an hour of burrowing headlong through tunnels of scrub, following pathways that petered out in gullies, fiddling back and forth, even gazing helplessly up to try to get his bearings from the noonday sun. (From: 'Land/scape', p. 14, ll. 199–201)

Character and Characterization

⚠ **Trouble spot**
When talking about the characters in a fictional text, do not use the words: ~~people/person~~.

Characters are the people in a fictional text. They are usually presented through their actions, speech and thoughts as well as by description. There are generally speaking two types of characters in fictional works:

a *round character*	A round character may be similar to real individuals and have several traits and behave in a way that is life-like. A round character usually changes in the course of a story.
a *flat character*	A character has only a limited number of traits or represents only a single quality. A crude representation of a character which is meant to be laughed at is called a *caricature*

The main character in a story is called the *protagonist* and is almost always a round character.

⚠ **Trouble spot**
An author *characterizes* somebody, i.e invents the traits of a character.
A reader *describes the character* of somebody when talking about his or her traits.

Characterization is the way in which the author presents his or her characters. We usually distinguish between two kinds of characterization:

Direct or *explicit characterization*	The reader is told about a character's personality directly by a) the narrator, b) another character or c) by the character him- or herself.
Indirect or *implicit characterization*	The reader is expected to draw conclusions about a character by a) studying his or her behaviour, b) opinions, c) choice of words and/or way of talking.

Authors often combine explicit and implicit characterization in the presentation of their characters.

Example: Ant was bright enough to be in the A class, bright enough to pass everything, even Maths and Chemistry. [...]
Ant wished he was stupid enough so he could get into Special class: they did Art, Metalwork, Woodwork, Tech Drawing, Carving and Casting, Photography, Screen Printing and Excursions. Even more to the point, Ant wished he could go to the Creative Arts High School [...].
(From: 'Land/scape', p. 9, ll. 36–37 and 43–46)

In the first example Ant is characterized explicitly ('Ant was bright'), so the reader is told he is intelligent. In the second example Ant is characterized implicitly as a creative person with artistic interests – this the reader learns from the subjects he wishes he could be doing and the school he wishes he could attend.

Useful words and phrases

main/central/major characters (*also* figures) • minor/secondary characters (*also* figures) • hero/heroine

Action and Plot

Action is everything that happens in a fictional story.
Action may be on two levels:

external action	The author describes what the ·characters do and the events that take place.
internal action	The author describes what is going on in the minds of the characters, i.e. the reader is shown the thoughts of the characters.

·Novels and ·short stories usually combine external and internal action to give an overall view of the ·characters and the plot.
Example: In 'Land/scape' (pp. 8–17) the trip that Ant and his father take is external action. Ant's reported thought when he is lost (p. 14, ll. 194–198) is an example of internal action.

Plot: The structure of events in a fictional story; the story is usually told through cause and effect. The English novelist E.M. Forster described plot in these terms: ' "The king died and then the queen died" is a story. "The king died and then the queen died of grief", is a plot.' (*Aspects of the Novel*, 1927)
The plot usually develops in a number of stages:

1. the *exposition*	The characters, theme, setting, etc. are introduced.
2. the *rising action*	A conflict is developed.
3. a *climax*	The conflict reaches its highest point.
4. the *turning point*	There is a change in the conflict or suspense.
5. the *falling action*	The suspense is reduced.
6. the *denouement* [ˌdeɪ'nu:mɒ̃] (also known as the *solution*) which may also be:	Some resolution of the conflict is achieved.
a *surprise ending*	The reader's expectations concerning the course of the story are not fulfilled but instead an unexpected solution of the conflict is presented.
or instead: an *open ending*	The conflict is not fully resolved and the reader is left wondering what might happen next.

A plot will have some element of *suspense* and *tension*. Suspense is created when the reader does not know the outcome of a *conflict* (the struggle or opposition between different forces, characters, etc.) or of the action. Tension is the emotional reaction to the conflict, which rouses the attention of the reader and makes him or her curious about the further development of the plot; this is usually achieved by the expectations concerning the outcome of the conflict.
Example: The plot in 'Land/scape' (pp. 8–17) centres around a father–son conflict. The turning point occurs in the scene in the cave (p. 14). The conflict is resolved when the father accepts that his son is different from him and lets him go his own way.

Useful words and phrases
open/surprise/unexpected/happy/sad/tragic ending • centre around sth. • a conflict between ... and

⚠ **Trouble spot**
Not: ~~happy end~~

Flashback: Authors do not always tell their stories in a chronological order. In some stories the authors make use of flashbacks, i.e. the ·narrator goes back into the past to describe a scene that has relevance to the plot.
Example: In 'Origami' (p. 186) the protagonist remembers an incident that happened to her in a restaurant which sheds light on her situation at the time of the narration.

Foreshadowing: Foreshadowing (also called *anticipation*) is the technique of hinting at later events in a fictional text so that the reader or audience is prepared for them or can anticipate them.
Example: In William Shakespeare's *Macbeth*, the three witches allow the audience to believe that Macbeth will become king.

⚠ **Trouble spot**
atmosphere ≠ ·tone

■ **Atmosphere:** The atmosphere is the feeling or mood created by an author in his or her work. The ·setting, use of language and ·characterization all contribute to the atmosphere of a work.
Example: Outside, the wind suddenly dropped, as if the storm had blown itself out like a candle.
(From: 'Land/scape', p. 16, ll. 256–257)
Here the description of the end of the storm reflects Ant's tranquil mood once the conflict with his father is resolved.

■ **Setting:** The setting is the time and place in which a literary work takes place. The setting can have symbolic overtones; it may serve to reveal something about the characters and also contribute to the ·atmosphere of the story.
Example: The short story 'Land/scape' (pp. 8–17) is set in contemporary Australia in winter. The season might be said to reflect the cold relationship that exists between father and son at the beginning of the story.

Non-fictional Texts

➤ Reading Non-fiction (p. 236)

■ **Non-fiction:** Whereas literary texts create their own fictional world, non-fictional texts (e.g. ·news stories, ·advertisements, ·speeches, ·letters, etc.) normally refer to the real world. They may serve a variety of practical purposes, e.g. to inform, persuade, express personal opinions, criticize, etc.

Text Forms

News story: The terms news story, *news item* and *news report* can be used interchangeably to refer to reports of recent events of general interest that appear in newspapers, on television or on the radio.
News items can be of any length. In theory, news stories are meant to be objective and unbiased presentations of the facts, providing answers to the *five w's*, i.e. the questions 'who?', 'what?', 'when?', 'where?' and 'why?'. In practice, totally impartial reporting is impossible. The choice of words, the ·style and ·tone, the choice of detail and examples, the emphasis given to certain aspects of the story, the position of the article in the paper and on the page, the headline and layout all contribute to influence the reader.
There are two common formulas used in news stories:

a) The 'pyramid', in which the most important item or element in the story is reported first and then the rest of the information is offered in descending order of importance.
b) The 'Wall Street Journal formula', in which the news story starts with a particular (usually personal) example to attract the reader's attention before the topic is discussed. It differs from a feature story, in that the latter puts more emphasis on the personal account in order to illustrate a topic, while the former uses the personal account merely to attract the attention of the reader.
Example: 'Work Stops and Starts on Wembley' (p. 110)

Feature story: A feature story deals with a topic by concentrating on a particular person or on particular people. It often takes an individual case as its starting point to discuss the different aspects of the topic on a personal level and leaves the reader to draw more general conclusions from this individual case. The writer of a feature story makes use of direct quotes from the people involved in the story and relies on first-hand reporting, i.e. the journalist writes mostly about things and people he or she has actually encountered. A feature story often opens with the description of an event or a person in order to attract the reader's attention.
Example: 'Young, Talented and Rebellious' (p. 18)

Editorial: An editorial (in British English also known as a *leading article* or *leader*) is an article that expresses the opinion of the newspaper's editor or editorial team about an item of news or a political or social issue, etc. In American usage an editorial can also be a comment on radio or television that expresses the opinion of the station or network. Unlike *columns, editorials are not supposed to be personal and do not appear with a *byline*, i.e. with a line that gives the writer's name.
Example: 'America Triumphant' (p. 171)

Column: **a)** A column is the term used for any of the vertical sections into which the printed page of a newspaper is divided.
b) A column is the term used for a regular item in a newspaper or magazine, which either deals with a particular subject (e.g. gardening, gossip, financial, agony column) or is written by a particular writer (called a columnist). Columnists often write highly personal essays on topics of their choosing. Unlike *editorials, columns appear with a *byline*, i.e. with a line that gives the writer's name.
Example: 'Doctor Sarah Brewer Says ...' (p. 45)

Speech: A speech is an address delivered to an audience. A speaker may try to establish contact with his or her listeners in various ways: by flattering them, addressing them directly, using the first-person plural (e.g. 'we', 'our') to involve them in what he or she is saying. A speaker may appeal to shared experiences and values, e.g. by quoting from or alluding to sources such as the Bible or history. A speaker often uses *stylistic devices to heighten the impact of what he or she is saying. *Contrast may be used to highlight differences between the speaker and his or her opponents. *Repetition and *alliteration often help the audience follow the speech and remember key ideas and phrases.
Example: 'Chicken Tikka Massala' (p. 144)

Essay: An essay is a text form in which the writer expresses his or her personal views on some topic. Essays can vary widely in length, subject matter and ·tone, some being serious and others light-hearted and entertaining.
Example: 'Assimilation, American-style' (p. 175)

➤ Writing Letters (p. 250)

Letter: There are many types of letters. They can be personal or business-oriented, depending on the relationship between the sender and receiver, the occasion and the purpose of the letter. Letters are a very flexible text form and comprise thank-you notes, e-mails, covering letters (in American English, 'cover letters'), letters of complaint, ·letters to the editor, etc. The beginnings and endings of letters follow certain conventions. Usually, letters consist of the following parts: **1** the address of the sender (and in the case of a business letter, the address of the recipient), **2** the date, **3** the salutation (e.g. 'Dear Mark'), **4** the body of the letter, i.e. the information the sender wants to convey, **5** a conventional phrase to close the letter (e.g. 'Yours faithfully', 'Yours sincerely', 'Love') and **6** the signature.

Letter to the Editor: A letter to the editor is a letter in which a reader expresses his or her opinion concerning an article in a newspaper/magazine or a problem which is of public interest. The letter may criticize or support an article, or state a personal opinion concerning a topic which is being discussed in public or attract the attention of other readers to a topic that has been ignored or is worthy of attention.
Example: 'A Letter to the Editor' (p. 114)

⚠ **Trouble spot**
spot ≠ advertisement

Advertisement: An advertisement (informally also called an *advert* or *ad*) is a text which attempts to persuade people to do something (e.g. buy a particular product or contribute money to a cause). It normally consists of pictures and text (called *copy*) and is designed to catch the attention of the reader through its layout. Common elements of advertisements are ·wordplay in the title or headings and ·humour to win the sympathy of the reader. Advertisers often use the 'AIDA' (Attention, Interest, Desire, Action) formula in their advertisements (cf. 'AIDA', p. 122).
Newspaper or magazine advertisements dealing with job offers, buying, selling or renting something, etc. are called *small* or *classified ads*. Advertisements on the radio or on television are known as *commercials*.
Example: 'The Ultimate Pain Relief' (p. 130)

➤ Working with Cartoons (p. 224)

Cartoon: A cartoon is an amusing drawing in a newspaper or magazine that deals with human nature or a current political or social issue. Complex issues are reduced to memorable pictures. Cartoons often include captions or speech bubbles. Techniques employed by cartoonists include *caricature*, ·exaggeration, ·wordplay and the use of ·symbols. Cartoons usually presuppose that the reader has background knowledge of the political, social and cultural issues being dealt with, which often makes them difficult for the non-native reader to understand.

Style and Language

Style: Style is the way in which a text is written. In order to examine the style of a text it is necessary to examine aspects such as the *register, the *diction and the *tone of the text, as well as the grammar and the sentence structures used in the text.

Tone: Tone is the way in which a writer treats his or her topic, thereby reflecting his or her emotional attitude towards that topic and also towards the reader. The tone can be formal, intimate, solemn, playful, serious, ironic (cf. *irony), humorous (cf. *humour), angry, etc.

Humour: Humour is based on the human ability to see and laugh at the incongruity or strangeness of a *character, an action or comment, etc. because it is unexpected or unsuitable in a particular situation. At one end of the spectrum, humour is gentle, understanding and tolerant and makes the reader smile at human weaknesses; at the other end, it is divisive, bitter or sarcastic, evoking contempt and moral indignation at human vices and corruption. Not all forms of humour will be appreciated by every segment of society, since humour relies on shared cultural values.
Example: I walk to town every day [...]. People have got used to this curious and eccentric behaviour now [...].
(From: 'A Sedentary Nation', p. 180, ll. 22–27)
Here the normal human activity of walking is described as 'curious and eccentric', which is a humorous way of commenting on the fact that Americans never walk anywhere any more.

Register: Register is the level of language (the choice of words, grammar, etc.) used in a particular situation. The register in a text may be formal, neutral or informal:

formal style	Formal style consists of difficult vocabulary, often of Latin origin, and complex sentence structure; it is usually only used for serious purposes, e.g. essays or academic publications, or in official situations, and would not be appropriate in normal everyday conversation.
neutral style	Neutral style falls between formal and informal style and is the style generally used by educated people; it is used in feature stories, news stories, etc.
informal style	Informal style is characterized by fairly simple, often elliptical sentences, short forms (e.g. 'can't', 'you'll'), phrasal verbs and colloquial words, often of Germanic origin; it is used between friends or in a relaxed or unofficial situation.
includes:	
slang	Slang is very informal language, mainly used in dialogue between people of the same age or from a similar background, etc.
taboo words	Taboo words are generally considered obscene, vulgar or shocking and are used only if the writer is trying to make a particular point or shock his or her reader.

Example of formal style: The collision of increased standards of living, more leisure time, the explosion of post-war consumer culture and wider psychological research into adolescents all contributed to the formation of this new social category defined by age.
(From: 'This Thing Called "Youth Culture" ', p. 38, ll. 2–5)
The writer uses difficult words and grammar in a way that the reader must examine the sentence closely to understand what the writer is saying.

Example of neutral style: Alexandria had always excelled in dance, music and art and shone academically, too. [...] To her parents' consternation she stuck to her childhood dream of becoming an actress.
(From: 'Young, Talented and Rebellious', p. 18, ll. 1–4)
The writer uses straightforward sentence structures and words that are formal (e.g. 'consternation') and informal (e.g. 'stuck to').

Examples of informal style: 'Why not?' Tony asked. 'You've got another week of holidays, I haven't got any work till August. We can go up to Broken Hill, poke around a bit, and then I can drive you back to Sydney.'
(From: 'Land/scape', p. 17, ll. 279–281)
The short forms, the use of simple words like 'got', 'go', 'drive' and phrases like 'poke around' indicate that the author is using informal style to relate a relaxed conversation between a father and his son.
That was all OK anyway, so we had a great night, spoke to a few guys and eyed up the talent.
(From: 'The Trouble with Mother', p. 22, ll. 29–30).
The writer uses slang words ('eye up the talent') as well as informal words ('OK', 'guys') in a written text in order to appeal to the readers of the teenage magazine, who are the same age as her.

Diction: The words a writer chooses for his or her text. Diction is very important as words influence the reader or listener. In many argumentative texts, for example, the writer will use words with positive *connotations* (i.e. the associations a word has beyond its literal or dictionary meaning) to support his or her arguments or words with negative connotations to attack those he or she opposes. The choice of words often reveals the writer's attitudes. A writer can also use emotive language (i.e. words and expressions with particular connotations that appeal to the reader's or listener's emotions) and so influence him or her to react in a particular way.
Example: The Lords in their wisdom have decided that scientists should be able to dabble in cells taken from cloned human embryos.
(From: 'Can Science Save Us from Ourselves?', p. 70, ll. 3–4)
The addition of the phrase 'in their wisdom' is ironic and implies that the Lords are not wise to take this decision; the word 'dabble' implies that scientists are playing with cells and are not doing serious work. Thus the writer seems to show that she finds the decision incorrect.

Layout: The way elements are arranged on a printed page is known as the layout. The layout includes elements such as the type and size of letters, the use of bold or italic typeface, underlining, headings and sub-headings, bullets (= dots or other symbols used at the beginning of a text passage), the size and number of columns, the length of paragraphs, the use of insets, the colour and the placement of illustrations. The layout determines whether a text attracts the attention of the reader and is pleasant to read, and it helps writers to structure their texts and to emphasize certain words, phrases or passages. The layout is particularly important when considering newspaper articles, *advertisements and brochures.

Stylistic Devices: Stylistic devices (also called *rhetorical devices*) refer to the methods and techniques used to produce a particular effect. Stylistic devices may relate to sound (e.g. *alliteration), structure (e.g. *repetition, *parallelism) or meaning (e.g. *imagery).

⚠ **Trouble spot**
Most stylistic devices are used mainly as uncountable nouns, e.g. *The author uses alliteration/ contrast/exaggeration/ repetition ...*
The exceptions are: allusion, metaphor, symbol, rhetorical question and pun, e.g. *In line 5 there is a metaphor ...*

Alliteration: Alliteration is the repetition of a sound, normally a consonant, at the beginning of neighbouring words or of stressed syllables within such words, to produce a usually rhythmic, but sometimes also comic, effect.
Example: Around the rugged rock the ragged rascal ran.

Allusion: Allusion is the direct or indirect reference to something or somebody the reader or listener is supposed to recognize and respond to. An allusion may be to a work of literature, a historical event, a religious text like the Bible, etc.
Example: ... then assume that Train A leaves Chicago traveling westbound at 47 mph, while Train B ...
(From: 'Remote Control', p. 59, ll. 64–65)
Here the writer humorously alludes to a maths question which is often asked in tests and is usually hated by students to show how difficult instruction manuals are.

Assonance: Assonance is the repetition of the same or similar vowel sounds within stressed syllables of neighbouring words.
Example: the poppies blow / Between the crosses, row on row
(From: 'In Flanders Fields', p. 131, ll. 1–2)

Contrast: Contrast is the term used when opposing views, words or characters are brought together to emphasize their difference and usually to highlight one of the opposing elements. In contrasting two characters, the author may be showing the goodness of one by emphasizing the evil of another; in contrasting two ideas, a writer may be attempting to show how the idea he or she opposes is not as worthy of consideration as the idea he or she expounds.
Example: In 'Sonnet 130' (p. 43) Shakespeare contrasts the ideals of beauty and his lover's beauty.

Enumeration: Enumeration is the listing of words or phrases in a text, with the last two usually connected by 'and'. Enumeration can be used to a) add emphasis, b) make a text more pleasant to read, c) list words in a climactic order, i.e. the most important elements come at the end of the listing, or d) highlight a *contrast, e.g. when after the enumeration of words or phrases with the same or similar meanings there follows a quite different word or phrase.

Example: It produced footballers, cricketers, graziers, senior executives, lawyers, doctors, and politicians of the Liberal and National Parties. It had produced Ant's father (Captain of the First XI; Dux of the School; Head Prefect; Barrister) and Ant's grandfather (Captain of the First XV, Sports Captain; Prefect; Judge).
(From: 'Land/scape', p. 9, ll. 20–24)
In the first sentence there is an enumeration of successful people, while in the second there is an enumeration of the achievements of Ant's father and grandfather. This is then contrasted (cf. ˑcontrast) with Ant's lack of ability (and interest) in any of the careers or achievements mentioned.

Exaggeration: Exaggeration is the use of a strong overstatement. It may be used to create either a serious or comic effect. A single phrase containing an exaggeration is called *hyperbole* [haɪ'pɜːbəli]. (Cf. also ˑunderstatement)
Example: Nobody walks anywhere in America nowadays.
(From: 'A Sedentary Nation', p. 180, l. 8)

Bildersprache / Metaphorik

Imagery: When a writer or speaker uses language beyond its normal dictionary definition and meaning, we speak of imagery. All non-literal (i.e. figurative) use of language falls into the category of imagery. Images are meant to stimulate the imagination of the reader or listener and give him or her a new perspective on a particular topic. Images can take many forms.
The following are particular forms of imagery:

metaphor ['metəfə]	A metaphor is a comparison between two things which are basically quite unlike one another without using the words 'as' or 'like' (cf. ˑsimile). **Example:** There's daggers (Dolche) in men's smiles. (From: William Shakespeare, *Macbeth*)
simile ['sɪməli]	Like a metaphor, a simile is a type of comparison. But while a metaphor says that something *is* something else, a simile says that something *is like* something else and uses the words 'like' or 'as' to draw the comparison. **Example:** the storm had blown itself out like a candle. (From: 'Landscape', p. 16, ll. 256–257)
symbol	A symbol is a thing, word or phrase signifying something concrete that stands not only for itself but also for a certain abstract idea. As in the case of a metaphor or a simile the meaning of a symbol goes beyond the literal. **Example:** A red rose is often a symbol of love.
personification	Personification is the technique of representing animals or objects as if they were human beings or possessed human qualities. **Example:** There was a nasty jolt as the wheels touched the ground, then a sort of shudder seemed to run through the body of the plane. (From: 'Land/scape', p. 10, ll. 61–62) Here the plane is personified when it shudders.

⚠ **Trouble spot**
symbol of sth.
Not: ~~symbol for sth.~~

s. im Gedanklichen / Theoretischen bewegend

Irony: Irony is the term used when a person makes fun of somebody or something without openly doing so. A person using irony may use certain words and actually mean the opposite of what those words normally mean. Also, a person may appear to support someone or something while at the same time making it clear (e.g. by his or her tone of voice or through his or her choice of words) that he or she is actually criticizing or revealing the contradictions in the other person's behaviour.
A text which uses irony to ridicule or make fun of an institution, person, set of beliefs, etc. is called a *satire*.

Onomatopoeia: Onomatopoeia [ɒnəˌmætə'piːə] is the use of a word which imitates the sounds it refers to, e.g. 'buzz' or 'hum'. In a group of words or a phrase it may evoke a particular feeling, mood, sound or movement.
Example: Only the stuttering rifles' rapid rattle / Can patter out ...
(From: Wilfred Owen, 'Anthem for Doomed Youth', 1917)
The repetition of 't's and 'r's sounds like the shooting of rifles which the words describe.

Repetition: Repetition is the deliberate use of a word or phrase more than once in a sentence or a text to create a sense of pattern or form or to emphasize certain elements in the mind of the reader or listener.
Parallelism is the deliberate repetition of similar or identical words, phrases, sentence constructions, etc. in the same or neighbouring sentences. Parallelism draws the attention of the reader to certain ideas that the writer may consider important. It may be used to show that the elements are of similar importance, or it may be used in a climactic sequence, with the most important element listed at the end.
Anaphora is a form of parallelism which repeats the same word or group of words at the beginning of successive clauses.
Example: Pile the bodies high [...]
And pile them high [...]
And pile them high [...]
(From: 'Grass', p. 131, ll. 1, 4–5)

Rhetorical Question: A rhetorical question is a question to which the answer seems obvious and is therefore not necessary. A rhetorical question pushes the reader or listener to a certain conclusion. As such it is popular in political speeches, etc. when a person is trying to influence others.
Example: How could he explain disability to a man who had been a Queen's Scout, Head Prefect, Captain of Cricket and (obviously) possessor of 20/20 vision? How could he say that he simply was not able to see with the rain coming down inside his specs?
(From: 'Land/scape', p. 12, ll. 122–125)
Here the rhetorical questions are used to emphasize the frustration Ant feels at not being able to meet his father's expectations and at not being able to express the things he wishes to say to his father.

Understatement: Understatement is a statement in which the true magnitude of an idea, event or fact is minimized, so that something is deliberately presented as being

much less important, valuable, etc. than it really is. Understatement is often used for ironic effect. (Cf. also ·exaggeration)
Example: The report of my death was an exaggeration.
(From: Mark Twain, *New York Journal*, 1897)
Twain wrote this comment following rumours that he had died.

Wordplay: Wordplay (also called *pun*) is the use of a word which may be understood in two different ways or which may be put into a different context to alter the meaning.
Example: Have sex after drinking and you could be nursing more than a hangover.
(From: 'The Morning After', p. 44)
Here the wordplay is on 'nurse a hangover' (i.e. suffer from a hangover) and 'nurse a baby' (i.e. feed and look after a baby).

Alphabetical list of words in the Glossary

Words in italics do not have their own entries.

Texts

All Internet pages were valid on 1 May, 2003.

Introduction

1/A Nadia Wheatley, *The Night Tolkien Died*, Random House, Milsons Point, Australia, 1996; **1/B** *Daily Telegraph*, 16 February, 2002.

I/All in the Family

1 *Jacky*, 15 June, 1991; **2** *High Windows*, 1974; **3** www.census.gov/prod/2001pubs/c2kbr01-8.pdf; **4/A** © 1999 by Laurie Halse Anderson. Reprinted by permission of Farrar Straus Giroux, LLC.

II/Youth Culture

Lead-in From 'Everybody's Free (to Wear Sunscreen)': © Mary Schmich; **1** *Guardian*, 18 December, 1999; **2/A** *Sugar*, March, 2002; **3/A** *Independent*, 16 October, 2000; **3/B** *Complete Sonnets*, Dover, New York, 1991; **4/A** *J-17*, December, 2001; **4/B** *Sugar*, May, 2001; **5** Copyright © 1999 by Alden R. Carter. Used by permission of Dell Publishing, a division of Random House, Inc.

III/Science and Technology

1/A *Independent on Sunday*, 19 March, 2000; **1/B** *Washington Post*, 5 March, 2000; **2/A** Reprinted by permission of Don Congdon Associates, Inc. © 1953, renewed 1981 by Ray Bradbury; **4** *Independent*, 28 February, 2002.

IV/Our Fragile Planet

Lead-in © Joe Miller, Moab, Utah, 1975; **1/B** *The Rose*, Puffin Books, London, 1997; **1/D** *Our Day Out*, Heinemann Educational Publishers, Oxford, 1976; **2** Copyright © 1993 by Jim Heynen. Used by permission of Alfred A. Knopf, a division of Random House, Inc.; **3/A** www.environzine.org; **3/B** *Eden, the Guide*, Eden Books / Transworld Publishers, London, 2001; **3/C** Copyright © 1998 by Paul Krugman. Used by permission of W. W. Norton & Company, Inc.

V/A Global Marketplace

1 copyright 1949, renewed © 1977 by Arthur Miller. Used by permission of Viking Penguin, a division of Penguin Group (USA) Inc.; **2/A** *New Internationalist*, March 1999; **2/B** *Faith in the Poor*, Lion Publishing, Oxford, 1998; **2/C** www.street-uk.com/sarah.htm and www.street-uk.com/leroy.htm; **3** 'The Great English Divide', *Business Week*, 13 August, 2001; **4/A** Milton & Rose Friedman, *Free to Choose*, Harcourt Brace Jovanovitch, 1980; **4/B** *The World We're In*, Little, Brown and Company, Boston, 2002.

VI/Inform, Educate and Entertain

1/A *Sun*, 1 October, 2003; **1/B** *Guardian*, 1 October, 2003; **1/C** © 1939, 1940 James Thurber; **1/D** *Daily Express*, 29 October, 2002; *Guardian*, 29 October, 2002; **2/A** *Economist*, 13 April, 2002; **2/B** Mike Storry and Peter Childs (eds.), *British Cultural Identities*, Routledge, London, 1997; **3/B** www.mhhe.com/mayfieldpub/webtutor/judging.htm; **4/A** *Martin Dressler*, Crown Publishers, New York, 1996; **4/B** www.danex-exm.dk/aida.htm.

VII/Turning Conflict into Art

1/A Reprinted with permission of Scribner, an imprint of Simon & Schuster Adult Publishing Group from *By-Line: Ernest Hemingway*, edited by William White. © Hemingway Foreign Rights Trust; **1/B** Reprinted with permission of Scribner, an imprint of Simon & Schuster Adult Publishing Group, and the Hemingway Foreign Rights Trust from *The Short Stories of Ernest Hemingway*. © Hemingway Foreign Rights Trust; **2/B** Jon Silkin (ed.), *First World War Poetry*, Penguin Books, New York; **2/C** *Cornhuskers*; **3/C** *Henry V*, Oxford University Press, Oxford, 2001; **4/B** Copyright © 2000 Martin Goldsmith. This material is used by permission of John Wiley & Sons, Inc.

VIII/The UK – Redefining a Nation?

1/A *Guardian*, 19 April, 2001; **2/A** http://files.fco.gov.uk/info/spotlight/ukdevolution.pdf; **2/C** *Economist*, 15 December, 2001; **3/A** *Richard II*, Oxford University Press, Oxford; **3/C** *Observer*, 30 August, 1998; **4/A** *Empire. How Britain Made the Modern World*, Allan Lane, London, 2003; **4/B** *Time Europe*, 20 January, 2003; **4/C** *Economist*, 19 December, 2001; **5** Zadie Smith, *White Teeth*, Hamish Hamilton, London, 2000.

IX/We the People

Lead-in Copyright © 1992 by Paul Auster; **1/A** *America the Beautiful: The Complete Verses*, Publishers Group West, Berkeley, California; **1/C** *Pass Through Fire: The Collected Lyrics*, Hyperion Books, New York, 2002; **1/D** *How Could Hell Be Any Worse?*, Epitaph Records, Los Angeles, 1982; **2/B** Luxembourg Income Study Working Paper, Luxembourg, 2000; *Statistical Abstracts of the United States*, U.S. Census Bureau, Washington, 2001; *Statistical Abstracts of the United States*, U.S. Census Bureau, Washington, 2001; **3/A** *Economist*, 7 September, 2002; **3/B** *Guardian*, 6 August, 2002; **3/C** http://news.bbc.co.uk/2/hi/americas/2544599.stm; **4/A** www.pbs.org/wgbh/pages/frontline/jesse/speeches/jesse88speech.html; **4/B** Copyright © 1995 by T. Coraghessan Boyle. Used by permission of Viking Penguin, a division of Penguin Group (USA) Inc.; **4/C** © 2001, Newsweek. Reprinted with permission; **5/A** *Boston Globe*, 6 October, 1986; **5/B** *Daily Mail*, May, 1997.

X/Who Am I?

1 Diane Glancy and C.W. Truesdale (eds.), *Two Worlds Walking*, New River Press, Minneapolis, 1994; **2/A** *Bend It Like Beckham. The Screenplay*, BILB productions, Ltd., 2002; **3/B** *Independent Magazine*, 6 April, 2002; **4/A** *Sugar*, February, 2002; **4/B** *Guardian*, 11 December, 2000; **4/C** *CosmoGirl*, February, 2002; **4/D** From *The Poetry of Robert Frost* edited by Edward Connery Lathem. Copyright 1916, © 1969 by Henry Holt and Company, copyright 1944 by Robert Frost. Reprinted by permission of Henry Holt and Company, LLC.; **4/E** *Complete Collected Poems*, Little, Brown and Company, London, 1994.

XI/Moving Out

1/A *As I Walked Out One Midsummer Morning*, André Deutsch Ltd, London, 1969; **1/B** *Junk*, Andersen Press, London, 1996; **1/C** www.ypp.net/fullarticle.asp?ID=19; **1/D** *Credit to the Nation*, The Refugee Council, London, 2002; **2/A** © 2002 Mapping Your Future, Inc.; **2/B** *Independent*, 14 August, 2002; **2/C** http://admissions.berkeley.edu/pdf/PerState.pdf; **2/D** *Never Far from Nowhere*, Hodder Headline, London, 1996; **3** Copyright © the Estate of James Joyce, 1967.

Skills Pages

p. 234 Reproduced by permission of Oxford University Press from *Oxford Advanced Learner's Dictionary* 6th Edition @ Oxford University Press 2000; **p. 237** *Guardian*, 24 April, 2002.

Illustrations

Action Press, Hamburg: pp. 142 (bottom left and cover, (Buckingham Palace, © Rex Features), 185 (F, © Rex Features); The Advertising Archive Ltd.: p. 39 (bottom); Agentur Focus, Hamburg: pp. 54 (B, © NASA/SCIENCE Photo Library), 71 (left, © James King-Holmes/ICRF/ SCIENCE Photo Library, right, © Petit Format/NESTLE/SCIENCE Photo Library), cover (scientist, © Geoff Tompkinson/SCIENCE Photo Library); agentur LPM/Henrik Pohl, Berlin: pp. 51, 204 (© Henrik Pohl); Airbus Deutschland GmbH, Hamburg: p. 54 (C and backdrop); AKG Images: pp. 55 (bottom left, second on the left), 64 (middle), 69, 102, 103 (top), 132 (all), 136; Albright-Knox Art Gallery: p. 75

(bottom left, © VG Bild-Kunst, Bonn 2003); AP Photo: pp. 170 (top, © The News Tribune/Peter Haley), 176 (© Cheryl Hatch); © Courtesy of Apple: p. 57 (right); The Art Archive: pp. 138 (top right, © Mireille Vautier), 155 (National Gallery, London, © Eileen Tweedy), 159 (Lords Gallery, © Eileen Tweedy); The Art Institute of Chicago: p. 200 (© mage); Auslöser-Bildagentur, Aachen: p. 84 (© H.J. Serwe); BBC World Service: p. 108; John Birdsall Photography: pp. 22 (photo, backdrop), 25 (photo, backdrop), 97, 98, 117, 146, 152 (left), 185 (A, B, C, E), 211 (all); Anthony Blake Photo Library: p. 144 (right, © Gerrit Buntrock); blickwinkel, Witten: p. 81 (top, © R. Rocholl); www.britainonview. com: pp. 78 (top right), 148 (all except The Crown Pub and Brighton photos); Caro Fotoagentur, Berlin: p. 198 (right, © Olaf Jandke); www.cartoonbank.com: pp. 24, 65, 82, 87, 88, 118 (top), 227 (© 2003 The New Yorker Collection from Cartoonbank. com. All rights reserved.), 194 (© 2003 The Cartoonbank.com. All rights reserved); www.Cartoonstock.com: p. 210 (© Nick Baker); Áine Chambers: p. 77 (top); Cinetext: pp. 93, 115, 116, 182 (all except top left), 193; Corbis, Düsseldorf: pp. 8 (© Penny Tweedie), 9 (left, © Paul A. Souders, right, © Patrick Ward), 11 (15, 17, © Penny Tweedie), 12 (© John Noble), 13 (© Michael S. Yamashita), 14 (© Diego Lezama Orezzoli), 16 (left, © Dave G. Houser), 26 (left, © Bohemian Nomad Picturemakers, right, © Henry Diltz), 30 (top, © Hulton-Deutsch Collection, middle left, © Royalty free), 43 (bottom left, © 2003 Andy Warhol Foundation for the Visual Arts/ ARS, New York, right, © Michel Arnaud), 49 (© Jose Luis Pelaez, Inc.), 52 (© Herrmann/ Starke), 55 (bottom, second on the right, © Bettmann), 60-63 (backdrop, © Dean Conger), 83 (bottom, © Richard Olivier), 85 (© Sygma/Caron Philippe), 86 (© Larry Lee), 90 (2, © Bob Krist, 3, © LWA-Stephen Welstead), 101 (© Guy Motil), 103 (bottom left, © Bruce Burkhardt, bottom right, © Eye Ubiquitous/Paul Seheult), 104 (left, © Tim Mosenfelder, right, © S.I.N./Martin Gilbert), 109 (right, © Martin Jones), 120 (© Bettmann), 121 (© Bettmann), 126 (© Nik Wheeler), 127 (© Hulton-Deutsch Collection), 131 (left, © Michael St. Maur Sheil), 133 (© Stapleton Collection), 135 (top, © Archivo Iconografico, S.A.), 139 (right, © Paul Almasy), 142 (right, © Sygma/Beirne Brendan), 143 (top right, © Peter Turnley), 154 (left, © Sandro Vannini, right, © Ric Ergenbright), 156 (left, © Sygma/ Polak Matthew), 158 (© Arvind Gary), 160 (© Barnabas Bosshart), 161 (left, © Robert Holmes, right, © Roger Wood), 165 (Coca Cola, © Jan Butchofsky-Houser), 166 (top, © David Muench), 168, 169 (all, © Wally McNamee), 170 (middle, © Robert Maass, bottom, © Viviane Moos), 173 (© Jonathan Blair), 174 (© Vince Streano), 175 (© Royalty free), 178 (© Natalie Fobes), 180 (© Kunio Owaki), 181 (© Joel W. Rogers), 188 (© Royalty free), 203 (© E.O. Hoppé), 208 (all, © Tom Steward), 212 (right, © Robert Holmes), 217 (right, © Bettmann), cover (newspaper, © Dennis Galante); Corel-Library: pp. 43 (top left), 47, 54 (A), 70-72 (backdrop), 74, 75 (top, bottom right), 81 (bottom), 83 (backdrop), 164 (left), 179, 219, cover (backdrop, bottom); Curtis Publishing Company, Cincinnati, Ohio: p. 21 (© 1943 The Norman Rockwell Family Entities); ddp, Berlin: pp. 138 (bottom, © Norbert Millauer), 165 (top left, © Michael Kappeler); dpa: p. 92 (5, © Berlin Picture Gate/ Christian Schulz); dpa-Bildarchiv: pp. 37 (top right), 64 (top left, bottom right), 94, 129, 137 (left), 167 (© Getty Sullivan); dpa-Fotoreport: pp. 30 (bottom left, © Stefan Rousseau), 36 (right, © Jens Kalaene), 55 (bottom right), 90 (1, © Oliver Berg), 91 (5, © Issouf Sanago), 95 (both), 99 (© Hector Mata), 131 (right, © Karl Mittenzwei), 142 (middle left), 144 (left, © Jonathan Utz), 157 (© Stefan Rousseau), 164 (top right, © Beth A. Keiser, bottom right, © Summers), 171 (right, backdrop, © Getty Platt, bottom, © Hondros), 172 (bottom, © AFP Jimin Lai); dpa-Sportreport: pp. 110 (© Empics Adam Davy), 190 (bottom, © Kent Gavin); © Bob Englehart: p. 107 (top); Mary Evans Picture Library: p. 135 (bottom); © Michael Fahrig: p. 198 (left); Das Fotoarchiv, Essen: pp. 154 (middle, © Jochen Tack), 162 (© Jochen Tack); gettyimages, München: pp. 27 (© Hulton Archive), 37 (bottom right, © Hulton Archive/James Jackson), 187 (© Royalty free/Steve Cole), 189 (© The Bridgeman Art Library), 206 (© Stone/Russell Kaye), 223 (© Hulton Archive/Douglas Miller), cover (skateboard, © taxi/Leland Bobbe, Wall Street, © Stone/Doug Armand); www.globecartoon.com: pp. 91 (bottom, © Chappatte), 225 (© Chappatte); www.goldenjubilee. gov.uk: p. 145; www. guardian.co.uk: p. 151 (all); Gabi Heinisch, Berlin: pp. 67, 187, 228 (4), 229; Peter Herlitze, Berlin: p. 226; HIPP-Foto: p. 182 (top left); © David Horsey: p. 107 (bottom); IBM Deutschland GmbH: pp. 56 (all), 57 (left); IFA-Bilderteam, München: pp. 118 (bottom), 143 (middle right, © Naegele), 201; Image Bank, Berlin: p. 31 (© copyright 2001-2002 The Image Bank, Inc. All rights reserved); Image State/ Premium: p. 205; © The Irish Image Collection: p. 148 (top right); Keystone Pressedienst: pp. 38, 109 (top, © Topham); © Kintop Pictures/Bend It Films/Road Movies/Roc Media: pp. 190 (top), 191; © The Kobal Collection: p. 134; © Dennis Kunkel Microscopy, Inc.: p. 55 (D); Friedhelm Maria Leistner, Berlin: pp. 34, 46, 65 (icons), 79, 100, 119, 140, 149, 177, 194 (icons), 216; Lokomotiv-Atelier für Visuelle Kommunikation: pp. 80 (© Thomas Willemsen), 165 (Dollar bill, © Thomas Willemsen); London Aerial Photo Library: p. 137 (right); Christina de la Mare, Berlin: p. 228 (1-3); © Carsten Mathaes, Berlin: p. 83 (top); Mauritius, Berlin: pp. 18 (middle, right, © age), 78 (left, © Dolphin Productions), 148 (bottom right, © Pigneter), 185 (D, © Kupka), 186 (top, © O'Brian, bottom, © IPS); Nicole diMella, Somerset County/NJ: p. 165 (bottom); © copyright: Joe Munroe, 1956: p. 36 (bottom left); The Museum of Modern Art, New York/ Photo Scala, Florence: p. 124 (125 © VG Bild-Kunst, Bonn 2003); Newsweek: p. 66 (© 2002 Newsweek, Inc. All rights reserved. Printed by permission.); NON SEQUITUR: p. 106 (all, © Wiley Miller. Dist. By UNIVERSAL PRESS SYNDICATE. Reprinted with permission. All rights reserved.); PA Photos, London: pp. 142 (top left-hand corner, © 2003 all rights reserved/Toby Melville), 196; Penguin Books Ltd., London: p. 202 (illustration: © Roger Coleman); Photofusion, London: pp. 91 (4, © Marc Campbell), 96 (© Edwin Maynard), 143 (left, © Jacky Chapman), 152 (bottom, © Judi Harrison), 153 (© Crispin Hughes), 156 (right © Bob Watkins), 192 (© Brian Mitchell), 207 (© Paula Solloway), 214 (© Ray Roberts); © Copyright Photolibrary Wales. All rights reserved: p. 143 (bottom right); Picture Alliance: pp. 138 (left, © dpa-Bilderdienste/ Tony Halliday), 139 (left, © ZB-Fotoreport); Reuters/E-Lance-Media: p. 114 (© Philippe Wojazer); Samsung Electronics: p. 39 (top); Schapowalow/Heaton: p. 166 (bottom); Skjold Photographs: p. 37 (left); Wieslaw Smetek, Seevetal: p. 172 (top); The Spectator: p. 68 (© E.Smith); St Hilda's College, Oxford: p. 215; Sugar Magazine, London: p. 45 (© Sugar Magazine 2001/Sarah Brewer); Tate Gallery, London: p. 76 (© Tate, London 2003); TG2: pp. 36 (top left, © Simmons), 150 (backdrop, © Zapf); Urban Alliance on Race Relations, Toronto: p. 122; VARIO PRESS, Bonn: p. 217 (left, © Susanne Baumgarten); VISUM: p. 213 (© Marion Losse, 2001); Voller Ernst, Berlin: p. 58 (© Gerhard Vormwald); WILDLIFE: pp. 77 (right, © J. Kottmann); Wildlight Photo Agency Pty Ltd: pp. 10 (© Lindsay Stepanow), 16 (bottom, © Grenville Turner); Zefa visual media, Hamburg: pp. 18 (left), 19 (all), 209 (all), 212 (left).